Piers Mackesy is Emeritus Fellow
a Fellow of the British Academy.
America, Statesmen at War and *W*
He was awarded the Templer Med<

'Piers Mackesy's account of the B<
is classic military history, a fine narrative based on high scholarship.

John Keegan

'Mackesy has here written military history of the best sort; humane,
perceptive and above all full of the sense of men taking difficult decisions under extreme stress.'   *Times Literary Supplement*

'A clear, readable account of an exciting and momentous campaign,
Piers Mackesy's study reclaims for the historical page an episode
wrongly consigned to the footnotes and restores to the pantheon a
forgotten Scottish hero.'   *The Scotsman*

'Based on extensive and wide-ranging research this is an excellent
campaign history that simultaneously covers an important campaign
and throws light on the potential and limitations of warfare in the
1800s...Aside from its scholarly interest and value, Mackesy's book
is well written...exciting and enlivening.'
Jeremy Black, *War in History*

'...military history at its best, humane, engrossing and related with
great verve and style...yet another superb account which blends
Mackesy's unique understanding of military matters and how human
beings operate under strain – quite outstanding.'   John Charmley

'By consulting every conceivable printed authority, French and English, and a quantity of new manuscript material, Mackesy has been
able to give a colour and a richness to his account absent from any
that have gone before, and he has made of it not only a very good
'read', as they say, but thoroughly sound history besides...a worthy
recipient of the Templer Medal'.
Journal of the Society for Army Historical Research

'Piers Mackesy...does full justice to the tale...his knowledge of the
sources is awe-inspiring...he writes clearly, and vigorously.'
Books in Scotland

'A fine example of classic military history based upon high scholarship and fine discussion . . . Mackesy has written a definitive study.'
David G. Chandler, *International History Review*

'What Piers Mackesy has given us here is military history of a high order, clear in its detail, and meticulously based on archival research.'
Journal of the Royal Asiatic Society

Tauris Parke Paperbacks is an imprint of I.B.Tauris. It is dedicated to publishing books in accessible paperback editions for the serious general reader within a wide range of categories, including biography, history, travel and the ancient world. The list includes select, critically acclaimed works of top quality writing by distinguished authors that continue to challenge, to inform and to inspire. These are books that possess those subtle but intrinsic elements that mark them out as something exceptional.

The Colophon of Tauris Parke Paperbacks is a representation of the ancient Egyptian ibis, sacred to the god Thoth, who was himself often depicted in the form of this most elegant of birds. Thoth was credited in antiquity as the scribe of the ancient Egyptian gods and as the inventor of writing and was associated with many aspects of wisdom and learning.

BRITISH VICTORY IN EGYPT

The End of Napoleon's Conquest

Piers Mackesy

TAURIS PARKE
PAPERBACKS

Dedicated with her approval to
Patricia
without whom this book
would have been finished years ago

New paperback edition published in 2010 by Tauris Parke Paperbacks
An imprint of I.B.Tauris and Co Ltd
6 Salem Road, London W2 4BU
175 Fifth Avenue, New York NY 10010
www.ibtauris.com

Distributed in the United States and Canada Exclusively by Palgrave Macmillan
175 Fifth Avenue, New York NY 10010

First published in 1995 by Routledge

Cover image: *Death of Sir Ralph Abercromby (1734–1801) March 21st 1801*,
from *The Martial Achievements of Great Britain and her Allies from 1799 to
1815*, by James Jenkins, engraved by Thomas Sutherland (b.c.1785) published
1815 (aquatint), Heath, William (1795–1840) (after) / Private Collection / The
Stapleton Collection / The Bridgeman Art Library

ISBN: 978 1 84885 472 7

A full CIP record for this book is available from the British Library
A full CIP record is available from the Library of Congress

Library of Congress Catalog Card Number: available

Printed and bound in India by Replika Press Pvt. Ltd.

CONTENTS

Part IV Honour redeemed

MAPS AND TABLES

MAPS

TABLES

INTRODUCTION

British Victory in Egypt is the concluding part of a trilogy on the British war against Revolutionary France, and the resolution of four years of twists and turns in search of a strategy. The three volumes cover the five years of the Second Coalition, an alliance of Britain, Austria and Russia to put an end to the adventurism and ideology of the Revolution. These were also the years that saw the rise of General Bonaparte to supreme power. As the Coalition began to form in 1798 he launched his Egyptian expedition, to find himself trapped in a distant cul-de-sac by Nelson's destruction of his battle fleet in Aboukir Bay. Abandoning his army in Egypt, he burst free from his bankrupt gamble to seize power at home: power which he confirmed with his victory over the Austrians at Marengo in June 1800.

The creator of the coalition was the British Foreign Secretary, Lord Grenville. He had become an ideological crusader. By 1798, the aggressions of the French Republic in the five preceding years had convinced him that the only road back to stability in Europe was regime change in France: Jacobinism must be 'attacked and subdued in its citadel at Paris'.

It was a goal of unlimited warfare without compromise. And to achieve it Grenville conjured a vision of a grand assault on France: an onslaught in 1799 by Austrian and Russian armies on a front stretching from the Mediterranean coast to the middle Rhine, with the decisive *Schwerpunkt* a breakthrough from Switzerland towards Lyon.

And the British contribution to this unrolling offensive? Here lay a new conundrum. In previous continental wars British expeditionary forces had been fed in to reinforce an established allied front in the west, whether in the Low Countries or in northern Germany. But now no western front existed. The Austrians had abandoned Belgium in 1795; the French Republicans had overrun Holland; and Prussia shivered in neutrality, more suspicious of the Austrians than afraid of the French, thus excluding British forces from northern Germany. This absence of an allied front in Western Europe was to persist across the Napoleonic Wars, not to be faced again until the Germans obliterated the French western front in 1940.

Thus, in 1799 the British Army could intervene in the west only by invading from the sea. In the past, many amphibious operations had been mounted on the coasts of the North Sea and the Atlantic, but these had been raids: this operation would be on a different scale. A beachhead seized by a picked force would be built up with reinforcements from England and a Russian expedition from the Baltic. The area chosen late in the day for this second front was North Holland, and Grenville hoped that the invasion would tilt Prussia into the battle. But even if Prussia still shrank back there were promises from Orangist exiles of a massive Dutch insurrection, enough to sustain a war front in Western Europe.

It was not to be. Prussia remained neutral, and no Dutch insurgents materialised in the rural polders of North Holland. In the east Masséna's defeat of the Russians at Zurich and the Austrians' focus on their own war aims allowed the enemy to exploit his interior position and rush reinforcements to Holland. The British beachhead was throttled, and the British and the Russian forces had to be extricated by negotiating an armistice.

These events were the theme of the first volume of the trilogy, *Statesmen at War: the Strategy of Overthrow, 1798–1799*. How British strategy was reconstructed as the Coalition unravelled is revealed in the succeeding volume, *War without Victory: the Downfall of Pitt, 1799–1802*. In spite of the allies' reverses Grenville remained determined to keep up the pressure on France, and his colleague the Secretary at War, William Windham, urged that the Army's operations should be switched to western France. But there was one strong man in the Cabinet capable of standing up to Lord Grenville. Henry Dundas, the Scottish Secretary of the State for War, had always been a sceptic about the Holland invasion, and now he would not hear of backing the promises of needy French émigrés who were clamouring for a landing in the insurgent Vendée. He had seen enough of exiles' promises in Holland. Step by step he downgraded the British army's commitment to Europe. At first it was to be an Anzio-style landing in the enemy's rear on the north Italian front; then demonstrations on the Biscay coasts of France. These operations fall within the derogatory 20th-century term 'sideshows', but Dundas saw no other choice.

Yet in his heart, Dundas believed that the Coalition would fail, and war would cease in Europe: that Britain must be ready to fight on alone towards a compromise peace. And for this two conditions were essential. First, the secure command of the sea, in which the Army's role was to raid enemy naval bases and destroy the battle squadrons lying in their harbours and roadsteads. Thereafter came the protection of colonial wealth and ocean trade to provide the riches which were the sinews of war. If the army which Bonaparte had left behind in Egypt remained there, it would be a standing threat to Britain's rich East India trade. Eventually, Dundas's courage launched the Egyptian expedition to dislodge it.

But strategic plans are mere vapour if the forces do not exist to execute them. Underlying the Cabinet's military hopes was the state of the British Army; and it was deplorable. Run down, starved of funds and neglected after the defeat in America, the regiments had been hastily filled on the renewal of war with recruits of poor quality officered by ignorant young men who had social connections. They had then been dissipated in the Netherlands and the West Indies. For the North Holland campaign the ranks were replenished at the last moment with volunteers from the militia.

It is a familiar story. As a child of the Army in the 1930s I saw and heard of its disappointment and frustration under a rule of neglect. As always it was the Cinderella Service, denied funds because the country's defence relied first on the Royal Navy and the Royal Air Force. I did not know at the time – but my father did – how heavy a responsibility the statesman Winston Churchill bore for cutting the Army's funding when he had been Chancellor of the Exchequer.

In the North Holland beachhead in 1799, the volunteering militiamen, though unsettled in mind and unknown to their officers, performed with some credit. But after their return from Holland and a harsh winter at home when little training was possible, they were floated around the coasts of Europe in the spring and summer of 1800 into a series of fiascos at Belle-Ile, Ferrol and Cadiz, and on the Italian Riviera, which did not improve their training but further diminished their reputation. *British Victory in Egypt* is the story of the Army's resurgence, which set it on the road to future victories in the Peninsula.

In the background were reforms at home under the eye of the royal Commander-in-Chief, the Duke of York, including a new drill book. But the force for Egypt was a ragbag of battalions thrown together from many places, and of varying quality. To fit the force for battle was the task of an elderly Scots general, Sir Ralph Abercromby. How he trained and melded his battalions, sorted out their rusty landing drills, won their devotion and led them to war is a central theme of this book. The deciding battle outside Alexandria on 21 March 1801 became the model for future combat. In the book I relate how the date 'the 21st of March' was shouted to encourage the troops going into an attack at Vimiero seven years later: seven years on again at Quatre Bras in the Waterloo campaign when the 28th Regiment of Alexandria fame was beset on three sides by cavalry, General Picton roared out, 'Twenty-eighth, remember Egypt'.

Abercromby himself died of wounds after the battle of Alexandria. It struck me, but too late, that this volume ought to have been titled *Abercromby's Soldiers*, picking up words from the closing quotation. And in my mind and heart *Abercromby's Soldiers* it remains.

PREFACE

1808, near Vimiero in Portugal; and Sir Arthur Wellesley has engaged in his first full-scale battle of the Peninsular War. The day is 21 August, and as the 43rd and 50th Regiments prepare to charge an advancing French column, Brigadier Anstruther rides forward and calls out: 'Remember, my lads, the glorious 21st of March in Egypt; this day must be another glorious 21st'.

His soldiers understand him. For the past eight years the battle fought by Sir Ralph Abercromby on 21 March at Alexandria has been the pattern of what a well-led British army can do. A week after his victory Abercromby died of his wounds on board the *Foudroyant* in Aboukir bay, where Nelson had destroyed Bonaparte's fleet two years earlier. Today the names of the two victors are inscribed together on Cleopatra's Needle, overlooking the Thames and in sight of the dome of St Paul's which harbours Abercromby's monument and the tomb of Nelson. Presented by Mahomet Ali of Egypt, of whom more later, the ancient obelisk bears a plaque which proclaims it 'a worthy monument of our distinguished countrymen Nelson and Abercromby'.

Of Nelson we have heard; but who is Abercromby? 'It ought to be unnecessary to speak in praise of such a man', one of his soldiers protested forty years after his death. While writing two earlier books on Britain's wars against Revolutionary France I was struck by the pre-eminent reputation of Sir Ralph Abercromby for courage, honour, and professional knowledge; and by his hold on the affection of his soldiers. In *Statesmen at War* I described his role in the expedition of 1799 to Holland; but the succeeding volume, *War without Victory*, relegated his final triumph and death in Egypt to the background of the strategic contentions in Pitt's Cabinet. With the present book I hope to render justice to Abercromby, and record his legacy to the British Army.

This book is also the life-story of an army: of the disparate and ill-provided battalions which assembled in the stormy autumn of 1800 in the Straits of Gibraltar, and disbanded a year later in the highest state of discipline and morale with their task of destroying Bonaparte's Army of the Orient completed. These units had been welded into cohesion by Abercromby; and his force became the model for the victorious British Army of the Peninsular War.

xiii

PREFACE

I wish to thank the Earl of Donoughmore for permission to copy his family manuscripts in Trinity College Library, Dublin; Viscount Sidmouth for giving me access to his papers in the Devon Record Office; and Mrs Enid Case for sending me copies of the papers of her ancestor Colonel J.H.E. Hill. The late Mrs Lavinia Smiley unlocked for me the papers of General Mackenzie Fraser at Castle Fraser; and the Earl of Elgin and Kincardine guided me through the records of the seventh Earl, adding pieces from his own store of knowledge. Finally I would like to thank my friends in the National Army Museum for their help and information.

Leochel Cushnie
June 1994

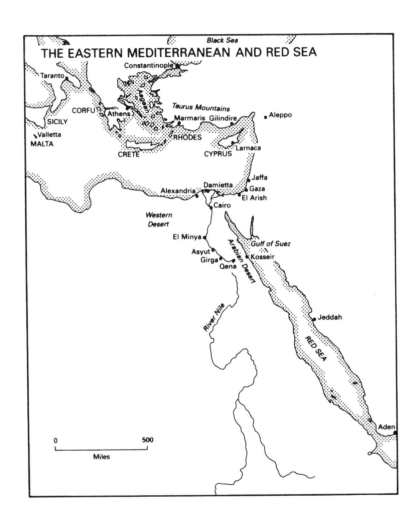

THE EASTERN MEDITERRANEAN AND RED SEA

Part I

FORGING AN ARMY

1

'SIR RALPH IS NOT A COURTIER'

'How harmless an English military force is against an enemy in battle array.' Lady Holland's fashionable sneer found an echo in many British hearts in the autumn of 1800. For nearly forty years the British Army had known little but failure. Driven out of the American colonies after a seven-year struggle, expelled from the Low Countries by the French Revolutionary hordes, the army had gone on to be exterminated by yellow fever and malaria in the course of cruel and inconclusive operations in the West Indies. The past twelve months had heaped humiliation on misfortune. In the autumn of 1799 it had been ejected from Holland by General Brune. The year 1800 was worse. In June an assault on Belle Ile was cancelled as the troops were boarding their landing craft; and in August a force under Sir James Pulteney landed near the Spanish naval base at Ferrol, to re-embark without a fight. The final fiasco was the massing of 22,000 men in Cadiz bay in October to destroy the Spanish fleet and arsenal. The first wave of troops embarked in assault craft; the admiral, Lord Keith, bungled the boat-plan and postponed the attack; a storm blew up, and the fleet sailed away. The reputation of the British Army plumbed its lowest depth. It had become, said Lord Cornwallis, 'the scorn and laughing-stock of friends and foes'.[1]

The contrast with the navy's record was bitter. Since the start of the war eight years earlier in 1793 British seamen had won great fleet battles and innumerable single-ship actions, bagging seventy-eight enemy ships of the line and 400 frigates and smaller vessels. Josef Haydn had celebrated their glory in song, and peerages had been showered on their admirals. Not one peerage had been bestowed on a military commander. Nor did the navy conceal its contempt for the sister service. 'Our Army does not stand very high in the estimation of the Navy officers', a military officer observed during the Cadiz fiasco; and the great seaman Lord St Vincent looked forward to the day when the whole army except the King's Guards and artillery would be abolished and replaced by an enlarged corps of marines.[2]

From the farce at Cadiz the angry and embarrassed general, Sir Ralph Abercromby, took his troops back to the Straits of Gibraltar to replenish the troopships' water and wait for fresh orders from London. Here on 13

October, while the ships' boats were ashore filling the water-casks at Tetuan on the Moroccan coast, the fleet was struck by a terrifying hurricane from the east. The ships abandoned their watering parties on the shores of Africa, cut their cables leaving a hundred anchors on the bottom of the bay, and raced through the Straits under bare poles to scatter into the Atlantic.[3]

Driven by furious gusts and labouring in mountainous seas, the troopships were taking in water everywhere through their leaky upper works. They were mainly old two-decked warships with their lower-deck guns removed, and as they heeled in the wind the waves spurted round the edges of the gun-ports, keeping the lee sides of the lower decks permanently awash. In the *Stately* the 92nd Gordon Highlanders were lying on the decks without bunks or hammocks; and when the ship heeled over to tack, the water which had accumulated on the lee side swashed across the boards and drenched the men lying huddled under their blankets. Constantly wet for days at a time, and half-dead from seasickness, the soldiers packed between decks were neglecting their food. The salt pork, maggoty biscuit and foul water which had been the main diet of many of the regiments for the past five months were bringing on scurvy, and fevers were beginning to appear in the crowded troop-decks. Little did these miserable and mostly inexperienced troops realise what test the government had planned for their future. Across the bay of Biscay a fast cruiser was racing southwards from England with orders which would bring them to battle in Egypt. There this 'wandering army' would face the hardened veterans of Bonaparte's old Army of Italy; the victors of Arcola, Lodi, and Mantua.[4]

The Cabinet's debate had been prolonged and agonising, and the critical decision to commit the country's only striking force to Egypt came at the end of a desperate summer. The Second Coalition which Pitt and his colleagues had so laboriously constructed two years earlier was dissolving. The Tsar Paul had summoned his armies home in the spring, and was moving towards a predatory alliance with Bonaparte and an armed neutrality of the Baltic Powers. The Austrians had been defeated by Bonaparte at Marengo and frightened into an armistice. At home two bad harvests had reduced the poor to starvation and riot, forcing the military to disperse in small packets around the country to keep order in spite of a threatened invasion. War expenditure was crippling the public finances. And the Cabinet was being torn apart by proposals for Catholic Emancipation. On top of all this came the bitter dispute over strategy, as the Cabinet came face to face at last with the problem of Egypt.

More than two years had passed since General Bonaparte had sailed from Toulon with his 40,000 veterans to seize Egypt from the Turks. Renamed the Army of the Orient, they had destroyed two Turkish armies, conquered Egypt, and invaded Palestine. It was true that their situation was now deteriorating. Nelson had severed their communications with France when he annihilated Brueys's battle fleet in Aboukir bay in August 1798; and Bonaparte had deserted his army and slipped away in a frigate to seize power in France. His splendid successor Kléber was murdered by a Muslim fanatic, leaving the command in the hands of the third-rate General Menou; and the Army of the Orient, receiving the barest trickle of news and supplies when an occasional frigate stole through the British blockade, appeared from the tone of intercepted letters to be a prey to disease and homesickness.

For the British the news of these difficulties had at first meant that the French could safely be left to moulder in Egypt: they could do far less harm there than in Italy or Germany where war was raging. The threat they had once levelled against British India had evaporated, now that a British naval squadron was in place to block the mouth of the Red Sea, and France's Indian ally Tippoo of Mysore had been defeated and killed in Seringapatam. The Army of the Orient could do little harm.

All this changed with the defeat of Austria and the collapse of the Coalition. Peace negotiations would soon be inevitable; and the Army of the Orient was still in firm possession of Egypt, the land-bridge and short route to the east: Egypt, which the British Consul had described as 'the master-key to all the trading nations of the earth'. His French adversary, Consul Magellon, had reported that from Suez 10,000 French troops could swoop down the Red Sea and expel the British from Bengal in a single campaign.[5]

There was one member of Pitt's Cabinet who viewed the prospect with peculiar horror. At the head of the War Department was Henry Dundas, the rough-hewn Scottish lawyer. He had devoted many years of his political career to restructuring the government of British India; and if Egypt remained a French colony and laid India under permanent threat, much of his life's achievements would be undermined and his vision of a great British trading empire dissolved. There was no doubt that the French were determined to hold on to Egypt at the peace. The Foreign Minister Talleyrand indicated that it would not be negotiable; and in numerous French and Spanish ports fast frigates and transports were loading troops and stores to run through the blockade to Alexandria. Egypt would remain a French colony; and when war broke out again as it surely would, their troopships would be waiting in the Red Sea and a battle squadron at Mauritius. Then would come the long-feared French invasion of India.

There was only one way to avert the future danger: an immediate strike by the British Army. For six weeks in August and September Dundas fought to persuade his Cabinet colleagues that Abercromby's army, gathered in the Straits of Gibraltar by the chances of war, must be sent to do it.

Yet the risks of invading Egypt were enormous, and Dundas's opponents were powerful. The Secretary at War William Windham, obsessed by dreams of a royalist counter-revolution in France, would have liked to bring the whole force at Gibraltar home and await an opportunity to land in Brittany. More influential than Windham was Pitt's cousin and Foreign Secretary,

Lord Grenville. Implacably hostile to Dundas's Egyptian plan, he wanted to keep the army in European waters and be ready to aid the Austrians if they re-entered the fighting, or defend Portugal against a threatened French invasion. To commit Britain's only strategic force at a distance of 3,000 miles in the furthest corner of the Mediterranean would mean the end of offensive operations in Europe; and even the British Isles would be left stripped of defences.

On 3 October Dundas at last steamrollered the decision through the Cabinet with the help of Pitt, and the invasion of Egypt was on. But he had won by a bare and shaky majority; and Grenville and Windham sent a strongly worded minute of dissent to the King. George III made it clear that he agreed with them. Kings outlast ministries and have long memories; and George remembered the American War twenty years earlier and Dundas's recent costly campaigns in the West Indies. Recalling the difficulties caused in America by ocean supply lines, he predicted that the force sent to Egypt would starve; and even if it found supplies, disease would make the country a graveyard as the West Indies had been. Windham added to the King's unkindness by a heated exchange with Dundas, telling him that he had lost one army fighting yellow fever and was now sending another to fight the plague.

Dundas shrugged off these warnings: supplies were plentiful in the Levant, and he intended the force to reach Egypt in the healthy winter months to avoid disease. But war is ruled by uncertainty, and he quailed at his responsibility. His own health was failing after nearly seven years at the heart of the war machine; and he felt the stresses of a ministry which was splitting apart under the pressures of war and the problems of making peace. In the coming months of political collapse the insomniac Dundas's sleepless nights would be haunted by fears for his far-flung campaign. In the remotest regions of the inland sea, where Asia and Africa merge, he had plunged 15,000 soldiers into danger and hardship. And the King's silent disapproval depressed his spirits, for he could not forget the duty and love which were owed to a monarch.

On one man above all Dundas depended for vindication: his hopes and his reputation must rest on the judgement, courage, and tactical skills of the military commander. On the day after the decisive Cabinet meeting, while the orders for the Egyptian expedition were being prepared, he took up his pen and began a long private letter to his Scottish kinsman Sir Ralph Abercromby. He explained the political imperative behind the plan, and gave Abercromby absolute discretion in its execution. 'In your hands', he concluded, 'I feel the interests of the country safe.'[6]

Sir Ralph Abercromby was approaching his sixty-seventh year, and a profile of him could be written which would make Dundas's confidence seem a mystery, were it not that the two men were 'Scotch cousins' related by blood and marriage. Abercromby's mother was a Dundas, and his eldest son had recently married one of Henry Dundas's Doric-speaking daughters. Sir Ralph was a small, quiet-spoken Lowland laird, surrounded by what the English tended to regard as a mafia of Scotch staff officers. Some senior members of the Cabinet regarded him with a distrust which he strongly reciprocated. Lord Grenville still resented his refusal to press on and exploit his successful landing in Holland in the previous year, and viewed him as the epitome of all that he believed to be wrong with the British Army's leaders, most of whom he thought were unenterprising, and defeatist. Pitt himself had mixed feelings towards Abercromby, in which there was a tincture of guilt; for when Abercromby had commanded in Ireland Pitt had allowed a Dublin lobby to undermine his position and force his resignation.

Ireland in 1797 had been seething on the edge of the rebellion which erupted in the following year, and Abercromby found that his motley forces of regulars, fencibles, and English militia were scattered about the countryside in small packets to protect the landowners from their angry peasantry. He knew Ireland well and despised its gentry, whom he regarded as the real cause of the country's troubles. They should have been providing their own protection by serving in the yeomanry instead of calling for troops, whose dispersal on security duties left Abercromby without a mobile force to meet a French invasion. The troops were also too scattered to be kept under supervision by their commanding officers and generals; yet strict discipline was essential to the new security system he planned to try. Under his predecessor the search for concealed arms had been conducted by seizing and interrogating individual suspects. Abercromby applied collective pressure instead. In refractory communities where arms were hidden, troops were sent to live at free quarters on the inhabitants.

Where the local commanders were good and the troops under discipline, the policy worked. But too often free quarters meant looting and outrage; and in a sharp General Order Abercromby informed his army – regulars, fencibles, and militia – that their indiscipline made them formidable to everyone but the enemy. His censure was justified a year later when a mixed force encountered a small French invasion at Castlebar and took to their heels.

Abercromby's cutting prose, honed in the Edinburgh of Adam Smith and aimed at the militia, offended the colonels of Irish militia who sat in the Dublin Parliament; and his next order gave the Irish lobby in London its chance. Determined to disengage the army from petty police-work and restore its discipline, he forbade the troops to open fire on civil rioters without a magistrate's authority, in effect countermanding an order of the Lord Lieutenant, Lord Camden. Camden liked Abercromby and had agreed to try his system of free quarters; but his Irish advisers persuaded him to rescind Abercromby's order. This removed the army from the control of the civil power, freeing the magistrates from responsibility, and opening the way to the military excesses in the Rebellion of the following year. Deserted by Camden, and rebuked by the Home Secretary Lord Portland for his General Order on discipline, Abercromby resigned his command. He never entirely forgave Pitt for supporting Camden, who had been the Prime Minister's crony since their undergraduate days in Cambridge and was now in the Cabinet. He told his son that the Prime Minister was nearly a great man: 'if his mind [i.e. character] was equal to his abilities and talents, he would deserve the name of a first-rate statesman'.[7] It was a cold appraisal of the nation's war-leader.

Lord Camden suggested that the General had resigned to escape from a task which alarmed him.[8] Perhaps this was unfair, but in the course of his career Abercromby had shown a tendency to change direction which might lend credibility to Grenville's suspicion of defeatism. He had given up a legal career in favour of the army, he had avoided service against the Americans, he had abandoned a brief parliamentary career. In the West Indies he had asked to be relieved on grounds of age and health, and then because of the excessive burden of his complex military and civil duties, particularly the management of the army's accounts. On the other hand, after coming home from the West Indies with broken health after his first campaign, he had returned for the next campaigning season.

Such requests for relief were not unusual in the army or indeed the navy; and if Abercromby was not a man of naturally sanguine temperament he had been schooled in adversity. He had seen the worst aspects of political control and administrative muddle; he had experienced defeat in Europe and the ravages of disease in the Caribbean. In war he had always commanded inferior troops under bad officers. On Abercromby, wrote Lord Cornwallis, 'the most difficult and irksome part of the service in the present war has principally fallen'.[9]

Abercromby's vein of pessimism, whether natural or acquired, was reinforced by scepticism about the objects of the war. In the political spectrum of the day his views were tinged with pink, and he had no patience with the Foreign Secretary's right-wing war aims. Lord Grenville was an implacable enemy of the French Revolution and would fight it to the bitter end, with the certitude that its poisonous influence could only be extirpated by storming its citadel in Paris and overthrowing its government. Abercromby believed none of this. Yet he might have been expected to hold the conventional opinions of a landed Lowland gentleman, for he was the third generation of Abercrombies of Tullibody in Clackmannanshire. He was descended, however, from a long line of Banff and Aberdeenshire lairds stretching back to the thirteenth century, and perhaps the more adventurous mixed blood of the north-east stirred in his veins.

For within the laird there lurked a complex personality and a liberal. He was reared in a cultivated family – they had supported the painter David Allen in Rome; conscientious lairds, the very opposite of the Irish gentry whom Sir Ralph despised. He had been educated for the law at Rugby

School, Edinburgh University, and Leipzig, where he had fallen under the military spell of Frederick the Great. He switched his career to the army, and served in the Seven Years War in Germany. But when the Americans rebelled in 1775 he privately sympathised with them, and admired Washington. In consequence he avoided serving in America and spent the War of Independence with his regiment in Ireland. The ten years of peace which followed were spent in Scotland as a colonel on half-pay bringing up his children, managing the estate for his aged father, and taking time for reading and reflection. He had a house in Edinburgh, and an active social life in the Athens of the North.

When war broke out against Revolutionary France in 1793 he volunteered for active service. Yet from the beginning of the Revolution in 1789 he had declared that opinion cannot be controlled by force; and he marked his disapproval of the prevailing backlash of intolerance by joining an Edinburgh society 'for the diffusion of useful information among the people'. He was heard to say that a youth who was not a republican at 20 would be a corrupt man when he was 40.

It was one thing to go to war to protect the Low Countries from the onrush of the French armies, a limited and attainable aim; it was quite another to fight to put down opinion, by the overthrow of the enemy's government. At the end of the first campaign in Flanders Abercromby warned Dundas that a new spirit was abroad which would spread and could not be contained by force; that the old monarchies of Europe were worn out and a new order was coming; and that England should withdraw from the war as soon as possible. Now, eight years into the war in the second half of 1800, his views were unchanged. He reminded Dundas's Under-Secretary, William Huskisson, that he had never hoped to change the French or achieve the ideological aims of the Coalition. 'I sincerely hope you are negotiating a peace', he wrote on 15 September from Gibraltar bay.

The tide of opinion was now running with Abercromby and against the belligerent views of the Foreign Secretary. When years of Coalition failure culminated in the battle of Marengo and the consolidation of Bonaparte's power, even members of the Cabinet believed that the news heralded an era of stable government in France and made a reasonable peace attainable. Lord Nelson, St Vincent, Cornwallis, even Pitt were convinced that to fight on alone would bankrupt Britain without hope of victory. 'I think you are now beginning to be sensible', Abercromby told Huskisson; 'I wish you had laid aside your buckram principles before.'[10]

Holding these beliefs, it may seem odd that Sir Ralph had applied for a command at the outbreak of war. His doubts about the allied cause were unlikely to breed the killer instinct which is sometimes said to be indispensable in a successful general. Abercromby was generous to the enemy, and praised their conduct in the Dutch campaign of 1799. He there found them to be more civilised than four years earlier at the height of the Terror, while their manners were more frank and candid than under the old monarchy.[11] About the merit of Britain's tangible war-aim, however, he can have had no doubt: it was the integrity of Holland and if possible Belgium, the principle which had governed British foreign policy since the reign of Elizabeth. Patriotic duty brought him back to the colours; and his devotion to the British Army made him determined to defend and restore its old reputation.

That ambition, combining with his natural independence of mind, set him further apart from his political masters. 'Sir Ralph, as we all know, is not a courtier', wrote an Irish official; and he was uncompromising in his warnings when a military operation was not properly prepared. 'No army can march without horses or wagons', he told the Secretary of State for War while the invasion of Holland in 1799 was being mounted. He added gratuitously that even the Tsar of Russia, who could reduce a general to a private by a stroke of his pen, could not make his troops march without their transport: 'It is only in a free country such as ours that a Minister has absolute power over the army'.[12]

The point was relevant, but the irony might have been tempered. Abercromby got away with it because the minister he was addressing was a Scotsman, a relation, and a friend. Dundas was the most powerful politician in Scotland, and one of Pitt's two closest colleagues. Sir Ralph, whose brother had succeeded him in his parliamentary seat, might have used his political clout to promote his own interests. Instead, he used it to speak his mind.

Ministers could be disconcerted by his criticism of their plans, and impatient with the low priority he conceded to the political considerations which governed their strategy. Pitt, while admitting his own ignorance of military organisation, became irritated by Abercromby's objections to the plans for the Dutch expedition of 1799, which had been conceived by the Foreign Secretary Lord Grenville for political reasons with no regard for military problems. 'There are some persons', Pitt pointedly complained, 'who have a pleasure in opposing whatever is proposed.' Grenville raged at the sacrifice of time 'to the laziness of clerks and staff officers'; but soon a letter from Pitt brought him the memorable assurance, 'All military difficulties are completely overruled'.[13]

This seemed to be the final triumph of political over military considerations; but after the successful landing Abercromby frustrated Grenville's hopes by his decision not to advance from the beach-head till his reinforcements arrived. Grenville's fury erupted again. He had planned the expedition as a military perambulation, confident that the sight of a red coat would detonate an irresistible Dutch rising against the French; and the sight of Abercromby digging in imbued him with a distrust of the general which was never to be eradicated. Abercromby, however, had seen the retreat through Holland in the winter of 1793–4, and had the measure of the Dutch. He detected no enthusiasm for the invaders, and was sure that the Dutch would not rise till British victory was certain. He backed his judgment and was not to be deflected: 'I know you will say why is Sir Ralph Abercromby so long inactive, but I am prepared for that. . . . I am certain that I have acted right'.[14] A few days later his caution was justified when enemy forces, whose very existence the Cabinet had denied, attacked his entrenchments in superior force and were beaten off. If Abercromby had advanced without cavalry or transport to encounter the enemy in the open, the outcome would probably have been disaster.

With the awaited reinforcements came the Duke of York to assume the supreme command of the Anglo-Russian forces. When the campaign ended in capitulation and withdrawal, Pitt saw fit to offer Abercromby a peerage for his successful landing and the capture of the Dutch fleet. Dundas believed that Pitt was prompted by his guilty memory of the Irish affair; but perhaps he merely wished to stop Abercromby's mouth on the subject of the Cabinet's military planning, about which the Opposition was waxing sarcastic. This would have been the first army peerage of the war, and if it had been offered promptly after the landing Abercromby's son believed that he might have accepted it. But when the offer was made after the failure of the campaign Abercromby refused it. Through Dundas he told Pitt that he was not rich enough to support a peerage; and it would bar his heir from every career except the army and navy. He did not want to debar his son from a profession, in which he believed that 'every man ought to employ a certain portion of his life'.

'Allow us', he replied to the Prime Minister's offer, 'to go on in the patterns of industry in our different pursuits.' As an alternative reward Pitt offered him a grant of land forfeited by the rebel Caribs in the West Indies, which looked even more like a bribe. Abercromby replied with indignation that he was not a beggar or a covetous man to profit from the forfeitures of black insurgents. Sir Ralph stood above the rapacious patronage of the age.[15]

Abercromby kept his silence when he returned from Holland, and slipped quietly away to Edinburgh to resume his duties as Commander-in-Chief in Scotland. When, in the following May, he was appointed Commander-in-Chief in the Mediterranean with the command of Britain's only striking force, there was perturbation among his political critics. Grenville's brother Lord Buckingham was incredulous: 'Most violently am I indignant at the reappointment', he exclaimed.[16] But the appointment lay with Dundas; and he got away with it for a sound reason. Abercromby's record showed that for all his diffidence and awkwardness he was a soldier who delivered the goods.

His war record was astonishing. In 1793, at the age of 58, he had gone to war for the first time since his service as a junior officer thirty years earlier in Germany; and he was so short-sighted that he could see nothing without a telescope. His brigade was the first command he had ever held on active service; and it was a rabble of old men and newly enlisted boys.

Yet this elderly soldier led the column which stormed Valenciennes that summer. In the spring of the following year he was publicly thanked by his Commander-in-Chief, the Duke of York, when he coolly extricated his division from encirclement near Tourcoing. In the winter of 1794 he commanded the rearguard in the dreadful retreat across Holland and Germany to Bremen; and, the Duke of York having been recalled and his successor General Harcourt proving insufficient, Abercromby effectively directed the whole army. By the end of the campaign his reputation was made; and Pitt noted that he 'seems to stand higher than any other officer in general opinion'.[17]

Abercromby was therefore the best choice from an indifferent selection to command the expedition to the West Indies in 1796, the largest expeditionary force ever hitherto sent abroad. His troops were mostly newly raised and again of dubious quality, and they sailed into a raging pandemic of yellow fever. With regiments reduced to skeletons by fever and malaria, Abercromby captured the main French base at St Lucia, taking the previously impregnable fortress of Morne Fortuné. He then recovered Grenada and St Vincent, and in the following year captured Trinidad. He went on to attack Puerto Rico; but here the Spanish garrison turned out to be much larger than the British government had led Abercromby to believe. Unable to subdue the island, Sir Ralph made a masterly withdrawal. Under cover of preparations for an attack he re-embarked his whole force undetected, and the Spanish cavalry arrived as the last boat pushed off.[18]

Such was the military record which placed Sir Ralph Abercromby in command of the Mediterranean theatre and the Egyptian expedition. It would be Britain's final offensive of the war, and the British Army's last opportunity to redeem its reputation.

2

A LOOK AT JOHN TURK

About 19 October the gale in the Straits abated, and the scattered shipping worked back towards Gibraltar. Lord Keith brought in forty of the most damaged ships to Gibraltar bay, ordering the 74-gun *Ajax* to escort the rest to an anchorage on the African coast. Abercromby, a notorious Jonah who never put to sea without raising a tempest, had fetched up in the bight of Cadiz. But the worst had been averted: thirty or forty ships, feared lost when they were trapped by the gale in the bay of Tetuan, had survived when the wind unexpectedly 'southerned'.[1]

While the fleet reassembled and began to repair the damage the Adjutant-General, Colonel John Hope, was sent off in the *Incendiary* to organise a supply of fresh provisions at Lisbon, though the fresh oranges which warded off scurvy were not yet harvested. The force's next destination was unknown; but to keep the great convoy cruising in the Straits for any length of time awaiting orders from home was out of the question. There was no safe anchorage, and the shipping had to shift between Gibraltar, Tetuan bay, and the west coast of Africa according to the direction of the wind. Abercromby and Lord Keith had decided to move the whole expedition northwards to Lisbon where there was a safe harbour and provisions when, on the morning of 24 October, the *Lavinia* brig raced in to Gibraltar from England with the Secretary of State's new instructions, thrusting the army into the next phase of its 'wandering and unsuccessful movements'.[2]

Abercromby, with his intimate knowledge of Dundas's mind, had already realised that the government would not have collected this great armada in the Straits of Gibraltar unless they were planning some distant operation. With his mind prepared, he had alerted the admiral to the need to plan for the shipping arrangements; and he had separated the regiments enlisted for general service from those confined to Europe. The new orders confirmed his guess. Eight thousand men of his limited-service regiments were to sail for Lisbon under General Pulteney to defend Portugal against a threatened Spanish attack; and Abercromby was to take 15,000 to Egypt, making up his numbers by dumping his remaining Europe-only regiments in the Mediterranean garrisons in exchange for general-service troops. From India and the Cape another force of European infantry and sepoys would assemble in the Red Sea to co-operate with Abercromby through Suez.[3]

Dundas's letters, though flattering in their compliments and candour, did not soften Abercromby's sardonic view of his political masters. 'Is it not astonishing', he wrote to the Under-Secretary on receiving his orders, 'that it should not be known in England that Gibraltar neither affords a safe anchorage nor a drop of water?' His astonishment was not shared by a former Cabinet minister, the Duke of Richmond: 'I suppose Mr Dundas drinks himself so little water that he does not consider it as at all necessary for an army'. To be fair to the bibulous Dundas, the reason for keeping the army in the Straits had been the Cabinet's delay in agreeing to his Egyptian operation; a delay for which he had angrily renounced responsibility.[4]

Disparaging though Abercromby might be about the Cabinet's planning, he knew the importance of the expedition, as a measured act of British policy which had been explained with remarkable frankness and breadth in Dundas's private letter. Moreover Abercromby felt deeply how severe would be the impact of yet another military failure, and how much it would 'affect the public mind'. 'This undertaking is not to be weighed in an ordinary scale', he wrote, 'you shall hear no more of difficulties. I believe we all feel that something must be done to wipe off the disgraces of this unfortunate campaign.' He saw the problems ahead, but the adventure lifted his spirits. 'Sir Ralph is quite keen about it', his best subordinate General John Moore observed, 'and is ten years younger since he left England.' An officer on the staff at home, sharply resenting the army's disgrace at Ferrol and the enemy's 'exultation and ridicule', felt that Abercromby's army could redeem the fiasco. 'Such a force', he wrote to Major Hudson Lowe, 'under the command and at the disposal of a General whom we well know, might yet re-establish the character of British troops.' Such indeed was to be Abercromby's mission.[5]

Several difficulties were, nevertheless, at once apparent. One of them was the government's timetable. Dundas expected the force to put in at some island in the eastern Mediterranean to collect intelligence and fresh supplies, and to buy horses which could not be shipped from England for the cavalry and artillery; yet still to land on the Egyptian coast in December. It was now nearly the end of October; and after months at sea and the recent storm-damage, Abercromby's transports were in no condition to sail direct to the Levant. Many required dockyard repairs and all needed fresh provisions to stem the growing sickness among the troops. Before the expedition could be launched into the eastern Mediterranean, there would have to be a pause at Malta, the superb harbour in the Sicilian narrows which had been surrendered by General Vaudois and his French garrison in September after a two-year blockade and siege. Some of the worst of the transports would have to be diverted to Minorca for repairs in the Port Mahon dockyard.

In the meantime preparations could begin for the force's eventual arrival in the Levant. To Rhodes Abercromby dispatched his Quartermaster-General, Colonel Robert Anstruther, and his assistant Lieutenant-Colonel George Murray, both of whom were later to be distinguished in the Peninsular War. Their task was to make contact with the Turkish army in Palestine, where there was already a British military mission, and arrange the purchase of provisions and the hire of small vessels for the coming invasion. Abercromby also enlisted the aid of the British minister at Constantinople, Lord Elgin, who was a member of Abercromby's Scottish social network. A neighbour and intimate family friend on the northern shore of the Forth, Elgin was also known to Anstruther, a fellow native of Fife, who was to ask him to buy horses for the British artillery and unmounted dragoons and negotiate for Turkish cavalry.[6]

Before leaving the Straits there was some further sorting and culling of the force. A regiment enlisted for service in Europe was put ashore at Gibraltar to join the garrison, releasing the 44th to join the expedition. The seriously sick, about 4–500 men, were left in the Gibraltar General Hospital; and all but three companies of the 2/27th, infested with fever, were sent north to Lisbon to recuperate. Now only a westerly wind was needed to get the fleet clear of the Straits; and on 27 October the worst of the ships – troopships, transports, and victuallers – were able to sail for the Minorca dockyard.

Abercromby himself reached Malta on 19 November. Here he had to leave the 1/27th and the remaining companies of the 2/27th to recover from fever, as well as 800 sick from other regiments, thus carefully purging the army of a source of infection. The force was now well below the 15,000 envisaged by the Cabinet, whose military arithmetic seldom erred on the side of realism. Fortunately the two battalions of the 54th, enlisted for Europe only, had volunteered for Egypt. So too did the two battalions of the 40th when they were put ashore at Malta to relieve two general-service regiments. Abercromby accepted their four flank companies, the grenadiers and light infantry, compensating a little for his defective numbers. One further cull affected the troops more than their general. Only three soldiers' wives per company would be allowed in Egypt, and when the signal was given on 12 December to prepare for sailing, there were heart-rending scenes as the surplus women were sent ashore.[7]

A fortnight later, the troopships were rolling through heavy seas towards the coast of Asia Minor, carrying 14,000 cold, wet, and seasick soldiers. On board the storm-tossed *Thisbe*, a converted frigate now 224 days out from England, were part of the 2nd Foot, the Queen's, with their commanding officer the Earl of Dalhousie, who in future years would command a division under Wellington. Cooped in his ship for thirty-two weeks apart from brief respites ashore at Minorca and Malta, he cursed the floating gaols of troopships and the ships' officers, 'vulgar blackguards, that would do anything to disoblige us or annoy a soldier'.[8] Eleven of his officers were crammed into one small cabin; and on the lower decks his soldiers were lying under blankets, their clothing in tatters because a storeship convoy due from England had not arrived. As the storm raged under the lowering winter sky, Dalhousie reflected that in three days' time the nineteenth century would dawn on this miserable army.

Lord Keith had intended to bring the fleet in to Rhodes or the Gulf of Macri; but as the fleet approached the Dodecanese, the south-east gale barred them from fetching either anchorage. From several sources the admiral had heard of an anchorage unknown to his charts at Marmaris on the mainland coast, and he hailed the *Peterel* sloop which had been serving in those waters, asking her captain, Inglis, whether he could lead them into the bay. Inglis undertook to do it; and in hazy weather on a perilous lee shore the *Peterel* led the fleet straight towards a line of towering brown cliffs at whose base a foaming line of savage breakers was crashing. Suddenly an opening appeared; the *Peterel* altered course sharply; and for the seasick troops on the lower decks a miracle occurred, and the seas were stilled. One by one the transports entered a channel so narrow that an Irish officer vowed he could have thrown a ship's biscuit to either shore. Instantly the rolling and pitching ceased, and the ships which had not dared to carry a top-gallant sail in the storm outside were becalmed in the still waters of a natural harbour that could have sheltered the whole navy of Britain.[9]

Flickers of lightning still lit the low sky as the boats were slung out to tow the ships up the gulf. The weather was clearing, and out of the lifting cloud wooded hills appeared, falling to the water's edge round the twenty-mile circumference of the bay. Behind them the Taurus mountains rose peak on wild peak into the distances of Asia Minor. Here on the shores of the gulf was to be the expedition's home for the next seven weeks while it made the final preparations for the invasion of Egypt.

And here at last was an escape from Dalhousie's floating prison. On New Year's Eve he made up a party with his compatriot Colonel Brodie of the Gordon Highlanders and went ashore to celebrate Hogmanay. In a few hours' time the Tower guns in London would be booming their salute to the nineteenth century, and the new Union flags would flutter on public buildings to signal the union of Britain and Ireland in the United Kingdom. Dalhousie's party pitched a tent and supped round a huge log fire on the shores of Asia, swigging bumpers of brandy which left them with crashing headaches in the morning.[10]

To cure their hangovers the party set out with their guns to roam the plains and hills in glorious freedom with the local Turks, shooting the partridge, woodcock, and wild boar. They discovered a land of ancient ruins and wondrous cascades – 'wild, picturesque and awful'. Romantic, beautiful, sublime: letters and journals piled on the epithets of sensibility. The January days were like an English summer, and on calm evenings the setting sun threw a rich glossy light on the bay and its enfolding hills. The nights were loud with the croaking of frogs and the howls of wild beasts. After the months at sea Marmaris was a paradise to be remembered later with nostalgia in the sands of Egypt. 'I never wish to be on board a man of war again', Lieutenant James Brown of the 44th wrote to his parents. Alas, for him there was only one voyage ahead.[11]

But for their general the idyllic weeks at Marmaris were a slow torture. Abercromby wished to sail at once to the coast of Egypt and surprise the enemy, and had hoped to find everything he needed for the invasion waiting at Marmaris, having sent Anstruther five weeks ahead of the army to collect horses and horse transports, landing craft and provisions. But Anstruther had had no success during his weeks at Rhodes: the Turks would not supply him. Abercromby immediately sent out commissaries to forage and purchase, and soon there was an adequate stockpile of pork, flour and wine for the coming operations. But there were no small craft for the landing; and the horse transports which were being hired at Smyrna were not ready and could not arrive before the middle of February, six weeks ahead. And still the army had no horses: for these Abercromby relied on Lord Elgin in Constantinople.[12]

When Thomas Bruce, seventh Earl of Elgin, arrived in Constantinople in November 1799 he was a mature 34. That might not seem a ripe age for an Ambassador Extraordinary and Plenipotentiary; but he had been a raw 24-year-old on his first diplomatic mission when he tangled with the skilful Emperor Leopold II and the slippery Prussian foreign minister Bischoffswerder. He was transferred to Constantinople at his own wish, intent on organising a study of the remains of Greek art in the Ottoman dominions. This ambition would culminate after many obstacles in a Turkish firman which enabled him to rescue the endangered sculptures on the Parthenon and elsewhere which became known as the Elgin Marbles. He would need all the maturity and experience he had acquired in Brussels and Berlin to deal with his Turkish allies whether in war or archaeology; and to cope with the pretensions of the colleagues he found in Constantinople: the Smith brothers.

John Spencer Smith, and his brother Captain Sir Sidney Smith of the Royal Navy, were the sons of an army officer. Their father Captain Jack Smith had been aide de camp to Lord George Sackville at the battle of Minden in 1759, and had been threatened with prosecution for perjury after giving evidence for the defence at Sackville's subsequent court martial.[13] For the past four years his son John had been in charge of the Constantinople embassy, and when Bonaparte invaded Egypt in 1798 the Smith brothers were given joint plenipotentiary powers to negotiate a treaty with Turkey, which was signed in January 1799. Elgin's arrival did not remove John Smith's rank as minister plenipotentiary, and he ordered all but one of the embassy staff to act under his orders. This interference soon caused him to fall out with the new ambassador.[14]

John's brother Sir Sidney Smith, ambitious and enterprising, had become famous when he escaped from the Temple prison in Paris during the Revolution. In the Mediterranean his dual role as naval captain and diplomatist brought him into conflict with Nelson when he claimed an independent command in the Levant, and he had to be rebuked and bridled by their superior Lord St Vincent. Sir Sidney's great achievement was the defence of Acre in 1799 which halted Bonaparte's invasion of Syria. Neither Bonaparte nor Sir Sidney ever forgot the exploit; and for the rest of his career Sir Sidney inflicted his boastful reminiscences on every military visitor, from generals to subalterns, who boarded his ship. Elgin was exasperated by his puerilities, but forgave them for his cleverness, spirit, and local knowledge. The siege of Acre had left Sir Sidney with a taste for operations ashore, and he was to play a prominent part in the coming campaign.[15]

To be fair to Sir Sidney, he harboured no delusions about the military value of his friends the Turks, and doubted that they could ever be brought to face the French army again after the defeats they had suffered. Besides this, they had reason to fear the Russians on their northern border, and had no ideological commitment to the crusade against the French Revolution. The French were stigmatised by the British as atheists, but the British themselves were Christian dogs; and they tried in vain to interest the Ottomans in the defence of the hereditary principle against the levelling Jacobins, for Turkey had no hereditary aristocracy and its imperial succession depended on the bowstring. Even British gold was suspect. The Turks refused to accept Elgin's gold sovereigns as payment for the British army's supplies; and he had to send to Vienna to buy obsolete Maria Theresa thalers, the international currency of the Middle East, losing each time on the exchange.[16]

When Abercromby's list of needs reached Elgin in November 1800, the most difficult requirement was 600 horses, of which 200 appeared to be needed for the British cavalry. Elgin was passionately interested in horses and competent to judge his purchases,[17] but local difficulties were insuperable. Constantinople was said to be the place to buy them, since the horses of Syria would not stand the work. But while there was plenty of Arab bloodstock for riding, the stallions were ungelded; nor was there a stock of trained cavalry horses, for each Turkish cavalier was required to bring his own horse to war, and the disciplined drill of European cavalry was unknown. Draught horses there were none; for wheeled vehicles were little used, and such as there were moved slowly behind teams of oxen; and the pack animals were not horses but mules and camels. Elgin, warned by Anstruther that speed was more important than quality, quickly bought 200 horses and sent them overland by Smyrna, ordering barley to be shipped to Marmaris for their reception. He contracted for a further 500 horses, his sense of urgency increased by a letter from Anstruther dated 2 January: 'Pray hasten on all other matters, small craft, canteens, pioneers etc.: we wait only for these and the horses'.[18]

The 190 horses which reached Marmaris by 21 January were a disaster, and Elgin was 'deeply mortified' by Abercromby's reception of them. They 'do not exactly answer our expectations', the General delicately wrote to introduce the subject. This was euphemism. Of the 400 horses which eventually arrived from Elgin, not one was fit for the cavalry. 'Our poor dragoons groaned dismally' when they saw them. To make matters worse, two regiments of light dragoons had just been added to the army from Lisbon, without their mounts, raising the cavalry's requirement to nearly 1,200 horses. Many of those which arrived from Elgin were suffering from sore backs or lameness, and numbers had to be shot or sold as unfit for service: and the army guessed that Elgin had been deceived by the dealers, or that his purchases had been exchanged during the journey from Constantinople to Smyrna.[19]

About 180 weedy beasts were considered just fit for the artillery. To equip them for hauling cannon the artillery's harness was taken to pieces, replacing heavy sections with light ones to reduce the burden on the poor creatures. About 130 horses were thus fitted, and some light guns and howitzers were landed from the transports to teach them to draw in harness. Each 6-pounder required ten or twelve horses to drag it through heavy sand or shingle, so a bare dozen guns could be equipped with a team.[20]

To mount the cavalry, purchasing parties were sent inland, and enough horses were eventually bought to mount 450 dragoons after a fashion. They were handsome, spirited stallions, infinitely better than what had arrived from Constantinople; but they were barely fourteen hands high, more like Cossack ponies than the horses of the French cavalry. Mounted thus, the British dragoons would be fit for patrols and vedettes (the chain of mounted sentries in front of the outposts), but would lack the weight on which the British cavalry relied for a charge.[21]

What was causing the Turks' obstructiveness? The question had a wider implication for the success of the British operations, for Elgin and Abercromby were agreed that the British expedition was not strong enough to dislodge the French without Turkish military aid. How far could this be counted on? The failure of the local officials at Marmaris seemed to stem less from ill-will than from incompetence. They cheerfully made up shooting parties with the British officers, and fraternised happily with the sailors till some Greek vessels arrived with cargoes of wine. 'Now Jack has got his grog on board', noted Captain Wyvill of the Camerons, 'he swaggers and kicks every John Turk he meets.' Such conduct was intolerable. The tall, grave, proud shepherds, each with his gun at his shoulder, would not bear such affronts; and the coming operations in Egypt would require the highest discipline to retain the goodwill of the population. A stern warning was needed. Four sailors who had stolen and killed a bullock were condemned to death; and though two were quickly reprieved, the others reached the foot of the gallows before they were spared.[22]

The Turks continued to be lavish with firmans and promises; but nothing resulted. Abercromby believed that nothing could overcome their languor and indifference except the presence of the Capitan Pacha, the High Admiral of the Ottoman navy. By origin a Georgian slave, the Capitan Pacha was the most energetic and competent of all the Turkish commanders and officials the British encountered, and he had been expected to meet the expedition at Marmaris. But he had sailed away to Constantinople, partly because he doubted that the British were coming,[23] and announced that he could not return for six weeks. Little could be achieved without him. Power was never delegated, and the local authorities either dared not or would not show initiative. The one British officer who might galvanise them into activity was Sir Sidney Smith, who had been ordered to meet the expedition; but he had been swept up by Admiral Bickerton off Crete and taken away to blockade Alexandria on a report that a French squadron was at sea.[24]

The most sinister interpretation of Turkish unhelpfulness and the absence of the Capitan Pacha was their fear of Russia. Abercromby had been alerted by the British government to Tsar Paul's growing hostility and probable alliance with Bonaparte to partition the Ottoman Empire. He had been warned to be ready to seize Russian shipping and to resist an attack; and he feared that the Russian threat in the north would divert the Turks' attention and resources from the Egyptian operation.[25] But even if Turkish inertia had no explanation more sinister than procrastinating temperament and bad administrative habits, what did this promise for their military co-operation? An answer to this question suddenly appeared with the return of Major Murray from the Ottoman camp at Jaffa. There he had joined the British military mission, and seen the Turkish army.

The commander of the military mission to the Turks was Brigadier-General George Koehler, an artillery officer of German birth who had distinguished himself in the great siege of Gibraltar and the defence of Toulon. He had been sent to Turkey, which he already knew, as a military counterpart to Sir Sidney Smith on the news of Bonaparte's invasion of Egypt. His party consisted of thirteen officers and fifty-four other ranks from the artillery and engineers, with two commissaries, two draughtsmen, and thirteen civilian artificers. The future chronicler of the mission was Dr William Wittman, a Royal Artillery surgeon. There were also eighteen women and children. Twenty-five of the group were to die of disease before its return to England.[26]

A year later when Lord Elgin arrived in Turkey the military mission was still kicking its heels in Constantinople, having been prevented by the intrigues of the Smith brothers from obtaining permission to join the Turkish army facing the French in Syria. Elgin was amused by Koehler's exalted view of the state which befitted a European in the east. He claimed, said Elgin, the respect due to a Bonaparte or a Suvorov: 'Seeing Englishmen in authority in Turkey takes away all delight in reading Don Quixote'.[27]

In spite of Elgin's derision, his arrival set the mission in motion. He discovered that Sir Sidney Smith, commanding the naval blockade of Alexandria, was negotiating a free passage home for the French army; a good bargain for the Turks who would get rid of the unwelcome intruders without further fighting, but a dubious one for the British at a time when the Second Coalition was preparing to deal a decisive blow in Europe. In January 1800 Koehler was ordered to Cyprus, Sir Sidney's supply base, to counteract his influence. He took with him an officer of the artillery and engineers, and a draughtsman. A travelling scholar from Cambridge University attached himself to the party, no doubt with Elgin's encouragement. The Rev. Joseph Carlyle, Professor of Arabic, was eager to travel the lands where the language he professed was spoken, and had plans to collect Greek and Syriac manuscripts for a revised version of the New Testament.[28]

The party left Constantinople secretly, disguised as Tartar couriers and guided by a Tartar and a janissary. Setting out on the Aleppo road, they soon struck south-eastwards into the Taurus mountains through country where no Europeans had been seen in living memory. Reaching the coast at Gilindire, they crossed to Cyprus by schooner; traversed the island from north to south; and at Larnaca found the British squadron commanded by Sir Sidney Smith. Koehler discovered, however, that Smith's negotiation with the French (the Treaty of El Arish) had collapsed; and with no more to be done in Cyprus the military party crossed the sea to Jaffa on the coast of Palestine at the beginning of July 1800. Here at the Turkish camp they rejoined the rest of the mission.[29]

And here at last Koehler met the Grand Vizir, the chief minister of the Ottoman Empire and commander of the army. Aged 66 (the same age as Abercromby), white-haired, and with only one eye, he had recently suffered a catastrophic defeat at the hands of General Kléber at the battle of Heliopolis. In spite of this he had retained his position through his connections in the Sultan's household. The venerable potentate was well versed in Persian literature, but totally ignorant of European politics and western knowledge. In every circumstance he was said to see the hand of irresistible fate, which he regarded it as vain and impious to attempt to deflect.[30]

He was surrounded by a feudal host. Its human material was magnificent, and the Turkish soldiers impressed the British immediately by their fine physique and bearing. 'Strength and gravity are displayed in their gestures', wrote Captain Maule of the Queen's: 'I have never observed meanness in the look of a Turkish soldier; pride and severity more frequently predominate.' 'They were invariably men of large stature', Major Lowe reported, 'who appeared to look down upon us with indifference if not contempt.'[31]

But their military merit lay in individual skirmishing; and they were totally without the discipline on which European tactics were founded. The only troops which could be called regulars even in name were the janissaries, who in peacetime lived at home like civilians, pursuing their own trades without parades or training. The rest were irregular levies which had joined the army as it moved through their districts, and in camp each levy pitched its tents in disorder round that of its pacha. Government ammunition was issued only for battle, and the men fired off their own powder and shot to the public danger whenever the fancy took them. Each man equipped himself as horse or foot according to his means, and there was a huge disproportion of cavalry. This jumble of fighting men of every hue – black, white, copper, tawny and yellow – was mingled with a mass of tradesmen, servants, and standard bearers.

The number of troops was impossible to discover, for the army was in constant flux. The levies deserted in large gangs which defied the pickets guarding the roads to the rear; but new recruits also poured in. The Grand Vizir claimed that he had 35,000 men; Koehler guessed 7–8,000; and when the Vizir tried to muster and count them his Albanian levies fired into his tent to deter him. In spite of this he held a three-day review, which confirmed Koehler's estimate of their numbers and presented an alarming picture of their battleworthiness. Field-day manoeuvres consisted of an advance of a few hundred yards in confused and disordered lines preceded by the artillery, with no intervals in the lines for cannon. The army then turned about, and repeated the manoeuvre in the opposite direction. No progress had been made in the art of war for generations, perhaps for centuries. These troops could never cope with the swiftness and precision of a well-trained modern army, and Koehler judged that 2,000 European troops would rout 15,000 Turks.

On 3 December Colonel Murray arrived at Jaffa from Gibraltar in the *Chameleon* sloop, bringing the first news of the approaching expedition. He formed an even worse impression of the Turkish army than had been gathered from Koehler's reports. Plague was now raging in the camp, with a death-rate of a hundred a day, and the corpses were buried among the crowded tents in shallow graves from which hands, feet and even heads projected. Around the camp hung the putrid smell of death. The carcasses of horses, camels, and asses lay unburied and rotting, and there was an epidemic among the dogs which swarmed in the camp. Everywhere offal and filth were heaped.[32]

After ten days of this scene Murray re-embarked for Marmaris to meet the approaching expedition and report to Abercromby, accompanied by Captain Richard Fletcher of the Royal Engineers.

In the cabin of the *Kent* Sir Ralph had been pondering on strategy in the intervals of his daily routine of inspections and administration. He commanded Britain's only striking force: how best could he use it? The political aim was clear enough: it was to influence the coming peace conference by loosening the French grip on Egypt. And the direct means to this end was to defeat and destroy the French Army of the Orient.

Yet this was too simple a definition of his instructions. As Abercromby observed, his orders were 'eventual in some particulars'; meaning that they gave him a wide discretion and choice of options. Though Henry Dundas had been optimistic about the enemy's strength and morale, he had realised that the picture might look different when the expedition reached the Levant, six or eight weeks distant from Whitehall. He had received Koehler's discouraging estimate of the Turkish army, and admitted that 'much I am afraid is not to be expected of them'. And there was the risk of disease, which the Caribbean losses had taught him to dread: was it wise for a British force to advance into the interior of Egypt? Dundas's answer was no.

He had therefore devised what he called 'a limited plan of operations'; a flexible response to the unpredictable. He believed that a campaign in the interior would not be necessary. If the garrison of the port of Alexandria could be attacked and induced to capitulate in return for a safe passage home to France, the French forces isolated in the interior would probably accept the same terms. Short of this, it would still be helpful to the peace negotiators if Abercromby held the Egyptian ports and coastline; or indeed if he merely seized a beach-head, allowing them to claim that the possession of the country was in actual dispute. Something might even be gained if the expedition was established at a base in the Levant, and could be said to be capable of disputing Egypt. Dundas made it clear that Abercromby was not required to take unjustifiable risks: 'No false point of honour or feeling will induce you to attempt what is too hazardous to be attempted'.[33]

Three months later, on the coast of Asia Minor, Abercromby could not take this sentence at face value. What was at stake was no 'false point of honour', but the redemption of the British Army's name. He was haunted by its undeserved disgrace at Ferrol and Cadiz. Nor was the army's honour alone at stake; for a further fiasco could destroy the British public's will to continue the war. Whatever happened, he was determined at any cost to wipe off the army's recent disgraces.[34]

Nor did Abercromby accept that victory could be won by negotiating with the enemy general or nibbling at his coastal garrisons. Weak in numbers and homesick the French might be, though this was impossible to confirm. But Sir Ralph knew the French of old as a bold, ruthless, and mobile enemy, imbued with the doctrine of the offensive. The moment he landed in Egypt, they would concentrate their force against his bridge-head and attack him. At some point the British army would have to fight a decisive battle; for this was not diplomacy, but war.[35]

Yet how poorly his force was equipped for its task. He had neither wagons nor draught animals; only a handful of mounted cavalry; few gun-teams for his field artillery. He had no maps of the theatre, while the French army had excellent maps drawn by its skilled surveyors during the long occupation;

and his information of the enemy was vague, contradictory, and, as it eventually proved, entirely false.

It was clear to Abercromby that he was once again to look adversity in the face. The coming operation would be amphibious warfare at its most difficult. Consul Baldwin even doubted that water would be found where the army was most likely to fight, on the Aboukir isthmus; in which case, lacking land transport to fetch it, the troops would be entirely dependent on the navy's boats to supply them from the sea in any weather. Reporting the water problem to Dundas, Abercromby added his famous comment on combined operations: 'there are risks in a British warfare unknown in any other service'.[36]

Lacking maps, Abercromby had to interrogate anyone who knew anything about the country, to try to establish such elementary facts as the distance between towns, and on which bank of which branch of the Nile the town of Rosetta stood. From close questioning of naval captains who knew the coast, Abercromby did gather that the winter sea was less rough than the Admiralty had informed him; and he identified two roadsteads on either side of the delta, at Aboukir and Damietta, where the fleet might put the army ashore.[37] His instructions had emphasised the port of Alexandria, whose fall would sever the enemy's communications with France and secure an all-weather anchorage for the British fleet. For attacking Alexandria the best landing place was in Aboukir bay, to the west of the delta and about a dozen miles east of the city. Abercromby's first instinct was therefore to storm ashore at Aboukir.

From Elgin, however, he learned that the Turks wished him to land at Damietta, where he could co-operate with their advance from Jaffa. Landing would present problems, for the water was so shallow that the fleet would have to lie twelve miles from the shore, and the beach was defended by a new French fort at Lesbeh.[38] But there were some operational attractions; for the Damietta option would avoid the water shortage expected on the Aboukir isthmus and the engineer problems of laying siege to the fortress of Alexandria. Moreover the eastern branch of the Nile would afford not only water but transport for the hundred-mile advance inland to Cairo. His instructions cautioned him against an advance into the interior; but they also promised much of the Turks, and at Cairo he would gain possession of the enemy's artillery depot, powder mills and hospitals while his own force was still entire and healthy. The threat to their resources would probably force the French to make a stand and fight the battle he sought; and Abercromby therefore was minded to comply with the Turkish request and land at Damietta.[39]

No sooner had Abercromby formed this tentative resolution, however, than Colonel Murray arrived from the Grand Vizir's camp at Jaffa, bringing Abercromby an up-to-date account of the Turkish army. Murray described the filth, indiscipline, and disease; and reported that the Turks had no supplies and were therefore incapable of crossing the desert barrier between Palestine and Egypt.

This news was even gloomier than Koehler's earlier reports; and Abercromby had to be sure of the truth. If he complied with the Turks' desire and landed at Damietta, his army would be operating on a wider front than on the Aboukir isthmus, with open flanks and over much greater distances. He would need Turkish cavalry to make up his own deficiency, and the main Turkish army would have to advance close on his flank and support his offensive. Could he rely on the Turks to provide either cavalry or flank protection?

There was nothing for it but to send a senior officer to Jaffa to make sure. Abercromby knew at once that the man for the task was John Moore: the quiet, smartly turned-out major general, son of a Glasgow physician, who had served under him in the West Indies and Holland and now commanded the army's crack brigade, the Reserve. Moore was an utterly dedicated professional soldier. Studious, brave, and decisive in combat, he was also probably the best trainer of officers and soldiers in the army. Abercromby would trust his judgement of the Ottoman army, and on 3 January he ordered him to visit the Turkish camp. Moore was to propose that the Grand Vizir should advance (it could not be for several weeks, till after Ramadan, which began that year about 18 January), and cross the deserts of Sinai and Suez to Salahieh on the edge of the Nile delta. From there they could co-operate with the British army, which would advance from Damietta on the Turkish right, taking the lead to protect the head of the Turkish column. Abercromby would need some good Turkish cavalry with his own force. Would the Grand Vizir accept the plan? Was he capable of executing it? Moore's mission was to discover the answers.[40]

Six days later he landed at Jaffa from the *Chameleon*. As he rode out from the port towards the camp he was met by Colonel Holloway of the Royal Engineers, and learned that death was stalking the terrified British mission. Koehler and his wife had died of fever, and two others of the plague. The bedding and clothes of the dead had been burned and their tents fumigated. Moore rode on. Holloway took him immediately to the palatial tent of the Grand Vizir, and thence to the Reis Effendi, the Foreign Minister. He found these grandees seated cross-legged on cushioned sofas, their long gowns of silk and brocade lined with fur and embroidered with gold and silver. For an hour they exchanged compliments over pipes, coffee, and sherbet; and in the evening business began, in a secret three-hour session with the Reis Effendi interpreting in French. More meetings followed in the course of the next few days, and the Grand Vizir agreed to Abercromby's proposals. He would advance from Jaffa on 24 February at the end of Ramadan.[41]

During these days Moore was living with the British mission, quartered in a luxurious tent supplied by the Turks and with a daily dinner sent from the Vizir's kitchen. His nights were disturbed by the yells of the jackals devouring the half-buried corpses of men and beasts. In the daytime he spent the intervals between conferences trying to discover the real state of the Turkish army's organisation and magazines, of which Koehler's knowledge seemed to have died with him. The Grand Vizir now claimed that he had 7,500 cavalry, the same number of infantry, and fifty field guns. He said he had enough ammunition and biscuit to allow his force to advance, but was waiting for ships to arrive with barley for the cavalry's horses and transport animals for the baggage.[42]

Moore remained unconvinced. He assessed the Grand Vizir as an unreliable, weak old man without talent or military knowledge. The one-eyed veteran knew nothing about the enemy's strength, although the communications with Egypt were open; and Moore's own investigation of the Turkish supplies indicated that not enough provisions were stockpiled for the desert march to the Nile. The death rate in the camp had soared to 200 a day. As for the army's fighting quality, the cavalry were well mounted and individually had their horses under good control; but the infantry were a miserable-looking horde, and neither they nor the horsemen were under any discipline. They were not an army at all, Moore concluded, but a wild ungovernable mob.[43]

Returning to Marmaris on 20 January, Moore went straight to Abercromby's headquarters on board the *Kent* to report his findings, and advised him not to base his plans on Turkish help. For this Sir Ralph was prepared. If only because of the plague, it would be folly to become involved with the Grand Vizir's medieval horde. Abercromby told Moore there and then that he would land not at Damietta but at Aboukir; and summoned a conference on board the flagship to plan the operation.[44]

3

THE FORGING OF
THE BLADE

The point of attack was settled, the horse ships were hourly expected from Smyrna; and Abercromby intended to sail for Aboukir bay as soon as they arrived. But no horse transports appeared. The days dragged by, and nearly five more weeks were to pass before the armada streamed out from the narrow mouth of the bay of Marmaris. Every day that went by gave the enemy more time to prepare his defences and receive reinforcements from France. Every day spent at Marmaris had to compensate for the lost opportunities by making the expedition better prepared to land and survive on the barren shores of Egypt. All branches of the force were at work on special training and the improvising of equipment.

For the artillery and engineers the most intractable problem would be siege operations. The battering train of heavy siege-guns, originally prepared for the attack on Belle Ile, were awkward to transport overland and 'very indifferently provided'. Easier to handle were the short carronades of the warships, which the artillery commander General Lawson considered powerful enough, in spite of their short barrels and low muzzle velocity, to batter the crumbly new earthworks and unhardened masonry-cement he expected to find in the French fortifications. Experiments were made, and the naval carriages of the carronades were successfully modified for service ashore.

Transporting ammunition would be a further problem. For the early stage of the attack before horses could be landed, hand-carts were constructed, and nine-foot poles with rope slings were assembled on which a pair of soldiers could carry ammunition boxes or kegs of musket-cartridges. Even when the few draught horses were landed the sandy soil was likely to be difficult for wheeled vehicles; and, as alternative load-carriers, wooden stretchers or barrows were designed to be carried by a horse between the shafts at each end. Artillery ammunition boxes were modified to take mixed batches of round- and case-shot and cartridges, suitable for carriage by camels. Gangways were constructed for landing siege-guns and rolling them across sand and ditches.[1]

The same resourcefulness was shown in other departments. The military artificers were landed to supervise working parties of soldiers in making the army self-sufficient in the timberless and possibly waterless terrain of Egypt. Timber was felled and cut into lengths to make the engineers' fascines and gabions, for filling ditches and constructing siege-batteries. To provide cooking fuel two regiments were landed daily and formed wooding parties which felled vast numbers of trees. Large quantities of tent-pegs and mallets were fashioned for pitching tents. In the fleet the ships' coopers were at work on containers for provisions: small eight-gallon casks for carrying water on pack-animals; barrels to hold a hundredweight of boiled meat; wooden buckets and pumps for drawing water from wells. The ships' carpenters made hand-barrows and sledges to drag or carry supplies across the sand. Improvisation was the word.[2]

These lost weeks at Marmaris gave Abercromby the best opportunity he had ever had to prepare an army for war. He had always commanded regiments filled with rubbish and officered by ignorant young stringpullers. Here there was time to polish the regiments' training, and to plan and rehearse the assault landing. But first the army's health had to be restored. Fortunately the most dangerous diseases like typhus had not appeared, and the sick rapidly began to recover. When Captain Rooke joined the 3rd Guards from England he found that his battalion had 140 sick; but they had all been put ashore in tents, where clean air and good food were working a cure. After the long diet of salt pork and foul water, the fresh meat and pure spring water of Marmaris were performing wonders.[3]

Soon the troops were in remarkably good health in spite of their months at sea; and with the belated arrival of the storeships' convoy the soldiers' tattered coats and breeches were replaced. Except for the highlanders in their blocked bonnets, most of the infantry were wearing the new felt shako or 'stovepipe', with its patent leather brim and coloured feather plume: red and white for the battalion companies, and plain white for the grenadiers who no longer wore their bearskin caps in the field. The light companies were still wearing a round broad-brimmed hat, due to be replaced in the coming year by a shako with a green plume. Officers still retained the bicorne, but in Egypt most of them exchanged it for a civilian top hat with a floppy brim as protection against the sun, adding a feather from the bicorne at the side.

Abercromby now had a healthy, well clothed army to take into battle. But would its tactics measure up to the French? It was not only misfortune which had caused the army's reputation to plummet: there had been a long history of maladministration and mismanagement. The old British Army which had shattered the French cavalry at Minden and had fought so skilfully and tenaciously through the long years of the American War had been ruined by peacetime neglect and hasty mobilisation. When the infantry regiments returned from America in 1783 their depleted strengths had been allowed to run down to a level at which scarcely a battalion in the British Isles was fit for active service. The uniformity of their drill collapsed, for there was no longer a common drill manual in use and in peacetime there was no

Commander-in-Chief to restore conformity. No two infantry battalions drilled exactly alike, and the rare brigade exercises were chaotic.

When war broke out again in 1793, rapid expansion of this skeleton army brought chaos. An expeditionary force was scraped together for the West Indies only by tearing the élite flank companies of grenadiers and light infantry from their battalions and sending them to be exterminated by yellow fever. The regiments at home were left mutilated and under strength. Wartime recruits were scarce and of poor quality; and the best of the regiments were tied up in imperial garrisons. It used to be said before the Second World War that one had to go to India to see the real British Army, because the units at home consisted of under-strength training battalions. The same might have been said in the 1790s. To find mature battalions of 'hard-biting' soldiers one had to visit the overseas garrisons. Gibraltar and Minorca had regiments of seasoned men such as the 28th Foot and the 42nd Highlanders, which were both to win distinction in Egypt. But in the Netherlands campaign of 1793–5 the Duke of York and Abercromby had to wage war with skeleton battalions filled out with old men and boys. Even a petty German prince with only one regiment could field a better force. 'We were ashamed of our service', Sir Herbert Taylor recalled.[4]

And so they should be, thought the navy. Shortly before the Egyptian expedition sailed from Gibraltar, Lord St Vincent pronounced the whole infantry of Great Britain to be unfit for a service of hardy enterprise, and hinted that even Abercromby's courage might be deficient. Naval arrogance was exasperating, and in the past year the army had taken pleasure in recalling 'our naval friends' boasting' when the Mediterranean and Channel fleets allowed a great enemy armada to sail unhindered through the Straits of Gibraltar and into Brest. Yet if St Vincent was right about the infantry, it was a gloomy outlook for British strategy.[5]

But beneath the surface things were better than they seemed, and the foundations of recovery had been laid although improvement was retarded by the demands of war. In 1792 a new drill manual had been adopted. Its author was Colonel David Dundas, who based it on his *Principles of Military Movements* published in 1788. Dundas had observed that the infantry regiments returning at the end of the American War in 1783 from America, the Caribbean, and India had brought home the divergent practices of their own theatres. And with no Commander-in-Chief, and at least two different drill manuals in use, officers commanding battalions freely adapted from different manuals and added variations of their own. Dundas believed that the most pernicious influence on British tactics was the experience of war in the American colonies.

Since the end of the Seven Years War in 1763 a distinction had been drawn in the British Army between an 'American' and a 'German' school of officers: the German typified by faith in rigid close-order infantry drill designed for open plains in the presence of a strong enemy cavalry; the American school characterised by a looser order, faster marching, and more emphasis on light infantry, which were practices suited to small forces in close country against an enemy skilled in aimed musketry but lacking cavalry. British officers returning from the American War were crusaders for a loose, shallow two-deep line with emphasis on light infantry work and skirmishing.

David Dundas, a veteran of the Seven Years War, emphatically belonged to the 'German' school; and his book was an explicit rejection of the American experience. These 'loose desultory movements', this 'want of solidity', would not do in European terrain against armies trained in the close-order manoeuvres which Frederick the Great's Prussians had brought to perfection, and against massed cavalry. These precise German evolutions the British Army was no longer capable of performing; and Dundas's manual brought British battle-drill back to Frederickian practice. A battalion was to form in three ranks, not two; the ranks closed up one pace apart, the files touching their neighbour elbow to elbow; the marching pace a slow seventy-five paces to the minute. It was a system designed to deliver massive shock and withstand cavalry. Dundas's answer to cavalry was 'superior order, regularity and weight of fire'; a truth which was to be proved in Egypt.[6]

Regulations alone, however, were not enough; for as Wellington once remarked, 'Nobody in the British Army ever reads a regulation or an order as if it were to be a guide to his conduct, or in any other manner than as an amusing novel'. The new *Regulations* of 1792 required a Commander-in-Chief to enforce them. On the outbreak of war Lord Amherst was reappointed Commander-in-Chief; he had held the office in the American War but without distinction, and was now too old to impose the driving authority which was required. Not till 1795 was a firm hand restored, when Amherst was replaced by King George's second and favourite son Frederick, Duke of York. From now on Dundas's *Regulations* were firmly enforced, and uniformity was imposed on British tactical training. But still no prototype force existed to test the new regulations in battle. The army was sucked into the final devastating phase of the campaigns on the Caribbean forests; and in 1799 the force which was thrown together at the last moment for the expedition to Holland was too raw and inexperienced to give the regulations a fair trial. Most of the battalions were cadres fleshed out with drafts of volunteers from the militia. Inevitably their first performance in battle was mixed; but the militiamen were the best recruits the army had seen since the war began. Instead of down-and-outs, they were young men who had been compulsorily balloted into their county militias for home service, and had liked the military life enough to be tempted into the regular army with a bounty. Abercromby immediately recognised them as 'a superior race of men, and a great acquisition'.[7]

With this one begins to discover a side of Abercromby which was quite different from the one seen by frustrated ministers, blinded to military reality by their political hopes. Pitt and Lord Grenville might see Sir Ralph as an obstructive creator of difficulties; but even Henry Dundas, who felt the sting of Abercromby's frankness, alluded in a letter to Grenville to his 'accommodating disposition'. General O'Hara at Gibraltar, comparing him with his predecessor in the Mediterranean, the difficult Sir Charles Stuart, described Abercromby as 'a reasonable, considerate good officer, [who] listens with temper and patience to every proposal made with him'.[8]

To his officers Abercromby seemed a pattern of leadership and honour. Everyone, Sir Henry Bunbury recalled, loved the old general, who peered out from under his shaggy eyebrows like a good-natured lion. The example he set originated from the good tone in his own quarters and at his own table. Colonel Christopher Hely-Hutchinson, encountering him for the first time in the crowded *Diadem*, found his private conversation 'extremely liberal, well informed and polite'. When Lord Dalhousie was invited to dine with the general in Minorca, he was charmed by the absence of constraint or formality round Abercromby's table. Everyone felt at ease, and the youngest officers were courteously listened to as the conversation flowed interestingly on the French Revolution and the war. On duty too, nervous subalterns who encountered Abercromby for the first time found him friendly, accessible, and completely free from the pride and ostentation which junior officers expected from generals. He had a keen though well controlled sense of the ridiculous, with which he occasionally discountenanced officers who experimented with showy dress. Going on deck at Marmaris to greet a friend returning from a mission to Constantinople, he was disconcerted to find that the officer had sprouted a pair of half-grown Turkish mustachios in the fashion of Sir Sidney Smith. 'Why, my good friend', he said (addressing him by name, after earnestly inspecting his face), 'I had no notion that you meant to be a character.' The mustachios disappeared in a moment.[9]

Every officer who served with Abercromby sensed his utter integrity. Forty years on Sir Henry Bunbury remembered him as 'a noble chieftain: mild in manner, resolute in mind, frank, unassuming, just, inflexible in what he deemed to be right, valiant as the Cid, liberal and loyal as the prowest of Black Edward's knights'. This cannot be dismissed as the hyperbole of an old man gilding the memories of his youth, for everyone who served under Abercromby used such phrases: 'an honourable sense of duty . . . perfectly upright as well as brave'. Wherever he had served, wrote Bunbury recording his death, 'he had been respected and beloved. There was an absence of selfishness in Abercromby, a liberality of feeling, and an independence of spirit which entitled him to the highest respect as a gentleman'.[10]

A gentleman: the term denoted honour rather than superficial demeanour; and Abercromby demanded high standards of honour and duty from his officers. His manner might be mild, but he was a strong disciplinarian. 'Sir', he had written to Henry Dundas in his laconic style during the winter campaign of 1794, 'if we are to have another campaign, order, discipline and confidence must be restored to this army.' But for him discipline had to be intelligent, humane, and caring. He enforced punctilious saluting; but obedience must be taught with 'prudence and sense', and he recognised that the fine new breed of militia volunteers were unaccustomed to proper discipline. 'To this they must be led by degrees', he wrote to a friend; 'they must not be treated with too much harshness and severity'.[11]

Ultimately confidence could be restored only in battle; and if any senior British general was capable of training a force for battle it was Abercromby. Lord Dalhousie instantly recognised him as a master of professional detail. When his regiment, the Queen's, had marched into camp in 1799 to embark for Holland, Sir Ralph subjected it to a close and detailed inspection; and Dalhousie discovered that the old general was 'intimately conversant with the interior economy of a regiment'.[12]

Wherever Abercromby commanded, he strove to restore high standards of discipline and training. But till now he had never been allowed enough time; and the regiments he took to Holland in 1799 had been hastily summoned from all over England on the eve of the embarcation. They performed surprisingly well when they went into action, considering how Abercromby's spearhead battalions had been rushed abroad without preparation and the reinforcing units had been packed with militiamen. Yet, as Abercromby had already learned on his winter retreat through Holland five years earlier, young soldiers and inexperienced officers lacked the resources to sustain adversity, however dashing they might be in the attack. If the British Army was to fight the intelligent and war-hardened French on equal terms, its expeditionary forces would have to be thoroughly trained under the generals who were to command them. As the Duke of Northumberland wrote after the Dutch expedition, no thinking general would accept the command of an operation unless he 'had the troops to himself for at least some months before he went on active service with them'.[13]

Abercromby would have agreed. In the months after the withdrawal from Holland he had stressed the importance of training the new soldiers from the militia. 'In the spring you will have a fine army', he urged Henry Dundas, 'if the brigades are put under major-generals who are capable of instructing young officers and raw troops.' But Abercromby returned to his command in Scotland, and played no part in the winter's training in England, of which there turned out to be little. Part of the force from Holland was sent to keep order in Ireland, where it picked up a mass of raw recruits from the Irish militia; and in England training was stopped by severe weather. When embarcations for the Mediterranean began in the spring of 1800 little had been done to improve the regiments. In the force's subsequent wanderings the time lost during the winter could not be made up, with each battalion dispersed between several ships and tossing miserably on the high seas. The Duke of York had warned that they still needed two months of uninterrupted training.[14]

In Marmaris bay Abercromby's floating headquarters were in the *Kent*, a 74-gun two-decked ship of the line, in which he shared the cabin with five officers of his 'military family' or personal staff. From this incommodious office he contemplated his force. The infantry were a conglomerate of about twenty-six battalions drawn together from several quarters. One element in the force was probably better than any that Abercromby had hitherto commanded. These were the ten seasoned British battalions from the Mediterranean garrisons, which in John Moore's judgement were better than any of the regiments he had seen in the Dutch campaign. Of the troops which had come from the British Isles the two battalions of Foot Guards were privileged units which had always been kept up to strength to guard the King and maintain order in the capital; and the two new highland regiments, the 79th and 92nd, were fully recruited and had served with credit in Holland. Both were in a high state of pride. Rivalry between them about which had most distinguished itself in the Dutch campaign had led to fighting in Chelmsford barracks, and the two regiments had to be separated by transferring the 79th to the Isle of Wight.[15]

The remaining dozen battalions were a mixed bag. Four were recruited from foreigners, well drilled in Minorca but still to be tested in the outposts where desertion was easy. The two battalions of the 54th, and the four flank companies of the 40th, were filled with militiamen who were exempt from service outside Europe but had volunteered for Egypt. The other six battalions were typical of the recent history of the infantry of the line, with fluctuating strengths, mediocre recruits, and diverse training. Dalhousie's regiment, the Queen's, seems to have been a solid battalion; so should the 2/Royals have been, but we shall see that they fell under Abercromby's censure: they will subsequently be referred to by their more familiar title the Royal Scots. Three battalions (the 13th, and the two battalions of the 27th) had all served in Ireland in the previous winter and had been padded out with recruits from the Irish militia. All three had been reported by the Duke of York in the spring to be altogether unfit for any service, though since that time they had had some training before embarking in August. A sad case were the 23rd Royal Welch Fusiliers, a regiment of high reputation, which had lost 265 men in a shipwreck returning from Holland, and had been made up with Irish militiamen. In the spring the Duke of York had judged them to be not yet fit for foreign service; and they too were to fall under Abercromby's displeasure.[16] The two battalions of the 27th had been left behind to recover from sickness, one at Gibraltar, the other at Malta, and were partly replaced by a battalion of Marines assembled from the ships of the fleet.

Abercromby knew the strengths and weaknesses of his force, and no one was better equipped to right their defects. Part of the army had come under his eye during the summer at Minorca before the Cadiz operation. He had immediately brigaded the regiments in two divisions under Moore and

General Hutchinson, ordering the brigadiers to inspect their battalions and prepare them for review by the Commander-in-Chief. Sheds were erected so that reinforcements arriving late from England could be shifted out of their troopships for the brief duration of their stay. When the regimental reviews were completed Abercromby issued a General Order which set the tone for his officers. In general he had found the regiments to be satisfactory. But some ought still to be considered as newly raised, and these required the greatest care and attention of every officer from the General to the Ensigns, 'in the forming of troops so worthy of their care whom they may command in action and on whose conduct their own honour and the welfare of the public depends'.[17]

Those roasting August weeks in Minorca welded fourteen battalions into a sharp striking force with high morale. In the bay of Cadiz Dalhousie judged it 'impossible to wish for a more compact and efficient little army', and saw good humour and joy in every face as his battalion prepared to land. General Doyle thought the troops were in 'excellent condition and high spirits, most of the troops *aguerri*, with a confidence in their commander'.[18]

The disappointment when the Cadiz landing was cancelled, and the miseries of the autumn storms which followed, called for all the good spirits and humour the army could muster; and eight more battalions arriving from England via the fiasco at Ferrol had to be sharpened up to fighting pitch. But Abercromby never relaxed his hold on the force, or his drive to make it healthy and efficient. Wherever the fleet called for provisions and repairs, the regiments were given their turn in the available accommodation ashore to train while their ships were cleaned. When the 44th had their turn ashore at Minorca in November, their exercises took Lieutenant Brown's company across the island from coast to coast through wilder mountain country than the young officer from Cheshire had ever seen.[19]

And all the time the relentless inspection and supervision continued. Every morning during his eighteen days' stay at Malta Abercromby reviewed troops, accompanied by Moore and Hope, and from noon till three he interviewed officers and others who wished to see him. He inspected Dalhousie's battalion again 'in the same close manner as he did at Minorca'. In these inspections he was entirely indifferent to military fripperies. What he looked for in the ranks was good health, cleanliness, and equipment in good order; and in their drill, for discipline and sound instruction. Nor did he hesitate to censure neglect, either publicly on the spot or in General Orders. Some regiments received his public approval, the 92nd Gordons passing their inspection as 'in every respect fit for service'. But not all the regiments which had come out from England escaped his displeasure. Two which had recently joined the army from the Ferrol expedition fell short of Abercromby's standards. The 2/Royal Scots were rebuked in General Orders; and to Abercromby's dismay the 23rd Fusiliers, which had served under him with distinction in Holland, were in poor order after their shipwreck and the Irish influx. Their temporary commanding officer had been ill during the voyage, and Abercromby ordered the brigade commander, General Oakes, to take personal command and restore their efficiency.

He was enjoying the prospect of the campaign. General Oakes described him at Malta as 'indefatigable in endeavouring to put the army in the best possible state, and to create an emulation among the troops by close and frequent inspections'. 'Creating an emulation' has a ring of the new discipline later associated with Sir John Moore's training at Shorncliffe; and Moore himself used the term in writing of Abercromby's training. The drill which Abercromby enforced was not for ceremony but for the battlefield; and his painstaking inspections and field days in Minorca and Malta were designed to prepare his army for war. His minute attention to detail had always a purpose. In Egypt, for instance, there would be no transport ashore for anything but water, food, and ammunition, and officers and men would have to travel light and carry their own necessities. At Malta the regiments were reviewed in full marching order, and as the old general inspected the line he peered carefully at the knapsacks and insisted that they must be worn high on the shoulders. He was not a teacher who believed in tight-lipped prescription, and he carefully explained how carrying the weight high reduced the straining on the chest and allowed the men to move their arms more freely. For Sir Ralph this detailed attention to the soldier's comfort was nothing new: in the West Indies he had adapted the uniform to the tropical heat and abolished the noontime drills. And so he continued. One day at Marmaris Lieutenant Macdonald saw him supervising the removal of sick grenadiers of the 42nd to another ship. As they were being lowered to the boat, he personally tucked in a blanket which had come adrift in the wind, and called for a pin to hold it. The example spoke more clearly than the words of a General Order.[20]

Pioneer though he was in discipline and hygiene, was he competent to teach his army modern tactics? By now, at the age of 66, Abercromby was not one of the great contemporary masters of the battlefield. His short-sightedness was no help, and Moore had noted in the West Indies that he could see nothing without a telescope, though with one 'he observes ground quickly and well'. One of his faults was commanding too close to the front, where he exposed himself unnecessarily and tended to lose touch with the general picture as the battle developed. At the beach assault in Puerto Rico he had pushed on ahead of the assault craft in a small boat accompanied only by his aide de camp; leapt ashore ahead of his troops; and, drawing his short hanger, cheered and ran into the bush like a skirmisher.[21]

This foible did not diminish the confidence of his men, nor his success as a trainer of troops. Abercromby had the advantage of varied experience, from the ranged battles of Germany to bush-whacking against black guerrillas and coping with the new tactics of the French revolutionary skirmishers. 'You have experience of the modern manner of warfare', his friend General Hely-Hutchinson had remarked, 'which the grandees of our army want.' He belonged neither to the 'German' nor to the 'American' school of officers. He supported the new 'German' manual, and fifteen years earlier he had twice written to Colonel Dundas urging him to publish his *Principles*.[22] But in the hedgerows of Flanders, and the dunes of Holland, and the forests and hills of the Caribbean he had also learned the growing importance of light infantry which Dundas's manual had neglected. Dundas had allotted only a few sketchy pages on outpost duties to the light companies, whose excessive prestige after the American War he blamed for the defects in the army's drill. Though the Duke of York had witnessed the effectiveness of French skirmishers in 1793–4 in Flanders, and took some steps to redress Dundas's neglect, little progress had yet been made in improving the training of the battalions' light companies. As late as the autumn of 1799 a highland officer reported from the dunes of Holland that the British infantry were 'perfectly unacquainted with the system of sharpshooting'. Nor had any specialist light regiments been raised to match the dozen battalions of *chasseurs à pied* which the French had raised before the war and incorporated in the light demi-brigades of the revolutionary armies.[23]

Generals of the 'American' school like Cornwallis and John Simcoe rightly deplored the lack of light infantry; but they sometimes spoke as if all that was needed was the total overthrow of the 'German' system. In fact the need was to strike a better balance; and the outcome of British tactical developments would not be the overthrow of the 'German' by the 'American' or more strictly the new French system, but a synthesis of the two. It was by combining these elements that Wellington was to win his battles: one element the legacy of Frederick the Great, close-order battle drill executed to a high standard; the other, the copious use of light infantry to overcome French skirmishers.

At Minorca in the summer of 1800, when Abercromby still expected his force to operate in the vineyards of Italy or the jungle of the Caribbean and central America, he stressed the importance of light infantry work. His predecessor Sir Charles Stuart, a soldier of the 'American' school, had laid a foundation when he grouped his light companies in Portugal and later in Minorca to be drilled as a light battalion by his Adjutant-General Major Kenneth Mackenzie. Mackenzie's own regiment, the 90th, had been dressed as light infantry since their raising by Thomas Graham in Perthshire early in the war; and when Mackenzie rejoined them he polished their drill to make them the nearest thing the British Army had to a specialist light regiment, if one excepts the newly raised 5/60th which was recruited from foreigners. Moore watched with interest as the battalion broke up into skirmishing line, supports, and reserves. Mackenzie was said by George Napier to be 'generally regarded as the best commanding officer in the army', and was later to have enormous influence in the development of British light infantry.[24]

The basis of Mackenzie's tactical training appears to have been a new light drill pamphlet which had been issued in 1798, *Regulations for the Exercise of Riflemen and Light Infantry*, a translation from the German of Colonel de Rottenburg. But when Egypt became the force's destination, David Dundas's Frederickian *Regulations* came into their own. Though Abercromby continued the light infantry training, and at Malta put normal battalion companies through light infantry exercises, Egypt was not ideal for skirmishing. The open terrain was cavalry country, and the French had a strong mounted force while the British had virtually none. In these conditions good close-order drill was essential. At field days during the journey to Egypt stress was laid on the *Regulations*. But as is often the case with training manuals, the *Regulations* with their eighteen manoeuvres were too complex for the battlefield, and in Bunbury's words 'led the large class of stupid officers into strange blunders'.[25] Abercromby therefore simplified them into a few basic manoeuvres. Defence against cavalry was emphasised, and during the stay at Marmaris the brigades paid special attention to forming a variety of squares, the conventional hollow square, a solid square formed from the column of march, and an experimental four-deep square. A new drill for marching in hollow squares was practised, so that the army could manoeuvre in the presence of enemy cavalry.[26]

When the time came to leave Marmaris for the battlefield, Abercromby's work had converted a conglomerate of regiments into a highly trained and cohesive army. By now he knew the state of every battalion and the character of its commanding officer, and reported that his force was 'in the best disposition'. 'Most of the regiments', he wrote, 'are amongst the best in the service; the general officers men of high honour, with the advantage of vigorous health joined to experience.' Commanding such an army, his historical imagination was fired by the task of 'defeating the most splendid project of modern times': the oriental ambitions of Bonaparte, 'a man of great and comprehensive mind'.[27]

4

REHEARSING INVASION

The army was ready for battle. But before Abercromby could take it to war it had still one lesson to learn: the opposed landing. Many of his officers knew the difficulties. Lord Dalhousie, for one, had taken part in three landing operations in the past eighteen months, and every one of them had been botched. On the Dutch coast in 1799 Admiral Mitchell had thrown the troops on to the beach without order, mingling battalions and even brigades so that as the line was forming to meet a possible counter-attack the men were running up and down the sand looking for their units. At Belle Ile the orders had changed with every contradictory report of the enemy's strength. And at Cadiz General Doyle had described the abortive landing attempt as 'most sadly bitched'.[1]

Cadiz was the worst; and the naval commander, Lord Keith, whose incompetence there had appalled senior officers in both services, was still with the expedition. 'It is not to be described', General Moore told his father, 'the bad management and confusion which attended the assembling of the boats.' Dalhousie deplored Keith's want of method and arrangement; he had collected a useless staff in the flagship, and took all the detail on his own incapable shoulders. The future Lord Collingwood would have endorsed this judgement, for about this time he judged that Keith 'always has about him a set of very dull men, very incompetent to the aid a Commander-in-Chief needs'. There was a shortage of boats to land the first wave; and while the troops were being transferred from the ships Keith stormed up and down on the deck of the *Foudroyant* cursing, blaming, and talking 'incoherent nonsense' in his Doric accents, but doing nothing to sort out the muddle.

'In the whole course of my service', General Thomas Maitland told Henry Addington, the Speaker, 'I have never seen anything so shamefully mismanaged.' He went on to suggest something more sinister: that Keith had never intended the landing to proceed. Naval officers to whom Moore talked had formed the same impression. The suggestion matched Keith's character. In contrast with Abercromby, he epitomised the qualities which perhaps unfairly made the Scots so unpopular in politics and war. 'It is a true Scotch principle', wrote the Northumbrian Collingwood, 'to claim everything and get what they can, or Lord Keith would not have been so rich by many a good estate.'

A selfish careerist who held the record for accumulating prize money, Keith would never share responsibility for a risky decision if he could dodge it. Off Cadiz it was his clear duty to advise the army commander about weather and navigation, but he avoided saying anything which might justify Abercromby in cancelling the operation. To have a reasonable chance of success, Sir Ralph required that the weather at sea should not prevent the navy from reinforcing his assault wave and later re-embarking his whole force. Keith allowed him to sail from Gibraltar believing that all was assured. In Cadiz bay, however, a different picture began to emerge. After the bungled first attempt to land had been cancelled, the glass began to fall and the sky to darken; and naval officers who knew the coast (as indeed Lord Keith did) warned the general that at that time of the year a south-west wind would force the fleet to put to sea and leave the army stranded.

But Lord Keith himself would not give this advice, though the question was wholly his responsibility as the naval commander. He seemed determined to say nothing that would earn him a share of the blame if the operation was cancelled. In vain Abercromby offered to share the responsibility and pressed for a clear answer. Moore urged him to obtain the opinion of Keith's senior officers if the admiral would not be explicit; and Colonel Anstruther warned him that he had overheard Keith telling his staff that the general was about to commit a very rash act. At last Abercromby was forced to put his question in writing, although he was sharing a cabin with Keith, and obtained the reply that the admiral could not promise to re-embark the troops, or advise the general to land them. The opinion, which ought to have been given at least thirty-six hours if not a week earlier, was immediately justified by deteriorating weather. In the night it began to rain and blow; and at daybreak the fleet got under way and cleared the land with the loss of some anchors.

Such was the naval commander on whom Abercromby would depend on the Egyptian coast. Were his abilities in decline? St Vincent, in a famous letter damning 'Scotch pack horses', described Keith at this very time as by far the best of the Scottish tribe he had ever met by land or sea;[2] and Keith was scarcely into his fifties. But the 'incoherent nonsense' he had uttered on the quarter-deck of the *Foudroyant* off Cadiz was noted again in calmer circumstances by an unbiased witness: 'There is much incoherency in his Lordship's conversation', Colonel Christopher Hutchinson recorded in November.[3] Hutchinson discovered Keith to be far from popular with the officers of the Mediterranean fleet. Senior naval officers fully shared the army's indignation at Keith's behaviour off Cadiz; and a later quarrel with some of his captains over the supply of fresh food for the sick was conducted on both sides with astonishing intemperance. Captain Alexander Cochrane, a fellow Scot, closed the correspondence by telling the Commander-in-Chief that he was incompetent and untruthful; that his energies were concentrated on private gain; and that his manner was often such as 'no gentleman can put up with'.[4] 'He indeed is either much changed', General Maitland judged, 'or never could be the respectable man I took him to be.'[5]

During Abercromby's quest for advice 'very high words' had been heard to pass between the two commanders. 'It is impossible Sir Ralph can ever place confidence in Lord Keith',[6] Maitland warned the War Department. Yet one of the qualities which fitted Abercromby for combined operations was the 'accommodating disposition' to which Henry Dundas referred. Some years earlier in the West Indies he had laid down a rule for himself that a quarrel between an admiral and a general was inexcusable.[7] He would certainly need all the patience and good temper at his command to deal with Keith, and would have liked to escape from the partnership. He wrote as much to a friendly Under-Secretary of State; the letter found its way to the Admiralty; and the First Lord who had heard rumours of trouble took the matter up with Keith. Keith prevaricated; denied that there had been a misunderstanding; and tried to blame the cancelling of the operation on the plague in Cadiz. At the First Lord's suggestion he made Abercromby an offer to withdraw from the expedition and remain in the western Mediterranean, sending a more junior admiral to Egypt. But it would not have been easy to find a suitable substitute, and such a visible breach between the naval and military commanders might have created its own difficulties. Abercromby resigned himself to the admiral's presence, and assured him of his confidence. But he was determined that the next landing should be better organised.[8]

'It is a wrong fashion to decry the American education', General Simcoe had recently written to Henry Addington, 'the conjunct expedition of army and navy had arrived at great perfection.'[9] The lessons appeared to have been lost, though Keith himself had served on the American coast in combined operations. Ever since the art of amphibious warfare had begun to be studied and systematised forty years earlier in the Seven Years War, the formula for success had been to delegate the organising of the boats to a commodore or senior captain. In the American War Commodore Hotham had made a reputation for smooth and successful landings on the American coast and in the Caribbean. But on the Dutch coast in 1799 Admiral Mitchell had ignored experience, and confusion followed. At Cadiz Keith had followed the rules to the extent of putting the Senior Captain, Alexander Cochrane of the *Ajax*, in nominal charge of the boats. But Cochrane was not briefed and was left completely in the dark; and so, naturally, were the captains in charge of boat divisions who streamed on board the *Ajax* in search of instructions. In practice Lord Keith took everything on himself; and when confusion overwhelmed him he could think of no remedy but to order the loaded boats to assemble round the frigate in which Abercromby was waiting inshore to take command when the troops had been landed, and let him sort it out.[10]

Even Lord Keith realised that his personal direction of the landing craft had been a failure. At Gibraltar he made some changes in the flagship *Foudroyant*, saying that he was too old to take on the duty of landing troops. The captain was moved to another ship and replaced as Captain of the Fleet by the assistant captain, the able though junior and contentious Philip Beaver. The new assistant captain was an expert in troop arrangements, the Principal Agent for Transports Captain William Young. He would understand how to marshal the shipping from which the landing craft would be launched. When detailed planning began at Marmaris Captain Cochrane was again given responsibility for organising the boats and putting the troops on to the beach.[11]

But still one ingredient was missing. At the Helder Abercromby had seen proof that to leave the arrangement of boats entirely to the navy invited confusion on the beach. Few seamen understood the importance of landing the troops in their correct order of battle; and Abercromby realised that if his assault wave was to be put ashore in fighting order and quickly reinforced he would have to intervene in the naval planning. His answer was to provide Cochrane with an army colleague, Colonel Anstruther, the Deputy Quartermaster-General. Anstruther would ensure that Cochrane was properly briefed, that the boats were matched with the troops, and that the regiments would land in their order of battle and from the boats in which they had rehearsed. The planning was thus firmly in the hands of two able sons of the Scottish nobility: the one destined to be an admiral and a Commander-in-Chief, the other to die in the retreat to Corunna.

In the coming operation there would be no reprieve for muddle. The enemy were not half-hearted Dutch or Spaniards, but Bonaparte's battle-hardened French. Their experienced commanders were evangelists of the offensive, and would strike hard and rapidly against a landing. For the British, minutes would count and mistakes would court disaster.

Rarely had British staff officers faced a more complex planning problem than Cochrane and Anstruther. They could draw on much past experience and custom, but the difficulties of this landing were unique. The shallow waters of Aboukir bay would force the larger warships and troopships to lie miles off the coast; the landing would be fiercely opposed; once ashore, the troops would have to be totally maintained by the fleet in the inhospitable interior. Cochrane and Anstruther had to put an assault wave on to the beach under fire in fighting order; to reinforce it rapidly; to build the force ashore to its full strength of 13,000 men and 800 horses; and to ferry in all the army's requirements – ammunition, ordnance and engineer stores, hospital equipment and tents, provisions, and probably water. Each phase demanded careful planning to maintain the momentum of the invasion and ensure the army's survival. But the most critical phases were the opposed landing and its rapid reinforcement. Here there was no room for error and improvisation.

The strength of the assault wave was prescribed by the available landing craft. The flatboats, combined with the boats of the warships and government troopships, could carry about seven and a half battalions. By using the boats of the hired merchant transports – the storeships and victuallers – Abercromby was able to give the planners two and a half additional battalions. But the merchant crews were not under naval discipline, and could look for neither rewards for courage nor pensions for mutilation. They might be less keen to face fire than the naval oarsmen.

Rapid reinforcement would be difficult from the larger ships lying seven miles out in the bay. If the assault wave was launched from smaller ships close inshore, and the first reinforcements had to be fetched by a long haul across the bay with tired oarsmen, there would be a dangerous gap of some hours in the landing timetable. The solution was to reverse the obvious arrangement; to hold the first reinforcements close inshore in small local vessels; and to embark the assault battalions from the distant large ships. Thus the boats would make their longest haul before the battle was joined, and after landing the assault wave they could pull back swiftly for the nearby reinforcements.[12]

The assault drills were tested in a first rehearsal on 21 January, the day after the planning conference in the *Foudroyant*. The boats were collected round Cochrane's ship the *Ajax* and directed to the ships where they were to embark troops. Two brigades were then marshalled in line just out of gunshot from the shore, and landed on the beach in immaculate order. In five minutes the battalions were formed and ready to advance. Behind them two field-guns were run off their launches on ramps, and three minutes after touching the shore they were in action.[13]

In the light of this trial Cochrane and Anstruther issued detailed landing instructions for the boats and troops, which were rehearsed by the other brigades with each landing timed and compared. On 2 February the 3rd, 4th, and 5th brigades held a landing exercise using the new instructions. The whole operation was tightly controlled by flag signals from Captain Cochrane's cutter. These were repeated to the assault craft by the captains of boat divisions, each of whom also had an officer in a rowing boat to carry their orders down the line. As the loaded boats arrived on the forming-up position they were marshalled in three lines: the first of flatboats and artillery launches, the second of cutters to rescue boats in trouble, the third of cutters towing launches with more troops. Between the boats of the first line there was an interval of fifty feet, to avoid bunching the troops on the shore and leave space for the rearward line of towing cutters to beach. Each battalion was identified by a camp colour in its right-flank boat, on the left of which its companies were formed in seniority. Direction was kept by the right-and left-flank boats steering for given marks on the shore; and when Cochrane gave the signal to advance the line of boats took their dressing from the flanks so that the whole force would touch the beach together. As the flatboats ran in to the beach they dropped their grapnels from the stern, ready to haul off as soon as their troops were ashore and return to the shipping for reinforcements.

This rehearsal was less orderly than the first, proving the value of the methodical training which the delay at Marmaris allowed. Lord Cavan's small brigade, reduced to two battalions by the absence of the 27th, seems to have landed successfully, Wyvill of the 79th reporting that as each soldier ran up the beach he found himself in his own place in the line. In Doyle's larger brigade, however, James Brown of the 44th recorded 'a little confusion', though his own regiment was first of the four in the brigade to be formed. Dalhousie, also in Doyle's brigade, was as usual more caustic. He had reported favourably on the earlier rehearsal, but of this one he wrote: 'I never saw greater confusion, or things of the kind worse conducted'. Evidently there was more to be learned before their D-day.[14]

One improvement suggested by the first trial had been to eliminate the preliminary assembling of the boats round Cochrane's ship to receive orders. Instead they were to proceed straight from their parent ships to those where they were to embark troops; a simpler arrangement, with the advantage of familiarising the troops and their landing craft before the battle. But it required staff work of a high order by the standards of the day, because the landing craft would have to collect the troops of the assault wave in the dark of the night if they were to reach the distant shore by sunrise. To achieve this required careful tabulation, since there were 180 boats for the infantry and twenty-eight for the artillery.

About fifty-eight of the assault craft were flatboats carried on the decks of warships and troopships. These were the unpainted landing craft designed in the Seven Years War. Drawing only nine inches of water, they could run up high into the shallows carrying fifty infantrymen, and were crewed by a naval officer, a gunner, and twenty oarsmen. The ships' boats consisted of thirty-seven white-painted launches carrying twenty-five men each, and eighty-four row boats for ten men. All these varied craft from many ships had to be mustered alongside seventeen troopships carrying the assault battalions.

Cochrane had organised his 200 landing craft in four divisions commanded by senior troopship captains. To illustrate their task, the division commanded by Captain Stevenson of the *Europa* had fifty-nine boats, drawn from twenty ships, and these were to embark men from six troopships. Twenty-four of his boats belonged to the ships from which they were to embark men and were already alongside; but the remaining thirty-five had to find and identify their embarking ships in the dark. One of these ships was the *Hermione*, a converted frigate carrying 280 men of the Welch Fusiliers. Hoisted out alongside were her own flatboat, launch, and two row boats; but to complete her embarcation she was allotted two flatboats, two launches, and four row boats from the *Dido*, *Experiment*, and *Regulus*, three troopships whose soldiers were not part of the assault wave.

These complex arrangements were tabulated by Cochrane, and the embarcation tables were distributed to the captains of boat divisions: a striking contrast with the haphazard arrangements at Cadiz. Regimental officers who had seen the confusion at the Helder eighteen months earlier were impressed. There whole brigades had been mixed together on the beach; in rehearsals at Marmaris even companies were being landed in their proper place in the line.[15]

Landing cannon was a problem for General Lawson and his artillery officers. Most of the guns had been stowed in ordnance ships in England as heavy freight at the bottom of the cargoes; and to reach them the water casks and other material which had been stowed above them had to be unloaded into light vessels alongside. In one ship at Cadiz 70 tons of water had had to be removed to get at the guns. For the Egyptian landing fourteen light field-guns were unloaded from the transports' holds and lashed on the poops of the line-of-battle ships. From there they would be lowered into launches for the landing; each with a crew of fifteen artillerymen and twenty-five seamen to haul and serve it. Gangways had been made to run the guns on to the beach, the most successful being the hollow rounded mast-fishings, designed to strengthen the outsides of masts, which formed guide-runnels for the guns' wheels. So successful were these devices that in two landing rehearsals the guns were ashore before the infantry.[16]

When the assault brigades held their first landing practice on 21 January they were rehearsing – though they did not yet know it – a landing on the western shore of Aboukir bay. For it was on the previous day that Moore had returned with his report on the Turkish army which had caused Abercromby to abandon the Damietta landing. His intention now was to win the beach-head at Aboukir, and then attack Alexandria; or, if Alexandria proved impregnable, to turn eastwards along the shore of the bay, seize Rosetta, and gain the supplies of the delta and open the western branch of the Nile for water transport. The conference which assembled in the *Foudroyant* was to examine the operation in detail.[17]

In the Admiral's cabin Abercromby and Moore found the two seconds-in-command, General Hutchinson and Sir Ralph Bickerton. George Baldwin, the ex-consul in Egypt who had joined the expedition at Malta, had been invited in the illusory hope that he knew the country. There were two naval captains with experience of the Egyptian coast: Hallowell of Bickerton's flag-ship the *Swiftsure*, and Sir Sidney Smith flamboyant in huge un-naval mustachios, his weasel body disguised in Turkish robes. The army was also represented by the two senior staff officers, Anstruther with his knowledge of the landing arrangements, and the Adjutant-General Colonel Hope. John Hope was yet another offspring of the landed families on the shores of the Firth of Forth, a younger son of the Earl of Hopetoun whose title he would eventually inherit. He was linked to the Abercromby–Dundas nexus through his sister Lady Jane, the doleful second wife of Henry Dundas. Like Moore, Anstruther, and his own half-brother Colonel Alexander Hope, he had served under Sir Ralph in the West Indies and Holland. An able negotiator, he was employed by the Duke of York in 1799 to arrange with General Brune for the army's evacuation of Holland; and by Abercromby in 1800 on a mission to the Austrian army in Italy after its defeat at Marengo. Now aged 36, a man of soldierly bearing, polished manners and strong judgement, his future was to be scored with wounds and distinction.

Sir Ralph joined the meeting in no doubt that a landing must be attempted. Time was pressing, against a background of Russian hostility; and the odds seemed acceptable, though estimates of the enemy's strength fluctuated wildly. Sir Sidney Smith's secretary had visited Cairo and maintained that the French had 20,000 troops or more; Consul Baldwin said 12,000; and local sources indicated that they had about 13,000 French troops and 3–4,000 Greek and Coptic auxiliaries. This roughly tallied with Abercromby's instructions, which supposed that the 40,000 men whom Bonaparte had brought from France had sunk in two years to a maximum of 13,000.[18] Henry Dundas was convinced that the morale of this remnant had collapsed, and that they were too homesick to offer serious resistance. But homesickness was the lot of soldiers abroad, and 'we all know', remarked Hope, 'that this is always overcome by the superior principle of military duty'. As for enemy numbers, the British government's source was tainted. The intelligence rested on a packet of letters intercepted early in 1800, when the French commander General Kléber had had motives for painting his situation in the darkest colours for the French government. Instead of questioning Kléber's figures, Henry Dundas threw doubt on the credibility and motives of his own witness, Sir Sidney's secretary, whose high figure of 20,000 men in good order was in fact still an underestimate. The enemy's real strength was 30,000. In retrospect Colonel Thomas Graham was to suggest that, had Abercromby known the truth, 'probably even Sir Ralph's determined mind would have yielded to considerations of prudence'.[19]

Happily unaware of the reality, Abercromby proceeded to develop his plan. He put little trust in the collapse of French morale, but calculated rather on their widespread defensive commitments. If his information was correct, the whole French force was about equal to his own; but they had to hold their populous and turbulent base at Cairo, and garrison the forts east of the delta which guarded the coast and the approaches from Palestine and Suez, soon to be threatened by the Grand Vizir moving forward to El Arish. They would concentrate all the troops they could spare, and attack the British; but they would not have enough. 'They will probably collect their force', Sir Ralph predicted, 'and I shall be happy if we can bring them to a speedy decision.'[20]

A speedy decision? Perhaps; but the *Foudroyant* conference had to plan for a longer haul. Once the landing had been made, the intractable problem would be logistics. Without beasts of burden or wheeled vehicles, the army would have to move provisions, equipment, and siege-guns along the isthmus towards Alexandria, a distance thought to be eighteen miles. And the daily need for water? Inside Alexandria the French would be supplied from the ancient storage cisterns which were filled by canal from the annual overflow of the Nile. But outside the city some 15,000 British troops would have to survive on the sandy isthmus and conduct a siege; and according to Consul Baldwin no water was to be found there.

If Baldwin was right, the army would depend utterly on the boats of the fleet for its daily water, as well as most of its other needs. Could the navy do it? Abercromby admitted that the task was 'Herculean'. The two captains who knew the coast reported that the beaches on the seashore of the isthmus were, till the last six miles towards Alexandria, not too rocky for boats to land stores or haul up in stormy weather. But the lake shore of the isthmus would be better. If lake Aboukir could be navigated, the army would have a completely sheltered supply route. Yet about the lake almost nothing was known. It had been formed only twenty years earlier when the sea-wall in Aboukir bay was breached by a storm, and though Baldwin had lived in the area he did not even know how far the waters extended.[21]

Whether on the lake or the sea, the demands on the navy would be massive. Besides the boat-crews providing water transport, large numbers of seamen would be needed ashore to haul and carry, bringing up heavy artillery and an immense supply of ammunition and engineers' stores for the siege. Could the seamen be spared from the fleet? Could Keith be trusted to provide them? Abercromby remembered past difficulties with the admiral and was uneasy; and some days later he wrote to Keith emphasising the crucial importance of naval help ashore, and reminding him that in previous expeditions as many as half the ships' companies had been made available. He reminded Keith that at Martinique Lord St Vincent had brought up seventy heavy cannon with their ammunition.

For Keith there were real problems, though his reply was a characteristic mixture of promises, objections, and acerbity. The navy had never failed the army in combined operations, he wrote. But on the Egyptian coast the fleet would not have a safe harbour, and the ships must remain adequately manned. The troopships in particular were so undermanned in proportion to the weight of their anchors and cables that they could spare no men at all to work on shore when their boats' crews were away. In Aboukir bay he would have five ships of the line (two others were at sea blockading Alexandria). From their total complement of 3,339, he intended to land 545 seamen to work ashore with the army, while the boats' crews and reliefs would require 820; altogether forty per cent of the ships' complements would be serving the army. Besides these he was to form a battalion of Marines to replace the regiment which had been left to convalesce at Malta.[22]

As soon as the meeting closed, Abercromby returned to the *Kent* and wrote an urgent letter to London asking for reinforcements. Now convinced that he must eventually be prepared to advance on Cairo, but unable to rely on the Grand Vizir or count on the arrival in the Red Sea of the force ordered from India, he needed more troops. He also wrote to Constantinople asking Elgin to press for the help of the Capitan Pacha on the British front with 7–8,000 good troops and a flotilla to deal with the French gunboats on the Nile. He was anxious for visible Turkish support to demonstrate that the British were not 'adventurers come to decide on the plains of Egypt a European quarrel'. He hoped for a Turkish proclamation explaining why the British had come, and that they did not intend to stay: if none was issued, he would conclude that, if Russia joined the enemy, the Porte should no longer be regarded as an ally.[23] With the plan settled, the expedition should have sailed at once for Egypt; but the days trickled by with no sign of the expected mules, horse transports, and gunboats. In February the weather turned stormy, and on the 9th a violent tempest brought the troops a reminder of the miseries of life at sea. Even in the sheltered waters of the bay several ships parted from their anchors and ran foul of each other. On shore the ground was awash, tents were flattened, and sickness reappeared.

The harm caused by the delay was sharply demonstrated by news that two French frigates had run into Alexandria at the tail end of a storm which had blown the blockading squadron off its station. They had brought 800 troops from France as well as artillery, ammunition, and stores. More were likely to follow. Bonaparte was striving desperately to save the Army of the Orient and with it the French claim to Egypt. '*La grande affaire est de soutenir l'Égypte*',[24] he had written on 15 January; and his frigates brought news to cheer the garrison. Admiral Ganteaume was on his way with 4–5,000 troops; and Austria, having re-entered the fighting in December, had suffered a decisive and final defeat at Hohenlinden and was making peace. Britain, deprived of her ally and on the brink of war with Russia, would soon be forced to follow Austria's example and sue for peace. The Army of the Orient must hold on at all costs, and Egypt would be theirs.

At Marmaris anxiety had time to breed. The troops remained cheerful and busy with their training and working parties, but senior officers confided their forebodings to journals and private letters. 'I cannot but think the enterprise in which we are about to engage extremely hazardous and doubtful in its event', Moore confided to his diary after the *Foudroyant* conference. He did not believe the enemy would solve the British problems by offering a pitched battle, and expected them instead to use their great superiority in cavalry to harass the British communications during the siege of Alexandria.[25]

Abercromby may not have been aware of Moore's forebodings, but the doubts which surrounded him were disturbingly revealed in early February by his second-in-command. General Hutchinson told him in Anstruther's presence that he was strongly averse to the operation and saw no rational grounds to expect success. Abercromby showed him the Secretary of State's correspondence and told him that he intended to persevere, characteristically adding that he hoped their difference of opinion would not cause a coolness between them. Hutchinson replied that it would not, and that having done his duty by declaring his opinion he was satisfied. He remained dejected and in low spirits, however; particularly, his brother recorded, when orders directed that officers were to land with nothing but what they could carry themselves.[26]

And this was the man who would command the expedition if Abercromby were killed or disabled! Sir Ralph himself had to maintain a front of confidence and serenity though beset by his own anxieties. The optimism he had felt during the voyage from Gibraltar had been dashed by the Turkish failure to supply his force's deficiencies; and on 16 February, when the long-expected horse transports at last arrived from Smyrna, he confided his anxieties about logistics to two friends at home, the Quartermaster-General Sir David Dundas and the Under-Secretary at the War Department, William Huskisson. The letters would not reach London for a month, and by then the outcome would probably have been decided. 'The enterprise', he warned General Dundas with reference to his supply problems, 'is arduous, and perhaps doubtful'; the Turkish army so torpid, weak, and diseased that little reliance could be placed on it: 'I do not wish you to consider this as a desponding letter. I certainly however am not confident of success'. To Huskisson he repeated the words 'arduous' and 'doubtful': 'No enterprise in my mind can be so hazardous as that on which we are now engaged. . . . You may rest assured that everything shall be done that it is possible to accomplish, but I cannot and will not promise success'.[27]

But these were private channels for his fears, and the doubts he aired may well have been intended to hasten the needed reinforcements. He never communicated his fears, by words or demeanour, to his troops. General Eyre Coote, himself depressed by the Turkish failure to provide the army's needs, told a correspondent at home that 'Sir Ralph, who must naturally feel upon this occasion, conducts himself with much good sense and propriety and bears well a very serious disappointment'.[28]

Commanding an army whose only fear was that it had become a laughing-stock, Abercromby continued to display the equanimity and determination that reassured the men whom he was preparing for battle. Inspections continued, and regiments were landed in turn for training while their ships were cleaned and fumigated. He would do all that could be done to prevent a repetition of the disgrace of Ferrol and Cadiz. He had 'made up his mind to the undertaking', Moore was to recall: 'he was determined, whatever might be the result of this expedition, that no disgrace should attach to him or the troops he commanded. This sentiment was ever uppermost in his mind. He often expressed it, and it would appear that he had infused it into his army . . . they loved their Commander, had complete confidence in his talents and experience, and were determined to submit cheerfully to every deprivation in the execution of his orders'.[29]

Moore, whose brigade was to form the right wing of the assault, had confided his own doubts about the coming operation to his diary. But he had added resolute words which echoed the feelings of his chief: 'We cannot, however, hesitate; we must attempt it'.[30]

The arrival of the horse transports on 16 February was the signal for which Abercromby had been waiting. The 500 mules ordered from Smyrna had still not appeared, but he could wait no longer. Though Turkish pilots said that the fleet could not lie off the Egyptian coast till after the equinox about 21 March, the risk of further reinforcements reaching the French was too great, and every day that passed allowed the enemy commander to strengthen his defences. The horses were embarked immediately; the landing place was revealed in General Orders; and two Engineer officers were sent ahead to survey the coast and the passage into lake Aboukir. On the following day, Abercromby summoned his generals on board the *Kent* to issue his final instructions. One of his chief concerns was still the army's water supplies, and he had sent a memorandum to all commanding officers about the conservation of water. The latest information indicated that enough water for drinking might be found on the Aboukir isthmus by digging three or four feet deep near palm trees: for washing and steam-cooking sea water would have to be used. The local horses would not need as much water as European ones, and were to be tightly rationed.[31]

It was time to be gone. On shore the tents were being struck and the troops were returning on board their ships, now crammed with provisions, fuel and makeshift equipment. 'Again begins another life of misery', Lord Dalhousie lamented: 'going on board is like going to prison.'[32] On the 18th the fleet was ready to sail, but the wind blew contrary and boisterous. Abercromby had not been called a Jonah for nothing, and four more days were lost before favourable weather returned. At daybreak on 22 February, fifty-two days after the arrival at Marmaris, the wind came fresh from the north-west, and Keith gave the signals to unmoor and weigh. One by one the ships moved out through the narrow passage to the open sea. At the head of the van squadron Sir Ralph in the *Kent* followed the *Foudroyant* out of the bay. From the *Kent*'s deck his son Colonel Robert Abercromby gazed back at 'the noble sight of this great fleet issuing from under the stupendous mountains of Asia Minor'. A hundred and seventy-five sail were spread on the sea: men of war, troop-ships, and transports from England; polacres, xebecs, and feluccas gathered from the ports of Asia, the Aegean, and the Adriatic.[33]

'Never was the honour of the British Army more at stake', Robert Abercromby reflected, 'but an equal number of Britons were never assembled who were more determined to uphold their own and their country's valour.' At five in the afternoon Admiral Bickerton signalled that all the ships were clear of the bay, and the fleet crowded sail for Aboukir.[34]

5

THE EVE OF BATTLE

Three days out from the shelter of Marmaris Abercromby's ill-luck with the weather struck again. The wind turned foul and a gale blew up. In the heaving troopships crockery smashed in the ward-rooms and four dozen bottles of English porter that Lord Dalhousie had been saving for the landing spilt their contents on the deck. When the storm abated on 28 February the entire day was lost in collecting the scattered fleet. The Greek horse transports and Turkish gunboats had vanished utterly.[1]

On 1 March the expedition at last sighted the Egyptian coast, its objective for the past four months. From the deck of his troopship Dalhousie descried the ancient skyline of Alexandria, broken by Pompey's Pillar and Cleopatra's Needle, monuments of imperial Rome and the older world of the Pharaohs. Perhaps the admiral should have stood off below the horizon till the sea was calm; but in spite of the unsettled weather Lord Keith held his course and closed with the land till he was so close that the colours were seen at the masts of the French shipping and the enemy could count every last ship of the British force. This needless parading of the expedition under the eyes of the French worried and puzzled General Moore; still more so on the following morning at daybreak when the fleet entered Aboukir bay though the weather was still too rough for a landing.[2]

Inside the great bight of the bay the leading ships of the line were still seven miles from the shore when soundings showed only six to nine fathoms of water, and the larger ships were forced to anchor. Lord Keith's flagship *Foudroyant* chafed her cable against a wreck lying beneath the waves: it was Brueys's flagship *L'Orient*, which had been anchored on that very position thirty-one months earlier when Nelson's attacking line swooped on his fleet and annihilated it. The British troopships and transports worked further into the bay, but five miles off the shore they too were brought to anchor by the shoaling water. A cutter went forward to take soundings, and plumbed only two fathoms when she was still three or four miles from the shore. As Abercromby had expected, the landing craft would have a long run in to the beach.

The sky had cleared; and hoping that the wind would drop Keith made the signal to cook three days' provisions for the soldiers' haversacks and prepare to land. Abercromby had still to make his final plan for the assault, and was waiting for a report from the Chief Engineer Major McKerras on his reconnaissance. All day the signal flew for McKerras to report to the general, but he never appeared. In fact he had done his work thoroughly, as was learned later, but it was to be of no use to Abercromby. Accompanied by Captain Fletcher, McKerras had boarded the *Peterel* sloop off Alexandria on 24 February and stood inshore to reconnoitre. From the Marabout fort west of the city to Aboukir castle on the point of the bay to the eastward he studied the coast, going ashore three times to map the terrain and reconnoitre lake Aboukir. Finally the *Peterel* stood into Aboukir bay itself, and finding the ship unable to approach close enough through the shallows, McKerras set off in her pinnace for a final reconnaissance, with a warning from Commander Inglis not to risk the boat by venturing too deep into the cul de sac of the bay. McKerras observed the coastline and made soundings near the entrance to lake Aboukir.

But all this careful work was thrown away. When darkness fell, McKerras ordered the pinnace to push in to the shore and landed on the actual beach where the assault was later made. But he had been seen by the enemy. A French gunboat came out from lake Aboukir to intercept him, and as the pinnace was returning to the *Peterel* at dawn, the gunboat bore down from the windward. The *Peterel* made sail to come to the rescue, but in shoal water and in the eye of the wind she could do nothing and Commander Inglis saw the Frenchman open fire with cannon and muskets. The disabled pinnace was brought to in the water. The enemy drew alongside to take possession of their prize; but the boat's crew showed fight, the French fired, and a musket ball smashed into McKerras's skull. As he fell forward his brains splashed into Fletcher's boot, a horror which Fletcher would never forget.[3]

That daybreak had deprived Abercromby of his two senior Royal Engineers, the army's scarcest experts, and of all the information they had collected. He had now with all speed to discover what he could for himself. Boarding a cutter with Moore, he went inshore to find a landing place. From the castle at Aboukir point the bay swept round in a vast crescent to the south and east, where the low shore vanished towards the distant mouth of the Nile. The only sector from which an advance could be launched towards Alexandria lay between the castle and the lake. Here the British generals saw a low line of sand dunes very like the landing-beaches in Holland, dominated in the centre by an abrupt sixty-foot sandhill which reminded them of the Dutch hill of Camperdown. To the right of this sandhill the beach was in range of the castle's batteries of eight heavy 24-pounders and two 12-inch mortars; while on the extreme left towards the lake the broken wooded terrain looked unsuitable for an advance. It was clear that a landing could be made only between the sandhill, which would have to be stormed to secure the right flank and the view over the landing beach, and the wooded ground on the left, a front of little more than half a mile. Abercromby and Moore could see French working parties on the summit of the sandhill; but the low crest of the dunes to the left concealed the enemy fighting force from fire and observation.[4]

At two in the afternoon Sir Ralph returned to the flagship to speak to the admiral, and orders were issued to land on the following morning. Abercromby needed ten hours of settled weather to get his force ashore; but at 6 p.m. it began to blow again from the north-west. A heavy swell rolled into the bay, and breakers were crashing into foaming surf on the beaches. All over the bay signals of distress were flying as transports parted their cables or struck on shoals. If the wind continued long the whole plan might have to be abandoned, and Moore for one felt let down by the naval advice that the bay was safe for a landing. It had good anchoring ground for warships, and though they rolled heavily in the gale the long reef which extended eastwards from Aboukir point broke the full force of the sea. But to try to land troops in these conditions was hopeless. The heavily laden flatboats could not make the long approach through the swell, let alone bring the infantry through the surf and on to the beaches. Once again Moore sensed the gap between naval and military requirements.[5]

For the next two days the bay was so rough that for long periods boats could not even pass from ship to ship. And while the storm blew, the *Romulus* joined the fleet with news from the outside world which added to the sense of urgency and wasted time. Britain was now at war with the Baltic Powers: 'I think we must have peace now', wrote Commander Inglis: 'We cannot fight the world'. Worse was the news that ten sail of the line had escaped from Brest and at least six of them had entered the Mediterranean. To Keith's tasks of supporting the army and blockading Alexandria was now added the threat of an enemy fleet. His shortage of force was exposed when two more French frigates slipped into Alexandria with ammunition and reinforcements; and again when a small French warship came boldly round the point of Aboukir and anchored under the guns of the castle, adding her firepower to the batteries which commanded the northern beach.[6]

On 5 March the sea had abated enough for Moore to reconnoitre the shore again. About a mile and a half from the beach a bomb-vessel was riding at anchor in seventeen feet of water, and Moore boarded her to search the shore-line with his telescope. He saw no sign of entrenchments, but the captain of the bomb thought that the movement of enemy troops had increased during the day and guessed that reinforcements had arrived. What force the French held concealed behind the dunes it was impossible to know, but one thing was certain: the bad weather was giving them time to prepare. With every day that passed more movement could be seen, and more cannon were appearing.

While the troops waited for the weather to improve, they had leisure to ponder on their situation and the daily indications of increasing enemy force. Colonel Paget of the 28th feared that if the delay continued a different landing place would have to be found. But still the French force remained a mystery, for their control of the coastline meant that not a scrap of information was getting through from the native population. This fog was pierced on 6 March when Sir Sidney Smith brought off a prisoner for interrogation, after bringing a cutter and some gunboats inshore and attacking the two-gun blockhouse which guarded the entrance to the lake. The French reacted swiftly and in force, and the landing party had to retire; but they took off a French corporal, who stated that the bay was defended by General Friant with 2–3,000 troops from Alexandria.[7]

On the same day the wind moderated, allowing the transports to weigh and work in closer to the shore where they were marshalled in three groups under the Agents for Transports. The general and admiral were out reconnoitring again in a cutter, and a landing was ordered for the early morning of the 7th. Again it had to be postponed, as the wind continued too fresh. During the 7th the weather improved, and three days' pack-rations were cooked. The infantry of the second wave began to tranship to the small craft which were to hold them in readiness closer inshore, the 92nd transferring after eating their dinners to seven small Greek vessels. Already the *Tartarus* and *Fury* bomb-vessels were anchored inshore near the forming-up line, and before dark the gunboats and armed launches which were to provide close fire support were brought forward to their battle positions. All but two of the Turkish gunboats which had separated on the voyage were still missing, so for close support the attack would rely mainly on naval launches with a carronade mounted in the bows.[8]

In the evening came the signal for all boats to be ready at 2 a.m. Daylight faded, and the dark line of the shore merged gradually with sea and sky. French picket fires twinkled in the night on the low crests of the dunes. What force waited behind those crests, ready for battle in the morning? On the answer depended the lives of the troops and the fate of the expedition.

Eighteen months earlier the answer would have been in the hands of Bonaparte; even nine months ago the disposition of the French forces would have been determined by the brilliant Kléber. But Bonaparte had slipped away to seize power in France, and in June 1800 Kléber had fallen to an assassin. The Army of the Orient passed by seniority into the lax hands of General Abdullah Menou as the senior *général de division*. His command was provisional, but he had attached himself to Bonaparte and now played on the First Consul's jealousy of Kléber. Instead of appointing the able Reynier, Bonaparte confirmed Menou in the command.

Menou, a paunchy 50-year-old, had acquired the name Abdullah as a convert to Islam, with exemption from the surgical penalty of that decision:

his reward was the pleasure of a native wife, whose father was said to keep a bath-house in Rosetta where Menou had been governor. Yet he had been born Baron Jacques Menou of an ancient noble family of Touraine. As a cavalry colonel in 1789 he threw in his lot with the Revolution; was wounded fighting the Austrians; and showed courage and leadership as a divisional commander on the north-eastern frontiers. Later he was disgraced and court-martialled for leniency to royalists during the civil war in the Vendée, but was saved by the intervention of Bonaparte, and attached himself to the rising star of the future Emperor and accompanied him to Egypt.

And in Egypt he remained when Bonaparte returned to France. But he was ill qualified for the supreme command which fell to him by the chance of Kléber's assassination. He had never held an independent command, and was long past his peak. Soon after landing in Egypt Bonaparte had replaced him with a younger officer in the command of his division, and appointed him governor of Rosetta. Thus superannuated, he saw less active service in Egypt than any of his senior subordinates. All of them were much younger, and of very different background. Of his divisional commanders the oldest was Friant, aged 42, while Reynier and Lanusse were both under 30. They had risen from nothing during the Revolution. Rampon, Friant, and the cavalry commander Roize had been rankers in the old royal army; Lanusse and Belliard had been promoted from the revolutionary National Guard; and Reynier, the ablest of them all, had been one of the heroic generation of the volunteers of '92.

An amusing story-teller and entertaining companion, Menou was neither stupid nor wholly ignorant of his duties. Yet he was a fool; restless but dilatory, active in trivialities but unable to take important decisions; reck-lessly generous and always massively in debt. He could not command the respect of his subordinates; and Reynier rapidly became the leader of an opposition to the balding, pot-bellied Commander-in-Chief with whom they maintained a constant state of bickering. They remonstrated against his innovations and his orders of the day; his declamations on morality, and his refusal to subscribe to a monument to their hero Kléber. Menou fell out immediately with his chief of staff Damas, and replaced him with Brigadier-General Lagrange whom he quickly promoted to *général de division*. Soon he was bypassing the military chain of command and cultivating direct relations with a lower tier of officers, triggering further protests.

Menou's conversion and marriage had made him a joke in the army: it also identified him as an enthusiastic member of the 'colonist' party, advocates of the permanent French colonisation of Egypt, a further recommendation in the eyes of Bonaparte. Kléber had regarded Bonaparte's Egyptian adventure as bankrupt; and the best of his officers, ambitious arrivistes like Reynier and Lanusse, longed to be back in Europe where their contemporaries were winning glory and promotion under Bonaparte's eyes. In June 1800

Bonaparte's victory at Marengo, on the day of Kléber's assassination, had spotlighted their lost opportunities; and as they waited for the British invasion an incoming French frigate brought news of General Moreau's decisive defeat of the Austrians at Hohenlinden. Reynier and other friends of Moreau wrote to him lamenting that they had not been there, and sought his influence with Bonaparte to bring the Army of the Orient home.

Menou learned of the correspondence with Moreau in February 1801, on the eve of the British invasion. Rightly suspecting his generals of conspiring for the evacuation of Egypt, he reported their conduct to Bonaparte. The four leaders of the opposition – Damas, Lanusse, Belliard, and Reynier, who were all to be prominent in the coming campaign – retorted with a joint letter to Menou deriding the colonist and anti-colonist parties as figments of his imagination and demanding the withdrawal of his accusation. Their letter was seditiously circulated in the army, further undermining respect for Menou; and Reynier wrote home to Moreau and General Gouvion St Cyr (a future Marshal of the Empire) urging them to tackle Bonaparte and obtain Menou's removal. Menou's relations with his best generals had reached the point of explosion. They were unlikely to approve his measures to meet the British invasion; nor he to heed their advice.[9]

The seven cavalry regiments and fourteen demi-brigades of Menou's field force had been much wasted by battle and disease during their two and a half years in the east. The cavalry were nearly forty per cent below their original strength; and most of the demi-brigades were thirty per cent down and had been forced to amalgamate their three battalions into two. The troops were weary of Egypt with its filth and disease, its squalid villages, and its hostile louche inhabitants. The soldiers were dressed in ragged motley, for shortage of cloth meant that the dark blue of the Revolutionary armies was reserved for the artillery, with dark green for the cavalry and light green for the light infantry, leaving the rest of the infantry to share out red, black, grey, or brown as available. For foreign service under a hot sun the bicorne hats had been replaced by peaked leather helmets crowned with coloured pouffes to identify the demi-brigades. Yet, strange though their appearance would have seemed to the army at home, they remained in good order, hardy and disciplined, though their resilience in adversity had still to be tested. Their units had a proud record. Victorious with Bonaparte in Italy, they had marched with him to the Holy Land; had pursued the Mamelukes up the Nile as far as Assouan, and inscribed their generals' names on the temple of Philae. Under their protection French scholars had surveyed every field of Egyptian science and art, discovering tombs in the Valley of the Kings, and accumulating material to fill twenty printed volumes.[10] The French achievements in Egypt had not been ignoble, and their army was not disintegrating.

Menou's 22,000 field troops were backed by 8,000 auxiliaries – veterans, seamen, marine artillery, native Greek and Coptic infantry, sappers and miners, and administrative troops – who largely manned the static garrisons and freed the field army for mobile operations (see Table 1 below). The numbers were formidable, and far greater than Abercromby suspected. But they were dispersed across Egypt, and their concentration for battle would depend on the quality of their high command.

Menou's strategic problem was far from straightforward. He knew that he faced a Turkish attack across the Sinai desert, and British landings in the Mediterranean and the Red Sea. Menou had to provide against all these threats, and they were even more diffuse than might appear. The Turks, for a start, were not negligible: the French had fought them already, and took them more seriously than the British did. The two British expeditions had the nebulousness conferred by sea power. The division approaching the Red

Table 1 French forces in Egypt, 7 March. The figures are based on embarcation returns at the end of the campaign and losses during it

Cavalry, infantry, artillery (embarked)	17,580	
Dromedary Corps and guides	491	
Sappers and miners, artificers, staff	456	
Invalids (i.e. older garrison troops)	740	
Sick embarked	2,187	
Greeks and Copts	718	
Mamelukes	160	
Seamen and marine artillery	1,864	
Hospital staff, and naval and military commissariats	529	
Casualties and desertions during campaign	3,460	
Captured other than at Cairo and Alexandria	2,030	
Total		30,215
Deduct men not of the field forces:		
Local troops (Copts, Greeks, Mamelukes)	874	
Sappers and miners, artificers, staff	456	
Invalids	740	
Seamen and marine artillery	1,864	
Hospital and commissariat	529	
		4,463
Total		25,752
Deduct:		
One third of casualties and desertions, and sick, and of surrenders other than at Cairo or Alexandria (to allow for men not part of field force)		2,259
Total field force (cavalry, infantry, artillery) on 7 March		23,493

Note: The total of the field force calculated above is slightly more than the calculations made by British officers on the same basis, which give the French between 21,000 and 22,450 field troops (Walsh, App., 138; Add. MS 35894, f.70). The discrepancy could be accounted for by army artillery posted in garrisons.

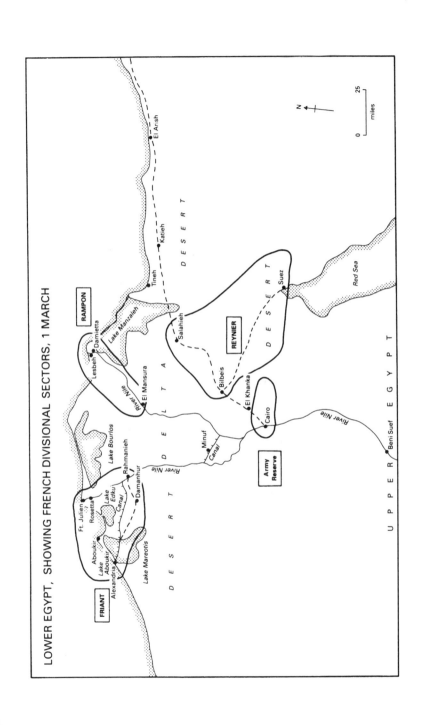

LOWER EGYPT, SHOWING FRENCH DIVISIONAL SECTORS, 1 MARCH

Table 2 French field forces: deployment on 1 March. Deployment of cavalry and infantry: strength in rank and file. DB = demi-brigade

---

Eastern Approaches (Reynier)

Reynier's Division:

Salahieh	14 Dragoons	25
	22 DB légère	430
	(garrison troops)	(110)
Suez	9 DB	100
	(garrison troops)	(50)
Belbeis	14 Dragoons	25
	22 DB légère	80
	(garrison troops)	(32)
Cairo	14 Dragoons	195 (and 67 dismounted)
	22 DB légère	234
	9 DB	794
	13 DB	841
	85 DB	890

Damietta Sector (Rampon)

Rampon's Division:

Damietta area	20 Dragoons	153 (and 60 dismounted)
(with Lesbeh,	2 DB légère	540
Mansura)	32 DB	542
	(garrison troops)	(530)
Rahmanieh and delta	20 Dragoons	80
Cairo	2 DB légère }	462
	32 DB }	

Alexandria Sector (Friant)

Friant's Division:

Alexandria and Aboukir	18 Dragoons	115 (and 75 dismounted)
	61 DB	750
	75 DB	950
	(garrison troops)	(2,350)
Rosetta, Fort Julien, Bourlos	3 Dragoons	150 (and 30 dismounted)
	25 DB	100
	61 DB	150
	(garrison troops)	(320)
Rahmanieh and delta	25 DB	580
	75 DB	80
	(garrison troops)	(125)
Cairo	3 Dragoons	75
	25 DB	230

Table 2 Continued

Upper Egypt (Donzelot)		
Beni Suef	21 DB légère	850
Kosseir, El Minya, Girga, Asyut	21 DB légère (garrison troops)	800 (110)

Army Reserve, Cairo (Commander-in-Chief, Menou)		
Cavalry (Gen. de brigade Roize)		
Bron's brigade:	7 Hussars	240 (and 30 dismounted)
	22 Chasseurs à cheval	230 (and 40 dismounted)
	15 Dragoons	129 (and 52 dismounted)
Infantry		
Lanusse's Division:	4 DB légère	790
	18 DB	794
	69 DB	859
	88 DB	883
	(garrison troops)	(2,602)

Source: Tables in Reynier

Sea from India could land at Suez to support the Turkish advance from Palestine; or 300 miles further south at Kosseir to threaten Upper Egypt. In the Mediterranean Abercromby's army had numerous options, among which Menou did not regard the Alexandria sector as the most probable. Damietta, which for a time had been Abercromby's first choice, seemed the likelier point of attack. The French also viewed as a serious possibility a British landing further east to join the Grand Vizir in the Gulf of Tineh (Khalig El Tîna) or on the coast of Palestine. This notion was nourished among the French generals by a delusion that the perfidious British had come to the Levant to partition the Ottoman Empire and would wish to eliminate the Turkish army. Thus could Abercromby's long delay at Marmaris be explained: he had been preparing a base against the Turks.

Menou faced three convergent threats, and had at least four sectors to defend on the circumference of his command. His situation called for a classic defensive on interior lines, with a central reserve to strike alternately at the approaching allies; and for such a campaign his dispositions were well conceived, with four covering forces on the periphery and a *masse de manoeuvre* at Cairo. Far off in Upper Egypt General Donzelot was posted with a strong demi-brigade and ancillary troops to block the Indian army's approach through Kosseir. The northern coast and frontier were organised as three divisional areas: Reynier's on the Palestine front, with forward posts at Salahieh (El Salhîya) and Suez; Rampon's at Damietta; and Friant's at

Alexandria and the mouth of the western Nile. There remained for the central reserve Lanusse's strong infantry division and General Bron's cavalry brigade. A third of Rampon's infantry was also held back at Cairo; so was the majority of Reynier's division, on the calculation that 120 miles of desert between his outpost at Salahieh and the Turkish advance guard at El Arish would give ample warning to send it forward. An intermediate post at Bilbeis guarded Reynier's communications with his forward elements.

These dispositions kept half the field army in reserve in the Cairo area and at Menou's disposal. The flaw in this prudent deployment was that too many of the reserves were held in a single mass as far back as Cairo.[11] The Turks could spring no surprise from Palestine; but the British could appear suddenly on any part of the coast and throw a force ashore. An immediate local counterstroke would have to be mounted, and to provide for this Kléber had kept 7,000 men lower down the Nile at Rahmanieh (El Rahmâniya), a communications centre from which the force could march rapidly to Alexandria, to Rosetta, or across the delta to Damietta. But wherever Menou stationed his reserves, success would depend on correct reading of the enemy's intentions and a swift response.

The first sign that the crisis was about to explode reached Cairo on 2 March with the news that two British engineer officers had been captured while reconnoitring Aboukir bay. On the 3rd came tidings, by a dromedary which had made the 115-mile journey from Alexandria in twenty-seven hours, that a British fleet had been sighted off the port. The British threat now pointed strongly towards the Alexandria sector. Was this the moment for Menou to begin the movement of his reserves? He was doubtful, still unconvinced that Alexandria was the point of attack. The fleet's appearance might be a feint. It might yet reappear a hundred miles to the eastward at Damietta; or much further east to join the Turkish army. The last far-fetched notion still appealed strongly to Menou's imagination.

His response was to begin a cautious movement of reserves towards all the sectors where he perceived a threat. The 460 infantry of Rampon's division which had been held back at Cairo were sent forward to rejoin him at Damietta. To counter an Anglo-Turkish advance from the direction of Palestine Reynier was ordered to move closer to his outposts, by advancing to Bilbeis, some thirty-five miles to the north-east of Cairo, with two of his four demi-brigades and all his divisional artillery. To the critical Alexandria sector, however, Menou at first sent little, because the local commander Friant made light of the danger. Two of Friant's demi-brigades had already taken part in the defeat of a Turkish landing in Aboukir bay in 1798 and knew how easily an amphibious force could fall into chaos. He could collect at least 2,000 troops at Aboukir by calling in his detachments from Rosetta and the delta, and wrote confidently that he could repel a landing. He asked only for an additional cavalry regiment; and Menou ordered the 230 troopers of the 22nd Chasseurs à cheval at Cairo to join him.

These diffuse movements provoked a vehement reaction from Reynier, who was being sent away from the British and towards the Turks. In the strongest terms he protested at his orders, urging Menou to march with the whole of his reserves to Alexandria and forget the Turks till he had destroyed the British. In his later memoirs he claimed that he had had serious thoughts of removing Menou from his command, but had shrunk from a step which only resounding victory could clear of the taint of mutiny. Perhaps Menou was affected by Reynier's pressure, for as an afterthought he prepared a strong eventual reinforcement for Alexandria. Lanusse's division was ordered to march in two days' time; and Menou himself, if he heard no more from Friant, intended to follow with a second cavalry regiment and one of Reynier's remaining demi-brigades. This would leave a single cavalry regiment and one demi-brigade in general reserve at Cairo.

Lanusse marched as planned on 5 March. But immediately the intelligence picture began to change as a succession of reports arrived to be misinterpreted by Menou. In the course of the day the commandant at Bilbeis reported that the Grand Vizir's advance was not due to start within the next two or three weeks; an indication that his offensive was not timed to synchronise with an immediate British landing at Aboukir. Menou took this reasoning further: the Vizir was probably waiting for Abercromby to transfer his expedition eastwards and join him, and the British demonstration at Alexandria was a feint. In that case, it would be wrong to commit the French reserves to the Alexandria sector, at the opposite end of the theatre and on the wrong side of the delta. At nine o'clock that evening came a contrary indicator that the British had anchored in Aboukir bay. But this did not shift Menou's appraisal. Friant still expressed doubt that the British would land, and believed that he was dealing with a diversion. If they did try to come ashore, he promised to knock them for six: *je les culbuterai*. Menou, who underrated the British troops and despised their unenterprising commanders, readily endorsed Friant's appreciation. He and his staff concluded that Friant had his local situation in hand, and prepared to strengthen the eastern defences. Menou cancelled his own move to Alexandria, and recalled one of Lanusse's demi-brigades to Cairo at the start of its second day's march. Lanusse himself was ordered to halt when he reached Rahmanieh with two demi-brigades and to send only one forward to Alexandria, though Friant was authorised to call the other two forward if they were needed. The wisdom of these changes seemed to be confirmed on the 7th by news from a Greek vessel which had slipped past the British fleet to Aboukir castle: it reported that there were few troops on board the British ships, and that most of the British force had remained at Rhodes to suppress an insurrection. Did not this confirm that Abercromby's real objective was to the eastward?

By this chain of reasoning Menou misread Abercromby's mind and dismissed the threat to Aboukir. It is true that, because the whole of the French reserve was initially back at Cairo, no reinforcement he might have sent could have reached Friant in time to oppose the British landing on 8 March: even the 22nd Chasseurs were not in time, though they had marched as soon as Menou knew that the British fleet had been sighted. But we shall see later that if Menou had marched in strength on 6 March when he learned that the British had anchored in Aboukir bay, the first French reserves to reach the front would not have been frittered in a partial attack, and Menou's concentrated counter-offensive would have been launched earlier and with forces intact.[12]

Thus Friant, asking for no reinforcements and receiving none, prepared to oppose the landing with his own resources. He was a gallant and experienced infantry officer, whose name is inscribed on the Temple of Philae at Assouan as one of Desaix's brigade commanders. He would serve Bonaparte loyally to the end, and received the last of his many wounds while commanding the grenadiers of the Old Guard in the final holocaust at Waterloo.

Friant was convinced that a landing from boats would produce confusion on the beach. Hence his confidence that with 2,000 infantry and cavalry he could defeat a British attack. He had a strong narrow front with fixed batteries defending the flanks. In his centre was a battery of three iron cannon on the beach; and his dozen field guns were dug in on commanding points on the dunes to batter approaching landing craft with round shot and grape. The main body of his force was concentrated south of the great sand-hill, the Monticule du Puits, and sheltered from naval bombardment by the dunes. As the assault craft drew close to the shore the ships would have to cease fire to avoid hitting them, and at that point the French infantry and dragoons would be unleashed on the invaders struggling in the surf. Thus Friant proposed to destroy them.[13]

Table 3 Friant's Force

Friant's numbers at the beach-head are difficult to determine. He claimed that he had 1,450 infantry and cavalry; Reynier gives him 1,700; and Walsh calls it 2,500. The total strength in Friant's command was 3,260 infantry and cavalry excluding officers. If the whole of each unit represented in the 8 March battle had been present, the total would have been about 2,995 (excluding the unmounted men of the cavalry who were left behind). But detachments from these units seem to have been sent to the Rosetta area. I think a reasonable guess would be:

Cavalry:	18 Dragoons	115	
	20 Dragoons	80	
Infantry:	61 DB	680	
	75 DB	950	
	51 DB	210	(recently arrived from France in *Régénérée*)
Total	2,035 excluding officers		

The above figures may underestimate the detachments absent in the Rosetta area: but, to balance this, some of Friant's battalion of the 25 DB were also present in the battle, though I have not discovered their numbers.

As the evening of 7 March drew on, the soldiers on the lower decks of the British troopships were packing and fitting their equipment for the landing. The assault wave were to leave their knapsacks on board, yet they had to carry food and shelter for the next few days. Into their packs and pouches they crammed two spare shirts, and two pairs of socks; sixty rounds of ball ammunition and two spare flints; three days' rations of freshly cooked bread and pork. On to this load they had to fit blankets, entrenching tool, and camp kettle. Each man had a full canteen of water on his belt: rum would be landed with the quartermasters and issued later. Officers' servants were ordered to be under arms in the line, and officers had to carry everything themselves like their soldiers. Non-combatant duties would be done by bandsmen: regimental surgeons were allotted orderlies to carry their field chests of instruments, while each brigade had medical staff attached from the General Hospital. The sick left behind in the troopships would be nursed mainly by convalescents and women.[14]

As darkness drew on, the battalion majors inspected arms and the adjutants made out their embarcation returns. The gale had dropped, and a gentle night breeze from the desert lifted the bows of the ships at their cables. Boats passed to and fro transferring the second wave of infantry to the small vessels lying inshore; and on the warships' poops the telescopes of the officers of the watch lingered on the distant watch-fires of the Army of the Orient twinkling beneath the stars of Africa. In the fleet occasional false fires and rockets flared to confuse the enemy. Midnight tolled in the 8th of March. One o'clock and the ships were astir. On the quarterdecks of the troopships the infantry of the assault wave formed up by companies: guardsmen in the *Delft*, *Dictator*, and *Trusty*; highlanders of the 42nd in the *Inconstant*, *Cyclops*, and *Kent*; Welshmen of the 23rd Fusiliers in the *Astra* and *Héroine*; the English of the 28th and 40th in the *Blonde*, *Druid*, *Winchelsea*, and *Vestal*; on the deck of the *Pegasus*, Hudson Lowe's Corsican Rangers. The warships of the fleet had hoisted their boats out ready for the two o'clock signal from the admiral.

There was subdued excitement and anxiety. What lay behind those concealing crests of the dunes? Would one acquit oneself well under fire? Adrenalin might not yet be pumping in the veins, but confidence was high.

Part II

BEACH-HEAD

6

ASSAULT LANDING

Out in the darkness to the eastward in the deep water where the great ships lay, a single rocket soared to extinguish the stars in a shower of sparks. It was the signal for the waiting boats, which began to pull away from the side of their parent ships towards their rendezvous with the troops. As each boat came alongside its appointed troopship and made fast, the infantry drawn up on the deck were given the order to embark. In the big two-deckers the men filed off by ranks through the upper gunports and down the gangways. In single-decked ships they handed their muskets to soldiers stationed at the bulwarks and clambered down the side of the ship on ladders. With their feet firmly planted on the bottom boards of the boat, they took the muskets which were handed down to them and found their places, sitting down in strict silence with their weapons between their knees.[1]

The boats were now loaded and ready, and at three o'clock a second rocket blazed its bright tail into the dark sky. The boats pulled clear and the oarsmen began the long haul towards the forming-up line. Some of the boats had five or six miles to row to where the *Mondovi* brig marked the flank of the line about a gunshot from the shore.[2]

Under the brilliant stars nothing disturbed the stillness of the night but the dipping of thousands of oars in the rippling water. The seamen kept warm as they hauled on their blades, but the silent immobile soldiers huddled against a chilly night breeze from the desert. Behind them darkness was dissolving into a grey dawn; the sky lightened in the east; and the sun rose on a bright morning as the boats lifted their bows to the wavelets of the bay. By six o'clock some of the boats were up by the *Mondovi* brig, where they were directed into their places in the line by Captain Cochrane and his captains of boat divisions. But it was eight o'clock before the boats from the most distant ships were up and marshalled, and for early arrivals the minutes had dragged into hours as they surveyed the scene of their coming ordeal. When the last boats were positioned and the line was dressed, there was a pause of about a quarter of an hour while the sailors rested on their oars before the final pull into the zone of cannon fire. All was happening just as it had been planned and rehearsed. The flatboats in the first line had taken station at their intervals of fifty feet, and behind them the rescue cutters were placed to assist sinking boats and save men floundering in the water. In third line were the cutters with towed launches.[3]

At the right of the attack were the six battalions of Moore's Reserve, the largest formation in the assault. Moore and his staff, with his second-in-command Oakes, were in Captain Cochrane's barge, placed a little ahead of the first line to control its alignment by signal. In the centre of the assault wave, on the left of the Reserve, was General Ludlow's brigade of Guards, and beyond them two and a half battalions of Coote's brigade in the transports' boats manned by merchant seamen. Interspersed with the infantry in the front line were fourteen artillery launches carrying field-guns and their crews. The whole force was about 5,500 strong.

The men had now been five or six hours in the boats. The tense minutes ticked away, and the silent soldiers glanced anxiously at the shore and at each other. For the past two hours enemy troops and cannon had been visible moving into position nearly a mile distant on the shore. Away to the right were the towers and bastions of Aboukir castle with its heavy batteries. To the left was the two-gun battery at the blockhouse on the lake. These guns were out of range, but at the foot of the great sandhill was the heavy battery of three iron cannon. Along the crest of the dunes the barrels of General Friant's field-guns and howitzers were dark against the pale sky, sinister black mouths waiting in the bright morning.[4]

A little forward on the flanks of the line small naval craft pointed the heavy gun in their bows towards the shore to provide fire-support: on the right, the *Cruelle* cutter, the *Dangereuse* and *Janissary* gunboats, and two launches with squat carronades in their bows; on the left, the *Enterprise* cutter, *Malta* schooner, *Negresse* gun-vessel, and more launches. Heavier sloops, the *Peterel* of 16 guns, the *Chameleon* of 18, and the *Minorca*, were anchored with their broadsides to the beach; and two bomb-vessels, *Tartarus* and *Fury*, were ready to lob explosive shells on to the dunes from their 13-inch and 10-inch mortars. But it would be long-range shooting and not very accurate. The warships could not risk anchoring close enough inshore for the enemy to sweep their decks with grape-shot.[5]

Lord Keith and Abercromby had taken their battle-post in the *Tartarus* bomb, but there was little they could now do but watch: they had issued their orders, and the next stage was up to the troops. Far off behind them, black against the morning sun, were the clusters of warships and transports from which the boats had come, their decks thronged with spectators. On board the 74-gun *Minotaur* two French officer-prisoners climbed the rigging to see the last of their British friends. Close in by the bomb-vessels were the small Greek vessels with the first reinforcements, their decks also crowded with troops watching the line of boats across the bright water. 'I contemplated the scene with an anxious aching heart', a highlander of the 92nd remembered. On the deck of the *Tartarus* Abercromby shared their anxiety.

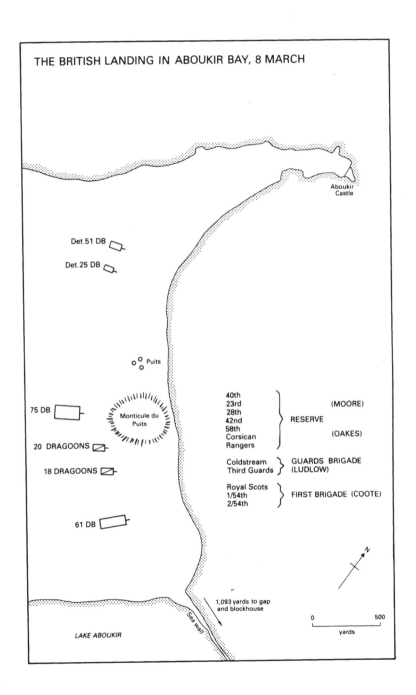

THE BRITISH LANDING IN ABOUKIR BAY, 8 MARCH

Aboukir Castle

Det. 51 DB

Det. 25 DB

○ ○ Puits
○

Monticule du Puits

75 DB

20 DRAGOONS

18 DRAGOONS

61 DB

40th
23rd
28th   (MOORE)
42nd   RESERVE
58th
Corsican   (OAKES)
Rangers

Coldstream   GUARDS BRIGADE
Third Guards (LUDLOW)

Royal Scots
1/54th   FIRST BRIGADE (COOTE)
2/54th

N

1,093 yards to gap
and blockhouse

Sea wall

LAKE ABOUKIR

0   500

yards

Table 4 Order of battle of British force, 7 March

	Regiment	Rank and file fit for duty	Joined from
First line			
Brigade of Guards	1/Coldstream	766 ⎫	Ferrol expedn
M. Gen. Ludlow	1/Third Guards	812 ⎬ 1,578	Ferrol expedn
1st Brigade	2/1st (Royals)	626 ⎫	Ferrol expedn
of the line	1/54th ⎱	⎪	Ferrol expedn
M. Gen. Coote	2/54th ⎰	974 ⎬ 2,129	
	92nd (Gordon Highlanders)	529 ⎭	Belle Ile expedn via Ferrol
2nd Brigade	8th (King's)	439 ⎫	Minorca
M. Gen. Cradock	13th	561 ⎪	Ferrol expedn
	18th (Royal Irish)	411 ⎬ 2,138	Gibraltar
	90th (Perthshire Vols)	727 ⎭	Minorca
Second line			
3rd Brigade	1/27th	left sick at	Ferrol expedn
M. Gen. Lord Cavan	2/27th	Gibraltar and Malta	Ferrol expedn
	50th	477 ⎫	Portugal and Minorca
	79th (Cameronian Vols)	604 ⎬ 1,081	Belle Ile expedn via Ferrol
4th Brigade	2nd (Queen's)	530 ⎫	Belle Ile expedn
B. Gen. Doyle	30th	412 ⎪	Malta
	44th	263 ⎬ 1,583	Gibraltar
	89th	378 ⎭	Malta
5th (Foreign) Brigade	Stuart's (Minorca)	929 ⎫	Minorca
B. Gen. Stuart	De Roll's	528 ⎬ 1,987	Portugal and Minorca
	Dillon's	530 ⎭	Portugal and Minorca
Reserve			
M. Gen. Moore	23rd (Welch Fusiliers)	457 ⎫	Belle Ile expedn via Ferrol
B. Gen. Oakes	28th	587 ⎪	Gibraltar
	42nd (Royal Highlanders)	754 ⎬ 2,726	Minorca
	58th	469 ⎪	Minorca
	40th (flank companies)	250 ⎪	Malta (ex-England)
	Corsican Rangers	209 ⎭	Minorca

Table 4 Continued

	Regiment	Rank and file fit for duty	Joined from
Cavalry Brigade			
B. Gen. Finch	11th Light Dragoons (one troop)	53 ⎫	England
	12th Light Dragoons	474 ⎪ 1,034	Portugal
	26th Light Dragoons	369 ⎬	Portugal
	Hompesch's Hussars	138 ⎭	Ferrol expedn
Artillery			
B. Gen. Lawson	13th, 14th, 26th, 28th, 55th, 69th, 70th, 71st Companies	627[1]	
Staff Corps		82	
Total		14,965	
Infantry		13,222	

[1] In addition 19 gunners (23 all ranks) were serving in the bombs *Tartarus* and *Fury* (dets from various companies in England).

His careful planning was about to throw 5,000 men into a fire-storm from the enemy's waiting guns. He began to take counsel of his fears. What if the enemy fire was too destructive to be endured? What if the steep front of the big sandhill where Moore was to land proved too steep, and the sand too loose to be scaled?[6]

There was just time for last-minute alterations, and shortly before the signal to advance he sent Hope off with a final message to Moore. If the enemy fire was unbearable he would fly the signal to retire, and Moore and Cochrane were to watch for it. Hope was also to ask Moore whether he now thought it better to land his brigade further to the right, and gain the hill by the more gradual slopes of its northern flank. Moore had no means of telling whether the sandhill was the left flank of the French position, or whether other enemy forces extended northwards beyond his own flank. But the hill certainly dominated the landing-beaches, and he had arranged to assault its front himself with his right-hand battalions, leaving the command of his left to Oakes. He could see enemy on the heights; but the hill did not seem unscalable, and once his men were on the beach they would be able to form up in 'dead ground' invisible from the crest. He told Hope that he would stick to his plan, and Abercromby smiled when Hope reported the answer. 'This is really taking the bull by the horns', he said.[7]

A moment later the *Tartarus* hoisted the signal to advance. The whole line sprang forward, and the guns of the warships roared their salvoes, sending the sand flying on the beach and the slopes of the dunes. But few of the enemy were visible. As the assault-line passed the two bomb-vessels their mortars lifted their range and began to drop shells on the tops of the dunes. For a while the boats moved on in silence, pulling hard against a strengthening breeze from the land. Smoke from the warships' guns was drifting back across the bay, and the shells of the bomb-vessels were bursting in little puffs above the dunes. Steadily the flatboats pushed on, every stroke of the oars bringing them closer to the enemy's defensive fire. Suddenly flame and smoke leapt from the muzzles of fifteen cannon, followed by the sound booming across the sea. Columns of water leapt from the waves and sprayed the boats. From the decks of the Greek vessels the kilted highlanders of the 92nd watched for the flash of an enemy gun, then turned their eyes to the boats to see where the shot would strike. Three boats were hit by round shot and sunk, but most of their heavily laden soldiers were picked up by the following cutters. A howitzer shell burst in a flatboat of the Coldstream and killed or wounded most of the men on board.

Now the assault line was only 300 yards from the shore, and the fire changed. Instead of the shot and shell which could send a boat straight to the bottom, there came a storm of grapeshot and canister ripping the water like hailstones. Soon small-arms fire thickened the tempest. In one unlucky boat twenty-two men were hit. 'The shower of grape and musquetry seemed so to plough the surface of the water, that nothing on it could live', wrote an eyewitness. Wedged together on the thwarts for the past six hours, the men were at last allowed to break their silence and answered the enemy fire with ringing hurrahs. On the left some of Coote's boats with their merchant crews were hanging back from the fire and veering to the left. But the centre and right kept their stations. Cochrane's barge was the first to touch the beach, below the sandhill; the crew put out their landing planks and held out their boarding pikes as if they had been landing at a pier. As Moore landed, the boats of the Reserve swept up beside him, and the soldiers leapt into the surf.[8]

Up to the last moment the French commander General Friant seems to have been incredulous that a landing was intended. If he was wrong, and the British succeeded in forming up 5,000 British infantry on the beach, he would face certain defeat. His own 2,000 soldiers could not prevail against such odds, and his only hope now was to break up the attack at the waterline. Friant had imagined a ragged line of boats breaking up in the storm of fire which would lash them; small groups of men struggling ashore through the blood-stained waves; and French horsemen sweeping along the fringe of spume and mercilessly cutting down the survivors as they clumped together trying to load their firelocks.

But nothing had gone like that. The lines of boats had advanced through the curtain of fire in parade order. When the assault craft burst through the final barrage of musketry Friant seized his last chance to break up the invasion before his force was overwhelmed. Infantry and dragoons were rushed through the gaps in the dunes. But the right of the Reserve came ashore under the protection of the great sandhill where they could not be charged. Officers and men ran up the beach, camp colours were struck into the sand as markers, and the line began to form. In a moment the 23rd and 28th were ready and loaded, with Colonel Brent Spencer's volunteers of the 40th rapidly ranging their line on the right. Without a pause Moore led his men straight up the face of the hill. The sand was sliding under their feet, and men were scrambling up on hands and knees in the deep loose surface. Bursting over the crest, they fired and charged with the bayonet. Outnumbered French infantry broke and ran, abandoning two 6-pounders and part of their horse teams. Moore had cleared the height which dominated the beach-head.

On the left of Moore's attack, beyond the shelter of the great dune, the fighting was more confused. Here the rest of the Reserve under Oakes landed under fire in the immediate presence of the enemy, but the 'steady and intrepid' 42nd Highlanders and the 58th fell into their ranks and loaded with the same composure as Moore's battalions. A column of French infantry which threatened their left flank as they were forming was held off by a party of brave Corsicans under Lieutenant Morati, who were then attacked by cavalry and had nine men cut down. A few moments after Oakes's landing, as the Guards touched ground, the French 18th and 20th Dragoons burst through a gap in the sandhills and charged them, riding into the sea to thrust and slash at the soldiers in the boats. But by now the 58th were formed on their right and opened fire, checking the French cavalry and giving the Guards time to form a front on the beach. Now Coote's delayed battalions began to come ashore on the left, at the moment when a column of French infantry were advancing against the left flank of the Guards. On seeing the Royal Scots and the 54th forming, the French hesitated, fired a single volley, and retreated.[9]

Coote's battalions and the Guards were now led forward by their dismounted generals and field officers, and gained the crest of the dunes. From every point along the front the French ran back, to rally on the rearward sandhills and maintain a scattered fire for some time till they were finally dislodged and pushed back into the plain behind. Friant sent a detachment to hold Aboukir castle, and with the rest of his force took up a position with his right on the lake, protecting his open left flank with guns and cavalry of which the British as yet had none.[10]

From the deck of the *Tartarus* Sir Ralph Abercromby had watched the marshalling of the assault line; but knowing his weakness for risking himself at the front, his staff arranged that the naval lieutenant in charge of the general's boat should not push off till the landing was secured, and then slipped away themselves to join the assault boats. Abercromby was not to be deflected by such machinations. As soon as Hope and Anstruther had left the ship, Sir Ralph called for his boat, pushed off, and was on the beach before the fighting was over.

As he landed he saw an intoxicated officer staggering on the shore. 'Colonel Darby', he called to the drunkard's commanding officer, 'look at that officer of the 54th.' Christopher Darby struck the delinquent with the flat of his sword and ordered him back on board his transport to await orders. Soon afterwards, moving to the right, Abercromby caught sight of Colonel Hall of the 23rd, who had recently arrived from England to resume the command of the regiment from the second-in-command whom Abercromby had temporarily removed at Malta. Abercromby had observed the discipline with which the 23rd formed on the beach and stormed the sandhill, and seized the moment to erase the slur he had cast on the regiment. Going up to the colonel he shook his hand and said: 'My friend Hall, I am glad to see you; I shall never abuse you again'.[11]

From the decks of the shipping nothing could now be seen of the infantry who had vanished beyond the crests of the dunes. On the beaches surgeons were dressing wounds and extracting musket balls before the casualties were embarked. The flatboats were hauling off with the grapnels they had dropped behind them, and hoisting sail to run back with the wind and embark reinforcements. The *Peterel*, her fire task completed, weighed and ran back to the fleet with wounded men, to return to the beach with 200 men of the second wave. On this run speed mattered more than tactical order, and as it had been impossible to predict which boats would survive the enemy fire during the assault they had not been given specific tasks for the second run. They were simply to head for any ship flying its ensign at the foremast, the signal that there were troops of the second wave on board. As soon as all the troops were out of a ship she hauled down her ensign. The artillery launches made for the ordnance transports, some to pick up four howitzers and the remaining pair of 6-pounders, other to ferry engineers' stores, ammunition, and hand-carts for delivering ammunition to the line. Immediate ammunition reserves were held in a vessel flying an ordnance flag which was brought in and anchored close to the shore.[12]

Nothing seems to have been overlooked in this meticulous operation. When the infantry were ashore Captain Scott's boat division was detailed to land the dismounted cavalry and pioneers, while the other three boat divisions began the complicated task of getting mounted troops and their horses to the beach. Dunnage of matting or brushwood was placed in the boats' bottoms for the horses, which were then hoisted out of the Smyrna transports and ferried ashore with their grooms or riders. Many of the cavalry horses were still absent in the missing Greek transports, but eventually nearly 800 horses were landed: 486 for the cavalry, 186 for the artillery, and 120 chargers for staff and field officers.[13]

While the boats pushed to and fro on these tasks, the first reinforcements were moving inland to join the line about a mile from the beach. There were chilling sights for the eyes of men new to battle, as they passed the scattered dead amidst the groans and cries of the wounded: Private Robertson of the 92nd began to wish he had never listed for a soldier. Beyond the debris of the battle they came upon the enemy's bivouacs, evidence of the French soldier's skill at making himself comfortable. The snug huts of date-palm planking had water ready to drink and camp kettles still bubbling on the fires. On marched the reinforcements, till the enemy skirmishers' bullets began to whistle past. Young Ensign Church of the 13th ducked at the sound. 'Don't be afraid, sir', said a burly sergeant, 'you'll soon get used to it'.[14]

The first line had now been halted for two or three hours waiting for the remainder of Coote's brigade and the arrival of reserve ammunition. No artillery had yet reached the front, but in mid-afternoon the advance was resumed in three columns with little sign of the enemy who were withdrawing in front of them. About three miles from the beach the columns halted and deployed to take up positions for the night.

The losses that morning had been heavy. The navy had lost seven officers and ninety seamen killed or wounded; the army 625, a toll which was to rise alarmingly in the coming fortnight. Of these soldiers 137 of all ranks were killed or missing (the thirty-five missing presumably drowned). Among the dead were Captain Warren of the Coldstream Guards, son of the distinguished fighting seaman and future ambassador to Russia, Admiral Sir John Borlase Warren; and the Hon. Frederick Meade, an ensign in the 40th, who is said to have been the only graduate of Oxford or Cambridge killed in the Revolutionary and Napoleonic wars.[15]

The enemy had suffered more lightly. Sheltered from the preliminary bombardment by the dunes, they had been saved in their retreat by the British lack of cavalry and horsed artillery to conduct a close pursuit. The French had probably lost two or three hundred men, among them General Martinet, who had been captain of a French ship of the line at the battle of the Nile and was now commanding the naval forces ashore. They had also lost seven guns, a sure measure of defeat.[16]

But the relative losses said little about the significance of the battle. Abercromby's force had accomplished a marvellous feat of arms, the result of careful organisation, planning, and rehearsal. French prisoners said they had had no fear that a landing could succeed. General Bertrand praised the admirable order of the landing, which in less than five or six minutes had presented 5,000 British troops in battle array: 'It was like a movement on the opera stage'.[17]

The effect on British morale was electric. This was the most spectacular success against the French for many years; and the courage and discipline of the regiments gave their commanders confidence for the future. 'Nothing but British valour could have effected the debarcation', asserted General Coote who had commanded the left brigade. 'The French were astonished and struck with awe at the boldness of the undertaking. . . . The undaunted courage and coolness of the troops was such that they never loaded until they disembarked from the boats and while loading were charged on the shore by the cavalry and infantry. Upon the beach they coolly fixed their bayonets and loaded. Nothing can exceed this disembarcation, certainly the first and most glorious act of valour that is imaginable.'[18]

General Oakes felt the same pride in his battalions of the Reserve. They had landed under 'the most tremendous fire I ever saw . . . the uncommon bravery and determined spirit of our glorious soldiers overcame every difficulty and danger . . . the order and discipline they also showed by first forming before they advanced was equally to be admired. . . . It was impossible for troops to behave better'. The dry laconic style of Moore's diary tells the same story: 'The fire of grapeshot and musquetry was really most severe. . . . Our attempt was daring, and executed by the troops with the greatest intrepidity and coolness'.[19]

In the command ship *Tartarus* the spectators felt that they had witnessed a turning point: the end of the bogey of French invincibility. 'The French', wrote Lord Keith, 'have read a lesson today they will not soon forget.' Consul Baldwin declaimed that the conquerors of Italy had fled before the British Army: 'the invincible companions of Bonaparte were vanquished'. In fact the British may have overrated their victory in the dunes, because they overestimated the strength of the enemy which was believed to be 3–4,000. There was nothing remarkable about 5,000 men dislodging 2,000, though it was an exhilarating experience for British troops to see the French running from them. But the landing itself had been a brilliant feat of arms: the long ordeal by fire, and the forming of the line and loading under attack as the men struggled out of the surf. Abercromby had shown his army that he could organise for victory; and they had proved that their courage could be fused with training and discipline. Abercromby expressed his satisfaction to the army's mentor Sir David Dundas, now Quartermaster-General at the Horse Guards: 'The moment the 28th and 42nd were on shore Paget [commanding the 28th] was formed in the best possible order and remained so, the 42nd the same, and many regiments in not so high order as them were little inferior'. Colonel Anstruther said that the troops had formed *as if on parade*: a comparison often to be repeated in the coming operations.[20]

The storming of the Aboukir beach had been a desperate risk; only to be justified by desperation, in the view of more than one witness. But it confirmed the power of boldness in war. It proved, wrote Major Robert Wilson of Hompesch's Hussars, 'that brilliant exertions, supported by persevering courage may surmount mathematical improbabilities, and snatch a victory where cold calculation would predict a certain defeat'.[21]

Was Abercromby wrong to run the risk: a risk which seemed the greater because the enemy's strength was unknown? That he feared the outcome he revealed during the last moments before the assault in his message to Moore. Yet he knew in his mind that the risk had to be taken. No other landing place was as good, or offered the fleet a safe anchorage. To sheer off for reasons of prudence after the recent catalogue of British humiliations would, in Major Wilson's words, have condemned the army to 'eternal and irretrievable obloquy'. Moore had written flatly that 'we must attempt it'; and now Abercromby had won a foothold which would enable far-off negotiators to dispute the French claim to Egypt. When the news of the landing reached Henry Dundas in London nearly a month later, he was no longer Secretary of State, for the Pitt ministry had resigned in February. Yet still the Egyptian expedition haunted his restless nights. Thus far his old general and friend had not failed him.[22]

7

'WE SHALL ALL FARE ALIKE'

The conquest of the Aboukir dunes had cracked the thin shield of the enemy's overstretched coastal defences, and only Friant's little covering force stood between Abercromby and his first objective at Alexandria. Now should have been the moment to dislodge Friant and unleash a force of boldly led cavalry, with the infantry marching hard on their heels in an irresistible torrent to rush the Alexandria defences. Then, with the only good port in Egypt in his grasp, Abercromby could have waited, as his instructions indicated, for the French forces trapped in the interior to fall like ripe plums, while the British fleet rode in safety in Alexandria harbour and supplies flowed ashore in all weather. And in England news of the capture of Alexandria would have cleared the way for the peace negotiators.

But where were the cavalry? Abercromby's light dragoons, poorly mounted and outnumbered by the excellent French cavalry, were not even ashore. For want of horses his guns had to be hauled across the dunes by seamen harnessed to the traces. And his infantry had only two days' rations left in their packs. On the day after the landing, wind and heavy surf on the beaches suspended the disembarcation of horses and stores, and when the weather allowed provisions to be landed again there would be no transport to move them forward. 'No army can march without horses or wagons', as Abercromby had once warned the Secretary of State. Shortage of transport and cavalry was the inevitable accompaniment of an amphibious operation, as Abercromby had experienced in the Dutch campaign. Sir Arthur Wellesley was to see it again in the Vimiero campaign of 1808, when for want of a few hundred more dragoons he was prevented from destroying Junot's army and rushing Lisbon.

Abercromby had no means of discovering what reinforcements were marching to join Friant; and if his largely unblooded army were to be counter-attacked after outmarching its supplies, a retreat might cause it to disintegrate, as he had feared with the young soldiers and inexperienced officers in Holland. He had to stand fast till his supplies were secured. Yet the price of immobility was high. Enemy reinforcements would build up along their short defensive front, and a slogging match could be expected with heavy casualties which Abercromby could ill afford.

For the moment all that he would do was to probe into the unmapped terrain ahead of him. On the morning after the landing Colonel Anstruther went forward to reconnoitre, escorted by Moore with the Corsican Rangers and a handful of the 11th Light Dragoons for whom mounts had been landed, with the 92nd Highlanders in support. Two or three miles to their front, and about five from the beach, they came to an abandoned redoubt at Mandara with a heavy 26-pounder cannon at a point where the peninsula narrowed to less than a mile between sea and lake. Here Moore posted the 92nd to secure his rear, and pushed on with the Corsicans and light dragoons till he met a strong cavalry patrol which forced him to retire. From the report sent back by Anstruther Abercromby learned of the narrow neck of land at the Mandara redoubt. By occupying it he would secure his start-line for the coming advance and deny a defensible position to the enemy. Moore was ordered to hold the Mandara isthmus with the rest of the Reserve, which advanced and joined the 92nd about noon.[1]

For the next two days Moore commanded this forward position. Abercromby had long recognised him as a most promising officer, and had commended his 'abilities and heroism' in the Dutch campaign. 'Every quality in Moore was real, solid, and unbending', Bunbury recalled: 'a man to whom every officer and soldier looked up with an entire confidence.' As commander of the Reserve he held the most important tactical command in Abercromby's force; and his storming of the great sandhill had been the start of outstanding service in Egypt.[2]

At daylight on the 10th Moore was out with his handful of dragoons and the Corsican riflemen to 'feel what was on my front'. It was a first test for his skirmishers. Before long he met the advance guard of a considerable force of cavalry which tried to push him back. But Moore had his pickets close behind to support him, and the ground provided enough cover to shelter the light infantry. The Corsicans dispersed and posted themselves, and forced the enemy to withdraw. Not content with their success, however, they followed the enemy who lured them on till they were close to their main body. The French cavalry then turned and attacked them, wounding several Corsicans and capturing a dozen.

Observing the enemy, Moore decided that their cavalry was no more than a strong escort for senior officers on reconnaissance. Skirmishing continued but pointlessly, and Moore ordered the Corsicans to stand fast and hold their fire unless fired on. Firing ceased on both sides, and in the afternoon the enemy cavalry withdrew leaving only a normal screen of pickets and vedettes. All through the afternoon, however, Moore could see French offi-cers reconnoitring his front, with such persistence that he suspected an attack was being hatched. His own front was so strong that he did not fear a break-in, but he thought they might try a raid to carry off a picket. With his usual thoroughness he reinforced his pickets at dusk, especially on the flanks. But the night passed quietly.[3]

The first night after the landing had been cold and showery. Bright starlit nights followed but the cold continued, with damp from the heavy dews. No tents would be ashore in the first week, so officers and men huddled under their cloaks or blankets, their sleep disturbed by the bitter chill. Abercromby planned to sleep under the stars like his soldiers. 'Baldwin', he said when the consul came ashore on the 9th, soaked by his boat being swamped in the surf, 'you will live with us a soldier's life; but we shall all fare alike.' The general's servants however made him a bivouac of palm branches, an example which the army followed since there was no virtue in discomfort.[4]

The army was settling down to its field routine. Guards and pickets were mounted, and the field officers of the day did their rounds and made their reports. An hour before daylight each morning the whole army stood-to under arms – the 'alarm post parade'. Seeing the ranks of cold faces in the grey dawn Abercromby ordered a half-ration of rum (a gill) to be distributed.[5]

Parties of seamen were burying the dead, and the captain of the *Peterel* took a walk across the battlefield and found it a shocking sight. In the meantime the landing of stores was proceeding when the weather allowed. The navy's boats completed the landing of horses, and transferred their efforts to the supply services. The boat divisions of Captain Scott and Captain Stevenson were bringing fresh water and provisions ashore for the commissary-general. Captain Larmour's boats were assigned to ordnance and engineers' stores, and they rounded up ships' carpenters to construct wharves, and to make ramps and plank roadways for rolling heavy cannon off the boats and across the sand. Captain Apthorp's division took charge of hospital equipment and the Quartermaster-General's stores. His boats were responsible for bringing the wounded back to the hospital ships lying out in the bay, but all returning boats were expected to take wounded men on board. As the landings progressed the captains would increasingly be guided by their own discretion and the wishes of the army staff.[6]

These were taxing days for the boats' crews and their reliefs, pulling the long miles out to the shipping and back across the bay under the hot afternoon sun. For the admiral the fleet's heavy commitment of men to the army was an anxiety when he knew that there was an enemy battle squadron at sea and had to keep his ships in constant readiness for action. Boat-crews, gun-teams and the marine battalion depleted his complements, and he complained to the First Lord of the Admiralty about the army's dependence on his fleet: 'I am convinced were I to refuse or withdraw a man the troops would re-embark and charge the failure to me'. If Abercromby had read the letter it would not have surprised him after Cadiz, where he had learned that it was Keith's nature to anticipate blame and try to shift it. Nevertheless with 6,000 men labouring in the army's service in all weather, and some of the ships seven miles from the shore, the navy's task was massive. 'It is a young army and has little resource', the admiral grumbled three days after the landing.[7]

The army's demands presented Keith with a hideous dilemma which was to last as long as the campaign. How could he shield the expedition against a French battle squadron, yet fulfil the army's requirements ashore? He had only two ships of the line off Alexandria to intercept Ganteaume's squadron of at least six; and his five sail of the line in Aboukir bay had been stripped of their fighting crews. The *Foudroyant* was already short by 107 men of its full complement of 719; and so many were now ashore that there were only 184 seamen on board to work the ship. The other ships were as bad. Keith's instinct on learning that Ganteaume was at large in the Mediterranean was to go off Alexandria with his line-of-battle ships and hope to intimidate the enemy by his appearance as he had once driven Admiral Bruix away from Cadiz. He proposed to take his boats' crews but leave behind the seamen and marines who were actually on dry land, and trust that the troopships and transports would fulfil the army's boat requirements. To this suggestion Abercromby responded that he could not do without the boats of the ships of the line, and asked that the fleet should not leave the bay unless a frigate brought intelligence that the enemy were actually approaching. He assumed that the Admiralty would have sent a squadron from the Atlantic in pursuit of Ganteaume; but Keith feared that the enemy, with fast ships and hulls clean from the dockyard, would outsail any British reinforcement and probably even his own scouting cruisers. If the enemy got into Alexandria the British expedition would fail. But if the removal of naval support from the army also made failure certain, he saw little choice but to remain in the bay.[8]

So Abercromby retained his naval auxiliaries, knowing that any military operation depends on the quality of its administrative support. To sustain a fighting front at any distance from the beach, transport had to be organised. It was impossible to carry the provisions and ammunition for 14,000 men across miles of loose burning sand with only two or three hundred horses and mules; and supply by boat along the rocky seaward coast of the peninsula was at the mercy of the weather. What saved the supply system and ultimately the campaign was the unknown lake Aboukir, so new that it was not mentioned in the most up-to-date manual on Egypt. The depth and extent of the lake were a mystery to be unravelled by surveys and reconnaissance. It was found to be navigable by boats and to extend to within three or four miles of Alexandria.

As the lake became known, Captain Cochrane took a decision to use its sheltered all-weather beaches for the supply-boats, protecting them against French gunboats by arming a dozen of his own flatboats with cannon. Soon the sheltered waterway was dotted with gunboats and supply boats, their sails hoisted to aid the oarsmen. Provisions, stores, and ammunition were delivered to a depot on the lake shore which was moved forward as the front advanced. Here carrier-parties from the regiments and batteries collected their requirements. The returning boats took the sick and wounded back to the base in Aboukir bay. Thus the army's critical supply line was secured.

Without the lake, wrote Anstruther, 'we could not have budged from the shores'.[9]

The strain on the boats' crews was heavy, as they toiled day after day under the hot sun, hauling on their oars to bring the heavy cargoes from ships far out in the bay to the advancing front. Exiled from their own ships, the oarsmen kept their rations and kits of spare clothing in the boats, and each flatboat was issued with two spare oars and a spare set of thole-pins or rowlocks.[10] To protect the crews and their boats from the sun, awnings or sails were spread over the boats whenever possible, and their timbers were kept wetted to prevent them from splitting. Teams of naval carpenters kept the boats in constant repair.

The only note of complaint was sounded by the admiral, and the navy's response to the needs of the army was magnificent. On shore the seamen serving with the gun-teams and on other military duties were commanded by Sir Sidney Smith, whose oddities did not bar him from being adored by the troops for his energy and courage. It was from him that they learned how to dig for water where the date-palms grew. All over the peninsula drinkable water was found, which relieved the boats of the frightening responsibility for bringing up the water the army consumed. For the fleet lying in the bay fresh water was found in the upper layer of the outflow from the Nile.[11]

Two days after the landing better weather in the bay allowed the last of the troops and most of the available horses to be brought ashore, and the remaining brigades joined the army, leaving the Queen's and 400 horseless dragoons to besiege Aboukir castle. On the evening of the 9th seven companies of the 2/27th arrived from their convalescence at Lisbon, and joined Cavan's brigade on the following day. The missing Greek horse-transports were beginning to straggle in, the last of them not till the 14th, six days after the landing.[12]

Abercromby, however, did not wait for these, and on the 11th he was ready to move and came forward to Moore's advanced position to brief him. He now knew that a supply route could be established on the lake; and in the meantime enough provisions had been brought up overland to enable the army to advance. That evening three days' rations were issued to the troops for an advance in the morning. The next trial of their training was about to begin. In the assault landing individual regiments had been tested. They had beaten off attacks as they landed and vigorously counter-attacked, proving that they could seize opportunities and support their neighbours. In the coming advance, however, their cohesion as an army would be tested. How would the brigades combine when manoeuvring together on an open front as General Dundas's manual prescribed?[13]

A methodical advance it had to be. There was no question now of rushing the Alexandria defences, for it was known that the enemy had been rein-forced. An officer reconnoitring the head of the lake had seen from the embankment of the Alexandria canal the rear of a column passing into the French lines. The advance was therefore likely to be a hard slog, for the terrain reproduced some of the problems Abercromby had encountered in North Holland eighteen months earlier. There the front had been a narrow defile flanked by the ocean and the Zuider Zee: here the enemy's flanks were protected by the Mediterranean and the lake of Aboukir. The country itself was a surprise. Abercromby had expected open level land on the peninsula, whereas Moore's reconnaissances had discovered innumerable palm groves, and uneven sandhills which broke the plain like 'the surface of a boisterous sea'. Much of the going was loose sand; hard work for marching infantry, and almost impossible for the seamen and gunners who had to manhandle field-guns through it. The artillery commander General Lawson was regretting the decision taken at Marmaris to give the cavalry the least bad of Lord Elgin's horses and allot only the rejects to his guns. The result was that neither the cavalry nor the artillery was efficient. What a difference it would have made if even a part of the artillery had been well horsed. The French had allotted the very prime of their strong horses to their artillery, which was mostly on the fast-moving Horse Artillery establishment with mounted gunners. Their teams were hauling 8-pounder guns, equivalent to British 9-pounders, and 6-inch howitzers, outranging Abercromby's light 6-pounders and 5½-inch 'royal' howitzers as well as outmanoeuvring them.[14]

A century and more later, in 1915, British troops stationed on Abercromby's line of advance were to find the deep sand unsuitable for wartime training. But across this terrain Abercromby had to force his way.

In the early morning of 12 March his main body closed up behind the Reserve, and at eight o'clock the whole force moved forward. The formation for the advance to contact was in two large columns marching on parallel routes, a more manageable arrangement than a deployed line which was neither speedy nor flexible. The head of each column was protected by a brigade of the Reserve, commanded by Moore and Oakes, each brigade of this advance guard marching in a column protected by skirmishers, the formation which had been tried and proved by the armies of the French Revolution.[15]

At first the skirmishing screen was provided by the Corsican Rangers, directed by the slightly-built, fair-haired Major Hudson Lowe, and the light companies of Moore's regiments of the line. But the Reserve had been holding the front for several days, and Abercromby soon relieved them of skirmishing duties by sending forward his two junior regiments, the 90th and the 92nd Highlanders. The 92nd Gordons we have already met when their state of training was commended by Sir Ralph at Malta. They were well known to Moore, for two of their men had saved him when he lay wounded on the dunes of Egmond aan Zee. Weakened by sickness, they had only 300 men to deploy ahead of the left column. At the head of the right column was one of the best regiments in the army, the 90th Perthshire Volunteers with their grey trousers and black Tarleton helmets. This was the regiment trained in Minorca as light infantry by Major Kenneth Mackenzie, now its second in command. Two of their officers were later to command corps under Wellington: Thomas Graham, the future Lord Lynedoch, who had raised the regiment but was on leave at home; and Lieutenant-Colonel Rowland Hill who was commanding the regiment in Graham's absence. Colonel Hill controlled his regiment in battle with a light infantry bugle horn.

The 90th and 92nd advanced each with its light company forward, reinforcing them several times from their battalion companies as the enemy pickets became stronger among the thick brushwood. By now the sun was high, as the skirmishers worked their way forward through a broken country of palm groves, scattered ruins and sandhills. About a mile to the front they made contact with the enemy's mounted vedettes who fell back, skirmishing with their firearms, towards a stronger screen of cavalry formed by the 22nd Chasseurs à cheval. Newly arrived from Cairo, they disputed the British advance with sharpshooting across the broken terrain. About 1.30 p.m. Moore reached a square tower with a flagstaff, the direction mark for his advance, from the top of which he could see enemy infantry advancing. If an attack was coming, the ground a quarter of a mile ahead seemed more favourable for defence, and the whole army was ordered to deploy into two lines and advance to occupy the position.[16]

This was the army's first deployment in contact with the enemy, and it was executed, wrote Major Lowe of the Corsican Rangers, 'in a more perfect manner than I have ever seen it at any review'. The army was proving again that the drill manual could be applied in the field. The advance was resumed in line, dressing by the colours of the 23rd on the right, a severe test of training as the companies were constantly forced to break the line and file round obstacles amid the brushwood and ruins. Yet the line was constantly re-formed, and when the new position was reached scarcely any correction was needed.[17]

The day's advance had been about three miles in the presence of the enemy, and Moore was well satisfied with the performance of his brigade, admiring 'the regularity and coolness with which they moved'. The army was settling down to its drill under field conditions. So far, so good. But as yet there had been no fighting apart from the advance guard's light skirmishing, and the day's toll had been only seven casualties. The test of battle had still to be faced.

On seeing the British advancing the enemy had halted and then retired. Their main body was now posted on a ridge of higher ground a mile and a half away, with their advanced posts close to the British lines. It was too late in the day to close up and attack before dark, and orders were issued for an attack on the following morning. The army settled down for the night, 'lying on their arms' in case of a surprise, while a summons was sent back to the siege-lines at Aboukir castle for the Marines and the battalion companies of the Queen's to join the army at once. They moved at sunset, and pushed through the dark on a loose desert track, the Marines suffering from the unaccustomed marching. At midnight a long line of lights was seen glowing through the darkness from the British fires, and the Marines found their way to their place in Lord Cavan's brigade to snatch a brief sleep before the four o'clock reveille.[18]

With the enemy so close, extra precautions had to be taken, and as usual in tricky circumstances Abercromby turned to Moore, though it was not his turn for outpost duty. But the Reserve had had several 'fagging' days holding the front and leading the advance, and to rest them the 90th and 92nd remained under Moore's command for the night. He divided them into six bodies at intervals across the front, with a third of their strength thrown forward to form a strong chain of sentries who were relieved every hour. All night the two battalions were on their feet or standing by in readiness for an alarm, though they had another hard day ahead of them; while behind them at headquarters there was grumbling that Abercromby was showing partiality to his fellow Scot, Moore, and his junior Scottish regiments.[19]

8

'A COOL INTREPIDITY': THE MANDARA BATTLE

Friday 13 March was to be a testing day for the reformed British battle drill, and the pivotal point of the army's regeneration. But no such reflections crossed the minds of the infantry as they dumped their knapsacks at daybreak in the charge of a soldier from each company and swallowed a tot of rum. Whatever the day might bring, they would do their duty. About 6.30 a.m. the columns moved off towards the battle.[1]

Abercromby had had no choice but to attack. With his pocket telescope he had seen the enemy strongly posted on a ridge of sandhills across his front; and he had to dislodge them before they received further reinforcements. But Sir Ralph was aware that he was acting on inadequate information. He knew that the French had been reinforced: but by how much? Had Menou arrived with his whole *masse de manoeuvre*? Even if he had not, the enemy had still the advantages of their strong position, their cavalry, and their well-horsed artillery which far outweighed the firepower of Abercromby's lagging cannon. As for the terrain they were defending, virtually nothing was known. 'It is vain', wrote Anstruther to his brother, 'to refer you to maps. There are none but what the French may *now* have that are not the greatest botchpennies possible, and perfectly erroneous.'

Abercromby's plan was to manoeuvre by his left, to cover his lakeside dumps and assail the weaker flank of the French. Their northern flank rested on the sea and was strengthened by a block of massive ruins dating from Roman times, and known to the French and Arabs as Caesar's Camp but to the British as the Roman Ruins. But their right was in the air beyond the head of lake Aboukir, no longer protected by the defile between lake and sea, for the Alexandria canal was dry at this season. If Abercromby could break out to his left beyond the head of the lake, he would win space to manoeuvre across the dry bed of lake Mareotis against the enemy flank.[2]

The army was organised for the battle in two 'divisions', a term which did not denote the permanent formations of all arms as known in the French army. The right division, formed from the brigades of the first line in the formal order of battle, was commanded by Abercromby; the left division, which had the task of attacking the enemy's right flank after passing the head

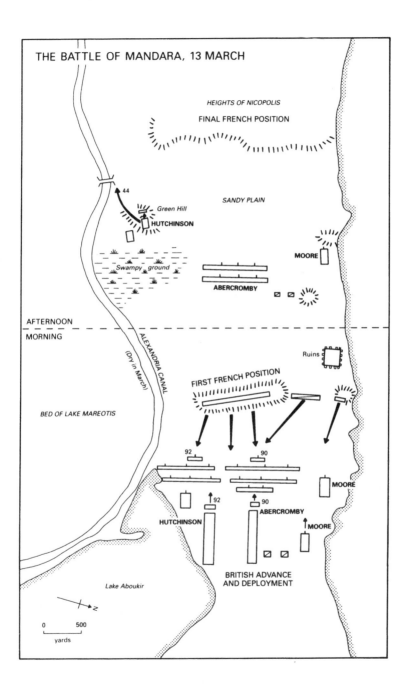

THE BATTLE OF MANDARA, 13 MARCH

HEIGHTS OF NICOPOLIS

FINAL FRENCH POSITION

SANDY PLAIN

44

Green Hill

HUTCHINSON

Swampy ground

MOORE

ABERCROMBY

AFTERNOON

MORNING

(Dry in March)

ALEXANDRIA CANAL

Ruins

BED OF LAKE MAREOTIS

FIRST FRENCH POSITION

92

90

92

90

MOORE

HUTCHINSON

ABERCROMBY

MOORE

Lake Aboukir

BRITISH ADVANCE
AND DEPLOYMENT

z

0   500

yards

of the lake, by General Hutchinson. For Hutchinson's brigades this was their first test in battle, none having taken part in the landing. The approach march began with each division formed in column of manoeuvre with the regiments stacked behind each other on a front of one company – the approved formation since the time of Frederick the Great for the approach to battle, the column being an infinitely more flexible body for manoeuvres and last-minute changes of direction than the long and cumbersome line. Between the infantry columns marched 120 poorly mounted cavalry commanded by General Finch; and to protect the open right flank against the superior French cavalry, the Reserve commanded by Moore marched slightly behind the head of the main body in an open column which could form a front in any direction to meet a flanking attack. The front and flanks of Moore's column were protected in the French manner by Corsican skirmishers.[3]

In a conventional approach the divisions would have deployed successively into brigade and then battalion columns as they drew closer to the enemy, before the crucial final deployment into line. But in this battle the left of the army would not have room for a full deployment till it was clear of the head of the lake and had open ground on its left. Only Hutchinson's leading brigade was therefore to deploy and close with the enemy, until the ground opened and the battle developed. Hutchinson's rearmost brigade would then remain in column, taking station on the left to provide flank protection against cavalry as the Reserve was already doing on the right. The heads of the two divisional columns were again covered by the 90th and 92nd, each with its light company leading and the battalion in column of companies behind it. Both regiments had an attached cavalry picket of thirty mounted men.[4]

Useful though a column might be for manoeuvre, it presented a dense target for artillery. The British columns had not been advancing for long when French guns pushed boldly forward from their main position and opened fire, correcting their aim accurately as the columns advanced. With no threat from the British cavalry, the enemy guns could manoeuvre with impunity close to the British front, some of their teams with as many as sixteen horses to ensure their safe withdrawal from position to position. Nor did they have to fear counter-battery fire, for the British guns were being dragged slowly through the heavy burning sand by seamen and were falling behind their infantry. French round-shot ricocheted through the columns from company to company as the infantry trudged through the loose sand.[5]

Moore, who was not given to superlatives in his diary, described the cannonade which was mowing down the Reserve as 'tremendous'. Colonel Paget had two captains and thirty or forty men of the 28th struck down without being able to fire a shot in reply, but the regiment marched steadily on in perfect silence, preserving its correct intervals. It was a sight, Paget wrote to his brother, which would have gladdened the heart of General

Dundas at a Phoenix Park review. There was not a moment when Moore did not feel confident that he could halt the column and instantly wheel to a flank to form a continuous line. Under that murderous fire 'nothing could overcome their cool intrepidity, discompose their order, or prevent their advancing'.[6]

As the British columns formed up with the early sun behind them, they had been watched by a new French commander. General Lanusse had reached the Alexandria front three days earlier from Cairo and assumed the command from Friant, bringing with him three fresh demi-brigades which raised his force to nearly 5,000 of all ranks. It was still much weaker than the British force, or than it need have been; but a whiff of the atmosphere in Menou's headquarters arrived on the 12th in the shape of one of Menou's aides de camp to explain why so much force had been withheld. 'My old general has not been fooled', he boasted: wherever the enemy might appear, the old fox had provided a force to stop him. 'Alas,' exclaimed General Bertrand, 'I thought the science of war consisted in concentrating at the decisive point, and ignoring the subsidiaries.'[7]

Table 5 Lanusse's order of battle, 13 March. Rank and file, totals rounded by Reynier. Strength on 1 March is shown in parentheses

Friant's Division		
25 DB (2nd and 3rd battns) (including Rosetta detachment recalled by Friant)	500	(680)[1]
61 DB	600	(750)[1]
75 DB	750	(1,030)[1]
Lanusse's Division		
4 DB légère	650	(790)
18 DB	650	(794)
69 DB	800	(859)
Cavalry (Bron)		
22 Chasseurs	230	(230)
3 Dragoons (det.)	150	(150)
18 Dragoons (det.)	80	(115)[1]
20 Dragoons (det.)	60	(80)[1]
Artillery		
19 cannon		
3 howitzers		
Total rank and file		
Infantry	3,950	
Cavalry	520	
Total	4,470	

[1] Unit present at landing on 8 March and incurred casualties.

Inferior though Lanusse was in numbers, he had chosen to hold a position well forward of the prepared defences of Alexandria. His intention was to cover the route by which he expected Menou to join him; for he and Friant believed that the bed of lake Mareotis was impassable at this season, and that Menou would have to approach by the narrow route from Damanhur along the banks of the Alexandria canal unless he made the immense desert detour to the west. Lanusse's aim was therefore to prevent the British from breaking out of the defile between lake Aboukir and the sea and establishing a blocking position on the canal which would prevent Menou's approach.

He had a defensive position on the ridge flanked by the Roman Ruins. Its weak point was the open right flank against which Abercromby's attack was aimed; but, if the British manoeuvre made Lanusse's position untenable, he had two successive positions to fall back on. Behind the ridge a wide sandy plain provided a perfect field of fire from the formidable heights of Nicopolis, a partially entrenched position from which French artillery could rake the plain below. Behind the Nicopolis line were the walls and batteries of the Alexandria fortifications, into which Lanusse could withdraw his force in the last resort till Menou could contrive to join him.

Withdrawal was the course advocated by General Bertrand – or so he later claimed. He urged that Abercromby should be allowed to develop his offensive and ponderously turn the French flank; whereupon Lanusse should fall back to his strong rearward positions.

Not for Lanusse, however, these sage but unspectacular options. He belonged to the Revolution's new generation of aspiring generals, and had served under the gambler Bonaparte in Italy and watched his daring operations. Ambitious and competitive, Lanusse was determined to bring lustre to the obscure theatre where fortune had buried the Army of the Orient, and wrest a share of the fame and glory which were being won in Europe. Besides, there was the doubt whether Menou could reach him if the canal route from Damanhur was abandoned; and even the Roman Ruins ridge was not forward enough to cover the canal. Lanusse resolved to launch a counterstroke, and beat the British before his incompetent and despised Commander-in-Chief arrived on the scene.

In vain Bertrand remonstrated. He warned that the French would be attacking against odds of nearly three to one; that defeat would shake the confidence of the troops and compromise Alexandria. Lanusse paid no heed. As he watched Abercromby's advance, an opportunity seemed to be developing. According to his friend Reynier (who was not present) he was unable to see the British centre which was concealed by rising ground, and believed that Hutchinson's turning force on their left was becoming isolated. He proposed to Friant that they should attack it. His plan was to contain Moore's advance on the British right with one demi-brigade, and hold back two battalions to guard the Roman Ruins and provide a reserve. The rest of the French force would attack the British left, with the cavalry wheeling across the front to assail Hutchinson's flank. The advance was launched, and from the valley between the ridge and the Roman Ruins the 3rd Dragoons and 22nd Chasseurs à cheval trotted forward, a mass of 400 horsemen, on an oblique line towards Hutchinson's column. The British were about to receive their first charge by the new cavalry of France.[8]

For the 90th Perthshire Volunteers the morning had started badly. They had not received their orders for the advance, and coming off their night's picket duty at daybreak they had marched back to camp to find that they were to lead the army. The day's work began with a hurried march almost at a run to regain their place at the head of the right column.[9]

As the advance proceeded, the pace of the columns was slowed to allow the field-guns with their teams of seamen or miserable horses to catch up, and the two battalions of the advance guard were allowed to push on too far ahead of their supports. As the 90th were emerging from a grove of palm trees they suddenly found themselves in the presence of the 22nd Chasseurs.

Both regiments were equally surprised. At the head of the chasseurs was Colonel Latour-Maubourg, newly arrived from France with heartening messages from Bonaparte. Sighting a somewhat scattered line of troops in black Tarleton helmets, he may have thought that they were dismounted cavalry forming a linking chain between the British left and right, and therefore a soft target. Moreover he probably had no suspicion that there was a strong column of infantry behind them. He instantly ordered the charge, and the chasseurs bore down on Captain McNair's light company in front of the battalion. Though they were, wrote McNair, 'unavoidably a good deal scattered, they individually stood firm to the cavalry and bayoneted some of them'. Major Mackenzie was in close support behind them with the grenadiers and two battalion companies, which he immediately formed on the left of the light bobs. Colonel Hill rushed up with the remaining six companies, but they did not have time to reach the end of the line and closed up behind the left, making it six or eight deep. As the chasseurs charged, the Perthshire men opened fire with a volley which rolled down the line from right to left 'like a rattling peel of thunder'.[10]

Latour-Maubourg was wounded in the head, and many of his horsemen were brought down and the rest thrown into confusion. The cavalry recoiled and swept off to their right where Cradock's brigade, not yet tested in battle, was coming up and deploying under a heavy fire. The French cavalry charged them, but were beaten off again by the disciplined fire of the 8th and 18th. A British eyewitness described the exemplary firing drill of the 18th Royal Irish: 'No impression was to be made upon infantry which coolly waited for the words of command, ready, present, fire, and this the 18th Regiment did; much greater proof of steadiness, coolness and discipline could not be given'. The 8th and 18th were both seasoned regiments from the Mediterranean garrisons; and together with the 90th they proved on that day, said Captain McNair, 'how futile the attempts of the most determined cavalry is [*sic*] on an infantry that meet them with resolution'.[11]

At the head of the left column the weak 92nd were struck by the frontal attack of Friant's 61st demi-brigade, 600 strong and with two guns in close support. Under cover of cannon fire the enemy column approached and deployed, partly concealed by the crest of a slight rise 200 yards ahead in front of the British regiment. As the French line completed its deployment and resumed its advance, Colonel Erskine waited till his men could see the feet of the French infantry crossing the rise, and gave the order to fire. The first volley stopped the advance, and a fire-fight developed which soon covered the front with a thick cloud of smoke into which the 300 Gordons fired where they guessed the French line to be. One of their privates counted twenty-two rounds as he loaded and fired, and the powder grains left in the men's mouths as they bit off the ends of the cartridges increased their parching thirst.

Two British guns came up to support the 92nd, but soon ran out of ammunition and retired again, allowing the enemy to push their own guns closer and open up at close range with grape-shot. Colonel Erskine was hit and carried off to die, and for some time the Gordons held their ground under this destructive fire with no support on their flanks. The first help to arrive was the Marine battalion which came up on their right. But the Marines, who had been dispersed in their warships till a few days earlier and had joined the army only that morning, had not undergone the thorough battalion training of the rest of Abercromby's infantry. In their hurried advance they had fallen into confusion; and with their line still eight or ten deep they opened fire before they were far enough forward to support the highlanders, killing some of their own men and the Gordons. At last two or three companies of Dillon's Regiment from Stuart's foreign brigade came up on the left and the enemy gave way. The highlanders' fire had already picked off the French gunners, and the survivors had to abandon their guns when they retired.

The losses of the 92nd were shattering. Out of only 300 in action, eighteen officers and 150 other ranks were killed or wounded. Colonel Brodie survived to record the combat, which was a far cry from his Hogmanay binge at Marmaris. 'Nothing could possibly exceed the bravery of our troops in this action', he wrote; 'but the cool, steady and most regular manner in which they advanced in the face of a most experienced and veteran enemy and the most regular and independent fire they kept up in spite of the enemy's artillery were particularly admired by Sir Ralph Abercromby.'[12]

The 90th and 92nd had blunted the French attack, losing both their commanding officers as they fought. Of all the regiments in the battle they alone were to bear the battle-honour *Mandora* thus spelt on their colours.[13]

The whole British front was now attacking. The right-hand column under Abercromby was completely deployed with the Guards in second line, and the Reserve was still moving in column on the right to protect the open flank. In Hutchinson's division on the left the two leading brigades were also deployed, with Doyle's 4th brigade in the rear still in column to protect the left flank as the line drew clear of the lake. The exhausted and depleted 92nd were ordered to lie down and let the 50th and their old rivals the 79th Camerons advance over them; but on the right the 90th were still fit to join the attack. Rather than remain halted under the heavy French fire, Colonel Hill advanced with a succession of volleys and drove the enemy from the first height on which they made a stand. Here he halted the regiment with the bugle horn, dressed the line, and advanced again with great regularity to storm the next sandhill where he was wounded. Major Mackenzie took command of the battalion: he must have been well pleased with the results of his training.[14]

The terrain through which the troops were now fighting their way was still a tangle of hillocks, level patches, and palm groves. Every hundred yards seemed to offer the French a new position, which they defended with skill and tenacity. The French cavalry continued to hover and threaten, searching for an exposed flank or a gap in the line, and covering the successive withdrawals of their artillery. Their gun-teams would unlimber and open fire every time the British infantry halted to wait for their own artillery, only to limber up and gallop off when the advance was resumed, and take up a new position to resume their cannonade. In these testing combats and small separate battlefields the British brigades remained unshaken and in good order. On the right in Cradock's brigade the 8th, 13th and Royal Irish were advancing with regular volleys which forced the enemy out of position after position. Without artillery support the infantry had to push forward almost to the muzzles of the enemy guns to dislodge them with musket-fire.

Still fighting staunchly but outnumbered, and with their cavalry galloping across the British front in a vain search for an uncovered flank, the French were gradually falling into confusion, so that when they reached the ridge from which they had advanced in the early morning they were unable to organise a stand. Hutchinson's column debouching beyond the end of the lake had outflanked their right, and about 11.30 a.m. they abandoned the ridge and continued their retreat across the sandy plain towards their rearward position on the heights of Nicopolis. If Abercromby had had cavalry and well-horsed artillery to exploit their disorder, a hard pursuit would have captured the whole of Lanusse's field artillery and taken a rich harvest of prisoners. On the left Dillon's Regiment made a charge and captured two guns. But on the right when Moore reached the rising ground near the Roman Ruins he could see the enemy retreating well ahead of him across a wide plain, in confusion but still virtually intact.[15]

The view which opened out from the crest of the ridge completely disconcerted the British commanders. Abercromby had been assured by Consul Baldwin that it immediately commanded the Alexandria defences;[16] and after the fighting advance through broken country and the enemy's increasingly disorderly retreat with the British infantry in full cry at their heels, there seemed to be a good chance of rushing Alexandria and capturing the city. This hope was dashed when Moore discovered two miles of open plain ahead, commanded by the distant heights of Nicopolis.

The Reserve had reached the ridge ahead of the line, not having had to deploy and fight, and Moore saw that if he followed the enemy into the plain without cavalry he could not overtake them but would merely bring his own troops within range of Lanusse's field artillery and of batteries on the heights of Nicopolis. Halting his column on the ridge, he rode over to the neighbouring 2nd brigade as it came up and persuaded General Cradock to halt till the rest of the army came into line so that they could discover Abercromby's intentions. The brigades on their left came up, but instead of halting level with Cradock they swept on into the plain, and Cradock and Moore went forward with them into the enemy's artillery fire.[17]

Perhaps Abercromby should have grasped the situation as instantly as Moore. But in hot pursuit and with his poor eyesight he failed to halt the advance when the country ahead was revealed: the fact that a horse had been shot under him may have placed him in the wrong position at the critical moment. When he discovered the true lie of the land and could see the enemy halted and regrouping, he realised that a fresh attack would have to be organised. A signal to halt was given, Moore met the General, and after consultation orders were issued to rush the enemy position by an attack on both flanks. Moore was to command the right thrust with the Reserve and the Guards, neither of which had been committed to the battle during the morning. On the left, Hutchinson's column which had been lightly engaged was to make a circuit across the dry bed of lake Mareotis and approach the enemy's right flank. Moore advanced the Reserve to its start line, and waited for Hutchinson to manoeuvre his force into position, so that the two attacks would be launched simultaneously.[18]

Hutchinson's first objective was a conspicuous hill of white sparkling sand, jokingly named the Green Hill, a mile and a half from his left front and close to the enemy flank on the heights. His brigades in the plain reformed their columns, concentrated towards their left, and advanced without opposition across a marshy area to occupy their objective. The crest of the hill was beaten by artillery fire from the heights of Nicopolis, from which the British columns found shelter on the reverse slopes while Hutchinson reconnoitred. The French, however, brought two howitzers forward along the bank of the dry canal to search the concealed ground with high-angle fire, and Hutchinson ordered the 44th from Doyle's brigade to advance and silence them. The 44th, a weak regiment less than 300 strong, boldly advanced and charged, taking and spiking the howitzers. In their salient position, however, they were caught in a converging fire from thirty cannon on the Nicopolis heights. Round-shot ploughed the ground around them, a counter-attack developed, and the regiment was hustled back. During this withdrawal Lieutenant James Brown was hit in the right side by a cannon shot. He shook hands with the men of the light company and was carried back to the lakeside, to be put on a boat and taken to Aboukir. His wish that he should never be on board a ship again was fulfilled, for he died that evening before he could be embarked.[19]

From the Green Hill General Hutchinson had been reconnoitring the ground ahead across which he was to attack. Wilson later suggested that he could have marched round the French flank and attacked the unfortified southern face of Alexandria; but this was armchair strategy after inspecting the French defences at the end of the campaign. It also assumed that the bed of the old lake Mareotis could be crossed by troops; but to British eyes at the time the salty, sappy surface of the lake-bed appeared to be marshy and certainly impracticable for artillery, as it also seemed to the French. The British intention was a more direct attack from the Green Hill across the valley beyond it, aiming at the right face of the enemy positions on the heights of Nicopolis.

Hutchinson's reconnaissance from the crest of the hill was the first good view the British had had of the Nicopolis position. From here he could see that the French lines were strongly defended and studded with artillery; and the bombardment suffered by the 44th in their sally against the enemy howitzers indicated how high the cost of an attack across the valley would be. The view also confirmed that the escarpment was not, as Consul Baldwin had stated, close up to the Arab walls but at a little distance from them, with a further defensive position close under the walls themselves. Moreover the escarpment appeared to be commanded by the guns of Fort Cretin and Fort Caffarelli inside the city.

Hutchinson concluded that the heights could not be stormed without heavy losses; and that the attackers would then come under heavy bombardment and could make the escarpment tenable only by rapid entrenching, for which they had no tools. He reported this to Abercromby, and asked for instructions. Sir Ralph sent Hope to look at the ground, handed over the command of his division to Cradock, and followed with Anstruther to see for himself. Time was slipping away, and it was now late in the day. The beaten enemy had had time to be steadied and reorganised; and on the right flank Moore could see that they had observed his column forming for an attack and were sending troops and guns across their position to oppose him. He no longer thought that the attack should be risked.[20]

Abercromby's conclusion after studying the ground on the left was the same, and he aborted the attack; partly because the immediate opportunity had been lost, but for more enduring reasons. The great military thinker Clausewitz was to learn in the coming years of war that the most dangerous situation in which an army could find itself was an arrested offensive. Such was the likely outcome of the intended British attack. The storming of the Nicopolis escarpment would not be decisive unless it caused the utter collapse of the enemy; and the British would find themselves perched on the edge of the escarpment close to an entrenched enemy and under bombardment. 'Without cannon, ammunition, provisions, or the means of entrenching ourselves', Moore noted, 'I doubt if we could have held it.' Ten days would have been needed to bring up heavy cannon for breaching the French fortifications; and the siege-guns, ammunition, food, and even water would have to be brought forward from the lake by a three-mile portage without draught animals. That frail thread of a supply line would be exposed to the French cavalry. And while the British clung to their exposed lodgement and laboured on preparations to storm the city, Menou's force would be approaching their strategic flank from Cairo.[21]

About four o'clock in the hot afternoon the order was given for the whole army to retire to the Roman Ruins ridge from which the French had been driven in the morning. The relief to Abercromby's right column was immense. It had been halted under fire in the plain throughout Hutchinson's protracted movements and consultations. The French field artillery had been supplemented by some heavy 24-pounders, brought forward from rearward emplacements when the enemy realised that the lines were unlikely to be rushed. The gunners loaded and fired deliberately without fear of attack or counter-bombardment, and they literally had a sitting target, for after the departure of Hutchinson's column the infantry in the plain were ordered to sit down. On the right the Reserve found some cover from the French cannon in broken ground, but even here the enterprising French gunners brought two field-guns forward to a commanding knoll to harass them. In the level centre of the plain Cradock's and Coote's brigades were completely exposed. Whole files were swept away, but the gaps were quickly filled. An officer of the Camerons recorded that before the regiment marched off to the Green Hill much of the enemy shot flew overhead or ran along the ground, and as the low shot could be seen approaching the words 'open to the right and left and let the ball pass' were constantly heard along the line.

For the troops who remained there was no relief till at last the order to retire was received; and after sitting patiently for several hours enduring an 'exterminating fire' the brigades withdrew deliberately across the plain in stages and 'with great order'.[22] Their losses in the plain had been tragically unnecessary; and the French General Bertrand blamed Abercromby for not withdrawing the troops out of cannon shot while he deliberated. Perhaps a less impetuous commander than Abercromby would have reined his men back while he co-ordinated his next attack; but one must sympathise with him. The advance from the ridge had been made in the heat of a pursuit; it would have been discouraging for the eager and elated troops to retire just before launching a fresh attack; and Abercromby did not foresee how long the next phase of the battle would take to organise.

9

'WE MUST MAKE THE ATTEMPT'

In the rear of the regiments which were doggedly retiring from the fire of the French batteries, their quartermasters had been marking out a camp site on the old French position, and as the tired troops returned from their ordeal in the plain they took up a defensive line across the isthmus between the Roman Ruins on the coast and the Alexandria canal. They were set to work immediately, digging wells under palm trees behind the ridge and burying the dead. As the chilly evening gathered, the soldiers drew together round the smoky camp fires to swap stories of the fighting.

There was the tale of the paymaster of the Royal Scots who had been seen lurking behind the protection of a large date-palm, looking out for wounded officers of the regiment as they were carried to the rear and anxiously scanning his list to see who was in debt or in credit: a good story not to be spoiled by the fact that there had been no officer casualties in the regiment. A tailor of the 92nd was said to have put out his foot to stop what he thought was a spent cannon ball and had his leg taken off at the knee; and a highlander's head had been carried off by a round-shot on the previous evening while he was eating his supper with the bread still between his teeth. This gruesome levity was tempered with more serious speculation. Why had the French musketry not been more effective? Some of their musket-balls had bruised without penetrating the skin: Sir Ralph Abercromby himself had been bruised on the thigh by a musket shot. The likeliest explanation was that the French in their haste to reload had not rammed the charge hard enough, reducing the velocity and accuracy of the shot.[1]

Outside the circles of the fires dusk dissolved into a clear, starlit night, damp with dew and bitterly cold after the torrid day. There were still no tents – even the officers had only the blanket they carried – and on the bare slope of the sandhills there were no palm fronds to make bivouacs. Many regiments dug pits in the sand for shelter, large enough to hold six sleeping men; and, lying dressed in full equipment ready to turn out instantly, some of the soldiers tried to keep warm by piling sand over their blankets. An hour before dawn the drums beat reveille, and the men rose stiffly to find their alarm positions for the morning stand-to.

With daylight the unremitting fatigues were resumed. Half an hour after daylight regimental parades were held when the men were told off for the day's duties. A flag of truce was sent across the plain to arrange for the burial of the dead lying between the outposts, and parties went out from both sides into no-man's-land to dig mass graves. Water parties excavated wells, sometimes uncovering ancient aqueducts, one of which flowed with pure water from an undiscovered source to the amazement of the natives. Everywhere there were signs of ancient habitations. 'We lay on the ruins of the city of Memphis', a guardsman of the Coldstream believed.[2]

Other parties laboured on the construction of field-works to strengthen the position, carrying earth in double-handled baskets to build the new breastworks and redoubts. But the most taxing and urgent of the soldiers' tasks was bringing forward supplies from the lakeside depot a mile behind the left of the line. For want of horses and camels, all the provisions and ammunition had to be carried by soldiers and seamen; heavy casks of spirits were rolled through the sand. The only cooking fuel was green palm wood, which had to be carried up from a distance.

Nightfall did not end the duties. Half an hour before sunset the regiments paraded again to form the relief pickets; and as the sun went down behind Alexandria a beat of drum sounded at the right of the line and was passed from regiment to regiment to signal for the pickets to march off. Out in the darkness of the plain pairs of sentries were posted, and the pickets behind them sat in instant readiness, not allowed even to unroll their blankets or lie down. During the night they were visited by their brigade field officer on duty. That could be a chancy matter in the dark, and on the second night Colonel Brice of the Guards strayed into the enemy's patrols and was fatally wounded by a vedette.[3]

A few comforts began to reach the front. On the 15th Surgeon Thornton received a hospital marquee, and in the following day a small issue of tents arrived for the regiments. Army rations were supplemented with provisions brought by the bedouin, who had begun to arrive from the interior within a couple of days of the landing. A native market was set up and strictly policed by Consul Baldwin, who was more useful as market superintendent than as topographer. The market was roped off to protect the Arabs from being robbed and cheated, and all buying had to be done across the ropes and between fixed hours. Sheep, eggs, scrawny poultry and excellent red mullet and other fish were sold at regulated prices; and there was a brisk trade with the highlanders in ostrich feathers to add to their bonnets.[4]

Nevertheless, life on the sandy isthmus remained hard and comfortless. Even the palm wood burned badly and gave off an acrid smoke which irritated eyes already beginning to suffer from ophthalmia. The sick list was increasing rapidly, and by the 18th, after five days on the Roman Camp position, there were 3,500 sick – nearly a quarter of Abercromby's force – of whom 1,100 were serious enough to be sent back to the hospitals.[5]

But in spite of the labour and discomfort, the army's morale had soared since the battle of Mandara. After a generation of setbacks, the past two days' operations had been a heartening experience. In the letters and journals of regimental officers the recurring themes were the soldiers' combination of discipline with their courage, the parade-ground precision of their drill, and the subduing of the enemy's confidence. 'It is impossible for troops to have behaved better', Colonel Paget of the 28th declared: 'indeed *I* did not think it possible for troops to have conducted themselves so well. There was a degree of system and regularity displayed on the 13th far beyond belief, and a cool intrepidity that never was exceeded.'

It was the combination of cool discipline with the courage which no one had doubted that struck all the writers. 'I want words', wrote Hudson Lowe of the Corsican Rangers to his father, 'to express my admiration of the conduct of the British troops. Their valour was only to be equalled by the exact discipline and order apparent in all their movements.' Also writing to his father, Moore praised the performance of the Reserve. 'I have always had the best opinion of British troops', he wrote three days after the battle, 'but their conduct since we landed in Egypt has surpassed every thing I had conceived, and I would not exchange these eight days service for all I had seen before.' He sensed that he had seen a turning point in the army's history; and the old British confidence in their military superiority was being regained. Captain Wyvill of the Camerons described 'the most steady and determined bravery' of his men, and believed that 'the French began to be convinced that nothing could withstand the ardour of the British troops'. 'Our people', wrote Anstruther, 'now feel as they used to do, and have the utmost contempt for the French, especially for their cavalry.' And this although the French were agreed to be an efficient force of good soldiers and to have fought most gallantly, particularly indeed their cavalry. 'I have never', wrote Captain Maule of the Queen's, 'seen in the army of any country superior men to those of the French cavalry in Egypt.' They were, Hope told his brother, 'badly mounted but understand the service', whereas our cavalry 'does not deserve the name'.[6]

If there was a lesson to be drawn from the battle of Mandara, it was the soundness of the drill manual and of the training Abercromby had based on it. The Reserve had advanced under cannon fire, said General Oakes, 'with the utmost precision of movement, indeed (without any exaggeration) as much so as I ever saw at *any* review in my life'. Hudson Lowe, who had been a sceptic about the realism of the army's training as practised at reviews, was astonished to see the same manoeuvres performed by the Reserve in battle. 'Every movement', he reported, 'was performed with more regularity and precision than I have ever seen it practised at any review or field day, tho' the men were dropping in the ranks under the hottest fire of the enemy's grape and musketry.'[7]

What Lowe had seen were the fruits of a tree nurtured by Abercromby but planted thirteen years earlier by General Dundas when he published his

Principles. And this the senior officers of the army recognised. When Colonel Paget wrote that the army had manoeuvred 'with all the system and regularity of a Berlin review', he obliquely acknowledged the Frederickian example which had inspired Dundas's work. Paget had often hoped to see a fair encounter between infantry and cavalry in an open plain; and now (though he forbore to write it to his distinguished cavalry brother) he had witnessed a large body of horse twice attempting to break a line of infantry, and completely routed by 'the intrepid gallantry of the 8th and 90th Regiments'. He may have remembered Dundas's formula for beating off cavalry: 'superior order, regularity and weight of fire'. It was the antithesis of the old loose order of the 'American' system.[8]

'Old Pivot' Dundas, now Quartermaster-General in London, was at last to have his work acknowledged from the battlefield. Anstruther wrote to him that he had '*formed the British Army*. In this, all here are unanimous.' Regiments of all kinds had been collected from everywhere, and had moved and deployed with a regularity 'of which no infantry in Europe, but one, is capable: following one system, speaking one military language. . . . All this we owe to you'. What a contrast it was with the early years of the war when no two regiments had drilled alike. Abercromby was delighted with his infantry's performance, and paid his own tribute to the work he had encouraged Dundas to publish. To the Duke of York he reported the success of the system, with the troops 'really manageable and always in order'. And he found time a few days later to pen a letter to Dundas: 'It is a pleasure to me to say that the principles you have laid down for the British troops have begun to operate. . . .' He had never seen such good order during the course of the war, and 'the courage of the troops was not checked by it'.[9]

Those two days of movement and fighting had given the army an ideal proving ground for its battle skills. The opposition had not been too strong, yet strong enough to give the victors confidence. The French had been skilful and courageous; but though they had used their great superiority in cavalry and artillery effectively, their infantry had been too few to nourish their attacks. The British infantry had been able to practise their manoeuvres in line and column under war conditions, and test their light infantry's ability to combine with conventional infantry in the modern manner. The whole force had gained confidence in each other, and the commanders in their troops. The British Army was beginning to come right.

Yet the 'blooding' had been costly for an army which was outnumbered by the enemy in the theatre. The battle of Mandara had cost the troops 1,240 killed and wounded including seventy-six officers, while the navy and Marines had lost eighty-four of all ranks. Of the army's casualties only 156 were killed outright; but most of the 1,084 wounded had been mauled by cannon shot, and of those who survived the hospitals many would be permanently crippled. Abercromby had been denied the harvest of a pursuit by his lack of horsed artillery and cavalry, and the French were believed to have lost only 700 men; so once again the balance of loss was against the British. Altogether the first six days of the invasion had cost Abercromby 2,000 casualties, about one in seven of his force. 'Our victories have been too dearly bought', General Oakes lamented when the difficulties ahead became apparent.[10]

For the truth was being faced that the campaign was as far as ever from victory, and Moore could form no clear vision of how it would end. The opportunity lost at Mandara for want of guns and cavalry would be dearly paid for. The defences of Alexandria still defied Abercromby from the skyline. To seaward the small modern city of Alexandria could be seen between the Old and New Harbours, guarded by its own wall on the neck of the peninsula. To southward on the mainland the Arab walls contained the ruined Arab town where lay the hutments of the French garrison, dominated by Fort Caffarelli; and on the heights outside them towered Pompey's Pillar, surrounded by redoubts and adorned with four immense flagstaffs from which flapped the colours of France and the Northern Powers. But between the British Army and the two towns stood the entrenchments of the Nicopolis escarpment. The city could not be reduced by blockade because it was open to supplies on its westward side: it would have to be stormed.

Hence the halt on the Roman Camp position, to cover the bringing forward of heavy artillery. The opening phase of the assault would be to storm the Nicopolis escarpment, and entrench there under bombardment. Breaching batteries would then be pushed forward against the old Arab walls and whatever defences the skilled French engineers had prepared. The fortifications would not compare with a European fortress; but they were defended by a large field army, not garrison troops. As the weather grew hotter the labour of digging the approach trenches and dragging siege-guns up the escarpment, and the insanitary conditions in the trenches, would propagate disease and further weaken the besiegers.[11]

And there was another sense in which time was not on Abercromby's side; for Menou was approaching with reinforcements. A reconnaissance by Moore had confirmed that the lake-bed was passable for troops; and on 17 March, four days after the battle of Mandara, natives reported that Menou with 1,500 cavalry had reached Damanhur, only thirty miles from Alexandria. Though no infantry or artillery had been seen, his cavalry screen effectively blocked reconnaissance.[12]

The concentration of most of Menou's force against the British now seemed certain. Could the Turkish threat prevent it? The Grand Vizir was known to have advanced from Jaffa three weeks earlier on 25 February, and his advance guard was rumoured to have reached Salahieh on the Egyptian side of the desert. If that were true, there was just a chance that the threat to Cairo might divert some of Menou's reserves.

In the British headquarters Colonel Anstruther still harboured a hope that Menou might be induced to disperse his force on several fronts against the Turks and the Red Sea expedition. But in this expectation he seems to have been alone, though we shall see that to a significant degree his prediction was fulfilled. One of the sceptics was John Hope. 'A Turkish army', he explained to his brother, 'exactly resembles one of our old feudal armies – a machine of so little consistency that it cannot keep the field long for any useful purpose, and probably never will be brought across the desert.' Abercromby would have agreed. 'The Turks will do nothing', he assured General Dundas on 18 March.[13]

In that case, what were the British to do? To the senior officers the outlook, with Menou about to enter the battle, was bleak. John Hope, though not quite prepared to say that the situation was desperate, dared to speculate on whether the British government might have protected India more easily by blocking the Red Sea or reinforcing the sub-continent rather than invading Egypt. Anstruther, though he did not think that the Alexandria defences would hold out long once the siege-guns were in position, expected heavy casualties in the preliminary assault on the escarpment, and 'a hard job or two before we can open trenches' with much loss of time and lives. Coote, the senior brigade commander, was equally guarded: he saw the enemy 'very strongly posted and upon very high hills – we must be cautious'. General Oakes, tired after a night on duty with the pickets, gave way to pessimism and had no idea what was to be done next – 'but I think I foresee disaster'. He feared that hot weather and enemy reinforcements would force Abercromby to raise the siege. 'If this *should* prove so what we are to do I know not. I hope I am only a croaker.' Moore went further, baldly stating in his diary, 'the operation is beyond our force'.[14]

Abercromby was as baffled as his subordinates. The situation which Moore had predicted at Marmaris had arrived: without a decision by battle, a stalemate had developed with an open flank threatened by enemy cavalry, a fair example of Clausewitz's 'arrested offensive'. 'You may fairly grasp my situation', Sir Ralph confided to General Dundas: 'I am sure no man however envious of military fame can envy me. God knows how this will end. ... In Alexandria there are seven thousand men, with a numerous artillery. It is not a fortress, but a very strong camp, and if we can carry it, of which I doubt, we must lose many men.'[15]

But he added, 'We must make the attempt'. Of this he felt no doubt, and had said so to Lord Keith on the 14th when the Admiral wished to take the fleet out of Aboukir bay in search of a French squadron: 'We are now fairly committed, and cannot stop short without national loss and national disgrace'. Moore believed that Sir Ralph's only hope of success lay in some unforeseen turn of the fortunes of war. But *virtutis fortuna comes*: fortune favours the brave. The army's honour was at stake; and the spirit which Abercromby had planted at Marmaris had grown and flourished in the soil of victory. 'Of this I am certain', Moore told his father, 'that what men can do will be done. . . . The honour of the country will not be tarnished.'[16]

But it was Abercromby alone who held the sky suspended, in the lonely responsibility of command. 'I pray God he may be saved to us', wrote Hope, wondering what would become of the army if he were removed by wounds or disease. It could easily happen: in the short campaign Abercromby had already had a horse killed under him and had been bruised by a musket ball. His presence in the thickest fighting endeared him to the troops, particularly to the Irish soldiers who would run out when he passed their tents calling 'Here he comes! here he comes!' Danger seemed to increase his composure, and his orders became the more clear and decisive. But would his luck hold? Forty years earlier, breaking a similar deadlock at Quebec, General Wolfe had been slain at the head of the 28th Regiment.[17]

The thought of his successor troubled Abercromby's mind. He had good brigade commanders who had shown up well in the recent fighting, though it was said that Lord Cavan 'knew little of manoeuvring troops, and when he attempted it, was apt to make sad mistakes'. Moore and Coote had confirmed the competence they had shown in the Helder campaign, and Abercromby was pleased by Cradock's performance at Mandara: the 'Town Bull of Dublin'[18] turned out to be 'a very sensible man, he managed his brigade with great judgment'.

But at their head, if Abercromby became a casualty, would be General Hutchinson, and Abercromby had lost confidence in him. His dejection at Marmaris had been a warning, and in councils of war his opinion had, as Lord Dalhousie heard, always been 'extremely cautious and timorous'. During the landing on 8 March he had been intended to command the second wave; but after watching the assault from a brig close inshore he felt unwell and returned to his ship. This, and his hesitations on the Green Hill on the 13th, may have been in Abercromby's mind when he reported to the Duke of York's military secretary that 'General Hutchinson has bad health and does not like responsibility'. The next senior general was Coote, a reliable brigadier, but Abercromby doubted his fitness for supreme command, and begged the Duke of York to send out a general who was fit to command the army.[19]

On 18 March the castle of Aboukir surrendered with its garrison 150 strong after a four-day bombardment by 24-pounders, for which most of the powder and shot had been carried from the beach on the horse-stretchers designed and made at Marmaris.

On the same day a cavalry skirmish caused losses which the army could ill afford. About three o'clock in the afternoon a small body of Menou's hussars and light infantry were seen reconnoitring along the canal from the direction of Damanhur, intercepting and killing Arabs who were on their way to the British market with provisions. The British cavalry commander,

General Finch, was absent, but Colonel Archdall of the 12th Light Dragoons hastily mounted a mixed body of eighty or a hundred men of his own regiment and the 26th Light Dragoons, some of whom had only just received their horses from the delayed Turkish transports. Without seeking orders or informing the General of the Day he galloped off to attack the enemy patrol. The light dragoons and the French hussars charged through each other; but while the French reined in their well schooled Arab horses and re-formed, the British on their raw mounts failed to check and rally, and ran into an ambush of infantry concealed behind the parapet of an old redoubt. Fired on by the carbiniers of the 21st légère on their flank, and attacked from the rear by the 7th Hussars, they extricated themselves with difficulty. Colonel Archdall lost an arm, and left thirty-three casualties and prisoners behind.

Harsh though the calculation may seem, the loss of forty-four scarce cavalry horses was almost worse than the loss of the men. Abercromby, angered by the needless casualties, issued a sharp General Order warning his troops against advancing without proper support, and 'pursuing advantages beyond what the occasion demands or prudence warrants'.[20]

The days of inaction while material was assembled for the next attack must have been a trying time for impatient spirits, explaining if not excusing Colonel Archdall's impulsive sortie. Sir Sidney Smith, a man of action and a loud-mouth, complained that he would have liked 'a little more activity *in our general system*', to dominate the surrounding country and show the French that they controlled only the ground they stood on. He was referring to the killing of Arabs by the French; but the fate of the British cavalry who tried to prevent it should have shown him the futility of hoping to control the countryside against superior enemy cavalry. Sir Sidney may also have had in his mind the damping down by Abercromby of skirmishing between the lines. In the first couple of days on the Roman Ruins position the French had lost a few men while attempting to drive back the British vedettes. Abercromby shared Moore's dislike of aimless skirmishing; and he suggested to the enemy general that the calamities of war ought not to be pointlessly aggravated at the expense of individual soldiers. He received a polite agreement from General Friant. Wellington was later to adopt the same philosophy, remarking that 'the killing of a poor fellow of a vedette or carrying off a post could not influence the battle'.[21]

By the daily toil of soldiers and seamen the accumulation of stores for the offensive was nearly completed. Since the landing on 8 March scarcely a day had passed when the weather was calm enough for delivering stores on the beach at Aboukir; and the army's supplies were totally dependent on the lake, on whose sheltered waters the boats rowed to and fro assisted by their sails, bringing material from the shipping in the bay to the Commissary's depot on the lake shore behind the front. Engineers' stores and entrenching tools for the siege were accumulating, and the barrels of heavy guns were being slid off the boats and hoisted on to their carriages. Ammunition was being stacked for the bombardment. When Captain Cochrane came up from Aboukir on 19 March to check the army's requirements, he learned that the demands of the artillery and engineers were virtually fulfilled except for 12-pounder guns which he promised to expedite.[22]

But on the same day it became apparent that the British were losing the race to attack before Menou's reinforcements joined the enemy garrison. Already Colonel Archdall's dragoons had encountered one of his cavalry patrols; and on the morning of the 20th a long train of camels and draught animals could be dimly seen through the haze in the far distance crossing the lake-bed towards Alexandria. During the day Abercromby visited Moore's quarters to discuss the increasingly critical situation. The British attack would have to be delivered against a force of equal strength, in a strong natural position protected by fieldworks. And if they succeeded in storming the escarpment, there was still no certainty whether they would then be in range of the guns in the Cretin and Caffarelli forts.

But Sir Ralph could see no alternative to his coming attack. He was distressed by the sacrifice of his fine army; but even failure was better than repetition of the fiascos at Ferrol and Cadiz. When the heavy guns were ready in a couple of days' time, his plan was to push them forward in the night, form the infantry under whatever cover was available, and advance at dawn to attack both the enemy flanks. If the assault failed, the army would fall back on its fortified position, and hold it while an intermediate line was prepared in the rear to cover a retreat and re-embarcation. Abercromby's situation was all too familiar to British commanders: an army with its back to the sea and the risk that if its offensive failed it would have to embark in the presence of the enemy. It had been the story of the Dutch campaign fourteen months earlier, and would be the story of Moore's last fight at Corunna eight years later. But however desperate the coming attack, it was clear to Moore that Sir Ralph was 'determined to do it'. Abercromby took his leave and departed; and Moore, little suspecting it had been the last quiet discussion he would ever have with the old general, went out to spend the night with the pickets as Major-General of the Day.[23]

In the course of the 20th Sir Sidney Smith had received a letter from an Arab chief with information that Menou had arrived in Alexandria with his whole force and planned to attack in the morning. Not much weight seems to have been placed on the warning at headquarters, for such a resolution of the British dilemma seemed too good to hope for: Wolfe's problem had been resolved on the Heights of Abraham by Montcalm's hasty attack, but such luck could scarcely be expected to recur.

If it happened, however, the British would be ready. On the 18th Abercromby had reinforced the standing orders for the dawn stand-to with a warning that it would be enforced with the severest discipline: any officer who was late at his alarm post would be arrested, and any soldier caught not wearing his accoutrements at night would face a drum-head court martial.[24]

On the day of Abercromby's last visit to Moore, Lord Darnley rose in the House of Lords to demand a committee on the state of the nation. He painted a dark picture of the war. Austria had made peace; Russia and the Baltic Powers had formed a hostile armed neutrality; and a British fleet was being sent to coerce the Danes at Copenhagen. At home Pitt had resigned over Catholic Emancipation; the gold reserves were sinking; bread prices had soared to a peak unheard of; and the army required for defence against invasion was scattered across the country in small packets to control a rising tide of riot spurred by hunger. And what news was there, Darnley rhetorically enquired, of Britain's only striking force, immured 3,000 miles away in the Levant? By the last account at the end of January Sir Ralph Abercromby had not been able to attempt a landing in Egypt. The expedition might yet succeed, Lord Darnley told the House; 'but I confess that I am by no means without serious apprehensions'.[25]

Abercromby had not been given the men or the resources to make success likely; and even as Lord Darnley spoke, Menou's army was assembling to drive the British leopard into the sea.

10

SURPRISED IN DARKNESS

The position which the British army occupied was by nature defensible; but it was rather too extended for its garrison, and less thoroughly fortified than it would have been if the labours of Abercromby's men had not been diverted to prepare for an offensive.[1]

The right flank on the coast, which was to see the most desperate fighting in the approaching battle, formed a salient of broken sandhills about 500 yards wide, crowned by the Roman Ruins. From the Ruins the sandhills sloped gradually to the south into a flat open valley several hundred yards across through which ran the road from Aboukir to Alexandria; and beyond the valley the ground rose again to a sandy ridge some 1,200 yards long, the main feature of the position, with several small redoubts mounting one or two guns at intervals along the crest. At its southern end the ridge fell away to a level plain 500 yards wide and bounded by the banks of the Alexandria canal where the line was anchored on a redoubt with a 12-pounder. From there the front turned back in a right angle along the canal to rest its flank on the waters of lake Aboukir, facing a possible enemy flank approach across the bed of lake Mareotis. The length of the front from coast to canal was about two miles, with a further half mile along the canal.

The defence of the critical coastal sector was confided to the Reserve commanded by Moore. The sandhills here were dominated by the Roman Ruins, whose vast roofless quadrilateral extended across most of their width. The beach on the right of the Ruins was commanded by the cannon of Captain Maitland's flotilla of anchored gunboats; and the left angle of the walls was covered by a big new redoubt with emplacements for two heavy 24-pounders. This redoubt had a raised parapet for infantry with a ditch in front; but Captain Jennings of the 28th described the work as 'unfinished and ill constructed', and 'entirely open to the rear'. Forward of the redoubt was a small redan, an angled field-work with a single gun.

It was here in the Ruins and the redoubt that Moore planned to fight his defensive battle, for he saw that their loss would open the unoccupied valley on his left and compromise the whole position of the army. Taking personal command of these forward positions, he placed the 28th in the redoubt and manned the front walls of the Ruins with the 58th. His second line, commanded by General Oakes in reserve behind the Ruins, consisted of the 23rd and 42nd, the four flank companies of the 40th, and the Corsican Rangers. He placed his handful of cavalry, a hundred badly mounted troopers of the 11th Light Dragoons and Hompesch's Hussars, to the rear of the unoccupied valley; and in the event of an attack Oakes was immediately to send forward the left wing of the 42nd to protect the valley flank of the redoubt.[2]

South of the valley, the ridge which formed the centre of the position was occupied by the Guards and by Coote's brigade, with a large battery and signal station between them; and on Coote's left the plain towards the canal was held by Cradock's brigade. The second line of the British force, behind the ridge, consisted of the three brigades which had formed Hutchinson's column in the battle of Mandara. On the left, Cavan's brigade, though stationed behind Cradock's, was already partially committed, being responsible for the flank approach across lake Mareotis, and was posted so that it could wheel to the left and line the canal with its flank resting on lake Aboukir. On the right of the second line, Stuart's foreign brigade was aligned in the rear of the open valley which intervened between the Reserve and the Guards, and would have to move up and close the gap if a serious attack developed in that sector. There remained in the second line, as a wholly uncommitted reserve to meet the emergencies of a defensive battle, only Doyle's brigade stationed in the centre behind the Guards, and about 120 mounted troopers, and 500 dismounted, of the 12th and 26th Light Dragoons in the rear of Coote.

It is impossible to be certain how many officers and men of the army were present and fit for duty. Moore believed that not more than 10,000 rank and file were present; but the returns of 18 March show 11,900 rank and file of infantry fit for duty, besides 625 almost useless cavalry of whom only 219 were mounted. Adding about 1,000 sergeants and drummers, the numbers would be about 13,000 infantry of all ranks.[3]

Such was the British position which General Menou surveyed from the heights of Nicopolis two miles distant across the stony plain. He arrived in Alexandria with his corps of guides, his dromedaries and his cavalry on the evening of 18 March, his infantry and artillery marching up behind him.[4] A week earlier, on 11 March, he had received the news of the British landing in Aboukir bay, which he greeted with his usual blustering confidence. 'I have just heard of the little English affray', he wrote to the defeated Friant: 'If they attempt as much every day they will have our troops scrambling like hounds for the prey.' He still relied on the British commanders' lack of enterprise; for he mistakenly blamed Abercromby for the fiasco at Ferrol and the defeat in Holland. Adding to this catalogue of failures the withholding of aid from the Austrians at the crisis of the Marengo campaign, followed by the farcical display at Cadiz, a clear pattern of hesitation and incompetence seemed to emerge. Abercromby would bungle again, Menou concluded, and it would be the end of the struggle. 'I think this is the last act of the tragedy', he had predicted to Friant, 'and that the British will be forced into peace.' His estimate of the British commander determined his response to the invasion.[5]

The news of the British landing resolved Menou's dilemma. No longer did he need to hold back most of his reserves in their central position at Cairo. The British had committed their force to the Alexandria front; and, freed from doubt, Menou began to concentrate the French forces for his counterstroke. From his central reserve he had already allowed three demi-brigades and a cavalry regiment to march with Lanusse and enter the battle. He now gathered up the rest of his reserves: Lanusse's remaining demi-brigade; another, which he had held back at Cairo from Reynier's division; a battalion belonging to Friant's 25th demi-brigade and a battalion of Greek auxiliaries; and three regiments of cavalry, the 14th and 15th Dragoons and the 7th Hussars.

Reinforcements were also summoned, by officers racing through delta and desert on dromedaries, from the other forward sectors. From the borders of Upper Egypt Menou had already called back two battalions of the 21st légère, leaving Donzelot to watch the Red Sea approach with only one battalion. In the Damietta sector most of Rampon's division was ordered across the delta to join Menou's march at Rahmanieh: the 20th Dragoons less 100 men, the 32nd demi-brigade, and the three élite carbinier companies of the 2nd légère, leaving the rest of the dragoons and of the 2nd légère to guard Damietta. On the Palestine front Reynier's division was ordered to send the 13th demi-brigade across the delta to join Menou at Rahmanieh, and the 9th to Cairo to reinforce the garrison troops commanded by General Belliard. Reynier himself was to stay and watch the Palestine frontier and Suez with the 22nd légère in scattered garrisons. This, however, the insubordinate Reynier was not prepared to do. He had no intention of hanging about on the fringe of the eastern deserts while victory was being won at Alexandria. Ignoring his orders, he put himself at the head of the 13th and his divisional artillery and led them to Rahmanieh in person, marching round through Cairo to avoid the delays of crossing the waterways of the delta.[6]

These movements concentrated virtually the whole of Menou's cavalry and the equivalent of eleven demi-brigades on the Alexandria front. About three demi-brigades and some garrison troops were left to guard the other forward sectors and the base at Cairo; and Reynier was to claim with hindsight that these were too many to leave out of the battle.[7]

By 15 March Menou was at Rahmanieh, where Rampon joined him on the following day. The cavalry were pushed forward to Damanhur, and their commander General Roize was ordered to reconnoitre boldly with an engineer and an artillery officer and discover a route across the lake-bed to

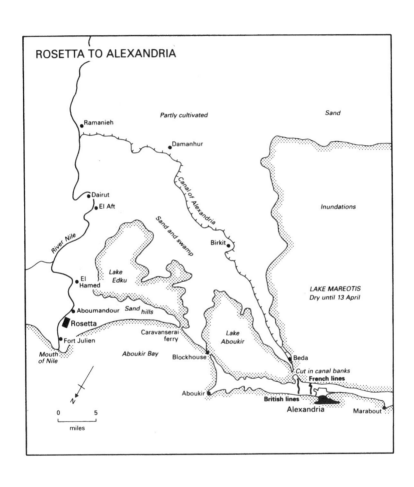

ROSETTA TO ALEXANDRIA

Partly cultivated

Sand

Ramanieh

Damanhur

Canal of Alexandria

Dairut

El Aft

Inundations

River Nile

Sand and swamp

Birkit

Lake
Edku

El
Hamed

LAKE MAREOTIS
Dry until 13 April

Aboumandour

Sand hills

Rosetta

Caravanserai
ferry

Lake
Aboukir

Fort Julien

Beda

Mouth
of Nile

Aboukir Bay

Blockhouse

Cut in canal banks
French lines

N

Aboukir

British lines
Alexandria

Marabout

0   5

miles

Alexandria, confident that the British had no cavalry capable of hindering the reconnaissance. 'Tell your troops', Menou charged Roize, 'that the general peace will be made in Egypt. The Army of the Orient opened the war in Europe, and it will end it in Egypt. This is the last effort of the English.'[8]

Roize succeeded in his reconnaissance, though the only route he could find that was fit for artillery led the army far to the west, reaching the coast near the Marabout fort and giving the British their blurred and distant view of the French column.

Excluding officers, Menou's force in the field was about 11,600 strong, of whom 1,460 were cavalry. Their numbers were thus inferior to the British by about 1,400 other ranks, but if one excludes the British cavalry as an almost useless battle-force, the British margin of superiority reduces to about seven hundred.[9] Neither army had the superior numbers needed to attack a resolute enemy in a strong defensive position; and, had either commander been able to read the mind of his opponent, each might have thought that his best course was to wait for the attack the other was planning. Yet neither felt that time was on his side. Abercromby, entrenched on a barren isthmus with the hot weather coming, could expect desperate measures by Bonaparte to land reinforcements; and with a French battle-fleet at large in the Mediterranean the indispensable support he received from his own fleet could be disrupted. He had also to remember the urgency of his mission to clear the way for peace negotiations.

Had Menou known that Abercromby was preparing to attack him, he too might have waited. But no more than Abercromby did he wish for a stalemate, for his force would soon be needed to stop the Grand Vizir. No doubt he overrated the co-ordination between Abercromby, the Grand Vizir, and Baird's expedition from India; but even if the Vizir did nothing, Menou could not afford to maintain his concentration on the heights of Nicopolis indefinitely. He had to control the country, maintain his flow of provisions, and cover Cairo. It was later suggested that he should have reinforced the Alexandrian garrison but then gone back into the delta to cut off the British supplies and ward off the Turks: 'What could we have done?' asked Colonel Thomas Graham.[10] But Lanusse and Reynier vehemently pressed Menou for an offensive to forestall the advance of the Grand Vizir and the Red Sea force. Victory, said Reynier, would be decisive, while a check would not make the situation much worse.

If there were rational arguments for delay, there were psychological pressures for an attack. Like Lanusse at Mandara, Menou had been reared in the Revolutionary armies' doctrine of the bold offensive. Time and again in the coming years French commanders were to follow the formula, and launch disastrous attacks against well posted British infantry. They were never to learn the lesson. At Alexandria Menou and Lanusse were not warned by Lanusse's defeat a week earlier at Mandara; and Reynier, who witnessed the disasters in Egypt, was to repeat the error five years later at Maida. Four years on at Busaco, Masséna, with fire-eating younger marshals breathing down his neck, would sacrifice his better judgement and attempt a frontal attack on Wellington's ridge position. The pattern would continue till the crowning blunders at Waterloo.

Here on the heights of Nicopolis Menou, like Masséna later at Busaco, was surrounded by impatient rivals, eager to emulate the glory of their contemporaries. If anyone had uttered a warning – perhaps General Bertrand, who had cautioned Lanusse at Mandara – it would have required a stronger intellect than Menou's to heed it.[11]

Time was lost in debate through 19 March, but by the 20th Menou gave way to the advocates of the offensive. Scarcely giving his infantry time to rest from their long march as they arrived on that day, he ordered an attack before dawn on the following morning, 21 March, a date long to be remembered in the British Army. There was now little time to deliberate on a plan, and according to Reynier Menou had sent his chief of staff Lagrange to consult Lanusse, who produced a plan of attack which he had concocted with Reynier himself. It was distributed that night at ten o'clock as an Order of the Day. In five hours' time the army was to be under arms, and at 4.40 a.m., an hour and a half before dawn, the advance would begin. Cloaked from the British batteries in the dark, the French columns would make their secret approach across the plain.[12]

The most open sector of the British front was the plain on their left by the canal. General Hutchinson's brother Christopher noted it as particularly weak; but that was not the view of Lanusse and Reynier, who observed that it was flanked by the guns on the southern end of the ridge which could pour a devastating cross-fire into an attacking force. The ridge itself was a natural defensive position, protected by field-works and by the flanking fire of the salient redoubt in front of the Roman Ruins; and stony ground and fragments of ruins made the approach unsuitable for cavalry.

The open valley on the right of the ridge was a much more promising approach, with good going for cavalry. If the way could be cleared by taking the salient of sandhills and ruins by the sea, a huge gap would be torn in the British flank. The position on the ridge could be turned and rolled up; and the French cavalry, pouring through the valley, would wheel round to envelop Abercromby's stricken army and drive it back against lake Aboukir. Menou accepted this bold and sweeping plan. Like Washington and Rochambeau eighteen years earlier at Yorktown, he would trap the British against an inland sea.

In the darkness before dawn it might be possible to deceive Abercromby about the main point of attack, the *Schwerpunkt* in the speech of a later race of warriors. If, as the French trusted, he was unaware of Menou's arrival at Alexandria, a diversionary attack on his left would persuade him that he was being attacked from the south by the reinforcements from Cairo. To create this impression 300 hussars and chasseurs were to demonstrate in the dark in skirmishing order across the lake-bed, while the 200 men of the dromedary corps and thirty cavalry would make a wider circuit and advance along the canal from the direction of Damanhur towards two small British redoubts.

While this diversion drew the British reserves towards the left, the real attack would be launched against the British right. The four demi-brigades of Lanusse's division would assault the coastal salient and the Roman Ruins; and as his advance cleared the flank, the French centre directed by Rampon would feel its way into the valley to lap round the British position on the ridge and dislodge it. In the meantime Reynier's powerful right wing, five demi-brigades in all, would attack the front of the ridge while providing a detachment to check a counter-thrust by the British left towards Alexandria. Behind the French centre, aligned with the mouth of the valley, were Roize's five regiments of dragoons, 900 strong, waiting for the moment to burst through the broken British right.

This phase of the battle was intended to overrun the prepared defences and dislodge the first line of the British right and centre. A brief pause would follow, while the demi-brigades, covered by their aggressive tirailleurs, rapidly re-formed to attack the second British line. Lanusse would again open the assault, to unhinge the broken British right wing and wheel round its flank. The centre commanded by Rampon would 'follow this movement', while Reynier's right wing paralysed the whole of the British left.[13]

The concept was striking, but Menou's orders had been hastily drafted and were riddled with ambiguities and flaws of detail. The diversion against the British left was to begin simultaneously with the real attack instead of preceding it, thus allowing no time to deceive Abercromby and lure the British reserves away from the *Schwerpunkt*. The plan of attack for the French left must have been orally explained, for Lanusse was clear about his objectives, though they were not stated in the written orders. But heaven knows what the commanders of the French centre were told: their actions reveal nothing but confusion. This vital force, which was intended to work closely on Lanusse's flank and exploit his success, was composed of two scrappy columns, referred to in the written orders as the *divisions* of Rampon and Destaing but not to be compared in numbers or cohesion with the permanent divisions of Friant, Reynier, and Lanusse.

Rampon's 'division', commanded in battle by Adjutant-Commandant Sornet while Rampon appears to have commanded the whole of the centre, was composed of the infantry which Rampon had brought from his division at Damietta, the 32nd demi-brigade and the three carbinier companies of the 2nd légère (the carbiniers of a light demi-brigade were the equivalent of the grenadiers of a demi-brigade of the line). Destaing's column, on the right of Sornet's, was an improvised formation built around the two battalions of the 21st légère newly arrived from Upper Egypt. To these were added a

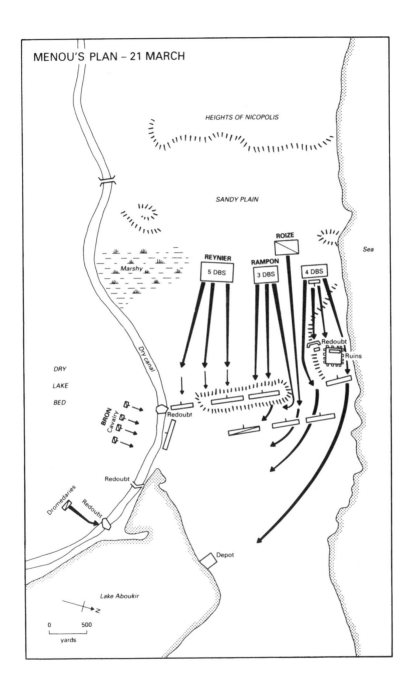

MENOU'S PLAN – 21 MARCH

HEIGHTS OF NICOPOLIS

SANDY PLAIN

ROIZE

Sea

REYNIER

5 DBS

RAMPON

3 DBS

4 DBS

Marshy

Dry canal

DRY
LAKE
BED

Redoubt
Ruins

Redoubt

BRON
Cavalry

Redoubt

Redoubt

Dromedaries

Redoubt

Depot

Lake Aboukir

N

0   500
yards

conglomerate of grenadier companies, three of them detached from French demi-brigades, and two from a native auxiliary unit, the *Grenadiers grecs*. The command of this hastily collected grenadier group was given to Eppler, *chef de brigade* of the 21st légère, who marched his force on the right flank of the 21st as a separate column, further subdividing the French centre. From such forces, unfamiliar with each other, little unity of action could be expected; and in the darkness there would be difficulty in orchestrating their advance with Lanusse's progress on their left.[14]

Underlying these flaws in the details was a fundamental weakness: the plan was too ambitious for the force available. Lacking the numerical superiority normally required for an attack, the French had to rely on surprise, concentration at the decisive point, and mobility. Yet the critical attacks on the British right and centre were made by the equivalent of barely six demi-brigades, while Reynier's right wing of five demi-brigades waited on their progress. The plan could succeed only if the British stood like dummies and yielded the initiative to the bold and experienced French commanders. Indeed the phasing of the battle into successive assaults on the British first and second lines anticipated a peculiarly passive defence, such as the French may have learned to expect of the Austrians in Italy. Yet Lanusse and Friant should have learned during the past fortnight that the British response to an attack would be vigorous. For Menou's plan to succeed, his left and centre should have been strengthened by reducing the right wing to the minimum needed to hold its ground and contain the British left. Even then success would require supreme skill and daring.

A gamble it might be, but the dice were cast. At three o'clock on the morning of 21 March, in the darkness which enveloped the heights of Nicopolis, the French formed their columns 200 yards in front of their camp. No drums had sounded the reveille, and in spite of a liberal issue of alcohol the columns moved off in silence, descending the escarpment and feeling their way across the rock-strewn plain.

On the right, Lanusse regarded the redoubt and the Ruins as outposts to be cleared before fighting his main battle beyond them, and he planned to rush them with a surprise attack by his grenadiers. Behind the grenadiers his division was advancing in two close brigade columns, ready to bypass the captured redoubt and Ruins before deploying for the battle. In the left column Brigadier-General Valentin was leading the 69th and 88th along the shore to pass on the left of the Ruins, while Silly led the 4th and 18th in the direction of the redoubt with the aim of keeping to the right of the Ruins as he advanced. Ahead of them, skirmishers and grenadiers were creeping towards the British sentries. Here, on the sector commanded by General Moore, the battle would be won or lost.

Through the hours of darkness John Moore had been out with the pickets as Major-General of the Day. Earlier in the night he had visited all the outposts along the front: first his own pickets of the Reserve in front of the Ruins; then in succession those of the Guards and Coote forward of the sandy ridge; Cradock's in the plain on the left; and Cavan's watching the line of the canal.

Returning from his rounds, Moore stationed himself with the left picket of the Reserve where he stayed till 4 a.m. The enemy had been quiet during the night, apart from firing some rockets which was not unusual. The regiments behind him in the lines were now getting under arms for the morning stand-to, and it would soon be time to withdraw the pickets. Leaving orders with the field officer of the Reserve pickets to retire his posts at daylight, Moore rode off along the front giving the order to the pickets of the other brigades as he passed. As he joined the further picket of the Guards, musket fire broke out on the left from the direction of the canal; but he was not uneasy, because during his rounds on the previous evening he had observed 'some stupidity and confusion' on the part of the officer commanding the pickets in that sector, and as the rest of the front was so quiet he guessed from the style of the firing that it was a false alarm. He set off at a trot to sort things out.[15]

What Moore had heard was the opening of Menou's diversionary attack. Dismounted men of the dromedary corps rushed a small field-work defending the southern approaches on the canal, and entering it simultaneously with the retreating British sentries, captured the garrison and turned the 12-pounder gun against the British positions. They had fired one shot into the darkness when the second redoubt in the rear opened fire on them, and they quickly withdrew, carrying off their wounded and a dozen prisoners and leaving the skirmishing line of light cavalry on the lake-bed to keep up the firing.[16]

Along the British front listening officers could hear continuing musketry and an occasional cannon shot on the left, and in the reserve line General Stuart began to march his foreign brigade across the rear of the army towards the sound of the guns, uncovering the valley on Moore's left flank. Surgeon Thornton, exempt from the morning stand-to, was still in his tent when the firing began, and emerged to find everyone around him peering into the darkness and straining their ears for clues to what was happening. Behind them on the eastern horizon the faintest suggestion of grey was beginning to show; but day seemed reluctant to break, and the terrain ahead was shrouded in mist and darkness. Gun-crews were still working by the light of lanterns.[17]

The 92nd Highlanders, reduced by sickness and casualties, had been ordered to leave the army and return to Aboukir that morning. Half an hour after reveille they began their march, and were passing Abercromby's headquarters when the firing began on the left. Abercromby was sending off his aides de camp and his staff were dispersing to the front line, while Sir Ralph remained outside his headquarters, sceptical about the seriousness of the attack and waiting for the situation to declare itself. Major Napier, commanding the 92nd since the death of Colonel Erskine at Mandara, halted the regiment; and the men began to call out to be sent back to their station in the line. Abercromby called the officers over to him, and told them it was only an affair of outposts and they were to proceed on their way to Aboukir.

In front of the Reserve, all had remained quiet for a time when Moore left the pickets to make his morning round. Then, ahead of the redoubt, the field officer of the picket heard the twitter of small birds roused from their roosts in the sand. A moment later a sentry saw French troops creeping towards him and fired his musket. French tirailleurs rushed forward, charging up the slope towards the redoubt.

Abercromby had just ordered the 92nd to be on their way when a furious cannonade broke out at the right of the line. The mystery was resolved. 'It is an attack upon our right', he said to Consul Baldwin; and calling for his horse he mounted and prepared to ride off. From the ranks of the Gordons came loud calls to be sent back into the line, and Abercromby let them go. Major Napier turned his fragment of a battalion, and marched it back to its place in Coote's brigade on the ridge. General Stuart, marching towards the left, heard the heavy cannon fire and musketry behind him, and halted his brigade.[18]

Moore, like Abercromby, knew instantly what the sound meant when he heard the firing from his own pickets. 'This is the real attack', he said, turning to his aide de camp, 'let us gallop to the redoubt.' As the two horsemen sped across the rough ground through the dark, the pickets of the Guards whom they passed were already falling back towards the line. When the redoubt came into their line of sight across the valley Moore could see that it was under heavy attack. The black sky was lit by gun-flashes, and blazing volleys of musketry sounded like the long roll of drums.[19]

11

THE BATTLE IN THE DAWN

The coastal sandhills towards which Moore was crossing the valley at a gallop were dominated by the Roman Ruins. The gaps in the long front of huge broken masonry were manned by the seasoned 58th Regiment, which had thrown up breastworks of loose stones across the openings. To their right, the hundred yards of open ground between the Ruins and the sea was covered during daylight by Captain Maitland's gunboats anchored off the beach; but in darkness they could not see their targets, and early in the battle the Corsican Rangers were brought forward from the second line to block the gap. The left angle of the Ruins was covered by the new redoubt with its 24-pounder.[1]

The redoubt, like the Ruins, was garrisoned by a seasoned regiment, the 28th 'Slashers' commanded by Lieutenant-Colonel Edward Paget. A younger son of the Earl of Uxbridge, he had commanded his regiment for the past seven years since the age of 18 and had been wounded at their head in Holland in 1795. Brave and firm, courteous and well connected, he had a distinguished future.

Most of Paget's battalion were standing-to on the parapet of the redoubt, but he had placed two companies outside it to protect his left flank and the open rear of the redoubt; and in case of attack it had been arranged that the left wing of the 42nd Highlanders were to come forward immediately from the second line and extend his flank into the valley. But though the 42nd had been standing-to for fifteen minutes when the attack began, there had been no warning of the enemy's approach, and the first shock had to be met by the 28th without their help.[2] Moore, however, was determined to fight the battle on his forward positions; and for the next four hours a deadly combat raged round the redoubt and the Ruins, as French reinforcements were sucked into the crucial assault to unhinge the British flank.

As Moore sped across the valley to rejoin his brigade, a heavy fire was whipping out of the darkness. Enemy drums were beating the charge, and loud shouts of *En avant! En avant! Vive la République!* warned the waiting defenders that a heavy attack was coming. Moore's aide de camp Captain Anderson rode off into the dark to bring up the rest of the 42nd, and to

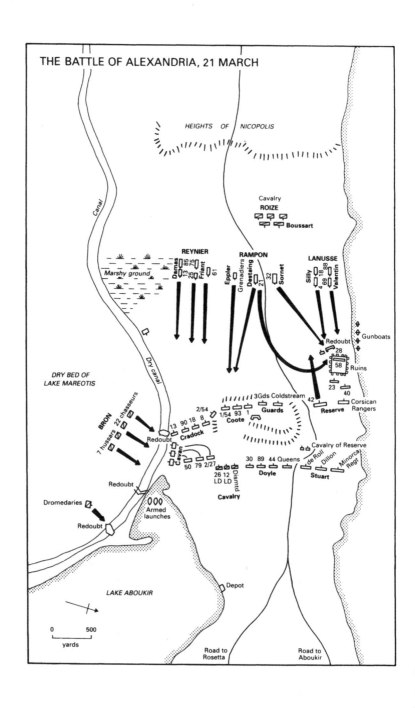

THE BATTLE OF ALEXANDRIA, 21 MARCH

HEIGHTS OF NICOPOLIS

Canal

Cavalry
ROIZE
Boussart

REYNIER   RAMPON   LANUSSE
Damas   Silly   Valentin
13 85   Eppler 32   4 18 69 88
25 75   61   Grenadiers Sornet
Friant   Destaing 21
Marshy ground

Gunboats

DRY BED OF
LAKE MAREOTIS

Dry canal

Redoubt
28
58
Ruins
23 40

3Gds Coldstream   42
2/54   Guards   Corsican
1/54 93 1   Reserve Rangers
Coote

BRON
22 chasseurs   13 90 18 8
7 hussars   Redoubt Cradock   Cavalry of Reserve
Cavan   de Roll
50 79 2/27   30 89 44 Queens Dillon
26 12   Doyle   Stuart Minorca
Redoubt   LD LD   Regt
Dismd
Dromedaries   Cavalry
000
Redoubt   Armed
launches

Depot

LAKE ABOUKIR

0   500
yards

Road to   Road to
Rosetta   Aboukir

order the 23rd and 40th forward to support the 58th in the Ruins. Moore's horse was hit in the face and became unmanageable, and fine horseman though he was he had to dismount. Entering the redoubt on foot he climbed on to the parapet to speak to Colonel Paget. While they were talking Paget was hit in the neck and fell, exclaiming that he was killed. 'And I thought so', Moore recalled crisply. Colonel Chambers assumed command; but Paget recovered enough to be carried down from the parapet and lifted on to his horse. He stayed to watch the fighting, and survived to command a division in Moore's last battle eight years later at Corunna.[3]

By now General Silly's leading demi-brigade, the 4th légère, was surging into the ditch in front of the redoubt and washing round its left side like a wave breaking against a rock. Unable to scale the parapet, and beaten back by the two companies of the 28th outside, the attackers receded. On the seaward flank General Valentin was leading his brigade along the beach; but probably realising that the Ruins were too strong to be cleared by his grenadiers alone as his divisional commander Lanusse had ordered, he deflected his main body inwards to tackle the mass of masonry. Still in column, his brigade pushed into the angle between the front of the Ruins and the redoubt. Inside the Ruins the 58th were ready. Colonel Houston held his fire to avoid killing his own pickets retreating in the darkness, and not till he could identify the glazed hats of the French did he give his grenadiers the order for the first withering volley. It rolled down the line through every gap in the walls, and the 69th demi-brigade recoiled from the close-range musketry with heavy losses. Falling back towards the shelter of the hillocks and hollows behind them, they were struck in the flank by grape-shot from the 24-pounder in the redoubt.[4]

Into this chaos of broken battalions rode the divisional commander Lanusse. As he struggled to rally the defeated infantry and reorganise the advance, a shot from the gunboats off the beach shattered his knee. He was carried to the rear and a surgeon amputated his leg, but in vain. At the age of 29 he was a veteran of many hard-fought battles and had already survived two wounds; but this was the end. As he lay dying Menou rode up and spoke to him, and he replied with bitter satisfaction that he was *foutu* like Menou's Egyptian colony.[5]

Lanusse's death left his division in disarray and leaderless, with each of its brigade attacks repulsed; and the resumption of their assault was further delayed by a new source of confusion. Into Silly's line of attack in front of the redoubt there blundered the left-hand column of Rampon's division, the 32nd demi-brigade commanded by Adjutant-Commandant Sornet. Drifting too far to the left in the dark it had already caused some confusion in Silly's first assault with the 4th légère, and was now blocking the advance of his second demi-brigade, the 18th. The appearance of the 32nd, awkward though it was, portended a change in the shape of the battle and an increasing threat to Moore's sector. For most of Rampon's division was feeling its way into the unoccupied valley between the Reserve on the coastal sandhills and the Guards on the central ridge. While the 32nd under Sornet was being sucked into the fight for the redoubt, Rampon's central column, the 21st légère led by general de brigade Destaing, was advancing down the Aboukir road in the valley and past the flank of Moore's position.[6]

On that threatened flank the left wing of the 42nd Highlanders was now coming up as Moore and Oakes had arranged. Major James Stirling led his five companies forward to form with their right on the redoubt, the red hackles on the highlanders' bonnets barely distinguishable in the darkness. As Stirling formed his line he encountered enemy in front, and his highlanders were coming under heavy fire when a message from his light company on the left reported a French column with a standard and a gun advancing along the Aboukir road beyond his flank.[7]

What the light company had seen was a battalion of Destaing's 21st légère from Rampon's division. Major Stirling rode across to the left to identify the enemy for himself, and warned the officer commanding the light company to be ready to form to his flank if the enemy tried to turn it. But he could not stay to see what happened, for the firing was very heavy along his whole front and especially to his right, and he rode back along the rear of his line. As he reached his right flank he heard a discharge of grape from the left, and galloping back he could see a French battalion in his rear, followed by a field-gun and two load camels.[8] They had wheeled to their left and were heading towards the undefended southern face of the Ruins. Without hesitation Stirling faced his rear rank about and charged. Bursting on to the rear of the French column, they broke it and captured the gun.[9]

Moments earlier an officer had come up to Moore where he had stationed himself at the rear of the redoubt, to report that the Reserve had been turned by an enemy column on the left. Moore's first thought was that the messenger had mistaken the 42nd for the French, for he could see the left wing of the 42nd forming exactly where he had intended it. But as he spoke, the wounded Colonel Paget loomed out of the twilight and smoke on his horse and interrupted: 'I assure you that the French have turned us, and are moving towards the Ruins'. Moore realised that his flank had been turned and an attack was wheeling in across his rear. At that moment the right wing of the 42nd came up. Moore ran on foot to their commanding officer, Colonel Alexander Stewart, ordered him to face his men about, and showed him the enemy at his mercy. As the French made for the Ruins, already pursued by the left wing of the 42nd, Colonel Stewart ordered the right wing to charge, and it rushed down on the flank of the enemy. The united regiment drove the French before them into the left face of the Ruins, pursuing without mercy. The highlanders, it was said, had been infuriated by various enemy acts in the preceding days, including the killing of a soldier while he was burying a dead Frenchman. The word had passed along the line not to give or receive quarter; 'which I understood they rigidly attended to', a naval officer recorded.[10]

Inside the sandy arena of the Ruins the flying French surged through the gaps in the wall, appearing unexpectedly on the flank of the 58th. Its left wing was commanded by Colonel Crowdje, who wheeled back two companies to face them. Sixty paces behind the 58th, the 23rd Welch Fusiliers had arrived from the rear and deployed into line. Lieutenant John Hill commanded the left flank company and recognised the Frenchmen's hats in the darkness. Wheeling his men to the left in silence, he gave the order to fire and delivered a volley at thirty-five yards. As his company fired a second volley two more Fusilier companies wheeled up on his flanks. The command 'Charge!' was given, the Fusiliers rushed forward, and the French were overwhelmed by a merciless torrent inside the quadrangle of ruins. Outside the walls their retreat was cut off by the 42nd. 'Our men attacked them like wolves', Captain Wyvill of the 79th Camerons was told, '. . . transfixing the Frenchmen with their bayonets against the walls of the buildings.' Later that day Moore may have been thinking of the fighting in the Ruins when he told Captain Beaver of the *Foudroyant*, 'The contest was so severe, that little of the humanity which mitigates the usual horrors of warfare was shown'.[11]

The survivors of the battalion of the 21st légère surrendered; their standard, emblazoned with Italian battle-honours, was seized by Major Stirling and handed to a sergeant of grenadiers; and about 340 prisoners were marched off to the rear by an ensign. The fight had destroyed a seasoned battalion of Bonaparte's veterans.

While the 42nd turned to crush the threat in its rear, it was fortunate that the frontal assaults had relented. But a fresh storm was about to break; and without a pause Moore led the regiment back to the slopes beside the redoubt, leaving Oakes in command of the troops in the Ruins. As the 42nd regained their station on the flank of the redoubt, fresh attacks began. Unable to break into the front of the redoubt, successive waves of French infantry were lapping round to their right trying to break through the 42nd and gain access to the redoubt by its open rear. Rampon's 32nd demi-brigade entered the fight, its commander Sornet was mortally wounded, and General Rampon's horse was shot under him. During this attack Moore was hit by a bullet in the leg, and though he stayed at his post he soon found it difficult to walk, and borrowed Major Robert Honyman's horse to fight the rest of the battle from the saddle.[12]

Abercromby now appeared as he always did in the hottest furnace of the fighting. Though it was still too dark to see much, Moore found Sir Ralph close in the rear of the 42nd without any of his staff, and gave him a report on the situation. Just then a heavy French column was advancing against the front of the regiment, and Sir Ralph rode up to Colonel Stewart and gave orders that the French 'should not be allowed to gain the height'. 'My brave highlanders', he addressed the regiment in words to which they always responded, '. . . remember your forefathers.' For the second time that morning

Stewart ordered the regiment to charge, and the highlanders drove the French column back down the slope of the sandhills.[13]

This time their boldness led them too far. The 42nd's attack took them into the thick of the dense curtain of smoke which hung across the airless battlefield; and concealed behind it the French cavalry commanded by Roize had moved up towards the mouth of the valley. Through their intervals the French infantry retreated, clearing the ground for a charge; and as the disordered 42nd emerged from the smoke five regiments of French dragoons were revealed close to their left flank. Colonel Stewart saw the tornado which was about to burst, and ordered his scattered men to retire and form quickly on the grenadier company by the redoubt. Some of his companies did not hear the order in the roar of gunfire; and while they hesitated to retreat or were still attempting to rally on the grenadiers General Boussart led forward the two dragoon regiments of Roize's first line, and with perfect timing charged to catch the highlanders with their companies in echelon and large gaps in their line.

'It was a moment', said a subsequent regimental report, 'in which a regiment pressing close on a retreating enemy cannot be supposed to be correctly in line.' Its right flank was protected by the fire from the redoubt; but on the open left the cavalry burst through the gaps in the line. The highlanders, however, rallied and kept firing, clumping together in compact bodies. Standing firm, they shot the enemy horses before they came within sword-length, and killed the fallen troopers with the bayonet. Other horsemen, galloping through the intervals, charged into broken ground among the sleeping pits dug by the 28th or became entangled in the guy-ropes of the tents which had been pitched on the previous day. Boussart was wounded and cohesion was lost; and the highlanders, in Moore's words, 'brought down so many men and horses that the rest were glad to get off'.[14]

While Moore's battalions were fighting their savage battle for the coastal dunes, the Guards on the ridge beyond the valley had been watching the continuous blaze of fire in the darkness round the redoubt and the Ruins. On their own front all was quiet for a time. On their left in Coote's brigade the gap created by the departure of the 92nd had been partially closed by extending the fronts of the neighbouring battalions, the Royal Scots and the 2/54th. But Major Napier and his Gordons were hastening back to the line, and as the enemy approached their leading files arrived to close the remaining gap. As the rest of the 92nd came up and took their place in the line, the 54th and Royal Scots closed their files to left and right to make room for them.[15] As day began to break the pickets fell back towards the line through the twilight, closely followed by enemy infantry advancing in *ordre mixte*, with a column of grenadiers embedded in a line of infantry.

The identity of these attackers remains a mystery. Menou's written orders allotted the attack on the British centre to Rampon's division; but most of this formation had been deflected into the battle on its left, where we have seen the 32nd demi-brigade joining the assault on the redoubt and the 21st penetrating into the valley to lose one battalion in the Ruins. This left only Rampon's right column, about five companies of grenadiers commanded by chef de brigade Eppler; and Reynier mentions no other units in the attack on the ridge though it is possible that the surviving battalion of the 21st demi-brigade was involved.

Yet despite the grenadiers being formed in column the attack on the ridge extended across the front of more than three strong British battalions. The uncommitted fragments of Rampon's division were not enough to form this front: other units must have been involved. And here one becomes entangled in a conundrum of the battle, the role of Reynier's five demi-brigades on the French right wing. Some of Reynier's troops must have been involved in the attack on the British centre; yet for reasons of self-interest neither Reynier nor Menou admits this. Menou's written orders had placed Reynier's strong force towards the canal, facing the extreme left of the British position; and he blamed the loss of the battle on Reynier's passivity. Reynier contradicts Menou by stating that the plan of attack destined most of his force to attack the British centre; but he goes on to claim that he did something entirely different. Striving to show that he had acted to overcome Menou's inertia, he asserts that he marched his force across the rear of the battlefield to revive the attack on the British right.

His story runs thus. The timing of his own attack was to be governed by the progress of Lanusse's enveloping movement on the left. When he realised that Lanusse's advance had been stopped and most of its leaders were casualties, he sought fresh instructions from Menou, but could extract none; and he decided to restore the momentum of the battle by an initiative of his own. He would throw his troops in to revive the attack on Moore's positions. Leaving General Damas with a single demi-brigade, the 13th, to contain the British left, he ordered Friant to march the other four demi-brigades across the front towards the sandhills. He then rode off ahead of his troops to reconnoitre the coastal battlefield; and in due course his narrative identifies three of his demi-brigades entering the battle in Moore's sector, the 61st and 75th, and the 85th at whose head General Baudot was mortally wounded. This leaves the 25th demi-brigade unaccounted for, and it may be presumed to have taken part in the attack on the British centre. Moreover none of the three demi-brigades which Reynier claims to have engaged in the coastal battles was identified there in British accounts; and one or more of these may have taken part in the attack against the Guards and Coote.[16]

As this attack emerged from the gloom behind the retiring pickets of Ludlow's Guards, the Coldstream and 3rd Guards sent out their flankers to oppose the enemy's progress; and when these in turn had been driven in, Ludlow gave the order to the line to open fire at close range. The deadly British volleys stopped the assault in its tracks. Foiled in his frontal thrust, the French commander tried to turn the left of the Guards which was thrown forward beyond the line of Coote's brigade. The officer commanding the left wing of the 3rd Guards wheeled back some companies to flank the penetration; the Royal Scots advanced from Coote's line; and thus assailed by fire from front and flank the French fell back with heavy loss. They had no reserves to renew the attack.[17]

Thus the assault on the British centre was decisively repulsed, and the raging *Schwerpunkt* of the battle continued to be the valley and sandhills defended by Moore's Reserve. Here the French were pouring in reinforcements to achieve a breakthrough, burning up the reserves which would have been needed to exploit success. The British were defending their outworks in desperate defensive fighting and bold counter-attacks, and the record of the swiftly changing battle falls into confusion. The fighting round the redoubt became a minute-by-minute struggle as fresh attacks emerged through the thick white smoke. Supported by their bold artillery at point-blank range, the enemy surged through the smoke in successive infantry attacks. Beaten back, they broke up into bands of skirmishers.

Abercromby, now joined by Colonel Hope, was still at the critical point, and the situation was increasingly being brought under control. British reserves were moving in from the second line to block the open valley on Moore's left: Stuart's foreign brigade advancing to hold the gap between the 42nd and the Guards, while behind the sand-ridge in the centre Doyle's brigade was marching across to form a new reserve line in the rear of the valley. By now there was enough daylight for the gunboats anchored off the shore to join in the battle and render the beach and the right face of the Ruins impassable.

Another French attack surged forward, with a line of infantry attacking the redoubt in front and extending out across both its flanks. Waiting in the gaps in the Ruins the 58th again allowed the enemy to come to close quarters, and at sixty yards opened a fire which dropped many of the enemy and broke up the attack. On the left of the redoubt the 42nd repulsed the attack with equal decisiveness.[18]

Every French assault had been beaten back with loss; and wherever the enemy had appeared Moore's men had defied the darkness and confusion and 'gone boldly up to them',[19] for in these conditions what counted most was individual courage and sense of duty. The French had had heavy losses; most of their commanders in the sector were casualties; and the momentum and cohesion of the offensive had been lost. Their infantry were now dispersed among the sandhills in front of the Ruins where they were keeping up a skirmishing fire. Menou in the meantime had been riding about at the rear of the battle, incapable of giving an order or taking a decision. No one was reorganising the broken formations; but according to Reynier he had arrived from the right wing and was reconnoitring the area of the redoubt from the hillocks of sand in front of it. No fresh attack could be mounted with the disoriented and leaderless troops of Lanusse and Destaing; and he was riding back to hurry on his own fresh demi-brigades when he met General Roize with the second line of dragoons. The three regiments were halted under fire and preparing to charge.[20]

They were Menou's sacrifice to desperation. He had failed to pull the elements of the battle together at its critical period; but now when his plan was in ruins he had ordered his cavalry to charge the still unbroken British position. Roize remonstrated with him. He could see that the battle had lost all impetus and was already a failure; and there were no fresh infantry at hand to support a cavalry attack. But all Roize's battle experience could not dissuade Menou. He repeated the order, and repeated it again; and Roize obeyed with a sense of doom. It was twenty-three years since he had enlisted at the age of 17 as a trooper in the dragoons. Still not 40, he had fought on the northern frontiers, in the Alps, and in Italy, and with Murat against the Turks. If this was to be his last charge it would be a desperate deed of glory.

When Reynier met Roize it was already too late to stop the cavalry charge; for the dragoons could not remain halted under heavy fire, and he had no authority to order Roize to retire.[21] Reynier galloped off to hasten on his own infantry, while Roize trotted forward with his three regiments in columns of squadrons, and at the correct distance pushed them into a gallop. From the parapet of the redoubt the wounded Paget saw the charge strike home: 'The shock was irresistible'.[22] The 42nd had just beaten off another column of infantry when the French squadrons crashed through them with the weight of an unstoppable torrent. The sergeant carrying the captured standard of the 21st légère was wounded and the standard was seized by a French dragoon. The highlanders were getting on their feet and fighting furiously with the bayonet; 'every man', wrote one of their officers, 'fighting on his own ground, regardless of how he was supported, facing his enemy wherever he presented himself . . . while strength or life remained'.

Through the broken line of highlanders the rushing horsemen swirled on round the commanders and their staffs. Moore's aide de camp Captain Anderson was in enemy hands for a time, till he fell wounded. Moore caught sight of the near-sighted Abercromby in the rear of the broken 42nd, and shouted and waved to him to retire. But in an instant Sir Ralph was surrounded and thrown from his horse. A dragoon lunged at him, and the sabre blade passed between his arm and his body, cutting the coat and grazing the flesh. At that moment a corporal of the 42nd shot the Frenchman, who fell leaving his sword in the old general's grasp.[23]

Part of the French cavalry wheeled to the left and charged into the open rear of the redoubt, pouring in behind the 28th who were under heavy infantry attack from the front. What followed gained the regiment an honour which was to live on down the years, the commemorative badge on the back of their caps. 'Rear rank 28th! Right about face!', shouted Colonel

Chambers. The rear rank turned about on the parapet, and fired a single volley inside the redoubt which destroyed the attackers. 'I was astonished at the execution which had so instantaneously been done', Sergeant Coates recalled: 'After the volley the 28th faced about and resumed their fire on their assailants in front, such as had ammunition'. A few minutes later the 28th's ammunition was exhausted. It had been a close thing.[24]

As the surging horsemen surrounded Abercromby, Moore had spurred his horse to get clear, and galloped across to the Ruins where he knew he could find troops still formed and in good order. Near the south front of the building were the flank companies of the 40th, and as a desperate measure he ordered them to fire a couple of indiscriminate volleys into the mêlée of horsemen and infantry, at the risk of hitting some of the highlanders. In a moment the field was strewn with stricken men and beasts, and riderless horses were careering about in the confusion. Roize was killed, and single horsemen and unhorsed dragoons were trying to make their way back through the intervals in the British line. On the left of the much reduced 42nd, Stuart's foreign brigade was coming into action. His own Minorca Regiment advanced in perfect order and completed the destruction of the cavalry, and a soldier recovered the French standard which had been taken and lost again by the 42nd. Many returning horsemen were brought down by de Roll's Regiment of Swiss commanded by Baron d'Huiller, one of the few *Gardes suisses* of the French monarchy to have survived the massacre in the Revolution.

The long fight for the Ruins was now won. The gap in the valley was closed by brigades from the second line; and most of the French attacking formations had been committed and broken. One enemy battalion still held the advanced flèche in front of the redoubt; but the rest had dispersed to skirmish in the sandhills and on the slopes of the ridge occupied by the Guards and Coote's brigade. Most of the British and some of the French infantry were now out of ammunition. Knowing that they were safe from musket fire, some Frenchmen entered the ditch of the redoubt and pelted the 28th on the parapet with stones, one of which struck a sergeant on the head and killed him. The 28th hurled the missiles back at their attackers. To put an end to this contest the two grenadier companies of the 40th, which still had ammunition, moved out to clear the ditch, and pushed on to drive the sharpshooters out of a hollow in front and retake the advanced flèche. But now the British cannon fired their last rounds and fell silent. For an hour they could not reply to the French artillery, which inflicted heavy casualties with close-range bombardment while their sharpshooters closed in again with impunity.

For the French this continuing engagement served no purpose. The battle was already lost, and Reynier claims that he repeatedly urged Menou to disengage and reorganise his battalions. If he would not retire, Reynier begged to be allowed to make a fresh attack with his own troops, imprudent though it might be to expend the reserves which would be needed to cover a retreat.[25]

But Menou would neither renew the attack nor withdraw, and his infantry continued to wage a skilful harassing action while his guns hammered the British lines. Moore gathered as many of his troops as he could behind the shelter of the redoubt to reduce casualties; but on the open levels on the left the 42nd and the Minorca Regiment suffered severely from ricocheting round shot. Along the ridge the losses of the Guards and Coote's brigade to the French sharpshooters were heavy and perhaps avoidable, though much of the round shot from the French cannon, fired with elevated barrels at targets on top of the ridge, flew over the crest causing random casualties in the British second line. All this would come to an end, however, as soon as the British ammunition came up. The inevitable French withdrawal across the plain would then have to be conducted under the fire of the British batteries.

One of the actors on the scene of carnage in the valley had been Sir Sidney Smith. Always to be found where the action was hottest, he had been the first officer to come up to Abercromby when the cavalry attack receded. He had accidentally broken his own sword, and Sir Ralph presented him with the one he had taken from the French dragoon. The subsequent cannonade offered Sir Sidney a macabre opportunity for one of the theatrical gestures he loved. Encountering Major Hall from Cradock's staff, whose horse had been killed, he offered him the horse of his own dragoon orderly. As he turned to order the dragoon to hand it over, the man's head was struck off by a cannon ball. 'This', exclaimed Sir Sidney, 'is destiny. The horse, Major Hall, is yours.'[26]

Not for Abercromby were such histrionics. Unnoticed by anyone, he had been hit by a musket ball in the thigh; and Dr Robertson, the surgeon who later attended him, was astonished that he could have moved at all with a ball lodged in the hip joint. With the crisis surmounted in the valley, he dismounted with the help of a highlander; and walking quietly along the line of the 42nd and Stuart's brigade he came to the ridge occupied by the Guards, where he had a view of the battlefield from the redoubt on the crest. Here he remained till the battle died away, watching the fighting intently.[27]

If the French infantry had attacked Moore's men again during the interval when they had no ammunition, the British would have had to repel them with the bayonet alone. 'Our fellows would have done it', wrote Moore: 'I never saw men more determined to do their duty; but the French had suffered so severely that they could not get their men to make another attempt.' At last ammunition came up for the British guns, and the French paid the price for hanging on too long. The field pieces opened a devastating fire, and in the redoubt Major Duncan of the artillery personally laid the 24-pounder to sweep the French files as they raced for the cover of the dunes. Two French ammunition waggons blew up with huge explosions; the enemy fire began to slacken; and about nine o'clock they began their withdrawal in very good order, harassed by British round-shot as they recrossed the open plain.[28]

There was no pursuit. The British inferiority in cavalry meant that the French horse artillery had no fear of being caught unlimbered, and covered the withdrawal with their usual skill and boldness. If the British infantry had advanced into the plain they would have been exposed to this fire without a hope of catching the retreating French columns, and would soon have come within range of the big 24-pounders on the Heights of Nicopolis. The enemy, harassed only by artillery, continued their march till they were beyond effective range, and by ten o'clock in the morning all firing had ceased. One of the last shots fired in the battle killed the horse Moore had borrowed from Major Honyman.

12

THE PRICE OF VICTORY

As the dead horse subsided between Moore's knees, his wounded leg took his weight and he realised that it was stiff and painful. For several hours he had commanded the storm-point of the battle with furious energy and courage. His second-in-command General Oakes had been hit at about the same moment and in the same part of the leg; and he too had remained in action. To retire from the battle while they could still manage a horse would have been unthinkable: '*we had both been able to continue to do our duty*'.

Now duty was done, and it was time to hand over the brigade and find a surgeon. The next senior officer was Paget of the 28th, who was also wounded; and Moore handed over the command of the Reserve to the fourth in rank, Colonel Brent Spencer of the 40th, a gallant battalion commander and a future Peninsular general. He then rode slowly off with Oakes down the fatal valley strewn with the debris of battle: 'I never saw a field so covered with dead'.[1]

The swathes of dead and wounded told the story of the battle. Nearly 90 per cent of the British army's 1,361 infantry casualties occurred on the right in the sectors commanded by Moore, Ludlow, and Coote. The entire action had been fought to stop the planned French breakthrough on the right. Pressure on the rest of the front had been slight, and all the British infantry reserves had been moved towards the threatened sector.

The distribution of infantry casualties also provides a comment on the tactics. Units which fought in the open suffered grossly higher losses than those which fought under cover. The defence of the redoubt and the Ruins, so costly to the enemy and so critical to the safety of the British position, cost only 10 per cent of the casualties, 138 dead and wounded shared among five units. In contrast the regiments defending the open ground on the left of the redoubt, fully exposed to the enemy's artillery and musketry and twice charged by cavalry, suffered nearly half the casualties in the army. Two of those regiments, the 42nd and Minorca Regiment, bore 38 per cent of the army's total, the 42nd alone nearly a quarter. On the ridge the Third Guards at the *Schwerpunkt* of Rampon's attack lost 15 per cent of the army's total.[2]

Table 6 British casualties, 21 March

By arms of service

Cavalry	14	
Royal Artillery	55	
Infantry	1,361	
Total		1,430 (243 killed)
Including staff		1,436

Infantry casualties		Percentage of: Brigade loss	Army loss
Total	1,361		
By sectors			
Ruins and valley:			
Reserve	451		33
Foreign Brigade	342		25
	793		58
Right sector of ridge:			
Guards	258		19
Coote	179		13
	437		32
Total of both sectors:	1,230		
By brigades			90
Reserve:			
42nd	313	69	23
28th	78	17	6
	391	86	29
58th	26		
23rd	20		
40th	7		
Cors. R	7		
	60	13	4
	451		33
Foreign Brigade:			
Minorca	206	60	15
Dillon's	60	18	4
De Roll's	76	22	6
	342		25
Guards:			
1/Coldstream	60	23	4
1/3rd Guards	198	77	15
	258		19
Coote:			
1/1st	82	46	6
92nd (half strength)	42	23	3
2/54th	45	25	3
1/54th	10	6	1
	179		13

Table 6 Continued

Infantry casualties			*Percentage of:*	
			Brigade loss	*Army loss*
By regiments				
42nd	313		23	
Minorca	206		15	
1/3rd Guards	198		15	
Three battalions		717		53
By terrain				
Ruins and redoubt		138	10	
Valley		655	48	
Right sector of ridge				
(3rd Guards 64%)		437	32	
Left sector of ridge		7		
Canal flank		70		10
Doyle's brigade (uncommitted)		54		

Moore was the hero of the battle. Though wounded early, he had fought on 'in an activity almost beyond belief' to save the hinge of the British front. Major Wilson predicted that he would one day be 'ranked amongst the most illustrious officers of the age'. But he added that General Stuart's advance at the head of the foreign brigade 'certainly decided the action', by defeating Menou's last vain throw with his cavalry. The heavy casualties in the brigade (Stuart's own Minorca Regiment had 206 casualties, or fifteen per cent of the army's total) lend credence to Stuart's claim to have played a crucial part. The son of the Superintendent of Indian Affairs in the colonial days of the American south, he had fought in Cornwallis's campaign in the Carolinas, and in the Netherlands in 1794–5: he was to meet Reynier again in 1806 at Maida and rout him. Sir Henry Bunbury, who served with him in Sicily during the Napoleonic Wars and acquired a strong bias against him, described him as 'vain, frivolous and sarcastic ... flighty and superficial, though there was a good deal of original cleverness'. Stuart always cherished the belief that he had won the battle of Alexandria; and ever afterwards his jealousy of Moore would rankle, and he could not bear to serve with him.[3]

Moore gave the glory to his men. 'Our troops', he recorded in his diary, 'seem to have no idea of giving way, and there cannot be a more convincing proof of the superiority of our infantry.' An infantry victory it had been. The British cavalry, too few to withstand Roize's dragoons, had not been committed, and the artillery had been outgunned. There was a feeling that the artillery had failed the army. Wyvill blamed the shortage of ammunition on some 'unaccountable negligence', and believed that by a 'dreadful blunder' reserve ammunition of the wrong calibre had been brought forward. Moore was scathing: 'Our artillery failed us as it did in Holland for want of arrangement'. In his own sector he claimed that there were only subalterns commanding the guns (three artillery lieutenants were wounded in the battle). When the ammunition in the boxes and limbers had been fired no fresh supply arrived. And the musket ammunition (also an artillery responsibility) had been held too far to the rear and took hours to bring up. 'There is certainly something wrong with our artillery', he concluded; 'it was formerly our best corps; it is now far from it. Among the officers there is a want of military spirit; they seem to me throughout to prefer situations of comfort to those which lead to distinction.'[4]

Moore was writing from his hospital bed, with no opportunity to check the impressions he had formed as an exasperated front-line commander in the heat of battle. Doubt is thrown on his belief that there were only subalterns with the guns by David Stewart, who fought with the 42nd alongside the redoubt and recorded how Major Duncan laid its 24-pounder as the French retreated. The most senior artillery officer, General Lawson, was wounded; and in fairness to other senior officers one might add that Major Thompson, commanding the 13th Company, was to be killed at Rahmanieh in May.

The failure of the ammunition supply may have arisen from the equal distribution of reserve ammunition along the front, while virtually the entire expenditure was on the right. Redistribution must have been hampered by the lack of draught animals, which both Wilson and Walsh point out. Turkish horses were trained for riding, and not to haul waggons; and the few miserable horses the artillery had been allotted at Marmaris had not yet been broken to the traces. The only other means of moving ammunition to the furthest flank from the lakeside depot or other dumps along the front was by seamen dragging or carrying it. Turkish carriers were also used in the battle, but were hampered by their custom of dropping flat on the ground whenever a shot flew near them.

Any deficiencies were redeemed by the glorious performance of the infantry, which set the seal on a fortnight of success. 'The business of this day has fairly proved the superiority of our troops over the French', the wounded Moore scrawled to Captain Beaver of the *Foudroyant*. Wounded officers had stayed at their posts and fought on; and French prisoners were saying to all and sundry that they had never faced such fighting. 'The wounded say they have fought in Germany, Italy and Egypt, but never met such resistance, or such bearing before', Lord Dalhousie recorded. Moore heard that prisoners were saying 'they have never been fought till now; that the actions in Italy were nothing to those they have fought since we landed'. French prisoners were usually arrogant and disinclined to flatter their captors, and when they did so they could be believed: 'these conquerors of Italy think as we do, that in all their campaigns they never saw such desperate fighting', wrote Commander Inglis. Italy was the magic word: the enemy were no ordinary troops, but the veterans of Bonaparte's early Italian victories. 'I have had the satisfaction', Moore told his father a few days later, 'of seeing the superiority of the British infantry over the French in three successive actions; we have beat them without cavalry and inferior in artillery. *This is the army of Italy!*'[5]

To the enemy's Italian triumphs the captured standard bore witness, with its emblazoned battle honours *le Passage de la Serivia, . . . du Tagliamento, . . . de l'Izonzo, la Prise de Graz, le Pont de Lodi.* Over this trophy there was bitter rivalry between the two regiments which had suffered most for the victory, echoing Stuart's jealousy of Moore. Sergeant Sinclair of the 42nd, to whom Major Stirling had handed the standard, had taken post with it in the rear of the left wing of the regiment. When the wing was ridden over by Roize's cavalry Sinclair received a sabre wound and lost possession of the trophy. The advancing Minorca Regiment saw it in the hands of a French officer a little behind the French skirmishing line; and an Alsatian private, Antoine Lutz, rushed forward from the ranks, shot the officer and seized the standard. So much was agreed by Lutz and the friends who testified for him. At the subsequent regimental enquiry Corporal Schmid declared that he had seen a body of French cavalry approaching Lutz, who threw himself to the ground in a hollow on top of the standard, later to rejoin the regiment with his trophy and a captured French dragoon. Lutz's own story was that after seizing the standard he had reloaded his musket and was making his way back when two French dragoons rode at him. He shot one of the horses and rushed at the rider whose foot was still entangled in the stirrup. The Frenchman begged for his life and surrendered his arms; and Lutz escorted his prisoner back to his own officer Lieutenant Markoff, who sent him to headquarters with the standard to receive a reward of twenty dollars.

Lutz's story was challenged by the 42nd. They suspected that, far from retaking the standard from the French, Lutz had picked it up from the ground near the wounded Sinclair. In the following year Moore and Oakes wrote to the commanding officer of the 42nd in Edinburgh, and a regimental court of enquiry was held which confirmed the loss of the standard by Sergeant Sinclair but shed no light on its recovery. Lutz retained the credit for his prize, and was awarded a special badge. He could not, however, be promoted sergeant because he was illiterate, while Sergeant Sinclair of the 42nd was commissioned in 1803 after his own regiment's enquiry.

If Lutz was a hero, he was not a saint. In August 1802 when the Minorca Regiment (renamed the Queen's German Regiment) was at Winchester, he was tried at the assizes for murdering a comrade with a knife, and was saved by the captured standard. His adjutant told the story and gave evidence of his good character; the jury returned a verdict of manslaughter; and 'the judge humanely ordered the very lenient fine of one shilling' as a newspaper reported: a bargain price for a soldier's life.[6]

We left Moore and Oakes riding back among the stricken men and horses in the valley. Behind the battle area the tents in their neat rows had been torn to ribbons by the French bombardment and several officers' servants had been killed; and hundreds of brass cannon balls glinted in the sand under the bright morning sun.[7]

On rode the two generals till they reached their own tents, where a surgeon was summoned to dress their wounds; and as it would be some time before they were fit for duty, they decided to speed their recovery by returning to the *Diadem* in Aboukir bay. Though any wound could be dangerous if it became infected, Moore was confident that he and Oakes would both recover: 'The bone is not touched in either, there is no danger'. He was relying on his own strong constitution and physical fitness; but infections respected no one. For a time the wound seemed to be healing well; but a fortnight after the battle the *Diadem* put to sea with the fleet to look out for a French squadron, and after five days of being flung about on the waves his leg was inflamed and his temperature had risen. The surgeons kept probing the wound without finding anything. Moore suggested an amputation, but the surgeons still believed that the leg could be saved. Poultices and fomentations reduced the inflammation where the ball had passed through; but a new inflammation broke out further down the leg. Cutting and probing, the surgeons fished out some pieces of breeches-cloth; accumulated pus was discharged; and slowly the leg began to heal. Moore progressed from bed to crutches, and he and Oakes transferred themselves from the *Diadem* to convalesce in a cool house in Rosetta.[8] Moore's leg and thigh were much wasted, and his illness had left him very weak.

His other companion was his aide de camp Captain Paul Anderson, who had lost a brother killed in the 42nd. Anderson was nursing a wound in the arm which he had received while temporarily in the hands of the French cavalry, probably inflicted by the very volley which Moore had ordered the 40th to fire indiscriminately into the mêlée. Nor was Anderson the last of the toll of staff and commanders wounded near the redoubt. The Adjutant-General, John Hope, had lost the index finger of his right hand, and his groin had been bruised by a spent musket ball.

Hope had been behind the 42nd with Abercromby, who had seemed to escape relatively lightly. The general was known to have received a graze from the sword of the French dragoon who had attacked him, and while he watched the final phase of the battle from the redoubt on the ridge in the area of the Guards he admitted to feeling pain from a contusion of the chest, probably caused by his attacker's sword-hilt. When his son, Colonel Robert Abercromby, noticed blood on his father's breeches and urged him to have his wound examined, Sir Ralph, like Moore and Oakes, was determined to '*continue to do his duty*'. He insisted that he had only been hit by a spent ball, and refused to allow a surgeon to be taken away from the 'poor fellows' who had been seriously wounded. He dispatched his orderly dragoon to fetch a bottle of wine and some water from his tent,[9] and walked up and down in the rear of the battery intently watching the enemy's movements.

But after half an hour Sir Ralph was overcome by faintness and subsided with his back against the wall of the redoubt. His son asked General Ludlow to send for a surgeon of the Guards, and though only a surgeon's mate could be found, he examined the wound and discovered that a musket ball had entered the thigh. Still Sir Ralph refused to leave the field; and only after all firing had ceased did he allow himself to be laid on a stretcher. The Assistant Adjutant-General, Lieutenant John Macdonald of the 89th, picked up a soldier's blanket that lay nearby and, removing the slings in which it was rolled, he arranged it as a pillow under the general's head. Abercromby asked what it was, and was told that it was only a soldier's blanket. He roused himself at the phrase. 'Only a soldier's blanket!', he exclaimed. 'A soldier's blanket is a thing of great consequence. You must send me the name of the man to whom it belongs, that it may be restored to him.'[10]

Bearers from the 92nd carried the stretcher down the rearward slope of the ridge, passing across the rear of their depleted regiment who were resting after suffering a further fifty casualties in the battle. When the word was passed among the highlanders that Abercromby was seriously wounded, everyone, a sergeant recalled, 'ran to get a sight of him whom we all loved'. The general was carried to his tent, where his wound was examined again, this time by an experienced surgeon. Dr Green did not think that the ball had gone deep, and made a large incision to extract it; but no ball could be found, and he advised that the patient should be sent on board a ship without delay. Abercromby ordered his son to return to his duties; and accompanied by his aide de camp and Dr Green he was carried off towards the lake, holding out his hand to Consul Baldwin as he passed. 'Don't be concerned, Baldwin', he said, 'I shall soon be well.' At the lakeside he ordered the blanket to be left for Macdonald to retrieve, and was embarked in one of the boats which were standing by to take off the wounded. The sailors heaved on their oars, and the flatboat gathered way for its twenty-mile passage to the flagship in Aboukir bay.[11]

Behind it the army was succouring the wounded and burying the dead. Seventeen hundred French dead and wounded were counted within the British lines, and 400 dead horses littered the valley where the cavalry had charged. Major Wilson rode out to see the battlefield: 'I don't remember to have seen a more shocking one', he scrawled in his journal, 'for the French were horribly mauled by grape, and some of their own guns had blown up, actually at the same time roasting the artillerymen.' Close in front of the 28th's redoubt lay the team horses and gunners of an abandoned French field-gun, which had been brought too close in the darkness and blasted with grape-shot. In the rear of the redoubt where the 28th had turned about to expel the French cavalry, General Roize lay dead with Menou's battle-orders in his pocket.[12] For some of the British their own losses had been shattering. The 42nd had lost 313 killed and wounded on top of nearly 200 earlier casualties since the landing. The fury of battle had died in the highlanders, and riding past their tents that morning Lord Dalhousie was distressed to see 'the most of them, officers as well as men, crying like children'.[13]

By nightfall almost all the dead within the lines were buried, including 1,040 French. On the following morning the 54th saw a dog lying out in front of their lines on the ridge. It would not be coaxed or driven away by the soldiers; and all through the next night it was scraping at the ground and disturbing the troops with its piteous howls. In the morning a prisoner told them that the dog's owner was a French captain, and a pioneer of the 54th remembered that he had buried a French officer on the spot after the battle. For two days and nights the dog stood guard over the grave, till a sergeant-major forced it away and adopted it. It eventually returned with its new master to England.[14]

For the wounded who could not walk, help and treatment were a matter of chance. As late as the 24th, when the weather turned to squalls and rain, several wounded Frenchmen were brought in to the General Hospital after lying out on the battlefield for nearly three days without water, food, or treatment. One grew hardened to death, but not to the wounded; and Major Wilson was lastingly affected by their suffering. 'Those who have never seen such a sight', he wrote, 'must not suppose that the effect of this scene altogether consists in the groans and lamentations of the dying; no, it is the gallant resolution with which these acute and terrible sufferings are borne . . . which excite the feelings, and annihilate the rage of hostility.'[15]

At the General Hospital there had been no time to indulge in such reflections. From the opening of the battle Surgeon Thornton had been surrounded by wounded men begging for help, and all through the hours of daylight he worked without cease dressing wounds, extracting musket balls, and helping with amputations. By nine o'clock in the evening when all the patients had been put to bed he and his party had dressed three or four hundred wounded, working without rest or food amid 'horrible and distressing groans and lamentations'. About nine he sat down to 'breakfast, dinner and supper', his first meal of the day, and afterwards visited the patients in his three marquees, administering medicines and comforts for the night.[16]

A regiment of whose wounded something is known was the 92nd Highlanders. The Gordons had paid a high price for their clamour to return to the line: three killed and forty-six wounded in a battalion which had gone into action only 150 strong. Among the casualties was Corporal Alexander Mackinnon the bard. A friend and admirer, Sergeant Maclean, found him unconscious but breathing and had him carried to the lake and taken on board a ship, where he recovered and composed two Gaelic poems on the campaign.[17]

The walking wounded fared differently. A private in the regiment was hit in the leg after firing twelve rounds, but stayed in the line till the enemy abandoned the attack on the ridge and withdrew out of musket range. He was then ordered to the rear. Painfully he limped back down the ridge and across a rough and sandy mile and a half to the depot on the lake, with round-shot flying past him from beyond the crest. At length he could no longer carry all his equipment, and had to abandon his musket. Dutifully he emptied the priming pan and left the weapon stuck upright with the bayonet in the sand, a device his successors would use a century and a half later to mark where the wounded lay in the long summer grass and corn of Normandy.

As he approached the landing place several surgeons were busy dressing wounds outside a hospital tent. Sitting down to wait his turn, the highlander removed his garter and pulled a piece of it out of the wound. He could see the musket ball prominent under the skin, and when his turn came the surgeon extracted it easily, together with another piece of his garter. The ball had flattened itself on the bone which was not broken.

After the surgeon's excruciating work, the Gordon lay down uncomplaining beside a bush to see what would be done with the wounded. Numbers more were streaming down from the fighting, all saying that the army would not be able to hold its ground; and for some time everyone anxiously scanned the skyline of the ridge for signs of a retreat. By ten o'clock it was clear that the battle had been won; but still the soldier lay patiently under his bush while the sun climbed overhead across the burning sky. About two o'clock he noticed that some of the wounded were boarding boats to be taken to the fleet. Struggling to his feet he joined a boat which pushed off into the lake and arrived in the evening in Aboukir bay; and with two comrades from the 92nd and two hundred other wounded he was put on board a two-decker out in the bay.[18]

The fleet was the army's only base, and it had been expanding its hospital accommodation to cope with the growing list of sick and wounded. Only two hospital ships had sailed from Marmaris, and after the landing the wounded had been evacuated to Rhodes. But as sickness and battle casualties mounted, additional transports were turned over to the medical service, among them the *Minerva* which was cleared of the 79th's baggage and converted to a hospital ship. On the day before the battle of Alexandria seven warships were each ordered to send ashore two carpenters to erect hospital huts on the bay. When news of the battle arrived the surgeons of three warships were summoned on board the *Braakel* hospital ship to receive the wounded, and the 80-gun ship *Ajax* was directed to send an officer ashore with materials to erect a 'large and commodious tent' for casualties. Three days after the battle six more ships were each ordered to receive up to 120 sick and wounded, and the women acting as nurses were granted full naval rations.[19] Thus the shipping coped with the soaring need for hospital beds and nursing. Six days later when only 12,697 rank and file of the army were fit for duty, there were 4,501 sick and wounded in the general and regimental hospitals, more than one man in four.

Wounded officers had the cramped comforts of a warship's cabin, and Lord Keith took a personal interest in those he knew. Moore would be up and about in a few days, he reported over-optimistically: 'he says a man cannot grudge to suffer for such a day'. Abercromby, when his boat arrived in the bay, had been hoisted on board the flagship *Foudroyant* on a grating,[20] and was put to bed in the admiral's cabin where Colonel Rowland Hill was recovering from the wound he had received on the 13th. Two days after the battle the general seemed to be on the mend. Keith reported that he had passed a good night; the doctors were cheerful, his fever was lowered, and his pulse was as good as could be expected.[21]

For several days Colonel Robert Abercromby received favourable reports of his father's progress. But on the evening of the 26th, five days after the battle, a warning arrived from Lord Keith that Sir Ralph had taken a turn for the worse. Robert set out for Aboukir, and travelled through the night to arrive on board the *Foudroyant* at four o'clock in the morning. He found his father feverish but clear-headed. In the course of that day Sir Ralph spoke to his son about various official matters, but never mentioned his own condition. In the meantime the report ran through the army that the general was not doing well. Lord Dalhousie felt a cloud of anxiety pass over the regiments: 'The dread the army is in of losing him is expressed in the almost universal conversation that passes about him'.[22]

That evening Sir Ralph seemed rather better and the surgeons were hopeful, not knowing that the musket ball which they had been unable to find had passed upwards from the entry wound to lodge in the thigh-bone near the hip socket, from where it could never have been extracted. During the night he grew worse, with pain and occasional delirium; and on the morning of 28 March Robert realised that his father was dying. Sir Ralph's mind was clear again, and whenever Robert spoke to him he replied as if he understood, though it was an effort for him to talk. Throughout the day the signs of approaching death grew more apparent. In the evening Robert left him for the last time at seven o'clock, and retired to a separate cabin; and about eleven at night Sir Ralph died quietly, 'with that composure and resignation one might expect from his character'.[23]

More than forty years later Sir Frederick Maitland, who had served as Abercromby's military secretary, reflected on that composure. Sir Ralph's physical bravery in action was well known: 'He was truly intrepid; danger never disturbed his mind. He was the first to lead and the last to retreat'. More profound, however, was his calm of mind when there was no action to excite his courage. Maitland remembered the voyage to the West Indies in 1796 when the *Glory* had turned on her side in a storm. The captain came below to tell Sir Ralph that he could not say whether the ship would sink or swim, and promised to return with more news. 'The General thanked him and he went back. Sir R's countenance bespoke the perfect tranquility [*sic*] that was within – as composed and serene as he would have been, had we not been in danger.' The captain returned with a reassuring report. 'Sir R thanked him again. He was as *un*moved by the *good* news as he had been by the *bad*, always self-possessed.' Maitland judged him 'the best, and wisest man I had ever known'.[24]

On 29 March dragoon orderlies brought the news round the regiments that the Commander-in-Chief was dead. The sense of loss was universal. 'A melancholy gloom overspread the whole army', wrote Colonel Brodie: 'No Commander-in-Chief at the head of an army was ever more beloved by those under him than Sir Ralph and no officer ever paid more attention to the comfort of the soldier. He commanded the highest respect and obedience from every rank . . . and was the perfect admiration of every one he had to deal with.' Lord Dalhousie echoed these feelings: 'Never did there exist a more admirably good, kind and amiable character than Sir Ralph; never did a General possess the confidence of his troops to a more unlimited degree'. 'His loss was a severe one', wrote Surgeon Thornton, 'his death was universally mourned, he was beloved by the troops, for his courage was their pride and example.' The navy shared the army's loss: 'The whole expedition', wrote Commander Inglis of the *Peterel*, 'from the highest to the lowest, adored him.'[25]

There were senior officers in other parts of the world who would have questioned this adulation. The American school of generals – Simcoe, Sir Charles Stuart, and Lord Moira – regarded Abercromby as too conventional to cope with the unexpected. Moira, who thought better of him than did Simcoe, conceded that he was brave, upright, and inspired by 'an honourable sense of duty'; but he doubted whether he had 'resources within himself if novel embarrassments occurred', and was puzzled (at a distance of 3,000 miles) at Sir Ralph's choosing to land in the face of an enemy army.[26]

Even among Abercromby's own brigade commanders there was a critical 'American': General Doyle had served with Moira and Cornwallis in the Carolinas. 'His talents', wrote 'Popularity Jack' to Moira, 'whatever they might have been in planning an action, were of no sort of use in action; his blindness which was nearly total, obliged him to depend upon the eyes of others, and the rashness of his gallantry often impelled him into situations, where one never thought of looking for the Commander-in-Chief of an army.'

'Of course', Doyle added, 'many necessary orders were wanting, and people were obliged to act for themselves.' The truth of this one cannot discover. Moore saw the Commander-in-Chief in the thick of the fighting unaccompanied by any of his staff; but they must have been detached on missions and probably knew where he was to be found, for Hope rejoined him. What orders did Abercromby give in the course of the battle? Was it by his orders that Stuart began to march his foreign brigade towards the left on the first alarm, and then counter-marched towards the valley to intervene at the crisis of the battle? Did Doyle move his brigade to the left to cover Stuart's rear on his own initiative or by Abercromby's directions? We shall never know. What is certain is that the course of the battle turned largely on the result of a series of determined brigade and battalion combats which held on to the forward positions or restored them when they had been penetrated. Major Wilson, too young to have served in America but with many opportunities on the 21st to observe the higher commanders, absorbed only the small-combat dimension of the battle: he did not consider Abercromby's death a great loss 'in regard to military operations, as our battles have not been gained by generalship but by courage'.[27]

He may have been right; and Moore conceded that Abercromby's poor eyesight made him dependent on having good executive generals under him in battle, though, as Sir Frederick Maitland added, he chose his subordinates well. Moore also admitted Doyle's complaint that he had always exposed himself too much in action. But in every other respect Moore was his devoted admirer, and recording his death he added this final panegyric in his diary: 'Sir Ralph was a truly upright, honourable, judicious man; his great sagacity, which had been pointed all his life to military matters, made him an excellent officer. . . . It was impossible, knowing him as I did, not to have the greatest respect and friendship for him'.

One further valediction deserves to be quoted. When the news of Abercromby's death reached his adjutant-general, John Hope, who had been with him in the fatal valley by the redoubt, he picked up his pen with his unwounded left hand, and wrote in large awkward characters: 'The army feels the loss to be irreparable, and laments him as a common father. Never were the qualities of his capacious and undaunted mind more wanted. I grieve for him on many a publick and many a private account'.[28]

Abercromby's army admired his courage, high moral character, and judgement. But above all, he had brought them victory. After eight years of disappointment, he had given the British Army the smell of success against good French troops. 'It has happened to no other general during this war to beat the French in three successive actions', Moore reminded his father: Abercromby was 'the best man, and the best soldier, who has appeared amongst us this war'.[29]

Part III

BREAKOUT

13

'UNGRACIOUS MANNERS AND A VIOLENT TEMPER'

Abercromby's successor as Commander-in-Chief, Major-General the Hon. John Hely-Hutchinson, was an odd creature though a talented one. His family background was in Irish law and politics. Born in Dublin in 1757, he was the second son of John Hely, a lawyer who had added the name Hutchinson on marrying a rich heiress. The father successfully climbed the ladder of patronage through the Irish House of Commons, acquiring the 'lucrative and honourable situation' of Provost of Trinity College, Dublin, and rising in politics to the Irish Secretaryship of State. His son John, the future general, was educated at Eton and Trinity College, Dublin, and commissioned in the army in 1774. Three years later he took his seat in the corrupt old Irish House of Commons, whose abolition he would later support by voting for the Union with Great Britain. On half-pay like Abercromby during the years of peace before the French Revolution, he studied tactics in France at the Strasburg Military Academy; and on the outbreak of war between France and the German Powers in 1792 he seized the opportunity to visit the French and Prussian camps and study their organisation and tactics. When Britain entered the war in the following year he served as a volunteer with the Duke of York's army in Flanders, acting as a supernumerary aide de camp to Abercromby. After the British withdrawal from Europe in 1795 he raised a regiment; became a major-general; and being present at the disgraceful rout of Irish troops by the French at Castlebar he was blamed by Lord Cornwallis for his misplaced confidence in unreliable fencibles and disaffected militia.

In the Helder expedition of 1799 Hutchinson again accompanied Abercromby as a volunteer, and in the final battle of Alkmaar commanded a brigade and was severely wounded in the thigh. Like Abercromby he had liberal views in politics, and supported the demand for Catholic 'emancipation'; an attitude shared by his elder brother Richard, who was rewarded with a peerage for supporting the passage of the Act of Union. A younger brother, Colonel Christopher Hutchinson, accompanied John as a volunteer on the Egyptian expedition, and sharing his radical opinions condemned the war against Revolutionary France as a 'mad crusade against opinions'.

145

At the age of 44 John Hely-Hutchinson was a reader and a scholar, intelligent and well informed. He had studied military theory, and his personal courage was proved. But he was no leader. Barely known to the army in Egypt, he had neither charm nor presence. He stooped and slouched, and his slovenly dress contrasted with the smart turn-out of Moore. This unsoldierly soldier, abstracted, reserved, and indolent, 'shunning general society', 'with ungracious manners and a violent temper', was unlikely to inherit the confidence the army had bestowed on Abercromby.[1]

And he was more than mistrusted: by many he was strongly disliked. Cooped up with him for weeks in the cabin of a ship of the line, his brother Kit had been dismayed by John's rudeness and ill-temper which threatened to wreck the successful career promised by his industry and his well trained mind. In conversation John's views were provocative, stubborn and aggressive, and he savaged anyone who disagreed. Christopher, a victim of his hurtful tongue, told him that 'even on the subject of the Gospels he would not converse with a decent reserve of temper'. Only the good humour and quick wit of the *Swiftsure's* captain, the admirable Ben Hallowell, averted a succession of inter-service rows. General Hutchinson's first General Order as Commander-in-Chief excited astonished disapproval when the army discovered that it ignored the death of his beloved predecessor; and it was typical of his failure as a communicator that many months were to pass before the arrival of the *London Gazette* revealed that his despatch on the battle of 21 March had recorded Abercromby's death with a moving panegyric. Colonel Brodie wrote that he was nearly as much disliked as Abercromby had been loved; and a diplomat complained of his 'nonchalance' as a correspondent and portrayed a 'naturally sullen countenance, bordering rather upon insult than reserve'.[2]

It was known in the army that Abercromby had valued his judgement and had applied for his appointment as second-in-command of the expedition; but during the fortnight's operations in Egypt he had changed his mind, and concluded that Hutchinson disliked responsibility and was unfit to succeed him as Commander-in-Chief. Lord Cornwallis would have agreed. 'I tremble for poor Hutchinson', he wrote on learning that he had succeeded to the command in Egypt: 'he is a sensible man, but he is no general – at least he was not one in 1798.' Swept along on this tide of disparagement, one stumbles with a jolt on the verdict of Moore: 'an accomplished man, and a man of sense'. Moore as usual was right. It was true that Hutchinson lacked the attributes of a leader; and even as a planner he would indecisively churn over all the facets of a problem. Yet he had brains and strategic judgement, and these qualities were needed in the situation the army faced after the Battle of Alexandria.[3]

For Hutchinson had inherited not a conclusive victory but a baffling military balance which called for patience, skill, and cunning. Six months later it would be possible to say, with Colonel Thomas Graham, that 'the 21st [of March] decided the fate of Egypt'. But when Hutchinson assumed command the battle's decisive consequences were not apparent. For there had been no harvest of prisoners and guns to crown the victory. Unable to pursue the defeated enemy, the British had collected a few hundred prisoners, a couple of guns, and a standard: insignificant trophies of a battle which had cost them 1,500 casualties or 12 per cent of their strength in action. They estimated the French losses at 3–4,000; but the British losses in the past fortnight and the ever-present sickness had reduced Hutchinson's force to little more than 9,000 'firelocks' in the field. The relative superiority of the French had actually increased since the landing.[4]

Faced with the complex terrain and the enemy's numerical superiority, Hutchinson had to feel his way from phase to phase, securing each foothold and testing the ground ahead. He had to keep his forces balanced, and avoid exposing detachments. This was not the style of generalship to appeal to an army which had tasted victory. It had taken the British only a fortnight to win a great battle and establish their moral ascendancy; yet it would require another five months to complete the task and clear Egypt. In the eyes of most of the army Hutchinson could do nothing right. 'We fear for the measures hereafter to be adopted', wrote Lord Dalhousie, 'the caution and wisdom of Sir Ralph cannot now guide us.'[5] In Abercromby caution was called sagacity: in Hutchinson, indecision.

The first need after the battle had been to strengthen the front against a renewed French offensive. Some 24-pounders were moved forward from the artillery park to the front of the Guards, and that evening Hutchinson warned the army to be ready for another night attack. The troops were to sleep under a blanket on their alarm positions, and not in their tents in the rear. Flints were checked and ammunition made up to sixty rounds per man, though the brigade commanders were warned not to waste scarce ammunition in the dark but to rely on the bayonet. If an attack was repelled the troops were warned not to follow the retiring enemy or be lured out of their defensive positions in the dark, and were reminded that the keys to a night battle were silence, order, and regularity. Hutchinson warned his men not to let their new sense of superiority undermine their prudence and discipline: 'with a little caution the British army in Egypt will find that they are invincible'.[6]

The night pickets were strengthened, and after a second night lying on the alarm positions the whole army continued to stand-to an hour before daylight. These short wakeful nights were followed by days of heavy toil dragging more guns into the forward positions, and carrying up not only provisions and fuel but vast quantities of ammunition to replenish the dumps emptied by the battle. Entrenchments were being dug to cover the whole front, including the open valley bottom whose defence on the morning of the 21st had cost so many lives. By early April nine redoubts were completed, requiring 1,200 men to man them, and the lines were now a formidable barrier.[7]

With heavy duties by day and pickets to mount by night, life was far from agreeable on the isthmus, which was infested with small snakes and scorpions. The nights with their frequent rotation of outpost duties were bitterly cold; and the days, often scorched by the hot sirocco wind, were made foul by the stench from shallow graves in the lines and unburied corpses of men and horses beyond the outposts. Filth was accumulating in the rear of some regiments, and orders had to be issued for butchers' offal to be buried at least three feet deep, or dumped far out in the lake. Officers had the privilege of keeping dogs in the camp, but in other respects they were little better off than their men: forbidden to use soldiers to carry their kits, and ordered to return their super-fluous baggage to the shipping.

There was a brighter side to this life, however. For some there was swim-ming in the clear Mediterranean from beaches strewn with beautiful shells. And now that the Arabs believed the British would win, local supplies flowed into the market to supplement the rations: sheep, poultry, pigeons, and excellent vegetables – spinach, lettuce, and onions. For some time there was not enough fuel for baking bread, and the army had to put up with biscuit and flour instead of fresh bread from the ovens. By early April, however, enough wood had been cut to allow the Commissary-General to supply the regiments regularly with the smoky palm wood. The camp behind the battle positions was garnished with trophies. In front of the tents French hats, caps, and helmets were stuck on pikes, some of them still covered with blood or full of the hair, skull, and brains of the late owner. As life became more comfortable in the tents, Hutchinson rejoiced that the uninhabited Aboukir isthmus had no houses to harbour vermin and disease.[8]

Whatever the discomforts in the British camp, they were no worse than what soldiers could expect in the field, and the troops were better off than the enemy. The British army was properly fed and had recently been reclothed; and desertion to the famished French was hardly an attractive option. Yet strangely, on three successive mornings in the vedette line a foreign trooper of Hompesch's Hussars made a dash across no-man's-land to join the enemy. The bad example could not be overlooked, because many of the infantry in Stuart's foreign brigade were deserters from the enemy and might go back. Hompesch's, commanded by the enterprising Major Robert Wilson, had served with credit as cavalry with the Reserve, but they had to go. Hutchinson ordered them to hand over their horses to the British cavalry and return to Aboukir for dismounted duties. They marched off in tears.[9]

In this fashion the army passed the fortnight after the battle, cooped up in the barren peninsula and grumbling at their commander's inactivity after one of the most brilliant victories since the Seven Years War. Yet Hutchinson's situation was far from straightforward, and when the guns fell silent on the battlefield of Alexandria he had little idea of how to complete the task which had been thrown into his hands by Abercromby's wound. The Cabinet instructions of the previous October were useless: he was supposed to capture Alexandria and occupy all the ports; but not to risk the health of his army by advancing into the interior. The Secretary of State had been confident that once Alexandria was captured the French forces in the interior would capitulate, for the evidence on his desk indicated their 'extreme and almost unanimous wish to go home'. Hutchinson was authorised to offer the Alexandria garrison a safe passage home to France, and to publicise the offer to the troops in the interior.[10]

But the real situation was not what Mr Dundas had imagined five months earlier in London. The French forces in Egypt were much larger than he had believed; and Alexandria was held not by a small demoralised garrison but by the enemy's field army led by its Commander-in-Chief, who was obstinately determined to hold on to Egypt. To starve the garrison was impossible, for the city remained open on the west and a deserter reported great quantities of flour and rice though meat was scarce and dear; yet with the present British resources it was inconceivable that the fortified city could be besieged and stormed. 'We keep the whole force of the French in check here', Hutchinson explained to Lord Elgin; 'we can do no more, it is impossible to go and attack them, they are probably as numerous as we are; and under the guns of Alexandria, according to the probabilities of war, an attack would not be successful and a defeat would be attended with ruin.' No senior officer seems to have disagreed. 'I do not think our force equal to the siege of Alexandria', wrote Coote, now second-in-command: 'What is to be done I know not'. Moore's view was identical. The government, he wrote, had been deluded about the enemy's strength; and, inferior as the British were in numbers and equipment, 'how is it possible we can force a strong position, and then carry on the siege of Alexandria?' It could be done only with reinforcements from home and the energetic co-operation of the Turks; and Moore, better than anyone, knew the deplorable state of the Grand Vizir's army.[11]

Perhaps bluff would work; and there was little to lose by testing the enemy's morale with Dundas's offer of repatriation. Though the Army of the Orient had served long together and shared a glorious history, there were enough signs of demoralisation to justify the experiment. The French attack on 21 March had been fuelled with liquor; and many of the prisoners were drunk, particularly one officer who entertained his captors with his tipsy staggering. At first the prisoners behaved 'in the most impudent manner'; but they were miserably clothed, and as they sobered up they seemed delighted to be in British hands. In the outposts the French cavalry vedettes were fraternising with the British sentries and complaining of their conditions.[12]

The bearer of the offer of repatriation was Sir Sidney Smith, who spoke French with fluency and charm. On the evening of 23 March he rode across to the French outposts with a flag of truce, and asked for the commandant of Alexandria. He was refused admission to the French lines, and handed over a letter in the names of Keith and Abercromby proposing the evacuation of the garrison to France. The reply, signed by General Friant as commandant of the city, pretended (though the British did not believe him) that Menou was not in Alexandria. He flatly rejected the British offer, and declared that the French would defend Egypt to the last extremity.[13]

But though the French command maintained its confident bearing, the soldiers in the line told a different story. While Sir Sidney was waiting for a reply he had chatted to the French outposts, who in the friendliest manner commiserated with the British over their coming occupation of this wretched land. In the following days Major Wilson often talked to the French vedettes who corroborated the miserable state of their army and its longing for home. On one occasion when he accompanied Lord Cavan to the British outposts and crossed over to the French vedettes, an officer galloped along the chain of mounted sentries forbidding them to talk to the Englishman. They ignored him, explaining with a shrug, '*Nous ne regardons pas nos officiers in telles affaires*'. Wilson gossiped with them for more than half an hour, and the drift of their talk was that 'there was only one man who was not anxious to return to France'. They meant the Moslem convert Menou – 'this haughty stubborn corpulent man', as a deserter described him.[14]

For the moment, however, Menou's determination was enough to hold his army together. His duty, defined by Bonaparte, was to hold out till reinforcements arrived or a peace treaty was signed. He remained loyal to the end to his patron Bonaparte, who would not prove ungrateful. Hitherto Menou had succeeded in containing the poison of homesickness and disillusionment on which the British government had relied to defeat him; and in battle discipline and courage had revived. Nevertheless he was aware that morale was fragile. Most of his units had now fought the British infantry and were reluctant to repeat the experience; and when he attempted to organise a fresh night attack it was made clear to him that his troops had had enough.

Even now a Bonaparte could have rallied the Army of the Orient and concentrated its scattered elements to fight again. But the French command was rife with dissension; and, knowing this, the soldiers regarded Menou as the single obstacle to their repatriation. His generals had no confidence in him, and Reynier's disloyal and insubordinate faction was still active. Menou took steps to strip him of his authority. Unit by unit Reynier's division was dispersed into other formations until he was left without troops, a vocal but powerless critic. Behind the Alexandria defences Menou could rely on his army to fight.[15]

14

'MUCH MORE AT EASE IN HIS COMMAND'

Across the stony plain of Sidi Gabir the two armies faced each other in dead-lock. What more could Hutchinson do to break it, now that his offer of repatriation had been rejected, an offer which his brother Christopher had regarded as ludicrous? If Menou was determined to sit tight in Alexandria and play for time, the British force might seal the eastern side of Alexandria and hope that enough reinforcements would arrive from Europe and India to allow siege-works to be opened. In the meantime the Grand Vizir might arrive from Palestine and deal with the remaining French forces in the interior – forces whose numbers Hutchinson greatly underestimated. For the moment he could see no surer course, and on the evening after the battle he sent off to Minorca and Malta for reinforcements from their garrisons. On 29 March he learned from an intercepted French vessel that Pitt had resigned and been succeeded by the ministry of Henry Addington, with Lord Hobart replacing Dundas at the War Department.[1]

It was soon apparent that the delays of submitting to Menou's waiting game were intolerable; and not only for the health of the troops in the flyblown Egyptian summer. Peace negotiations, the very reason for the army's presence in the east, could be hindered by delay; and the naval situation was also critical. Hutchinson received an alarmist letter from Lord Keith warning him that in no circumstances could the fleet remain in the shallow open roadstead of Aboukir after October; but the admiral wanted a much earlier end to the campaign, fearing the darkening international scene and the constant threat of a French relief expedition. Tsar Paul, as Keith knew, was planning to combine with France and partition the decayed Ottoman Empire; and the prospect had made Bonaparte more determined than ever to secure Egypt as part of his share of the loot. His troops were pushing down into the heel of Italy, where ports like Taranto afforded a short run for relief ships to Alexandria.[2]

Keith was barely beginning to perceive these wider threats when he learned that the Toulon fleet under Ganteaume was at sea again with troops on board. On 27 March, with Hutchinson's consent, he sent Admiral Bickerton out of the bay with six sail of the line to block Alexandria harbour against Ganteaume's reinforcements, leaving the residue of the fleet at anchor in the bay with the transport shipping, a vulnerable prey to a squadron attacking under sail as Nelson had attacked in '98. Worse news followed. On 6 April the *Pearl* frigate came in from the westward to report that Ganteaume's squadron, with hulls clean from harbour, had eluded Admiral Warren's barnacled ships in the western Mediterranean and was approaching the Egyptian coast. Keith made sail with his remaining ships of the line and joined Bickerton off Alexandria.

No wonder that the navy was racked by impatience at the slow pace ashore. When Bickerton put to sea, six days had passed since Abercromby's victory and the army was still static in the defensive position it had occupied before the battle. 'Neither army nor navy', Sir Alexander Cochrane confided to the Secretary of State Henry Dundas, 'have much confidence in General Hutchinson, who tho possessing many good qualities has not those necessary for the commander of an army.' Moore, wrote Cochrane, was 'our principal hope, and it will be well for General Hutchinson if he follows his advice'. 'Our operations drag along with more than Turkish languour', Captain Beaver of the *Foudroyant* complained on 7 April, even as Hutchinson was moving part of his force into position for an initiative to break the deadlock. As for the admiral, he was often beside himself with anxiety. 'Our progress is like the creeping of the snail', he grumbled on 21 April, a month after the battle of Alexandria at a moment when the strategic picture ashore was about to be transformed: '. . . Be assured our misfortune in Sir Ralph was great indeed and Moore's wound continuing so long ill is much felt by the army. . . . We go on very slowly here, are there no men of sense in our army, if so why not employ them?'[3]

This was perhaps wholly unfair. The admiral overlooked Hutchinson's strategic problems, his shortage of troops, and the operations actually under way: he ignored also the administrative difficulties of moving an army. Seamen carried their guns, ammunition, and provisions in ships which required only wind to propel them, and it had always been difficult for them to understand the problems of supplying war on land, with its train of horses and forage-wagons. It was in the face of Keith's uncomprehending criticisms that Hutchinson, lacking the confidence of his army and perhaps without much confidence in himself, doggedly pursued the cautious operations which circumstances demanded. On the very day when Keith put to sea to join Bickerton, he made his first move to break out of the barren Aboukir peninsula.

Hutchinson had neither the force, nor the mobility, nor the advantages of geography which would have enabled him to seize the initiative and impose his will on an active enemy. Menou still held an interior position between Hutchinson's army, the plague-stricken rabble of the Grand Vizir, and the British force believed to be approaching the Red Sea. And he had sufficient force to exploit this advantage. In the past the French had defended Egypt by taking the offensive with a mobile army; and Menou could still have assembled a decisive force if he had evacuated the minor posts of the interior and abandoned the city of Cairo, withdrawing the garrison to the citadel.

With this in mind Menou's generals urged several offensive plans, or so they later claimed. Bertrand advised him to concentrate all available force at Alexandria to attack and destroy the British: he calculated that 6,000 reinforcements could be brought in from Cairo, and even criticised Hutchinson for exposing his force on the over-extended Roman Camp position instead of falling back to the shorter line at Mandara. Reynier had a different proposal, and urged Menou to reconstitute the central *masse de manoeuvre* which Kléber had maintained at Rahmanieh. He would then have the choice of attacking the British, or driving the expected Turkish invasion back into the desert and gaining a year's security on the Palestine front.[4]

To assemble a field army at Rahmanieh would have meant reducing the Alexandria garrison; and Reynier argued that this could be done by withdrawing from the extended entrenchments on the heights of Nicopolis to a shorter line based on the Arab walls. But Menou would hear none of this. Rather than risk a bid for victory in the field, he would defend Egypt by static warfare, and win time for the arrival of Ganteaume's reinforcements or the signing of peace: '*Gagnons du temps, et nous nous tirerons d'affaire*'. Instead of regrouping the entire force in Egypt to regain the initiative, he ordered a few minor changes in his garrisons. Donzelot's remaining battalion in Upper Egypt was recalled; and instead of assembling an offensive *masse de manoeuvre* at Rahmanieh, he intended to collect there piecemeal a small force for the defensive role of guarding that communications centre where the routes from Alexandria converged with the Nile. The troops for the Rahmanieh force would be scraped out of Alexandria, Cairo, and the delta forts. The ostrich-vision which had blinded him before the British invasion now persuaded him that Hutchinson would remain inert, while the Grand Vizir would continue to lurk behind his desert barrier in Palestine.[5]

Hutchinson and his staff, however, were searching for a way to break the deadlock. The solution was not immediately obvious, given their unanimous agreement that with present resources the cost of storming the heights of Nicopolis was unacceptable. Yet eventually Alexandria would have to be taken, a point on which Anstruther harped obsessively to his chief: 'I never cease repeating to him that Alexandria is Egypt; at the same time all agree that the conquest will cost us dear. It is however what we must eventually come to'. But this advice merely expressed the dilemma without suggesting a solution; and Anstruther, who underestimated by two-thirds the enemy forces in the theatre, was taking a less realistic view than his commander.[6]

What initiatives were open? Though the French force was divided, neither part was immediately vulnerable. Alexandria with its garrison and fortifications was impregnable; and Cairo too distant until the Nile could be opened for the movement of British supplies and siege equipment. Even then the French would enjoy superior lateral communications between their forces unless they could be dislodged from the nodal point at Rahmanieh. Finally, the British lacked the numbers to contain one enemy force while they attacked the other: unless, that is to say, the Grand Vizir would supply additional force by pressing towards Cairo, but all the evidence indicated that his force was not capable of conducting a joint strategy, and at worst was a useless rabble.

Some staff papers retained by General Hope show several ideas being canvassed towards the end of March. A deliberate siege of Alexandria with concentrated resources? A secondary operation against Damietta to connect with the Vizir's advance? The navy was anxious to flood the dry bed of lake Mareotis. By cutting the canal banks which held back the waters of lake Aboukir, it was believed that a new lake up to ten feet deep could be formed. The inundation would open a vast extension to the range of British gunboats and supply boats; would cut off the French in Alexandria from supplies and reinforcements except by a long desert detour; and would protect the flank of the British lines. That it could be done, and that Menou feared it, was confirmed by a letter found on the body of General Roize.[7]

The flooding of the lake would overturn the military geography of the Alexandria front. The advantages were obvious; but Hutchinson's complex and diffident mind could see drawbacks too. No one could predict how far the rising salt water would extend, and with what economic consequences for Egypt. Though the new lake would allow the British army to manoeuvre by boat against the southern and western faces of the city, it would also strengthen the right flank of Menou's Nicopolis defences, and fill the dry canal to form a moat protecting the southern front. Moreover, while the supplies which were entering Alexandria across the dry bed of the lake would be stopped, so would much of the native provisions which were reaching the British market. Dwelling on these disadvantages, Hutchinson postponed the decision, at least till he could obtain alternative local supplies in the delta by opening a route through Rosetta. In the meantime the army and navy grumbled at the delay.[8]

Before any decision was taken, Hutchinson received an unexpected kind of reinforcement. On 26 March the Capitan Pacha appeared in the bay of Aboukir with three warships, followed by transports carrying 3,600 troops. He had already, two days before the battle, landed 500 soldiers, but they had not made a favourable impression: 'little better than a rabble', judged Captain Aeneas Anderson of the 40th, 'with a gaudy flutter about them, from the great number of their colours'. It would have been dangerous to integrate these untried irregulars into the British front, whatever their merits might be as skirmishers; and Abercromby had encamped them three miles behind the lines where they could cause no confusion.

The Turkish troops which appeared on 26 March, however, were of a different quality. The Capitan Pacha claimed that while 1,600 were irregulars as before, 2,000 were regular troops. On closer inspection Hutchinson confirmed that 1,200 of the new arrivals were Greeks or 'Albanians', trained and disciplined like European troops in two battalions under German officers. The Capitan Pacha, who came ashore to command the force, was the most vigorous and able Turkish official encountered by the British. The navy had been much improved under his command, and he was the only Turkish commander who had trained and disciplined his troops in any degree. With a predilection for everything European, he viewed the Grand Vizir with unconcealed contempt and intended to keep his own troops separate from the Vizir's.[9]

The Capitan Pacha seemed convinced that his arrival would induce the immediate surrender of the French; and on 29 March the offer of terms was renewed, in a letter signed by the Capitan Pacha, Keith, and Hutchinson, and delivered by Sir Sidney Smith, with the same result as before.[10] By now Hutchinson had been observing Menou's supine behaviour since the battle for more than a week and had confirmed the fragility of French morale; and a report had arrived, which he mistakenly believed, that the Grand Vizir had crossed the desert from Palestine and entered Egypt, as he had promised to do the moment the British had a firm foothold. The time seemed ripe for a probe to test the French response. Hutchinson resolved to push for Rosetta, where there was a small French garrison, using two and a half British battalions commanded by Colonel Brent Spencer, and the Capitan Pacha with his 4,000 Turks. The plan was tentative, and depended on how Menou would react. He might detach a force round the unmapped southern shore of lake Aboukir and attack Spencer at Rosetta; and for lack of cavalry Hutchinson would probably be unable to detect the movement. Spencer's orders were therefore to fall back if he met serious opposition.

If the operation went well, however, it would create new opportunities. Rosetta would give the British army access to the provisions and forage of the delta; it would open the western branch of the Nile to allied shipping; and it would, Hutchinson supposed, open a communication with the Grand Vizir and enable him to provide the British force with Turkish cavalry as he had promised. Beyond that, the possibilities were far-reaching. Depending on Menou's response, Hutchinson planned to strengthen Spencer's force and advance up the Nile against the communications centre at Rahmanieh, using the waterway to move his supplies and equipment. The capture of Rahmanieh would sever Menou's direct links with Cairo, Damietta, and the delta garrisons.[11]

Spencer's advance, scheduled to begin on 3 April, was delayed for three days by violent winds which lashed the troops' faces with sand, filled the tents with grit, and whipped up a storm in the bay which prevented the fleet from sending boats for the crossing of the two ferries on Spencer's line of march. But at length on 6 April, sixteen days after the battle of Alexandria, Spencer was able to begin his thirty-five-mile march to Rosetta, in command of the Queen's, 58th, the flank companies of the 40th, thirty mounted troopers of Hompesch's Hussars, and three guns. With them marched the Capitan Pacha and his 4,000 Turks. A mile and a half of narrow causeway took the force along the shore of lake Aboukir to the Blockhouse ferry, a crossing of nearly a quarter of a mile; thence to the caravanserai ferry at the mouth of lake Idku (Etko to the British of the day). Avoiding the beach with its debris of sun-bronzed corpses from the hospital ships, the little force marched across sultry desert country by day, lying at night in the open under a heavy dew in bitter cold. On the morning of 8 April they were in sight of Rosetta, with its fertile gardens and a glimpse of green and cultivated land in the delta beyond the Nile. A little to the south on the high sandhill of Aboumandour 800 French troops were drawn up; but as Spencer advanced, most of them crossed the Nile in native djerms and the rest retreated south towards El Hamed. Rosetta was occupied without a fight by the Queen's and 500 of the Capitan Pacha's Albanians, while the rest of the allied force advanced and pushed the French out of El Hamed. There Spencer took up a strong position with his flanks on the Nile and lake Idku to cover his next task, the clearing of the mouth of the Nile.[12]

A few miles downstream from Rosetta on the left bank the river was barred by Fort Julien, a low square Turkish work which had been repaired and improved by the French engineers. It was here in one of the thick bastioned towers that the French had discovered the Rosetta stone, the key to the ancient hieroglyphics of Egypt. The fort was garrisoned by a unit of *invalides* (in British parlance pensioners or Veterans) stiffened by a squad of infantry of the line from the 61st demi-brigade. Its heavy guns commanded the broad final reach of the Nile, with a distant view of the turbulent boghaz or bar where French gunboats blocked the passage from the open sea. The fort was now invested by Lord Dalhousie with the Queen's and 1,000 Turks.

Here in the navy's eyes was further delay. Eight days were consumed in investing the fort and preparing the bombardment, while Keith grumbled at the 'snail's pace' of the army. In reality the artillery commander General Lawson was working miracles to bring siege-guns up to the batteries and gunboats into the river. Robert Lawson was a typical artillery professional. With forty-three years' service behind him since he had entered the Royal Military Academy at Woolwich in 1758, he had risen slowly and predictably as Ordnance officers did, by seniority instead of purchase. In the American War he had invented a carriage to adapt mortars as field-howitzers; and in 1793 he had commanded the first experimental British horse artillery and devised their manoeuvres.

For the siege of Fort Julien he needed gunboats in the river. He could sail them some of the way on lake Idku, but the eastern end of the lake shelved to a depth of a few inches, and seven gunboats were dragged for three miles across sand and mud to be launched again from the banks of the Nile. For the siege batteries Lawson calculated that short-barrelled naval 24-pounder carronades, much lighter than the standard 24-pounders, would be sufficient to break up the fort's unhardened new cement and crumble the dusty local earth. The carronades were landed on the open seashore and dragged for four miles across desert and swamp to arm the batteries. To balance Moore's criticism of the artillery it is right to weigh the Herculean efforts of Lawson and his men with the siege train. They had already mounted seven 24-pounders for the siege of Aboukir castle, and had transhipped thirty more from the bay to the redoubts of the Roman Camp position. They would achieve much more before the campaign was completed.[13]

The British gunboats, launched into the Nile, soon forced the French gunboats to seek the protection of the fort, opening the bar at the mouth of the river to other British and Turkish gunboats which rapidly sank or blew up their opponents. On 16 April the arming of the batteries was complete, and Lawson's carronades opened fire against the south-west angle of the fort. Ammunition had to be conserved; but after two days' bombardment a section of the wall began to collapse, exposing the French gunners to Turkish sharpshooters. A newly completed mortar battery opened fire at 900 yards and dropped its bombs into the fort with astonishing accuracy, one shell bursting on the centre of the roof and tearing away the flagstaff and colours which were not replaced. At 11 a.m. on 19 April a white flag was cautiously raised above the parapet, and Fort Julien surrendered. Some 264 men grounded their arms on the glacis, and allied vessels could sail the Nile.[14]

While Colonel Spencer's operations were proceeding on the Nile, the Commander-in-Chief had been wrestling with the dilemma of flooding lake Mareotis. His strategic options would be governed by the decision. If the occupation of Rosetta was to lead to a major operation on the Nile, additional force would have to be taken from the Roman Camp position. Yet the garrison was already overstretched; and a further reduction could scarcely be afforded unless the left flank of the lines was secured by flooding. The new lake would moreover sever Menou's direct route to reinforce the Nile front against the British offensive.

Yet the consequences of cutting the dykes were incalculable. Anstruther feared the indeterminable extent of the flooding; and Moore was concerned that the flow of water would reduce the depth of lake Aboukir and hamper the British supply boats, by emptying the water into the lower levels of the new lake faster than it could be replaced from the sea. Hutchinson continued to doubt the advantages of the flooding even after it had been done, and remained convinced that it would have been wrong to do it before the occupation of Rosetta had opened the delta for supplies. According to his aide de camp Captain Proby he was never reconciled to cutting the dykes; but he yielded, wrote Moore, to the pressure of the army and navy against his own opinion.

These doubts about the long-term effects were outweighed by operational necessity: in Major Wilson's words, 'the urgency of the present service at last superseded general philanthropy'. This was scarcely fair to Hutchinson, whose doubts were based on reasons less nebulous than philanthropy. And he was beginning to see the way ahead as he gained confidence. 'General Hutchinson begins to feel himself much more at ease in his command', Anstruther reported on 5 April when the Rosetta expedition was under way, 'and if successful in his first operations will be induced to take bolder measures.' On 10 April news of the unopposed occupation of Rosetta cleared the way for an offensive on the Nile; and to release the necessary force he sanctioned the flooding of lake Mareotis. On 13 April the waters of lake Aboukir rushed through two cuts in the canal dyke, dropping in violent ten-foot cataracts which carried away three hundred feet of the banks. The flood spread slowly westwards towards the low horizon.[15]

The flank of the Roman Camp garrison was now secure, and on the same day the transfer of units to the Nile began. Between 13 and 17 April six battalions of infantry departed for Rosetta with the 12th Light Dragoons and the troop of the 11th Light Dragoons. Cradock and Doyle were sent to command brigades on the Nile; and on learning of the surrender of Fort Julien on the 23rd Hutchinson sent off his headquarters staff, and arrived in person on the Nile on the 26th looking far from well. Coote was left in command on the Alexandria front.[16]

For the next three months, from the end of April till the beginning of August, Coote was to hold a static front on the Aboukir isthmus, covering the British base against the enemy's main force in Alexandria and enabling Hutchinson to take the offensive on the Nile. Communication between the two British forces was swift and reliable, by bedouin couriers riding their own horses on the shortest route across the desert.

Coote's was not the glorious role, but it was a vital and an anxious one. The lines had been strengthened since the battle and were covered by breastworks and redoubts; and by the end of March there were fifty-six guns and howitzers in batteries. But the position was thinly manned, and there were no troops to form a reserve line. On 25 April Coote had 7,000 infantry fit for duty, and there came a time when sickness and the transfer of reinforcements to the Nile reduced his infantry to a bare 3,200 in the line, of whom 1,600 were the foreigners of Stuart's brigade. At this time Menou was thought to have 7,000 troops in Alexandria, and Admiral Ganteaume was attempting to land 3,000 reinforcements on the coast to the westward. If the Roman Camp lines were breached by these superior forces the British base at Aboukir would be swept away and Hutchinson cut off in the interior. 'Should an accident happen to my position', wrote Coote, 'our whole depot will fall.'[17]

Coote kept his force in a state of unremitting alert. With the enemy only fifteen minutes' march away the troops continued to stand-to under arms an hour before daylight, which by mid-June meant 3 a.m. Since the landing on 8 March Coote had never taken his clothes off at night, and for most of the day he was on horseback maintaining his troops in vigilant efficiency. His headquarters were moved forward close to Number 5 Redoubt on the crest of the ridge where he commanded a view of the whole encampment. A mile in front of the works British and French vedettes confronted each other at a distance of twenty yards, conversing politely, and officers visiting the two chains of sentries took off their hats to each other.

The fortifying of the lines continued under the direction of Captain Ford of the Royal Engineers, whose working parties toiled by day to consolidate the crumbling sand of the redoubts. On 21 May a post of 200 infantry, with twenty cavalry and two guns, was established at Beda beyond the breach in the canal dykes to protect the flow of Arab provisions to the market; but within three weeks this detachment had to be withdrawn to economise force when two more regiments were summoned to join Hutchinson on the Nile.[18]

Coote's left flank should have been secured by British gunboats patrolling the new lake; but the French had dragged their own gunboats across the isthmus east of Alexandria, and the British gunboat commander Captain Hand refused to reconnoitre the waters and dominate the enemy gunboats. Coote appealed to Lord Keith, who supported Hand and refused to transfer control of the gunboats to the army though he was himself twenty miles away in Aboukir bay. There was no point, he told Coote, in wearing down the boats and seamen on the lake by cruising and reconnoitring before active siege operations began. Colonel Thomas Graham later described Keith's refusal as 'very proper'; but Coote was bitter, and warned the admiral that if Menou received reinforcements across the lake from Cairo it was on Keith that the blame would rest.[19]

But blaming Keith for his anxiety was small consolation to the general as he rode out before daybreak on his daily inspection of the line. On 23 June one ill effect of the navy's refusal was apparent when Coote noticed water creeping across the low swampy ground on his left front. Unimpeded by British gunboats, French working parties had breached the bank of the canal, now filled with water from lake Aboukir. A flood was released across the British front; and if the inundation was allowed to flow to the limits of the low ground a future attack on Alexandria would be restricted to a narrow front and the reoccupation of the dominant Green Hill made difficult.

Coote reacted swiftly, pushing his vedettes across the marsh and supporting them with a strong picket of infantry and cavalry and two light 3-pounders. Under their protection a working party 600 strong was marched down from the lines at nightfall to start work on a dam to contain the creeping waters. At midnight they were joined by a further 200 labourers, and the work continued till daylight. It was resumed on succeeding nights till an earth dyke 300 yards long, thirty feet wide and seven feet high was completed, covered by two 24-pounders in a redoubt at its rearward end.[20]

The major medical scourge was ophthalmia, which at one period infected a third of Coote's force: by the end of the campaign 160 men of the army in Egypt were blinded and the sight of many more was permanently damaged. More deadly was the plague which broke out in the Aboukir hospitals. To prevent the infection from spreading to the lines Coote posted a quarantine chain of sentries across the neck of the isthmus at Mandara; and with strict enforcement of cleanliness the plague was kept out of the camp till it died away in the hot weather.[21]

Aside from the long hours of duty and the diseases, new arrivals discovered that life in the camp outside Alexandria was better, at least for officers, than they had been warned to expect. Even in the hot season the weather on the coast was bearable, with cool nights and a sea breeze from the north-east to freshen the heat of the day. Shelters of palm fronds provided shade from the burning sun; the thermometer rarely rose much above 85 degrees; and at sunset the evening began to cool and there was an hour for pleasant riding before dark.

To bring provisions forward across the fine deep sand from the Commissary's lakeside depot, a train of camels and mules was organised with a corps of Armenian drivers. Relief from the salty monotony of the army rations was provided by the native market which was improving daily, as the 'nasty looking Arabs' brought in their scrawny poultry, thin lop-eared sheep, and fresh mullet. The fruit – oranges, grapes, melons, and apricots – was excellent. The railed enclosure swarmed with Arabs and their asses which had brought the provisions forty miles from the delta. 'Not many luxuries but very comfortable', was Colonel Dyott's verdict after dining with Coote on the night of his arrival from England. Apart from the swarming flies and the shortage of cash, life would have been very tolerable; but for eight months no pay was received. Unless officers lent cash from their private means (losing more than 20 per cent on the exchange) there was nothing but salt rations for the soldiers. The French should have requisitioned the fresh grapes and melons and the supply would have dried up: the British had to pay or go without, but at least the supply continued.[22]

Coote seems to have been a popular commander. Arriving from England, Captain Dalrymple thought him 'one of the pleasantest men I ever met with. Shook me in so friendly a way by the hand. His open frank manners have much endeared him to the troops'. But in the fleet there was rising discontent with Keith. Much of the trouble, as usual, was about prize money. Officers from the *Ajax* and *Northumberland*, detached ashore on dangerous and exhausting duties with the army, found that their shipmates still on board were disinclined to allow them their share in the ships' prizes; and ships supporting the army in Aboukir bay feared that they would be denied a share of the prize money won by those cruising off Alexandria. Keith settled both complaints judiciously, ordering that the ships in the bay should be treated as part of the blockading force, and instituting a ten-day rota for officers' shore duty. More prolonged trouble, venomously aimed at Keith in person, was instigated by Sir Alexander Cochrane and Captain Hallowell over the price of shoes and the supply of vegetables to the sick. On both issues the Admiralty eventually supported Keith and formally censured his critics; but one may doubt whether the reverberation of these discontents would have travelled as far as Whitehall if Nelson or St Vincent had been in command. 'We stand much in need of such a man as Lord St Vincent', the exasperated General Coote remarked during the gunboats' dispute; a sentiment not perhaps shared by naval officers, who knew what short shrift St Vincent would have allowed them for their insolence.[23]

Inevitably there was trouble with Sir Sidney Smith; but feelings in the fleet and army were mixed when on 25 April he was ordered to return to his ship and relinquish his command of the seamen serving ashore and on the Nile. The ostensible reason was that the enemy fleet was expected and he was needed on board the *Tigre*; but his admirers attributed his removal to 'some low intrigue'. The fact of the matter was that Keith and Hutchinson had been forced to sack Sir Sidney for a characteristic piece of impudence. The taste for diplomacy he had acquired at Constantinople had earlier led to a clash with Nelson; and the Grand Vizir and Capitan Pacha harboured deep resentment of his role in the abortive Convention of El Arish, the repudiation of which by the British government they blamed for the Turkish defeat at Heliopolis. Smith's latest impertinence was to inform the Grand Vizir after his mission to Friant that he had been authorised to offer peace to the French. Hutchinson disavowed Sir Sidney and assured the Grand Vizir that he had been no more than the bearer of a letter; but the Capitan Pacha insisted on Sir Sidney's removal to his ship. His large head with its crop of black hair was seen no more ashore, and he was replaced by Captains Morrison and Stevenson.

Sir Sidney's charm and enterprise deceived those who knew him only by his reputation for courage and by the tales of his own claque of admirers; but the senior army officers seem to have been relieved by his departure. One of his gaffes had been to station Turkish troops in front of the British right wing without authority after the battle of 21 March, a potential source of confusion. 'All who . . . have acted with him', a diplomat accompanying the army informed Lord Elgin, 'were constantly thwarted by his ill-timed interference, and have never found him of the smallest use. Others who knew him by his reputation for gallantry and bravery, and had listened to the romantic tales of his followers have looked up to him as the Hero of the Army, and the person to whom we owe our conquest of the country.'[24]

15

THE THRUST ON THE NILE

Menou's first response to the fall of Rosetta was to dispatch General Valentin with a small reinforcement to recapture the town. But he soon realised that he had underestimated the British thrust, and on 14 April he sent his chief of staff Lagrange with further reinforcements to take command on the Nile front. Lagrange reached Rahmanieh on 17 April and on the following day marched down the river to El Aft, where he joined Valentin and began to entrench the position with 3,900 men.

Menou's critics were urging him to concentrate his force on a single front and take the offensive; but instead he was dispersing his field army in three separated groups at Alexandria, El Aft, and Cairo, each of them too weak to attack. His purpose was to impose delay, for his hopes of victory did not rest on his own resources but on Admiral Ganteaume's relief expedition from Toulon. Ganteaume was indeed on his way. After two abortive departures he had sailed again on 25 April, with orders to land 5,000 troops at Derna on the Libyan coast. If they could have been landed close to Alexandria on the western side of the city Coote's situation would have become critical; but a desert march of 500 miles from Derna was lunacy. Perhaps Bonaparte hoped that local craft could be found to ferry them along the coast; but his plan was not to be tested. On 8 June Ganteaume landed a few soldiers on the coast of Cyrenaica; but they met a hostile reception from the natives, and Ganteaume, alarmed by the sails of a British convoy which he mistook for Keith's squadron, re-embarked his troops and ran for home.

Menou had long been counting on his arrival; and as the days crept past without news of the French fleet he gave way to anguish. '*Mais Ganteaume, Ganteaume, où est-il? Qu'a-t-il fait?*', he demanded of the Minister of Marine on 3 May: 'Egypt would have been saved . . .' Was his delaying strategy to be in vain? Four days later his spirits surged again at unofficial news of peace negotiations, and he issued an upbeat Order of the Day: 'Courage, patience and energy, brave soldiers! Remember the importance of Egypt in the balance of the negotiations'.[1]

Here he touched on the crux. Hold on and all may be well, Egypt may yet remain French. But the defeatists had to be contained, and within the week he struck a decisive blow at his anti-colonist opponents. In the night of 12 May a force of infantry and cavalry led by Destaing, with a gun and a party of sappers, surrounded Reynier's house. Reynier and his gang were arrested, embarked in the *Lodi* brig, and deported to France. The opposition was left leaderless.[2]

Till 5 May Alexandria had continued to be supplied across the lake-bed by great convoys of 4–500 camels, though much of their burthen was forage for the army's horses. But on 5 May the flood waters creeping across lake Mareotis reached the coast at the Tour des Arabes twenty-five miles west of Alexandria, and camel convoys became more difficult.[3] The meagre rations were augmented with horse meat and camel. None but fighting men were now wanted in the garrison, and Menou was dismayed by the unexpected arrival from Cairo of the *savants* of the Commission of Sciences and Arts. In terror of the raging plague and the approaching Turks, the scholars had persuaded General Belliard to send them away, and on 16 April they embarked in a provision-convoy on the Nile. Arriving at the unloading point at Rahmanieh, they were ill received by the commandant who wanted to return them to Cairo; a fate from which they were saved by Colonel Cavalier of the dromedary corps, who escorted them through the spreading waters of the lake on camels which sank to their knees in liquid mud.

The unhappy *savants* did not find life to their taste in the blockaded city, and after a few weeks of camel-meat they asked to be sent home to France. Menou was happy to be rid of these useless mouths and embarked them in *L'Oiseau*. When the ship sailed after a month's delay, the captain confiscated all their letters and papers and dumped them overboard to prevent a leak of information to the enemy; a wise precaution, for the ship was immediately intercepted by the British sloop *Cynthia* and taken into Aboukir bay, where Lord Keith refused them passage. He would not allow Menou to shed useless mouths from a city under blockade, and ordered *L'Oiseau* back to Alexandria. Menou greeted the returning *savants* with fury. The ship was anchored under the guns of a frigate and ordered to sail in a quarter of an hour or be sunk: '*le commandant a ordre de vous foutre à fond*', in the elegant words of the Commander-in-Chief. Time ticked past, Menou paced the quay with watch in hand, the frigate's guns were run out; and five minutes from perdition the scholars joined the sailors at the capstan, the anchor was raised, and the ship sailed. Again she was intercepted, but this time Keith threatened to land her passengers on the desert coast and burn her, and Menou agreed to readmit them to Alexandria. When the message arrived Sir Sidney Smith was on board *L'Oiseau*, chatting in French and picking up information, and there was a farcical rush of scholars to board his boat from the crowded gangway. Under the loaded guns of the *Cynthia*, *L'Oiseau* was forced out of Aboukir bay and returned to Alexandria, where the *savants* were conscripted into the *Garde nationale* for internal duties.[4]

While Menou prepared to stand a siege, the British initiative had been developing on the Nile. When Hutchinson set out on 21 April to assume the command at Rosetta, he was acting on premature information of the progress of the other allied forces. He had heard that General Baird's force, which was reported to be 5–6,000 strong, was approaching Suez; and that the Grand Vizir's army from Palestine had already crossed the desert to Salahieh and might even have reached Damietta and Cairo. The Vizir in fact was not yet across the desert, though he reached Salahieh a week later; and the news of Baird was wholly misleading, as will appear, though the belief that he was about to land at Suez was to exert a constant pull on Hutchinson's strategy.

By advancing up the Nile and dislodging the French from Rahmanieh, Hutchinson would deprive Menou of his interior position between the British and the Grand Vizir. He would also sever the supply chain which connected Menou's army in Alexandria with the arsenal at Cairo and the provisions of the delta. At the river depot at Rahmanieh, supplies coming down the Nile from Cairo were transhipped on to camels and carried overland to Alexandria, shielded from interception by the superior French cavalry. Hutchinson assumed that when Rahmanieh fell Lagrange's force would fall back into Alexandria. Hutchinson's army would then close in and besiege the city while the Grand Vizir and General Baird dealt with the isolated Cairo garrison, aided by British siege-guns which would be sent up the Nile to bombard the citadel.[5]

If Hutchinson played his cards with skill, the converging allied forces would divide the French and drive their separate parts into corners where they could be trapped and destroyed. The one thing which could save them from the remorseless allied pressure was a daring counterstroke; and Hutchinson, aware of the Revolutionary armies' boldness and speed, was determined not to expose his force to a defeat. He intended to gain his objects with the least risk and at the lowest cost; for he could not afford casualties, and a British reverse would be disastrous for the confidence of the Turks. Dining with the convalescent Moore at Rosetta, he confided that he 'would be cautious of risking what, with a little patience, would be rendered certain; as a check of any kind to us in our present circumstances might have most serious consequences'. The remark explains much about the subsequent operations. Hutchinson had no margin of superiority over the French, who were 'much more inured to the climate and to every sort of fatigue' and likely to remain much healthier than the British. With only 5,000 British troops on the Nile, many of whom would fall sick, he had to rely on the Capitan Pacha's 4,000 Turks and auxiliaries.

In these he had no confidence: 'they are not even the shadow of an army . . . without officers, order or discipline. . . . It is a fearful experiment to act with them. But bad as they are we must make use of them, we have no other resource'. The speed of Hutchinson's operations would be regulated by the

ROSETTA TO CAIRO: THE NILE OPERATIONS, MAY–JUNE

Lake Bourlos

Rosetta

Aboukir

Damietta

Lake Aboukir

Alexandria

Lake Edku

El Hamed
8 April

Dairut
6 May

El Aft
8 May

Disuq

Lake Mareotis

Canal

Damanhur

Rahmanieh
9 May

River Nile Damietta Branch

El Mansura

Shubra
11 May

River Nile Rosetta Branch

Kafr Houdig
12 May

Tanta

Mit Ghamr

To Salahieh

Algam
16 May

Canal

Minuf

Benha

Bilbeis
Grand-Vizir
11 May

Lockmas
4 June

Birchamps

To Suez

Wardan
6 June

Charlahan

El Khanka
16 May

Burtus
9 June

Heliopolis

Cairo
Armistice 22 June

Giza
Old Cairo

0   25

miles

Pyramids

River Nile

progress of Baird and the Grand Vizir; and if the pace he set was slow, he pointed out that the peace negotiators at home could already assert that 'our allies and we have full as much of the country as the French'.[6]

By advancing up the Nile Hutchinson was flouting his government's warning against pushing into the interior. The risk was justified because the climate had hitherto been healthier than the Secretary of State had feared, and local supplies more plentiful. Though the British force had only a hundred draught horses and camels to haul its guns and carry its ammunition and stores, the shortage of land transport could be overcome by using the river, on whose surface the native djerms skimmed under their huge pairs of striped lateen sails with five or six tons of cargo.[7]

River transport was organised by Captain Stevenson of the *Europa*, ferrying stores from Aboukir bay through the furious breakers of the bar which drowned eight British seamen in two days. The shallow bar prevented heavy gunboats from entering the river to oppose the strong French gunboats, well constructed with musket-proof mantlets to protect the gunners. Captain Stevenson had to make do largely with adapted flatboats whose crews had no protection from small arms fire. On the subject of the gunboats, and a shortage of transport craft in the river, Hutchinson started another acrimonious correspondence with Lord Keith. The Admiral retorted that the Quartermaster-General was ignorant of water transport and mistaken in his calculations; Hutchinson countered with the *tu quoque* that it was Keith's figures which were wrong.[8]

Hutchinson was still short of cavalry for the open country ahead. Six hundred horsemen sent by the Grand Vizir were a rabble of the worst description; and the 500 mounted British light dragoons were still poorly horsed and no match for the French. To support them General Lawson applied his experience with horse artillery, and improvised a troop of light 3-pounders with the gunners riding on the caissons and the off-side draught horses. Ammunition camels were too slow to keep up with this flying artillery, and in action they were often reluctant to kneel down to unload and became unmanageable. Lawson replaced them with four-horse curricles by converting the hand-carts which had been made at Marmaris. Guns and curricles survived the long road to Cairo, and Lawson believed that they 'gave considerable confidence to the Dragoons'.[9]

By the early days of May the preparations on the Nile were complete. On 4 May three days' rations were issued; ammunition was completed to sixty rounds per man with two good spare flints; and on the following morning the advance to Rahmanieh began. The British marched in two columns while the Turks trailed behind in their own disorder, in a 'most laughable procession' under their innumerable flags and colours. On the further bank of the river Colonel William Stewart of the 89th was advancing level with the main body at the head of a small battle-group composed of his own regiment, twenty troopers of the 12th Light Dragoons, a detachment of artillery, and 1,200 Albanians. His task was to sweep the right bank of the river and clear the way for allied gunboats and djerms.[10]

Table 7 British order of battle on the Nile, 5 May

Cradock's brigade: 8th, 18th, 79th, 90th
Doyle's brigade: 2/1st, 30th, 50th, 92nd
Reserve (Col. Spencer): Queen's, 58th, 40th (flank companies), Corsican Rangers
Stewart: 89th
Cavalry: 11th Light Dragoons (50), 12th Light Dragoons (380), 26th Light Dragoons (80)

Winding along the course of the Nile, the army advanced seven miles to Dairut. That night all ranks slept as usual in their clothes, and the soldiers in their accoutrements. At three o'clock in the morning they were under arms for an early start before the heat of the day, for the hot weather had arrived and they had left the sea-breezes of Alexandria. Three or four miles ahead the French were entrenched at El Aft. In the course of the day the position was outflanked by Colonel Stewart's progress beyond the river and a passage was cleared for the British gunboats through a barrier of sunken vessels. Outnumbered and outflanked, Lagrange evacuated his entrench-ments during the night, retiring with about 2,300 infantry and 5–600 cavalry; but he failed to clear all his boats up river, and Stewart intercepted thirteen djerms laden with rice and stores. Some Albanians pushing ahead overtook five French soldiers and brought in their severed heads to claim a reward. Hutchinson protested warmly and the Pacha issued a severe order against the practice; but the Turks had not forgotten Bonaparte's massacre of prisoners on the beach at Jaffa and head-hunting was not extinguished. Its effect on French morale was salutary.

The Nile valley was a fertile and fascinating country after the bleakness of the Aboukir peninsula and the Idku desert: a rich alluvial plain more like the Po valley than the bare polders of North Holland which many remembered. Trees and orchards, lines of poplars, and tall pigeon houses of mud-brick broke the levels of the delta. The green fields of wheat and barley were inter-spersed with plots of melons and cucumbers, maize and tobacco. Everywhere ingenious pumping machines, driven by a circling ox or ass, a camel, or a blindfolded horse, raised the green Nile water into the irrigation canals and ditches which criss-crossed the fields. Yet in this benign countryside the condition of the friendly, warm-hearted peasantry shocked the British troops. Crushed by oppressive taxes through untold centuries, huddling in mud-walled villages against the marauding bedouin, they dwelt in hovels which made the cabins of the Irish seem like palaces. To avoid infection

British soldiers were forbidden to enter the villages, and the huts left by the French troops were burned. But in spite of precautions sickness began to increase. Flies swarmed on food and faces; and scorpions infested the sand on which the troops slept, stinging three men of the Queen's in one night. Instead of the sand-filtered water of the Aboukir wells there was only the raw Nile to drink; 'muddy and dark but tastes very well',[11] a highland officer conceded, putting from his mind the clear burn water of his native hills.

From El Aft it was a distance of only a dozen miles to the communications centre at Rahmanieh, the objective of the British offensive. Here Lagrange was now posted, and he was expected to fight for this key to French strategy. A captured commissariat statement showed that his force was now 3,000 infantry and 800 cavalry, and the position was reported to be strong though Hutchinson possessed no map of the terrain. The French right flank was supposed to rest on the Nile, backed by the fort which protected the French magazines; and the front facing the British advance was covered by the dry bed and banks of the Alexandria canal. Hutchinson's intention was to push forward on the 9th and close with the enemy's position; to make a thorough reconnaissance, and attack on the following day.[12]

At daybreak on 9 May the approach march began, and by eleven o'clock Hutchinson was able to reconnoitre the French position. What he saw was as disconcerting as the discovery had been in the battle of Mandara of the long open plain of Sidi Gabir. At Rahmanieh the French were not aligned on the Alexandria canal to face the British advance. Instead Lagrange had occupied a position with his back to the Nile, covering the Rahmanieh depot with both flanks resting on the river. His front was entrenched, with thirty-three field-guns and seventeen heavier pieces in place. The French situation was wholly unexpected, and required a rapid recasting of the British plans.

Though apparently strong, Lagrange's was not a tenable position. With a depth at one point of only 150 yards between his entrenched front and the river in his rear, it would become unendurable for the defenders as soon as Colonel Stewart's force on the opposite bank could bring artillery to bear in their rear across the hundred yards of water. Moore, when he later examined the ground, was convinced that the French commander had never intended to fight there, though he had lingered a little too long for safety.[13] Moore's hindsight was correct. Lagrange was making his final preparations to withdraw up the river to Cairo.

But of this Hutchinson had no suspicion. In spite of some indications of Lagrange's real intentions, he still assumed that if the French retreated they would make for Damanhur and Alexandria; and this might well have been the more dangerous outcome for the British. If Lagrange's force had reached Alexandria Menou could have attacked Coote long before Hutchinson could arrive on the Aboukir position by the long detour through Rosetta. Hutchinson's impression was confirmed when French cavalry were seen moving out from the Rahmanieh entrenchments and along the Alexandria canal.

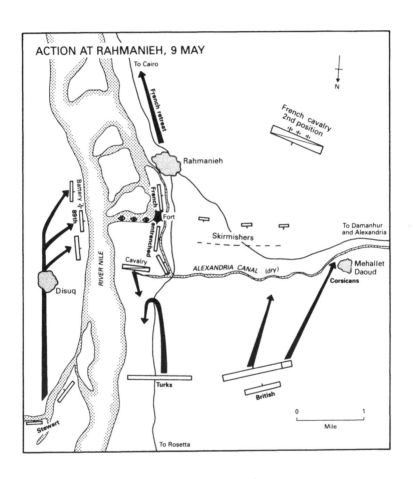

ACTION AT RAHMANIEH, 9 MAY

To Cairo

N

French retreat

French cavalry
2nd position

Rahmanieh

Battery

89th

French entrenched

Fort

Skirmishers

To Damanhur
and Alexandria

RIVER NILE

Cavalry

ALEXANDRIA CANAL (dry)

Mehallet
Daoud

Disuq

Corsicans

Turks

British

Stewart

0   1

Mile

To Rosetta

Lagrange appeared to have changed his plan of defence and to be holding the line of the canal to cover a retreat to Damanhur. His cavalry made a show of a serious counter-attack. Four squadrons advanced, supported on their flanks by sharpshooters whose shots were flying round the British infantry. Trumpets were sounding the charge, when the cavalry suddenly wheeled to right and left, unmasking eight horse artillery guns which caught the infantry in squares to resist cavalry. As the French artillery opened fire at close range the regiments hastily deployed into line, returned the fire, and forced the artillery to retire.

The British infantry now remained deployed, with the Queen's still in column to protect the right flank; and Hutchinson proceeded with his reconnaissance and made his plan. His aim was to place himself on the flank of the French escape route towards Alexandria, with his line beyond the canal and his right occupying Mehallet Daoud. He could then wait for Colonel Stewart's advance on the further bank of the Nile to bolt Lagrange into his waiting jaws.

There is no evidence that this manoeuvre was intended to force Lagrange away from Alexandria and deflect him towards Cairo; indeed Hutchinson seems to have thought only of intercepting Lagrange and bringing him to battle, an outcome for which he counted on Stewart's force beyond the river. Stewart was by now making good progress to close the trap. He had begun his advance at 5 a.m., and after marching some five miles and being reconnoitred by a group of French officers, he encountered three or four hundred French infantry and artillery which had been sent across the river to oppose him. It was possible that these might be reinforced to a strength which could overwhelm him, and he halted to wait for the supporting fire of his gunboats which had been stopped at dawn by a dead calm on the river. At 8 a.m. the expected breeze arose; the gunboats set their sails and pushed up the river; and Stewart's 89th Regiment advanced boldly and drove the enemy back across the Nile. With the way cleared, Captain Adye of the Royal Artillery brought up field-guns to the river bank, trapping seventy laden djerms which were trying to escape from Rahmanieh harbour; and work was begun on a battery for heavier cannon to bombard Lagrange's rear. In the late afternoon Hutchinson learned that the guns would be ready to open fire in eight hours' time.

He was now ready for his own advance. Time had been expended in reconnaissance, and in deploying the British force in response to the French cavalry; and it was nearly four o'clock in the afternoon when the line of infantry rose and moved forward, through level cornfields which had been set ablaze by cannon fire. The French cavalry hovered and skirmished, and the shot from their horse artillery flew through the British ranks. The line marched on, the canal was crossed, and the Corsican Rangers occupied Mehallet Daoud. Soon, Hutchinson knew, Lagrange's position would become untenable.

Evening was drawing on. The French had successfully occupied the British force during daylight and remained active into the dusk, with an attack on the Turks opposite the Rahmanieh fort which caused confusion and required a rapid move to the left by Doyle's brigade. The front was stabilised, darkness fell, and the sharpshooting died down. Lagrange was ready to go, and while Hutchinson planned for the destruction of the French on the morrow they stole silently into the night. They abandoned the djerms trapped in Rahmanieh harbour, and left forty men in the fort to protect their sick and wounded, besides a handful of drunken looters in the stores. They had sunk their gunboats, overturned their heavy artillery into the river, and destroyed their ammunition; but in the magazines they abandoned a huge quantity of provisions which were not so easy to spoil as powder. When day broke on 10 May the French lines were empty and a white flag was flying over the Rahmanieh fort.[14]

16

THE VERGE OF MUTINY

With the flag of truce flying over Rahmanieh, Hutchinson had gained the object of his offensive, the key to the enemy's communications; and gained it at a cost of only thirty casualties. Small gratitude had he earned from his army, however. There had been much impatience at the delay in starting the advance from Rosetta, an agitation which took no account of the transport problems which had to be surmounted. 'We are sadly in want of a Sir Charles Stuart', Colonel Paget had complained on the day before the start of the advance, comparing Hutchinson's delay after the fall of Fort Julien with General Stuart's bold and swift capture of Minorca three years earlier. Many officers were now beside themselves with frustration at Lagrange's escape. They held that if Hutchinson had begun his march earlier in the day, or had pushed on when he met the enemy, he would have had time to wheel his army to the left and pin Lagrange's force against the Nile.[1]

Was this a brilliant opportunity thrown away by Hutchinson's dilly-dallying? Lagrange, trapped against the river and enfiladed by Stewart's artillery, would have had no choice but to sortie against Hutchinson and try to fight his way out, or capitulate like Cornwallis twenty years earlier at Yorktown when he too had been trapped in earthwork defences with his back to a river. Lagrange would have been destroyed, Menou's command ripped asunder, and the ultimate fate of Egypt decided.

There were some who argued that Hutchinson should have assaulted the French entrenchments before darkness cloaked their flight. But Hutchinson had not timed his approach march with the intention of attacking that day; and a long wheeling manoeuvre to face the Rahmanieh entrenchments would have left little daylight in which to organise and launch an attack on a fortified position. Such an assault would have invited the costly repulse which Hutchinson had resolved to avoid; and as Moore concluded, 'if we had attacked it improperly, we might have been worsted'.[2]

The envelopment without the assault might seem more alluring; but it would have involved a change of front in the presence of an aggressive enemy with superior cavalry, a difficult manoeuvre which would have had to be executed in large part by Turks who were half-trained or worse. Had it succeeded, the allied army would then have had to hold a three-mile front through the night; a cordon too lightly manned to be proof against a sortie by Lagrange's mobile troops. It would not have been difficult for them to break out through the Turks on the allied left, and then outmarch the British – to whom, as Kit Hutchinson confessed, 'they were as superior in marching, as the British were to them in many more essential points'.[3] Covering their retreat with their cavalry and horse artillery, they could have joined Menou in Alexandria to attack Coote, or marched down the Nile to destroy Hutchinson's base and means of supply.

Neither of these courses, the assault or the envelopment, seems to have been urged on Hutchinson during the action; nor did Moore find them plausible. The most he thought Hutchinson could have achieved, and then only if he had begun his approach on the previous day, would have been to harass Lagrange's rearguard and pick up a few guns. How much could really have been done is doubtful, given the direction of Lagrange's flight to the southward and the speed of his march. Critics quickly forgot the exhaustion of the British infantry after sixteen hours of marching and skirmishing on the hottest day they had yet experienced.[4]

But the army which Abercromby had forged was bursting with confidence. Nothing could deter them. Marching with the 79th Highlanders at Rahmanieh was Lieutenant Patrick Ross, the son of a Jacobite hero of the 'Forty-five. On 21 March his arm had been amputated close to the shoulder; but refusing to be evacuated to Britain, he had mounted picket with his regiment five weeks later on 25 April before the skin had closed over his stump. 'We have men that would conquer hell itself', an officer wrote.[5]

Little did men in this frame of mind care that Hutchinson had gained his strategic objective cheaply. They could see only that the enemy had survived to fight again. 'Never was so fair an opportunity lost of a dashing action, completely surrounding their 4,000 men', Dalhousie complained in his journal: 'But we now find the loss of Sir Ralph'.[6] Of the larger picture the army knew little and cared less. They weighed neither the strategic gain, nor the damage a reverse would have inflicted on Turkish confidence, nor the crippling effect of heavy British losses.

At dawn on 10 May, as the French came out from the fort to negotiate a capitulation, the way ahead for Hutchinson seemed clear. He appears to have assumed that Lagrange's southward retreat towards Cairo was a feint, and that he would make a circuit in the desert to regain the Alexandria road. With the spinal cord which connected the enemy forces in Alexandria and Cairo broken, the next task was to turn back and drive Lagrange into Alexandria, closing the ring round Menou. The enemy's field army would then be trapped inside a besieged city, while to the southward Belliard's garrison in Cairo was believed to be a minimal force[7] which could safely be left to the Grand Vizir and General Baird. At midday, however, Lieutenant Drake of the 12th Light Dragoons rode into camp with news to overturn these hopes. He had been out with a watering party of thirty men when he heard firing; and riding to the sound they came upon fifty well-mounted French cavalry surrounded by sharpshooting Arabs. Their tormentors hung round the French like a swarm of bees and were picking them off one by one; and, astonished by the sight of the British dragoons, they gratefully surrendered. They had been escorting an officer with despatches from Alexandria to Cairo, and had made a circuit into the desert to bypass the Corsican Rangers at Mehallet Daoud. Interrogated, they revealed that they had seen no sign of Lagrange's troops on the Alexandria road. Hutchinson, who had spent the morning arranging the capitulation of the French fort, now did what perhaps he should have done at dawn, and sent General Doyle to reconnoitre towards Damanhur on the Alexandria road with the 12th Light Dragoons and a regiment of foot. Doyle found no sign of Lagrange, who was retiring by rapid marches towards Cairo.[8]

Lieutenant Drake's information confronted Hutchinson with the most racking choice of the campaign: to pursue Lagrange, or return to Alexandria. The Secretary of State's instructions had emphasised Alexandria as the key to Egypt, and had warned against pressing into the interior; and the longer the French held the port, the greater the risk that reinforcements would reach them from France and enable Menou to overwhelm Coote and the Aboukir base.

Yet if strategy and policy required the capture of Alexandria, operational imperatives now demanded the elimination of Cairo. Lagrange would provide Belliard with a *masse de manoeuvre* in a key position between the Turks and British. And to judge by the troops of the Capitan Pacha no Turkish force was fit to face the French without British support. Though his Albanian battalions were not contemptible, especially since their training had been improved by Colonel Lindenthal's appointment as their Quartermaster-General, the action at Rahmanieh had demonstrated the incapacity of Ottoman troops as a whole to face Europeans. As for the rabble headed by the Grand Vizir, whose advance guard at Bilbeis was only two days' march from Cairo, Belliard could certainly destroy it or drive it back to Palestine. Baird's expedition would thus be deprived of the means to cross the desert from Suez; and with Baird neutralised and the Grand Vizir routed, Belliard could march down the Nile to raise the siege of Alexandria. If the Grand Vizir could be persuaded to fall back from Bilbeis and avoid a battle, he would be saved; but his withdrawal would compromise Baird's approach from Suez. Only the intervention of Hutchinson's force could disperse the danger. There was a further consideration which drew Hutchinson towards Cairo. South of the city hovered the Mameluke cavalry, a force reputed to be incomparably better than the mounted troops of the Porte. By origin Circassian slaves, still recruiting from the same source and bonded by sodomy, they had ruled Egypt for centuries in defiance of their nominal suzerains in Constantinople. For fear of the Turks they had made their peace with Bonaparte's army of occupation; but their leader Mourad Bey had recently died of the plague, and his successor Osman Bey was now watching in the wings to discover which European army would prevail. On 3 May at Rosetta Hutchinson had received a letter from Osman asking for British protection; and by advancing towards Cairo he might tilt Osman's balance of doubt and acquire this useful cavalry.

Yet still there remained the intractable problem of logistics. While Lagrange was falling back towards a well stocked base at Cairo, Hutchinson's line of supply was already strained by the difficulty of navigating the shallow summer river, and for days at a time the bar at Rosetta was impassable.[9] There was also the risk of disease. To march on for a hundred miles amidst the flies and scorpions in a heat which could rise to 120 degrees under the scorching sun would soon waste the little British force, in the presence of Belliard's acclimatised and well provided troops.

For a commander of Hutchinson's temperament the dilemma inflicted on him by Lagrange's march to the south was excruciating; and the hostile criticism which had enveloped him ever since he had assumed his unwanted command rose to a crescendo. His generals and heads of departments were clamouring against a march to the south. The Commissary, the medical staff, and the Quartermaster-General all reported that the troops were worn out; that no supplies were available for the advance; and that if the enemy were brought to battle there was not a reserve cartridge nearer than Rosetta. The generals emphasised the strategic risk, that to move further up the Nile would expose the base at Rosetta and the army's communications to attack by a detachment from Alexandria.[10] Hutchinson withstood this pressure, resolving that operational necessity must override logistical difficulties. He would pursue Lagrange; and orders were issued to march on the following morning, 11 May.

All the generals seem to have joined in the protests; and they were backed by the Quartermaster-General, the influential Colonel Anstruther, though he later concealed the fact and claimed to have been a consistent supporter of Hutchinson.[11] The dissent was loud and public; striving, wrote Christopher Hutchinson, 'incessantly and indecently . . . in the most public manner to defeat the expedition'. 'I hear great complaint is made by our Generals against this march', Lord Dalhousie's journal recorded, 'but Hutchinson will listen to none of them, they have stated it will be the certain ruin of the army and of the expedition. . . . He won't listen to a word.' Some officers were shocked by the tone of this opposition. When Colonel Graham later arrived from England he was told that the criticism had been 'very unmilitary and improper', and that 'there has been much, and unjustifiable cabal in the army'.[12]

In the face of this barrage of remonstrance Hutchinson persisted, and the march to the southward began as he had ordered at 5 a.m. on 11 May. Major Wilson's journal contrasted with the bellyaching of Dalhousie's. It was certainly a daring enterprise, he noted, to advance into a country on a sudden resolve, unprepared in any way, ignorant of the terrain ahead, and very little superior in numbers to the enemy. 'But what may not be expected from an army which has gained such miraculous successes? . . . Such an army I never served with before. Brave the British *always* are; but such an order and discipline reigns here throughout this army that one might suppose every individual to be a noble gentleman.'13

The army's march under the early morning sun did not quell the opposition; and unknown to Hutchinson his generals had concocted a desperate plot to deprive him of his command. The only record of this conspiracy is preserved by Bunbury, who though not present himself must have had the story from Moore and other witnesses with whom he served in later years in Sicily. The cabal, wrote Bunbury, became little less than a mutiny. The dissidents wrote letters to Coote and Moore, 'inviting their concurrence in a plan which tended virtually, if not absolutely, to deprive Hutchinson of the command of the army, and their mad project was defeated mainly by the stern and uncompromising answer which they received from Moore'.14 No doubt they persuaded themselves, like Reynier in his opposition to Menou, that their plotting was true patriotism and that they were the saviours of the army. But their minds seem to have been transfixed by the danger of Hutchinson's plan, and closed to the balance of risk and gain and of French and British morale. In the words of Christopher Hutchinson when his brother's strategy had been crowned with victory, the critics 'only saw the difficulties and dangers of our march and never once fairly brought their judgments to bear on the question'.15

While the plotters waited for Moore's response, their conduct during the march continued to be 'most unmilitary, subversive of discipline', and was widely known. On 19 May Major Hudson Lowe reported that the pursuit of Lagrange 'was disapproved by several of the principal officers'; and by 2 June news of the trouble had even reached Admiral Bickerton cruising off Alexandria. Two colonels (identified by Christopher Hutchinson only as 'Colonel D and C') visited the General during the march to say that they 'were ready to come forward and declare that very improper language had been held in their presence'. Christopher believed that the mainspring of the dissidents' behaviour was wounded conceit because their advice was unsought or rejected: they 'tried first to govern and next to bully him'. He was convinced that if his brother had 'condescended to hold councils of war', every member would have left the headquarters tent assured of the General's clarity and strength of mind, and that the decision to march for Cairo 'was founded on a great and comprehensive view'. But Hutchinson as usual kept his silence. He did not open his mind even to Anstruther, whom the army mistakenly regarded as his *éminence grise*, and his only confidant was the absent Moore at Rosetta, with whom he kept in touch by letter.[16]

'Great and comprehensive' though Hutchinson's grasp may have been, he soon swithered between his own judgement and the pressure of his staff and commanders. The first day's march covered the twelve miles to Shubra in great heat; and here the hard facts of logistics began to bite. The heads of departments hammered the arguments against a further advance: the crushing heat; the diseases of Egypt – ophthalmia, dysentery, plague; the lack of hospitals. No magazines or transport had been collected to supply the hundred-mile march to Cairo.

Hutchinson's nerve faltered, and he decided to turn back to Rosetta. But first he had to secure the safety of the Grand Vizir, and would therefore follow Lagrange for two more days and drive him back towards Cairo to prevent him from turning east across the delta and attacking the Turks. By that time he hoped to have persuaded the Grand Vizir to move back from the reach of a French counterstroke. That evening he sent an aide de camp, Major Montresor, across the delta on a mission to the Turkish camp. He was to persuade the Grand Vizir to pull back from Bilbeis to Salahieh, beyond the immediate reach of Belliard.

Two evenings later Major Wilson followed Montresor to reinforce his message. But scarcely had he set out when news from the Red Sea overturned this intention and made it imperative that the Turks should hold their ground at Bilbeis. The British were now at Kafr Houdig, where they had been held up through 13 May by a suffocating sirocco wind which prevented the supply boats from coming up the river; and during this pause a report arrived from Admiral Blankett's squadron, of which news had been interrupted by the use of code books which differed from those of the Mediterranean fleet. He had at last succeeded in beating up to Suez with troops from Baird's force, and Baird himself with the main convoy had reached Jiddah. If this was true, the expedition might at any moment be landed at Suez, and the Grand Vizir's presence at Bilbeis would then be vital. For it was here that the route from Aden emerged from the Suez desert; here that camels would have to be collected and forwarded to enable Baird to march. Instead of urging the Turks to fall back to Salahieh, Hutchinson would have to push closer to Cairo to support their exposed position at Bilbeis: he was even prepared to cross the delta and recover the position if it had been abandoned, hazardous though the movement would be to his own communications with Rosetta. There was no question now of turning back to besiege Alexandria, before the Red Sea expedition crossed the desert to join the Turks and deal with Belliard.[17]

Accordingly the army resumed its march to the southward over parched and cracked soil, and reached Algam on 16 May. Here it was half way between Rahmanieh and Cairo, and close to the mouth of the Minuf canal, the 'noble' artery which connected the two branches of the Nile. The fertile plain through which the army had advanced was narrowing, and ahead lay a forbidding defile where the drifting desert sand closed in to the river.

Hutchinson, reserved and hesitant, had hitherto managed to impose his will on a rolling succession of problems. But on the evening of the army's arrival at Algam, Major Wilson rejoined from the Turkish camp with tidings which threatened finally to destroy his control of the situation. The effort to dissuade the Turks from giving battle had failed. Wilson had reached the Turkish camp on the previous day to learn that Lagrange had already joined Belliard and that their concentrated forces were advancing to the attack. Hutchinson's hopes of averting a collision had been defeated, in Anstruther's phrase, by 'the inconceivable rapidity' of Lagrange's march. Leaving Rahmanieh in the night of 9 May, he had arrived at Cairo on the fourth day, and with Belliard attacked the Grand Vizir on the 16th, having covered 150 miles. Instead of falling back from the French attack, the Grand Vizir had advanced to meet it, telling Wilson that his army would disband if he denied it the promised plunder of Cairo.

By the time Wilson arrived with this news the expected battle was probably over. Hutchinson imagined the Turkish levies straggling onwards into the jaws of Belliard's demi-brigades which would scatter them to the winds. On 17 May the British remained halted at Algam waiting for news. It came on the 18th. Major Montresor arrived from the battlefield with an incredible report. The Turks had defeated the French.

Our last sight of the Grand Vizir and his army was in the chaotic camp at Jaffa in January when Moore formed his damning assessment of the Ottoman force. Few would then have imagined that by May it would be only two marches from Cairo. The story of the Turkish advance across the deserts is an extraordinary one. Faithful to the promise he had made to Moore,[18] the Grand Vizir began his forward movement from Jaffa on 25 February, three days after the British expedition had sailed from Marmaris. For lack of provisions the Turks moved slowly, advancing through desert country by Gaza; and passing between a pair of granite pillars which marked the boundary of Asia and Africa, they reached El Arish on 30 March. Here they learned of Abercromby's three victories on the Aboukir peninsula; and in the first days of April, while Colonel Spencer and the Capitan Pacha were setting out from Aboukir to capture Rosetta, the Grand Vizir's advance guard of cavalry and Albanian light infantry resumed their march. Skirting the Sinai coast by Katieh, they plunged into the worst of the desert and crossed the Suez isthmus towards the forward enemy outpost at Salahieh, which the French evacuated and destroyed on 8 April. On 19 April the Grand Vizir followed with his main body from El Arish; detached a force at Katieh to follow the coast and occupy Damietta; and plunged into a wilderness of sand and scrub. He reached Salahieh on the far side of the desert on

27 April; and on 11 May, already aware that the French had been dislodged from Rahmanieh, he was at Bilbeis where he halted to reorganise his force.

'Reorganise' is a euphemism. He had advanced 250 miles from Jaffa, including 170 miles of desert; no mean feat, but by British standards there had been no organisation whatever. It had been the march of a rabble. The army had snowballed with the adhesion of local Syrians, bedouin, and fellaheen, fired by the prospect of the loot of Cairo.[19] Every foot soldier felt free to mount himself by seizing a horse and ravaging the country to feed it, so two-thirds of the force were mounted though they could not be called cavalry. The official cavalry, perhaps 5,000, had no discipline and were incapable of acting in a solid body like European cavalry.

Long periods without provisions or forage littered the line of march with dead beasts and men. As the mob of followers accrued, the filth in the camp grew beyond even what Moore had described at Jaffa. The soldiers camped in disorderly bunches round their chiefs; and the intervals between the groups of tents were jammed with horses and camels, carts and cannon. Within a yard of each tent was a latrine formed from a piece of canvas; but no hole was dug, and when the army moved on the abominable canvas was packed in its filthy state on the back of a camel. A British colonel who arrived from the Red Sea was amazed by the Turkish encampment with its total absence of recognisable discipline, regularity, or supplies. The Turks were constantly driving cattle over the tent-ropes of his little detachment; and at night 'thousands' of mares and stallions broke loose and roamed the lines, 'making love in their own way. All the consolation we had, was saying with Shakespeare, "Let copulation thrive" '.[20]

Turkish discipline and commissariat were beyond correction; but their operations at least were open to British influence. The Military Mission was now commanded by Colonel Charles Holloway of the Royal Engineers, a veteran, like his predecessor Koehler, of the great siege of Gibraltar where he had been severely wounded.[21] Stationing himself with the Grand Vizir, he sent forward Captain Lacy of the Royal Engineers and Captain William Martin Leake of the Royal Artillery to advise the advance guards, with the guiding principle of preventing the Turks from engaging in a pitched battle. Leake (later a distinguished numismatist and topographer of classical Greece) was attached to the cavalry spearhead led by Tahir Pacha; and Lacy to the Albanian infantry commanded by Mahomet Ali, the future founder of modern Egypt. Lacy's instructions were to reconnoitre the enemy, and, if Mahomet Ali insisted on closing with the French, to take precautions against being surprised; while if he decided to entrench, Lacy was to select positions and plan field fortifications. Lacy's advice was heeded; and when the Grand Vizir arrived at Bilbeis on 11 May he found his advance guard in an entrenched camp protected by redoubts. Here, while he was reorganising his force, he learned that General Belliard was advancing from Cairo to attack him.[22]

Augustin-Daniel Belliard, *général de division* and a future count of the Napoleonic Empire, aged 31 and born three months before Bonaparte, was a short, well built soldier of youthful appearance. He had been with General Bonaparte at the bridge of Arcola in 1796, and had been promoted brigadier-general on the spot. But brave and competent though he was in battle, he had in the past refused commands which entailed independent responsibility. Fate had now overtaken him, and since March he had been left in command at Cairo when Menou marched off to fight the British at Alexandria.[23]

The teeming, restless city of Cairo was not a comfortable charge, and beyond its bounds Belliard was responsible for the upper delta, Upper Egypt, Suez and the Palestine frontier. With only 2,500 troops of all kinds he awaited a Turkish overland invasion and a British landing from the Red Sea. After garrisoning the Cairo citadel and the outer forts and walls of the city, he had only 500 mobile troops to protect convoys, collect provisions from the surrounding country, and take the field against the Turks. He immediately summoned his friend Donzelot to evacuate Upper Egypt and join him by forced marches. Donzelot's arrival on 6 April with 500 men of the 21st légère doubled his field force to 1,000; but even this was quite inadequate to delay the Turkish advance while Menou defeated the British.

Diffident of responsibility Belliard might be; but unlike his chief he had massive fighting experience, with nine campaign and thirty battles and combats behind him. Dismayed though he was by news of the defeat at Alexandria and the tone of Menou's subsequent letters, which seemed to mean that Cairo was left to its fate, Belliard began to strip his force for action. The stores in the outer forts and depots were removed to the citadel; permission was obtained from Menou to withdraw the garrisons from Salahieh and Bilbeis; and on his own responsibility the force at Suez was recalled. The *savants* of the Commission were embarked on the Nile for their ludicrous adventures at Alexandria.

Belliard calculated that to take the offensive against the mobs of Turkish horsemen he needed 2,000–2,400 infantry, enough to form two good squares. But even with the troops recalled from the forward posts he could still only muster 1,700. On 23 April, with the Grand Vizir's advance guard scarcely two marches away at Bilbeis, a Council of War agreed that it was out of the question to sortie against the Turks unless it was certain that they would accept battle. If they would stand and fight they could be defeated; but if they avoided battle it would be impossible to prevent their mounted hordes from slipping round the flank and entering Cairo, whose restless population would explode into insurrection. A further deterrent for Belliard was the doubtful loyalty of the Mameluke cavalry in his rear since the death of Mourad Bey.[24]

Belliard resigned himself to a static defence of Cairo; and with plague thinning the ranks his officers grasped at a life of desperate pleasure with their houris as if there were no tomorrow. On 11 May the news that Rahmanieh had been lost severed the last link with the outside world except by the desert, a route only fit for dromedaries; and the soldiers were cursing Menou for not having brought his army to Cairo in a final bid for victory.[25] Help was at hand, however. Two days later Lagrange marched into Cairo at the head of his 4,000 men, having covered the hundred broiling miles from Rahmanieh in less than four days.

Lagrange's force gave Belliard enough troops to take the offensive. And with Hutchinson approaching on the Nile and the Grand Vizir less than fifty miles away at Bilbeis, there was little time to lose before the converging allies united. The French force would be vastly outnumbered by the Grand Vizir, but Kléber had prevailed over heavier odds at Heliopolis. Belliard took the plunge; and at dawn on 15 May he marched for Bilbeis at the head of 4,600 infantry, 900 cavalry and twenty-four guns, leaving General Almeras with the garrison troops to hold the city in his rear.[26] Halting for the night beyond Heliopolis, he advanced again at six o'clock on the morning of 16 May and encountered the Turkish advance guards of Albanians and horsemen near El Khanka.

For the British mission this was the climax of their long wanderings; an odyssey which had brought them to Constantinople and across the Hellespont; through Asia Minor, Syria, and the deserts of Sinai and Suez; and at last to the edge of the Nile delta. For the past five days they had been imploring the Grand Vizir at Bilbeis to draw back from striking range of the French at Cairo. But the old man reiterated that withdrawal was impossible; his loot-inspired hordes would disperse, and he would be forced to retire beyond the desert which he had crossed with such tribulation. Rejecting British advice, he sent forward his advance guard to meet the enemy; and as they became engaged he advanced with his main body to support them.

Though Colonel Holloway had argued in vain against the advance, the battle was fought as he wished, in the style best suited to an army whose only virtue was skirmishing. The horsemen swarmed like a cloud in the open plain, and to resist them Belliard formed his two squares of infantry with his cavalry in column between them. This was no formation for victory. He had to destroy or drive out the Turkish army: nothing less would enable him to turn on the approaching British. But he found that he was thrusting into a vapour which parted before his solid masses. His infantry squares were wasting ammunition and frittering lives to no purpose against the loose swarms of irregular sharpshooters, and he could not send out his own skirmishers in the presence of the Turkish horsemen. On his right the Turkish horse overlapped his flank and extended far into the desert beyond; and a body of cavalry had vanished entirely. Were they making for Cairo, as they had done during the battle of Heliopolis? In any case time had turned against him, for he was failing to destroy the Turkish army and the British would soon break into his rear. He resolved to fall back and defend Cairo.

For the first seven miles his withdrawal was harassed by the Turks urged on by the British mission; but his rapid and well conducted march brought him to safety. The day's fighting had cost him fifty killed and 300 wounded.

For the first time the Turks had prevailed in battle against the legions of the French Republic. So bizarre was the news that in the British camp French prisoners burst into incredulous laughter whenever it was mentioned; and a British general described the action as a parcel of sheep running from tooth-less dogs.[27] But the Turkish success was real enough; and the Grand Vizir camped that night near Heliopolis, the victor where he had once been routed by Kléber.[28]

17

ONWARD TO CAIRO

The road ahead for Hutchinson might now seem clear. With Belliard driven back into his lair in Cairo, the British and Turkish forces had only to advance in a deliberate converging movement to force his surrender. They would then turn and settle the fate of Menou in Alexandria. The current estimate of the French forces was 8,000 in Alexandria including seamen, and in Cairo 6,000 including natives.[1]

Belliard's force was still initially intact after the battle of El Khanka; but there were many signs that French morale was cracking. French officers dining with Hutchinson after the surrender of Rahmanieh and the capture of the dragoons were very content to be prisoners. They complained that their men would not fight; and the cavalry officers, with no patriotic regrets, were delighted to be allowed to sell their horses.[2] French detachments were now being rounded up all over the theatre. In the ten days following Lagrange's retreat from Rahmanieh 1,600 were captured: 150 of them in the Rahmanieh fort and the courier's escort and, from the forts at the Damietta mouth of the Nile, 700 who had embarked on the sea to escape the Grand Vizir's detachment and were intercepted immediately by British cruisers. A further 150, taken by Colonel Stewart on the Minuf canal, had been escorting a valuable convoy destined for Rahmanieh, Lagrange having failed to warn them of his retreat. Why the French were thus exposing their troops in small packets puzzled Moore, who sensed that it signalled the disintegration of the French command. Little could now go right for them.[3]

The most dramatic of these captures had occurred on 17 May while the army was waiting for the news from El Khanka. On a day so hot that drummer boys were roasting eggs in the sand,[4] a bedouin appeared at the tent of Lieutenant-Colonel Robert Browne of the 12th Light Dragoons and reported that a French convoy was on the move in the desert. Colonel Browne immediately sent out Lieutenant Francis Raines with a patrol, followed by a linking detachment under Lieutenant Caton; and as soon as the horses had been fed and watered, Browne himself came on with 250 mounted men of the 12th and 26th Light Dragoons. General Doyle's brigade of infantry was turned out to toil through the hot sand behind them.

Raines and his patrol were soon overtaken by Colonel Abercromby and Major Wilson; and riding on in the sweltering afternoon they perceived through the heat-haze a vast caravan of baggage camels escorted by 600 French infantry, cavalry, and dromedaries. The force, commanded by *chef de brigade* Cavalier of the dromedary corps, had been sent out from Alexandria four days earlier by Menou to forage in the Buhayra district round Damanhur; but finding no stocks of grain and the villages deserted Cavalier had decided to push on to Cairo and collect provisions for Alexandria from the depot. To victual his own force he skirted along the edge of the cultivated country of the delta, misled by reports that the British were still at Rahmanieh; but he was surrounded and harassed by Arab horsemen who prevented him from patrolling ahead of his convoy.

The sight of the British cavalry was therefore a complete surprise. Cavalier halted and formed a square to protect his baggage camels, the dromedaries kneeling obediently in unison at a word of command to form a parapet for their riders along part of the front, while a light 4-pounder gun kept the British at a respectful distance. The chances of capturing the convoy seemed slim. The British infantry struggling through the loose sand under the blazing sun were still three or four miles distant; the dragoons were too few to charge the square; and Cavalier's camelry could take to the desert, where the British dragoons could not follow them for more than half an hour for lack of water.

As Abercromby and Wilson considered the dilemma, the resourceful Wilson remembered how Sir William Erskine had once taken two battalions with a handful of men simply by asking them to surrender. Colonel Abercromby agreed that he should try the bluff; but he had to wait till the main body of dragoons came up in order to borrow a white handkerchief. As the dragoons approached, Colonel Browne deployed them into a single rank with extended intervals so that his force appeared through the haze to be a much larger body of cavalry. Wilson stuck a borrowed handkerchief on the point of his sword and galloped forward. The handkerchief flew off, but he galloped on; and reining up before Cavalier he proposed that the French should surrender on condition of being sent home to France. Cavalier instantly refused.

But his men had caught the word *France*; and as Wilson wheeled his horse away he could hear them asking each other whether he had said 'return to France'. Cavalier called him back, but he pretended not to hear and rode on. An aide de camp galloped after him and asked him to return and repeat his proposals. This time Wilson added an undertaking that the French should retain their personal effects and even send to Cairo for their baggage; and officers could retain their horses and camels. The generous terms were in harmony with the British government's instructions, and too good for Cavalier to refuse with his troops murmuring behind him. His force marched to a field near the British headquarters at Algam and grounded their arms; and the same evening they were embarked on the Nile for Rosetta and France. The Army of the Orient was weaker by 600 officers and men; and the British gained 200 horses, 660 camels with 300 Arab drivers, and seventy dromedaries, all helping to ease the shortage of cavalry and transport.[5]

A common factor in all these French surrenders was their fear of the native population, enraged by requisitions and ill-treatment, and dread of the cruel customs of the Turks. Harassed by bedouin who prevented them from reconnoitring, and terrified of being left wounded on the field to be maimed and decapitated, or of being captured by the Turks and enslaved, French detachments were seizing any chance to put themselves under British protection.[6]

But it did not follow that the main forces secure inside the defences of Cairo and Alexandria would cave in so easily. In Moore's judgement the French would no longer fight in the open, but would hold on in the two cities hoping that the hot weather would wreck the health of the British troops in the siege trenches. Nor did he believe that Hutchinson and the Grand Vizir were strong enough to reduce Cairo without the aid of Baird's force from India. In fact Hutchinson did not plan to squander his own force by attacking Cairo. Still expecting Baird and his larger force at Suez, his plan was to hold his present position on the Nile only till he had covered Baird's junction with the Grand Vizir. He would then turn back with the Capitan Pacha to deal with Alexandria, leaving the siege of Cairo to Baird and the Grand Vizir.[7]

In any case he would have had difficulty in moving further up the Nile. Above Algam the Rosetta branch of the river was now so low that his djerms would be forced to diverge by the Minuf canal and the Damietta branch, separating his water transport from the marching troops.[8] Already supplies were filtering through too slowly over the shallow bar at the mouth of the river; and if heavy guns and ammunition had to be brought up to bombard Cairo the delay might be long. For the moment, while he waited for Baird, the essential task was to deny Belliard another chance to destroy the Grand Vizir. Fortunately the Turks were forced by shortage of provisions to withdraw from their exposed position beyond El Khanka; and moving back towards the Nile they drew closer to the British. About 20 May the Grand Vizir and his army were at Benha on the Damietta branch just below the mouth of the Minuf canal, and only twenty-eight miles from Hutchinson. In this position the British could support the Turks and contain Belliard till the expected approach of Baird. A pontoon bridge was thrown across the Rosetta branch of the river to open a lateral communication; and Colonel Stewart's battle group, with the 30th Regiment joining the 89th to replace the Albanians, formed a link at the head of the Minuf canal.[9]

It was time for the two commanders to meet, and on 23 May Hutchinson embarked on the canal in the Capitan Pacha's barge to visit the Grand Vizir.

He spent several days in the Turkish camp, exchanging slow compliments and conferring, and established that the Grand Vizir had no more than 15,000 men, of whom 8–9,000 were mounted. It was 'the worst army that ever existed', wrote Hutchinson, 'but bad as they are they will fight to a certain degree in their own way'. If they remained at Benha all should be well. But at a conference on 28 May the Grand Vizir revealed that his levies would disband if they were not allowed to advance and plunder Cairo. The British mission confirmed that this was true.[10]

It was a blow to Hutchinson's intention of covering Baird's approach without compromising his own force; and he returned to his headquarters at Algam loaded with rich presents but in some dismay. Almost at once, however, the scene shifted again, when he learned that Baird would not be coming to Suez. The seasonal north-west wind had set in, barring the passage up the narrow Gulf of Suez for the rest of the season. Bitter news indeed. If Baird had reached the Gulf of Suez in time, the battle for Egypt would have been virtually won. But without the Indian force, Hutchinson faced again the old dilemma between Cairo and Alexandria.

Must he after all advance with the Turks and besiege Cairo? It would mean sending for his siege train, with all the delay which that would entail; and he would probably expend the siege material which was wanted at Alexandria.[11] He did not expect the siege of Cairo to be difficult, for the supposed garrison of about 5,000 French had a long circumference to man and the fortifications were of bad stone and new cement. But if it delayed the attack on Alexandria, the siege of the port might consume many months of hot weather, the French being strongly fortified and apparently well provided with rice and flour though short of meat.

Yet he dared not leave the attack on Cairo to the Grand Vizir alone. If the Turkish army was defeated, Belliard could make it very difficult to provision the British army at Alexandria from the delta, and would threaten the siege lines. Belliard had to be eliminated; and two further factors reinforced the argument. An advance to the southward would secure the Mamelukes' support and thus deny the resources of the countryside to Belliard's garrison; and further news of Baird revealed that he now intended to land 300 miles south of Suez at Kosseir (Quseir). His force would then have to cross 150 miles of desert to the Nile at Keneh (Qena) some 330 miles above Cairo by river. His arrival there would close Belliard's final option of retiring into Upper Egypt, while Hutchinson, by pressing Belliard from the north, would protect Baird's long approach down the Nile.[12]

There was no real choice: till Cairo fell Alexandria was impregnable. Hutchinson sent for his siege train, and to replace his sick he summoned from Coote's force the 28th and 42nd Regiments, the heroes of the battle of 21 March.[13] Since the storm which had greeted his earlier decision to advance from Rahmanieh, supplies had improved: the country was fertile, the corn was ripe; and the inhabitants remained friendly because the army, in spite of the shortage of cash, was under strict discipline and paid for what it consumed. The transport problem, as the army separated from its boats on the Minuf canal, would be eased by the camels taken from Cavalier's convoy, lightening the burden on the backs of the soldiers and ensuring a regular supply of water.

Nevertheless the hardships could be great: of this a hot sirocco wind on 23 May had left no doubt. The sky was darkened by blowing sand and dust, the thermometer rose to 109 degrees in the shade, and the wind was like the glow from the mouth of an oven. The metal on muskets, buttons, and knives became too hot to touch; and Wilson believed that one more day of such weather would be disastrous. But as night drew on the wind cooled and shifted to the north-west.[14]

The Mameluke Beys did not wait for the British advance before descending from the fence on which they had been perched. The Turkish success at El Khanka was enough, and on 29 May a messenger arrived from Osman Bey to announce that his Mamelukes were on their way to join the British force. Two evenings later 1,200 superbly mounted horsemen arrived, each accompanied by a servant on foot. They were not trained to act as a formed body in close order, and their small Arabian horses would have been ridden down by an equal body of heavier European cavalry. Nevertheless their equipment and their individual skill at arms were superb, and acting as scouts and vedettes they would prevent the French from foraging.[15]

Four days after the Mamelukes' arrival the final advance to Cairo began with a nine-mile march to Lockmas, while the sick and baggage diverged by the Minuf canal, not to rejoin the army till it reached the head of the delta. It was 4 June, the King's birthday, and the officers drank his health that evening in the water of the Nile. The daily routine began with a warning drum only half an hour before the time to march off, in order to keep the troops under arms for as short a time as possible. At 4 or 5 a.m. the drums sounded the long roll when the regiments immediately marched off without further orders. Two companies of infantry and ten dragoons brought up the rear, sweeping the stragglers and followers along to protect them from being set upon and robbed by the Arabs. If a halt was ordered close to a village the nearest regiment sent a guard to prevent soldiers from entering it. This was by now a disciplined and experienced army whose procedures were steady and fluent. The first officer to mount his horse in the morning and the last to lie down at night was the Quartermaster-General, Colonel Anstruther, who rode on with his staff when the army halted for the night, to reconnoitre the next day's camping ground.[16]

The marches were short because the army was crossing the belt of encroaching desert sand which here crept down to the banks of the Nile. Over this loose sand Colonel Hill described the troops plodding in conditions of 'unparalleled fatigue'. In the blazing heat of the day, sweat drenched their clothing and soaked through the buff belts as if they had been dipped in water. Officers and men 'all fared alike', wrote Wyvill echoing Abercromby's phrase. Officers had no baggage except a knapsack slung on the shoulder, and like their men carried a canteen with three pints of water. When tents came up the officers lived three to a soldiers' tent whose conical shape concentrated the rays of the sun to create an oven; at night they lay in their cloaks on the sand, overrun with scorpions and fearsome spiders. The daily ration was a piece of salt meat, or sometimes an issue of fresh buffalo, and biscuit of the worst kind baked by the Capitan Pacha's Turks.

Hitherto the health of the troops on the Nile had held up well, thanks to what Hutchinson called the 'Saturday night privation' of being unable to buy liquor; but now sickness began to soar. Fifty men a day were dropping out with dysentery, and almost everyone had sore eyes. By the end of the march 1,122 sick had left the force, 284 of them sent down the river to the General Hospital at Rosetta, and 838 to a second General Hospital organised by Staff Surgeon Webb when the force reached the point of the delta. A further 346 men were sick in the regimental hospitals. These deductions left Hutchinson at most 4,000 fit for duty.[17]

On 5 June the army halted at Wardan where it rested on the 6th; and on the 7th the march was resumed in insufferable heat, with the sand drifting in the men's faces and flying round in choking whirlwinds. In these conditions the ten-mile march was worse than forty miles in England. But relief was near. Ahead lay the fertile delta, and the blowing sand cleared to reveal the distant Pyramids of Giza. Three months earlier in the troopships off Alexandria the British had had their first sight of Pompey's Pillar, a granite wonder of the Roman world. Now they were moving into a still older civilisation, 'striking the mind with the most awfull sensations'.[18]

On 8 June the army marched clear of the sand, as the river turned away from the desert into a lush irrigated plain of standing corn. Passing the point of the delta where the two branches of the Nile divided, Hutchinson halted near Burtus. Here the tribulations of the long advance from Alexandria ended. The British and Turkish armies were firmly astride the main channel of the Nile, with Colonel Stewart's battalions at Charlahan to provide a connecting link.

For the siege of Cairo Hutchinson would need every man he could muster, and he sent for the detachment of infantry which Admiral Blankett had brought to Suez. Camels were sent across the desert by the Grand Vizir to fetch them, and on 10 June Colonel Lloyd joined Stewart with 200 men of the 86th. Lloyd gave a 'dreadful account' of his two-day march across the waterless desert in a heat of up to 116 degrees. He was said to have had his own baggage cut from the back of a camel, an example followed by the rest of his officers so that the weaker men could be carried. Lord Dalhousie received this tale of hardship and sacrifice with his usual scepticism: it had

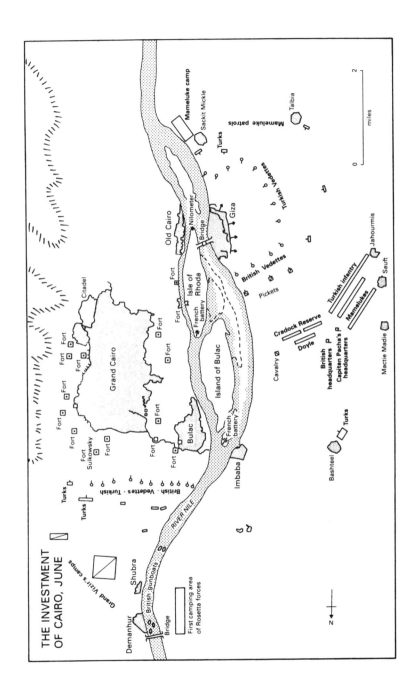

THE INVESTMENT
OF CAIRO, JUNE

Grand Vizir's camps

British gunboats

First camping area
of Roseta forces

Demanhur

Shubra

Bridge

RIVER NILE

Turks

Turks

British Vedettes - Turkish

Fort Sulkowsky

Fort

Fort

Fort

Fort

Fort

Fort

Fort

Grand Cairo

Citadel

Fort

Fort

Fort

Fort

Fort

Bulac

Island of Bulac

Imbaba

French battery

French battery

Isle of
Rhoda

Old Cairo

Nilometer

Bridge

Giza

Mameluke camp

Sackit Mickle

Turks

Mameluke patrols

Talbia

Turkish Vedettes

British Vedettes

Pickets

Cradock Reserve

Doyle

Cavalry

British
headquarters

Capitan Pacha's
headquarters

Turkish infantry

Mamelukes

Jahourmis

Sauft

Mactie Madie

Bashteel

Turks

N

0   2
miles

to be judged by the luxuries of an Indian campaign. He was told that Lloyd's own light baggage had included a hundred dozen bottles of madeira and twelve dozen shirts; and he felt that the officers who had set out from Aboukir with three shirts apiece and as many bottles of wine (long since finished) could have performed the journey with less trouble than the spoilt children of the East India Company's victories.[19]

But it must be confessed that Dalhousie's views were often abrasive. Even the distant pyramids disappointed him. As for Hutchinson's operations, they were 'all idleness, nothing going forward . . . we now find the loss of Sir Ralph'. He heard that the army was to remain at Burtus while British heavy artillery was belatedly summoned, because the Turks had not been able to bring a siege train across the desert. In fact General Lawson of the Royal Artillery and Captain Brice of the Royal Engineers had already been sent back to Rosetta to speed the siege-guns, and twenty 24-pounders were on their way. After the battering of Fort Julien, the ponderous cannon had been returned to Aboukir for the attack on Alexandria; now they had to be shipped back to the mouth of the Nile and transferred to djerms for the hazardous passage of the bar and the voyage up the shallow river.[20]

While Hutchinson waited for his siege equipment, he edged forward a mile on 16 June to within four miles of Cairo, the Grand Vizir moving level with him on the right bank to Shubra. On the 19th a new pontoon bridge made up of sixty djerms was completed to span the 180 yards of river between the British and Turkish camps. From the new British camp there was a spectacular view of the towers and minarets of Grand Cairo cutting the bleached sky.

Hutchinson's intention was to cross the Nile and combine with the Grand Vizir to attack the fortifications on the east bank, where the walls were not protected by the river and the terrain would be less liable to flooding when the annual rise of the Nile began. But it was soon apparent that before the British force could cross the river the fortified Giza bridgehead on the west bank would have to be taken, to prevent the French from breaking out into the desert, or sallying against the bridge to cut off the British force on the east bank. At 8 p.m. on 19 June orders to cross the river were cancelled.

On the following day the siege-guns arrived, only twelve days behind the army, a considerable achievement on the part of the artillery and the navy; and on 21 June the 28th and 42nd Regiments completed their eighteen days' march from Alexandria. The forces on the west bank now closed to within a mile and a half of Giza. Cairo was effectively encircled, with the British, the Mamelukes and the Capitan Pacha's Turks forming a chain of outposts and vedettes across the western face of the French defences. In the meantime the heavy siege-guns and their ammunition were being disembarked and dragged overland for twelve miles from their landing point to their battering positions, in a daytime temperature of 120 degrees. The batteries would be ready on 22 June, and should reduce the Giza bridgehead within four or five days. Hutchinson would then cross the Nile and join the Vizir to besiege Grand Cairo. He had only 4,000 British fit for duty, besides the uncertain Turks, to assault the French garrison which he believed to be 4–5,000; but the extensive city walls with their fourteen towers would be undermanned, and he knew from deserters that French morale was low and that they were anxious to surrender themselves to British protection.[21]

Hutchinson's deliberate movements of the past three weeks, designed to preserve his own strength and overwhelm Belliard's garrison with converging forces, were bearing fruit. Two or three steps more, and his task at Cairo would be done. But even those steps were not to be required. On 22 June, the day when his batteries were due to be completed, the gates of Giza opened and a party of the enemy emerged under a white flag of truce. The siege was over.

Part IV

HONOUR REDEEMED

18

FORTY CENTURIES
LOOK DOWN

Belliard's fate was now inevitable; but it could still have been deferred. He could have forced the allies to open laborious siege operations; and when his curtain wall was breached he could have withdrawn into the citadel and prolonged the defence for three more weeks. Thus he would have won time for Menou and delayed the attack on Alexandria.

But ever since his return from the botched offensive at El Khanka Belliard's spirits had been corroded by a sense of hopelessness. He felt isolated inside a closing trap. For many weeks past he had heard nothing from Menou; and from the north and east allied armies were closing on him, moving with a caution which offered him no opportunity for a counterstroke. To the southward he learned that another British force was landing at Kosseir (Quseir) on the Red Sea coast to threaten his only refuge in Upper Egypt. The Mamelukes were almost certainly about to desert him and make the countryside round Cairo unsafe for his foragers. Indeed on 8 June his cavalry patrols were turned back by the enemy, and no further foraging was possible. His horses and camels would starve, and his men would have only the stocks in the magazines to eat, amounting to less than two months' ration. If the city was invested the garrison would have twenty-five kilometres of outer walls to man.

On 13 June the silence from Menou was broken at last by the arrival of a courier, escorted by a dromedary detachment which had circled through the desert to evade the closing enemy. But Menou's letter was a month old, and bore no relation to the reality perceived by Belliard. The Commander-in-Chief had been living in a world of fantasy, reporting in his despatches to Bonaparte that the British had suffered horrible carnage at Rahmanieh, and that Belliard had crushed the Turks and was descending the Nile to combine with him and attack the British. Four days after Belliard received this letter, Menou was assuring the Minister of the Interior that Belliard had beaten the British on the outskirts of Cairo and Hutchinson had been killed: 'The Army of the Orient will fight to the death for a colony which, in every way, would be one of the finest possessions of France.'[1]

The letter to Belliard assured him that help from France was certain and Cairo must be held till it arrived. But for Belliard the time for such illusions was past. With nothing to delay the opening of the allied siege but Hutchinson's pause to await his heavy cannon, Belliard replied that to expect help from France was mere hallucination, since Admiral Ganteaume had already failed to break through the British blockade and Bonaparte had now turned his naval effort against the British Isles. Belliard described the true situation of the Cairo garrison, and implied that the game was up: 'The Army of Egypt has done its duty; whatever happens, it will always win the admiration of the universe'.[2]

Within a week of penning this despondent letter Belliard was closely invested, with British and Ottoman outposts covering the whole front on the west bank of the Nile. Was there any option left but to defend Cairo to the last or capitulate? None, he concluded. If he attempted a sortie against the siege lines he would leave his 27,000 yards of wall stripped of troops and open to escalade; while a retreat up the Nile was precluded by lack of boats to evacuate his stores and ammunition, and the reported presence at Kosseir of Baird's force from India.

How long could he hold out in Cairo? He had only 150 rounds per gun; and the inhabitants, who would soon be starving and desperate, were likely to rise in his rear when he was attacked. He might succeed in retiring to the citadel, and hold out there till his provisions failed. But what then? Surrender at discretion, with the British unable to restrain the ferocity of two Turkish armies. What that could mean is illustrated by the fate of Captain François of the dromedary corps, who was set upon by the Turks while escorting a flag of truce. A British unit intervened to avert a massacre; but François and two wounded companions were carried off into slavery, François bearing as trophies for his captors a pair of bleeding French heads.

Belliard concluded that his best hope was to obtain the terms of the aborted Convention of El Arish of 1799 (which the British had already offered to Menou), allowing him to capitulate with honour and return under arms to France. But although he was commanding half of the Army of the Orient, he had no authority to parley. Flinching at the responsibility, he sought the cover of a Council of War, which assembled on 20 June in a building surrounded by anxious soldiers waiting to hear the outcome. The most junior and least responsible officer present adopted the macho stance that the garrison should attack the British force to test its strength which was as yet unknown, and if need be die gloriously in the attempt. The most senior, Belliard himself, wanted to negotiate while he still had some cards to play. Between these poles a variety of opinions were aired, with Menou's creature Lagrange urging that nothing be done until an officer had been sent through the desert to Alexandria for orders. Eventually Belliard obtained a majority; and when Donzelot emerged from the building and told the waiting soldiery that the meeting had voted to treat for repatriation, many of his audience dissolved in tears.[3]

As the white flag of truce was borne out through the Giza gate, a British staff officer rode out to meet it and learned that Belliard proposed to treat for the evacuation of Cairo. Time would be expended in marching the French garrison to the coast and embarking it; but the loss of time was finite, while the delays and losses of a siege were incalculable, and it would almost certainly be drawn out till the Nile, which had begun to rise as early as 17 June, flooded the British bank and interrupted communications with Rosetta. On 23 June negotiations were opened with the Grand Vizir's consent. Escorted by the grenadiers of the 90th, General Hope went forward to meet Donzelot and General Morand in tents pitched on the bank of the Nile. An armistice was agreed immediately; and five days later on 28 June the capitulation was signed. The French would march with their arms, baggage, and field artillery to Rosetta, where they were to be embarked within fifty days at allied expense and shipped to a French port. On the same evening the 79th Highlanders took possession of the Giza gate, and on the Turkish bank Colonel Stewart occupied the Sulkowsky fort with the 89th.[4]

So ended Hutchinson's campaign on the Nile. All that remained was to escort the French to the coast; and for the British there was a period of rest and recuperation while the French prepared for their march. The force was reviewed by the Grand Vizir, who rode along the lines apparently asleep till his single eye was startled awake by the sound of the kilted 42nd's bagpipes to behold with surprise a line of men without breeches. During the inspection French and British minute guns were booming solemnly while Kléber's coffin was transferred from its tomb in the citadel to a djerm for shipment to France.[5]

To pass the time, Hutchinson organised parties of all ranks to visit the Sphinx and the Pyramids of Giza six miles off on the edge of the desert, where Bonaparte had told his troops that forty centuries looked down upon them. The entrance to the Great Pyramid of Cheops had not yet been discovered,[6] but it was possible to climb down into the depths of one of the others, and Colonel Cameron of the 79th obtained a souvenir by ordering a soldier to attack the Pharaoh's sarcophagus with a sledgehammer: 'thus, in an instant, was destroyed by this barbarian what time, the most merciless of destroyers, had spared'. Captain Dalrymple judged his compatriot 'a blunt honest Scotchman, but a great *Goth*'.[7]

Reactions to the Pyramids were mixed. Were they wonderfully vast, or vastly boring? The highlanders of the 92nd explored them with simple wonder, for they had neither read nor heard that the world contained such colossal structures, dwarfing even the mansions of the greatest chiefs of the north. Officers were also impressed. 'They far surpassed every idea I had formed of them', wrote Captain Jennings of the 28th; and even the astringent Lord Dalhousie now admitted that when one reached their base they were 'certainly awfully majestic'. Captain Maule was awed by the mysterious origins of these 'stupendous monuments', reflecting that he was seeing a wonder which 'few men in existence can ever behold. . . . The difficulties and dangers in that country were always great and in future will be still greater'.[8]

Not for all was mere size enough. Colonel Harness of the 74th, who had seen some of the wondrous buildings of India, mused that 'the only idea they invited, was that so much labour should have been thrown away in productions of neither use, beauty or profit'. Moore, who had explored Rome in his youth, saw here only 'immense piles of building without beauty', recalling perhaps the words of the sage in Samuel Johnson's *Rasselas*: 'I consider this mighty structure as a monument to the insufficiency of human enjoyments. A King . . . is compelled to solace, by the erection of a pyramid, the satiety of dominion and the tastelessness of pleasures'.[9]

Cairo was not the splendid city it had seemed from a distance; its streets narrow and unpaved, the heat unbearable, and many of the houses falling into ruins as a result of depopulation by the plague. Visitors found the French officers friendly and agreeable behind their huge mustachios. Their general sent breakfast to the officers of the 79th at the Giza gate; and Wyvill was given a tour of the city and discovered the French genius for making themselves comfortable. They grew every French vegetable except the potato; were still drinking good wine and rum; and had brightened their lives with Coptic or native women.[10]

General Moore had rejoined the army on the day after the capitulation, though his wound was still not quite closed. Riding round the French outer defences, he thoroughly approved of Hutchinson's terms of capitulation. Had the general known the weaknesses of the long perimeter he might, Moore considered, have imposed harsher terms. Yet the outer works could not have been carried by *coup de main*; and after breaching and storming them, the capture of the inner defences and citadel would have cost further time and lives.[11]

At first not everyone would have agreed with this verdict. Dalhousie recorded that outside the circle of Hutchinson's headquarters 'those who think for themselves' thought the terms too soft, and that the time allowed for the French to embark would unduly delay the siege of Alexandria.[12] Hutchinson himself, however, was convinced that the speedy capture of Cairo had decided the fate of Egypt. Its capitulation had cost Menou almost the whole of his cavalry and most of his field artillery, and he no longer possessed a balanced force to take the field and fight for supplies. Thus Alexandria must eventually fall to blockade, or earlier by assault. Hutchinson was conscious that his progress in Egypt would influence the peace talks which had opened in Paris; but he assured his government that the fall of Cairo had been decisive, and that even if Menou was able to hang on in Alexandria for a time, Bonaparte was no longer entitled to claim possession of Egypt or compensation for relinquishing it.[13]

Evidence was emerging that Hutchinson had made an even better bargain than he had supposed. At the time of the capitulation he believed that the

French had fewer than 6,000 fighting troops to defend the city; so he was surprised when the French commissary demanded rations for 17,000 people. But it was not yet possible to count the garrison, which was screened behind the walls of Giza while it prepared for the march to the coast.[14]

While Hutchinson was waiting for the French to complete their preparations, an officer arrived from Baird to report that the Red Sea force had at last appeared on the scene. It was now at Keneh on the Upper Nile, where Baird was awaiting instructions.

This was Hutchinson's first solid news of the force from India. Admiral Blankett's arrival at Suez in April with Colonel Lloyd's detachment had shed no light, for he had previously been cruising for three years off the mouth of the Red Sea to block the passage of Bonaparte's army to India, and knew nothing of the force the Indian authorities were sending. The Secretary of State's instructions of 6 October to the Governor-General, Lord Wellesley, had been to send 1,000 European infantry and 2,000 sepoys to Suez, where they would be joined by a British battalion from the Cape; and, little suspecting the strength of the French field force, Dundas had explained to Abercromby that Baird's troops would occupy the Red Sea ports in order to constrict the French occupation and bring additional pressure to bear on them.[15]

The East India Company could spare an expeditionary force from the turbulent sub-continent because it had received reinforcements of British troops in 1798 to stop Bonaparte's eastward thrust; and when Dundas's instructions arrived in India Lord Wellesley had already made some preparations and was able to assemble a considerably larger force than his orders required. About 8,000 were despatched, and though many were scattered at sea by bad weather 5,822 rank and file of all arms eventually assembled in Egypt.[16] From the Bengal Presidency came the 10th Foot and 1,200 Bengal sepoys, with a detachment of the Company's artillery; from Madras the 80th, 86th, and 88th, with further artillery; and from the Bombay Presidency two battalions of native infantry. These were joined in the Red Sea by the 61st with a troop of the 8th Light Dragoons and some British horse artillery, escorted from the Cape by Commodore Sir Home Popham. Their general, David Baird, was an experienced soldier with rude manners and a vocabulary to match.

Global strategy in the days of sail was no more predictable than the weather; and though the first of these troops had embarked in the Ganges on 1 December, the voyage of 3,800 miles round the sub-continent to Bombay and across the Arabian Sea had been slow and stormy. When the convoy entered the Red Sea in April the seasonal wind had changed and was blowing down from the north. Against this wind the ships had to proceed in small detachments among the uncharted reefs of the Arabian coast, groping their way under easy sail and often lying-to at night. When the fleet reassembled at the beginning of May at Jiddah, Baird faced a new dilemma.

Against the prevailing wind the troopships would not be able to work their way up the narrow Gulf of Suez, and it was therefore no longer possible to join Hutchinson by way of Suez and Bilbeis. The alternative was to land at Kosseir and cross the desert to the Nile at Keneh; but even with the logistical skills of an Indian army it would be a difficult and dangerous march. Moreover reports from the Arabs estimated the French force at Cairo as 15,000 French troops and 10,000 Greeks and Copts, enough for them to spare a blocking force at Keneh which would trap the Anglo-Indian force in the desert. And weighing these risks, Baird was not even certain that Hutchinson still needed his force.

While he waited, he sent part of his force under Colonel Murray across the Red Sea to Kosseir, where it arrived on 17 May. But it was not till 15 June that his ignorance of the situation in Egypt was cleared by the arrival of Admiral Blankett from Suez. He brought a despatch from Hutchinson, written five weeks earlier after the capture of Rahmanieh when Hutchinson had still expected Baird to land at Suez. He wanted him to join the Grand Vizir and besiege Cairo, while Hutchinson's own force would return to attack Alexandria.

From this letter Baird also discovered that the French at Cairo were nowhere near as formidable as he had been led to believe; and assured now that he was needed in Egypt he resolved to risk the desert crossing to the Nile, and worked his way up the Red Sea to join Colonel Murray at Kosseir.

The desert track from Kosseir to Keneh was an ancient commercial route between Asia and Europe. The Romans had used it to bring silk and spices down the Nile to the Mediterranean; and later the Arabs had preferred it to the Suez route and the contrary winds in the gulf.[17]

But it was no fit route for an army. The roadstead at Kosseir was dangerous; the town a cluster of mud-and-shell hovels where all fresh water had been imported from Asia till the enterprise of Donzelot's 21st légère discovered a local source. Behind the port lay a desolate hinterland. A dozen miles inland rose a low mountain range which the explorer James Bruce had described as perhaps the most barren hills in the world. Through them ran a wide desert plain, the route to the Nile 120 miles away; a terrain where no shrubs or vegetation survived the arid heat; no birds, no snakes or lizards moved under the burning sun. There were wells on the way where bedouin levied tribute on passing caravans, but their location was unknown to Baird; the longest gaps between them proved to be thirty-four and thirty-eight miles, each a good three days' march in the summer heat.

On 21 June Baird's desert march began. His army moved in small detachments so that the few available camels could carry their water supply in skin bags between the wells. The troops set out at a funereal pace, men and horses drooping as they slowly entered the desert; at first through ravines of red rock slabs; then over a sea of loose sand, followed by hard gravel covered with loose flat stones. Sixteen miles inland a strange discovery was made: on the top of some scorching rocks lay the desiccated corpses of six British marines, still identifiable by their uniforms and buttons. How and when they had died there was unknown.

The artillery was drawn by small bullocks from India; and the European troops were allowed beasts of burden to bear their provisions and knapsacks. The sepoys, however, carried their own knapsacks, cooking pots, three days' provisions, and sixty rounds of ball cartridge. Laden with these impedimenta they bore the march less well than the British, and two sepoys loaded their muskets and shot themselves. In the British contingent the paymaster and twelve soldiers died of sunstroke, and the 8th Light Dragoons lost fifteen horses from thirst.

Each detachment took twelve to fifteen days to complete its march, and in early July most of the force was at Keneh, slaking its thirst in the Nile and revelling in the grapes and oranges. What was Baird's next move to be? He had orders to undertake subsequent operations against Mauritius and the Dutch East Indies, and if he committed his force to the 400-mile journey down the Nile he would miss the northerly monsoon for his return to the Indian Ocean. Was he still needed at Cairo? News reached him by way of Kosseir that the city had surrendered, and while an aide de camp sailed down the Nile to learn Hutchinson's wishes, the force prepared to face a return march across the desert.

Hutchinson's own inclination was to summon Baird, and thus make sure of enough force to capture Alexandria; for at this point no reinforcements had reached him from the west. When Baird's aide de camp arrived on 10 July the question had been placed beyond doubt by a despatch from the new Secretary of State, Lord Hobart. Though 6,000 reinforcements were being sent from the west to hasten the conquest of Egypt, the army would then be required for services in other theatres as yet unspecified. When Alexandria fell, therefore, it was to be garrisoned by Baird's 'sepoy' force. For this purpose Hutchinson summoned Baird to join him, and would leave a garrison in Giza as a staging post for his boats as they descended the Nile. Baird cancelled his arrangements to return to Kosseir, collected djerms at Keneh, and prepared to float down the Nile to Rosetta.[18]

On 9 July the French had evacuated Cairo, withdrawing to Giza and the island of Roda while Colonel Stewart moved in to occupy the citadel with the 30th and 89th. As the French departed the Turkish army entered the city, and fell to the looting and murder which had lured them across the deserts from Palestine. About that the British could do nothing, and the Grand Vizir's army dissolved into anarchy.

By 14 July the French were ready to march. On the river 300 djerms flying the tricolour carried the baggage and provisions, the sick, and the corpse of Kléber. And the women. Those belonging to the Alexandria garrison would be delivered to Menou, and if he refused to admit them they were to be embarked for France with the women of Belliard's corps. The French baggage contained a mass of loot and public property which they should have surrendered under the terms of the capitulation, but in view of Belliard's superior numbers Hutchinson was not inclined to enforce the conditions too strictly if he could get the French out of the country without trouble.[19]

Belliard's troops marched in cheerful and boozy disorder. They had had enough of Egypt, which had tormented them for the past three years with all its diseases from gippy tummy to bubonic plague. But straggle as they might they were still armed and numerous, and their well horsed artillery had a full complement of ammunition. The task of escorting them fell to Moore, newly recovered from his wound, while Hutchinson and Cradock remained in sick quarters at Giza guarded by the 89th. Moore could obtain no returns from the French, but they were certainly stronger than his own British force of 3,500 though he did not guess how much so. With him marched the Capitan Pacha's force and 2,000 of the Grand Vizir's Albanians. When the armies moved off at 5 a.m. on 15 July the Turks took the lead followed by the British, with the French in the rear. From the second day 2,000 Mamelukes followed the French and provided desert patrols on their flank.

Table 8 Belliard's embarcation

All ranks		
Cavalry, infantry, artillery	10,856	
Etat major	45	
Dromedary corps	177	
Sappers and miners	150	
Invalids (fit only for garrison duty)	500	
Seamen	344	
Horse and foot guides	40	
Sick	800	
Auxiliaries:		
Greeks and Copts	600	
Mamelukes	160	
		13,672
Employées		
Mathematical School	30	
Library and bureau central	15	
Printing press	26	
Civilians	11	
		82
Total (excluding women and children)		13,754
Deserted to join Mamelukes		500

Source: Wilson, 178–9

The daily march was ten or fifteen miles, with a halt every fourth day. At night the French camped on ground chosen by the British Quartermaster-General, forming a three-sided square on the bank of the Nile, while about two miles ahead Moore ranged his camp to face the French in order of battle. Communication between the armies was prevented by a strong screen of outposts, and no disorders occurred.[20] On the first evening the mustachioed General Morand came over to the British camp with a message from Belliard and stayed to dinner. An agreeable and communicative man with 'gentlemanlike manners', he proved to be the new type of French general, a lawyer's son who had left college about the beginning of the Revolution and had served throughout the nine years of war.

Among the British troops ophthalmia continued to rage, and besides 600 cases who had been left behind at Giza, 300 were transferred to the boats after two days' march. The only threatening sign from the French was Belliard's thwarting of Moore's wish to see his column pass and count it; but no other problems had occurred when the columns reached El Hamed on 29 July, the fifteenth day of the march. Here Belliard's numbers had to be discovered in order to calculate the tonnage for his embarcation. Moore's opportunity came as the columns approached the El Hamed defile between lake Idku and the Nile. The Turks led on through the pass and camped near Rosetta; but Moore had no intention of being cornered in that pocket and leaving the French free to break away and join the Alexandria garrison.[21] The British troops halted and changed front to face the French as they filed towards Rosetta. Two officers of the Quartermaster-General's staff were stationed where they could count the enemy as they passed, and their total was startling: 8,000 'very fine stout fellows' including 800 cavalry, with fifty well horsed cannon. There were at least another 2,000 fighting troops in the river boats, so Belliard must have surrendered Cairo when he still had 10,000 fighting men rather than the 6,000 Hutchinson had supposed. Moore castigated the surrender as 'one of the basest acts I have heard of'.

At their final camp near Rosetta the departing French were selling swords, horses, and black girls. The horses enabled the British to complete the mounting of their cavalry and replace the worst of their artillery horses which were shot. The navy was better able than the army to take the black girls on their strength, and a party of sailors clubbed together and bought one for seven Spanish dollars. She wept during the auction, but allowed herself to be quietly led by a cord to the lake where her new owners stripped and scrubbed her before carrying her off to their ship in a boat. But the trade in girls languished, and at last the French were offering a premium to anyone who would take care of them.[22]

From the Rosetta camp the French were sent forward in small detachments to embark at the caravanserai (the sea-entrance to lake Idku). By 5 August 13,672 troops of all ranks had been embarked, besides women, children, and civilian officials; and on 9 August the last convoy sailed for France. One week later Moore's troops from Cairo launched an attack on the Alexandria front, and the final battle for Egypt began.

19

THE FINAL MANOEUVRE

The first report of the victory of 21 March had reached London from Paris in the last days of April. Even Lord Grenville, so sceptical of Abercromby's merits, judged it at first to be 'a brilliant and decisive success', though he played down Abercromby's credit by insisting that the battle proved the enemy in Egypt to have only 6,000 field troops, even fewer than the ministers had originally supposed.[1]

A fortnight later came the news of Abercromby's death; and, about the same time, of the death of Lieutenant James Brown in front of the Green Hill on 13 March. James's death was broken to his parents in Cheshire in a letter from his company commander, Captain Phillips of the light company of the 44th, who had sat down to write it ten days after the battle. He told them that their son had known his wound was mortal, and had said, 'If this is death I die happy, I feel no pain, write to my mother but break the news of my death as tenderly as possible'. 'I offer my best wishes', Phillips continued, 'that you may be able to bear up against it with the same fortitude and resignation to that power which governs the fate of us all, as your late esteemed and gallant son preserved even to the last moments of his life, and be assured, Madam, that no one ever fell more gloriously, or more deeply regretted by all who knew him.'[2]

In London the news of Abercromby's death brought the family of Henry Dundas to his house in Clarges Street, where they found the ex-Secretary of State 'in very deep affliction'. A letter of condolence arrived from the new Prime Minister Henry Addington on the death of 'this great officer'. Replying, Dundas told Addington that he had lost 'one of the dearest friends I ever had and one of the best men I ever knew'. They had been friends since early in life, he wrote, and were now linked by marriage: 'When I persevered in this expedition, under many discouraging circumstances, my chief confidence rested on the thorough knowledge I had of the union of enterprise and judgment which marked the military character of the General from his first onset as a soldier'.[3]

The House of Commons immediately voted a monument to Abercromby in St Paul's; and the barony which he had refused in his lifetime was conferred on his widow with remainder to his male heirs. But it was easier to honour Sir Ralph's memory than to replace him. His death, the Duke of York told the King, was a 'cruel loss . . . at this moment not to be fully repaired'. The senior officer in the Mediterranean was now Lieutenant-General Henry Fox at Minorca; but Hutchinson would continue to exercise the command in Egypt for months before Fox could supersede him, and the King unhesitatingly agreed that Hutchinson should retain the command with the local rank of lieutenant-general.[4]

Hutchinson's despatch called urgently for reinforcements, and the victory no longer seemed as decisive as had been hoped at first. The Cabinet agreed to send the strongest reinforcement that could be spared; but in England there were immediately available only two battalions enlisted for service outside Europe, the 25th and 26th, the only other two in that category being scattered all over Devon and Cornwall suppressing bread riots. After some discussion with the King, the Duke of York added the 24th and a draft from the Guards in London; and from Ireland the remainder of Hompesch's Hussars, and a British cavalry regiment which had to be dismounted because the Transport Board was unable to supply horse transports. To these reinforcements from home the Duke added three or four battalions from Minorca, reducing the garrison below the accepted safety level, and a regiment of French royalists from Trieste.[5]

None of these reinforcements arrived before July, and by then Hutchinson had completed the conquest of Cairo with no addition to his force except the 1/27th, which had been left at Malta to recover from sickness and had been forwarded by General Pigot in response to Hutchinson's appeal. To his original army Hutchinson issued a General Order on 14 July conveying the King's thanks for the victory of 21 March. 'Such', he added, 'are the effects of order, discipline, and obedience; without which even courage itself must be unavailing.'[6]

Inside the entrenchments of Alexandria Menou continued to proclaim that death was better than surrender; and when a copy of Belliard's capitulation arrived on 6 July he forthwith rejected the British offer of the same terms. Denouncing Belliard's surrender in a letter to Bonaparte, he declared that he would defend Alexandria to the last extremity: 'I know how to die, but not how to capitulate'. To Bonaparte's care he commended his wife and daughter, emphasising the good breeding of the bath-house keeper's daughter. 'She is . . . of the blood of Mahomet on the side of both her father and her mother – what is called *chérif*. My son Soleyman Mourad will equally be *chérif*. They are distinguished by a green turban.'[7]

On Menou's rejection of the Cairo terms, Hutchinson expected an obstinate defence of Alexandria; and reports of some great expedition being prepared in the ports of France and Spain suggested a massive effort to relieve the beleaguered city. Baird's reinforcement from India could not be expected for some weeks, since he had still to requisition boats at Keneh and pass his troops down the 400 miles of flooding river to Cairo; and indeed it was not to be till 27 August that his whole force was assembled at Giza for the final passage to the coast. But from the middle of July reinforcements were pouring in from Europe; and before Hutchinson's Nile expedition returned to Alexandria, Coote's force holding the Roman Camp position had received some 4,000 rank and file of infantry, raising its strength to about 9,000.[8] With these numbers it was possible to release the Marine battalion, which was dispersed to its ships.

Among the Nile force disparagement of the Commander-in-Chief had abated. Critics of the lenient capitulation were taken aback by the strength and quality of the garrison which marched out from Cairo. They were further confounded by a thirty-foot rise of the Nile, which would have interrupted a siege of Cairo and hampered communications with the base at Aboukir. There was now no denying that Hutchinson, far from having acted with excessive caution, had underestimated the risks of his Nile operations. He had subdued Belliard's force with a bare 4,000 British troops fit for duty, and a rabble of Turks on whom he could never rely. 'Leave the Turks to assemble the whole force of their Empire', he assured the Secretary of State in August, '10,000 good European troops, or perhaps less, would beat them in the course of an hour.' His success also silenced the school which had opposed the advance to Cairo as excessively risky and a misjudged priority; for with Belliard's strong force in his rear, the siege of Alexandria could not have been safely prosecuted. When Captain John Colborne arrived from England at the beginning of August he discovered that Hutchinson was now 'thought to have acted very politically' in getting Belliard's force out of the country without a fight.[9]

Opinion softened further in the Nile force with the arrival of the *London Gazette*. The army could now read Hutchinson's fine tribute to its gallantry on 21 March, and his grand and poignant eulogy of Abercromby which Moore was moved to copy into his diary. His silence about Abercromby's death in General Orders was forgiven.

In Coote's force, however, there was no relenting: the further one went from the Nile force the more virulent and persistent were the critics. Ill-informed hearsay still blamed Hutchinson for Lagrange's escape from Rahmanieh; and envy was roused by the news in the same *Gazette* that he had been made a Knight of the Bath and promoted to the local rank of lieutenant-general (hitherto he had held the same rank as his second-in-command and some of his brigade commanders). Little did he deserve the red ribbon of the Bath, snarled Coote and Dalhousie, pointing out that he had played little part in the early battles under Abercromby for which he had received it. Coote, moreover, had already been disappointed by the omission of his own name from Abercromby's despatch on the landing at Aboukir, and no doubt wanted a red ribbon for himself. 'Alas, I fear he is very unpopular', he wrote of Hutchinson.[10]

Newcomers quickly picked up the prevailing tone in the camp. Captain Robert Dalrymple heard the Commander-in-Chief 'pretty well abused' at his first dinner on joining the Third Guards. 'General Hutchinson's manners are haughty', he was told, 'his temper peevish and obstinate: hence no cordiality between the other General Officers and Headquarters, nor between the Commanders-in-Chief of the Fleet and Army.' The Guards found time in the tediousness of their routine to work up indignation about a slight on the privileges of guardsmen. General Ludlow had been given the colonelcy of a regiment of infantry of the line by which he ceased to belong to the Foot Guards; yet although the Guards were entitled to be commanded by one of their own, Ludlow remained in command of the Guards Brigade, confirming their conviction that Hutchinson was 'taking every opportunity of keeping down the Guards'. A petition to Hutchinson worked the trick, and when brigades were reorganised to incorporate the reinforcements, Ludlow was removed to the first brigade of the line (formerly Coote's) and replaced by Lord Cavan.[11]

All this fuss was probably a symptom of boredom. The watch at Alexandria had been tedious, and since the arrival of the reinforcements was not even demanding. 'One leads a terrible idle life in camp', Dalrymple discovered. Coote's officers were impatient for action, and anxious to match the glory of the force on the Nile. Dalrymple was told that since receiving the reinforcements Coote had written seven letters to Hutchinson proposing to send a force to the westward of Alexandria and cut off Menou's overland supplies, but had received no answer: 'Colonel Anstruther, a wary Scotchman, seems to carry everything'.[12]

Coote and Lord Keith had been exchanging complaints of Hutchinson's dilatoriness. For the admiral some of the urgency had been removed since early May by news of the assassination of the Tsar Paul, whose machinations with Bonaparte had threatened the Ottoman Empire, and by the British bombardment of Copenhagen which broke up the armed neutrality of the Baltic Powers. Yet reports of enemy naval concentrations in the west continued, perhaps portending either a relief expedition to Alexandria or, worse, a dash for Constantinople which would force Keith to abandon the army and pursue the enemy into the Aegean to save the Ottoman Empire. Such a threat to the Porte would also draw away the Capitan Pacha and his fleet, leaving his troops to dissolve into an ungovernable mob; and if the Grand Vizir also withdrew, his horde would lay waste the country as it retreated and leave Baird's force to starve if it landed at Suez.[13]

Haunted by these fears, Keith had continued throughout the Nile operations to harass Hutchinson for speedier results. Reluctantly accepting the need to push for Cairo to cover Baird's arrival, he had urged the general to move swiftly and return to finish the work at Alexandria. How could he dawdle thus between Rahmanieh and Algam? He wished the general would take a leaf out of Lagrange's book, and march with some of the French speed:

'The national enterprise will be questioned all over the world. How much we have to lament the misjudged intrepidity of Sir Ralph'. Evidently he had forgotten his impatience with Abercromby in the fortnight after the landing.[14]

Shortly before the capitulation of 10,000 troops at Cairo Keith was asserting that there were not 7,000 Frenchmen in the whole of Egypt. Yet after the fall of Cairo he continued to harass Hutchinson shamelessly about the terms of capitulation and the burden of transporting Belliard's force to France; complaints which Hutchinson refuted convincingly and with wit.[15] As the French began their march to the coast, the naval threat from the west was dissolved by news of Admiral Saumarez's victory at Algeciras over the combined French and Spanish fleet of Linois, the final defeat of Bonaparte's efforts to relieve the army he had abandoned in Egypt. Yet there still remained the political imperative to dislodge the French; and Keith sounded a warning that, unless Alexandria harbour could be opened to provide shelter in the September equinox, the transports in Aboukir bay would have to leave the coast.

Hutchinson remained an invalid at Giza through most of July, while Moore was escorting Belliard's garrison to the coast. Did he really intend to attack Alexandria, or would he continue the slow process of blockade? Coote feared the latter. No orders to prepare for an attack arrived from the ailing Chief; nor were the commanders of the artillery and engineers sent down the river to plan the siege. 'Alas! Slow measures are pursued', Coote lamented. It was being said that the Cairo force ought to have come down the Nile without delaying to escort the French garrison. Colonel Graham recognised that this was absurd; but he was critical of other delays. Hutchinson himself should have come down weeks earlier; and when the Nile force eventually arrived nothing had been prepared for a siege. Artillery and engineers' stores were only now beginning to be assembled, and the only gabions and fascines available were those which had been rotting on the beach for six months since their arrival from Marmaris.[16]

Coote, as rumour reported, had been planning to send a force up the lake and approach Alexandria from the west. As early as 7 July he predicted that, if Hutchinson would launch this operation quickly, Alexandria would fall between 15 August and 1 September; a shrewd forecast. Three days later he reconnoitred the sea-coast west of the city from a naval brig, with a view to occupying the narrow neck of land with 4–5,000 men. His intention was probably to stop the provisions which were enabling the enemy to survive. For a good price Arab caravans were still crossing the desert from the interior. To block this traffic, Captain Chollet of Hompesch's Hussars had been sent on a long circuit by Damanhur to organise bedouin patrols in the desert twenty miles west of Alexandria. Near the Tour des Arabes his patrol encountered a camel convoy with a flock of 700 sheep, escorted by nearly 400 Arabs who beat off the patrol and made their way into Alexandria. A party of Mamelukes who had followed Chollet across the desert met the same Arabs returning, and charged them. The Mameluke leader, Achmet Bey, was shot, and in consternation at having killed a bey the Arabs retreated into the city.[17]

It was not till 29 July that Hutchinson arrived at Rosetta by river. He still looked very unwell, and left no instructions with Moore who was mounting guard over Belliard's embarkation. He told Lord Keith, however, that he intended an immediate attack on Alexandria, and went on board the flagship *Foudroyant* where he remained convalescent for another fortnight. Coote implored him to come ashore, urging 'the absolute necessity of a Commander-in-Chief to be present to give his directions on the spot for an attempt of such magnitude which is now in contemplation'.[18] Hutchinson, however, judged otherwise. The extensive operations he was planning could not begin till Moore's brigades and the boats of the fleet were released by the departure of Belliard's final convoy for France. In the meantime he nursed his health and issued his instructions from the cabin of the *Foudroyant*, where he was planning the details of the coming operations with the admiral. From 4 August the army was put to work bringing up bombardment materials from the lakeside artillery depot.

This activity seemed to promise an early start for the big attack, and rumours of the plan had leaked out, though Colonel Dyott was still grumbling on 9 August – the sailing date of Belliard's last convoy – that 'procrastination appears to be the order of the day'.[19] Such complaints were the price of Hutchinson's remoteness from his troops. But on board the *Foudroyant* he was far from idle, for the requirements of the coming attack were massive. On the central question he had made up his mind: he would not risk failure and heavy loss by an unprepared assault on the deep belt of enemy redoubts, batteries, and entrenchments which now crowned the heights of Nicopolis. Always reluctant to expend the lives of his splendid troops,[20] he planned more subtly. He would proceed by a two-front operation. From the Roman Camp position he would begin regular siege approaches to bring heavy guns to bear on the French fieldworks and force Menou to man them. Simultaneously Coote would be shipped up the lake with three brigades to open a new front on the western side of the city.

Of the terrain and defences on the western isthmus very little was known, owing to Keith's earlier refusal to put his gunboats into lake Mareotis; for the gunboats which the French had dragged across the isthmus from the Old Harbour commanded the waters of the lake and prevented reconnaissance. But they were unlikely to have developed a defensive system in the west as strong as their works on the heights of Nicopolis. To discover more, Lord Keith now pushed some of his boats into the lake, and in company with Colonel Anstruther reconnoitred the enemy's lakeside positions and counted the French flotilla. They concluded that a landing would not be difficult.

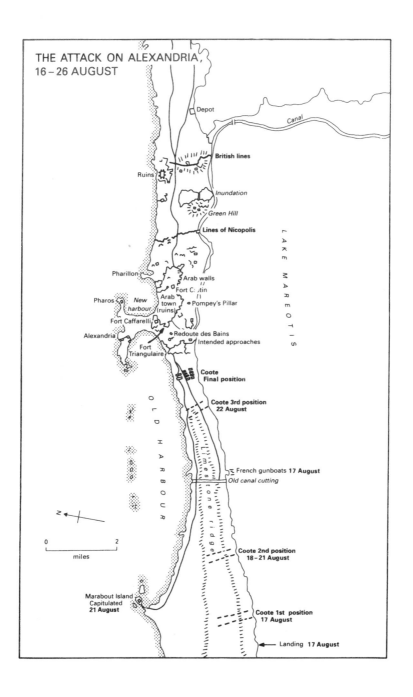

THE ATTACK ON ALEXANDRIA,
16 – 26 AUGUST

Depot

Canal

British lines

Ruins

Inundation

Green Hill

Lines of Nicopolis

L
A
K
E

M
A
R
E
O
T
I
S

Pharillon

Arab walls

Fort C: .tin

Pharos

New
harbour

Arab
town
(ruins)

Pompey's Pillar

Fort Caffarelli

Alexandria

Fort
Triangulaire

Redoute des Bains

Intended approaches

Coote
Final position

Coote 3rd position
22 August

O
L
D

H
A
R
B
O
U
R

French gunboats 17 August

Old canal cutting

L
i
m
e
s
t
o
n
e

r
i
d
g
e

0   2

miles

Coote 2nd position
18 – 21 August

Marabout Island
Capitulated
21 August

Coote 1st position
17 August

Landing 17 August

Whether the western manoeuvre would become the decisive one would depend on the strength of the enemy fortifications; but it would certainly draw French troops away from the heights of Nicopolis, and sever Menou's last supply route. Hutchinson as always was moving step by step; and without supposing that a regular siege would be easy or rapid, he knew that the enemy were discontented and ill fed, and that Menou was on good terms with only two of his eighteen generals. The collapse of resistance could be sudden.[21]

The effort required to supply the coming operations was immense. Two armies would have to be provisioned in desert country, one of them twenty miles from the fleet in Aboukir bay, the other thirty, and every djerm and ship's boat would be needed. To reduce the commissariat's problem, all but one regiment of cavalry and all the horses of the field artillery were sent back to Rosetta where they could be foraged from the delta; and with them went most of the train of horses, camels, and asses which had been bringing up provisions and stores from the lakeside depot to the lines. The final link in the chain of supply would depend on manpower as it had done in the first days of the campaign.[22]

By 13 August the preparations for the ground offensive were nearly complete. On that day the last of Moore's three brigades which had been watching Belliard marched in to the Roman Camp position, and were ready to relieve Coote's regiments whose fifteen weary weeks guarding the lines had earned the right to an active role.[23] Moore's arrival was the signal for the navy's preliminary movements to begin. Keith had moved twenty-six shallow-draught craft into lake Mareotis, including several large square-rigged Turkish vessels each carrying a 24-pounder and two 12-pounders. As Moore's men marched in from Rosetta the flotilla advanced across the lake to close with the French gunboats and, after forcing them in to the shore, formed a blockading crescent around them. Colonel Anstruther sailed on up the lake in a small boat with Captain Brice of the Royal Engineers. Landing on the isthmus and climbing the ridge, they reconnoitred the Marabout fort which commanded the entrance to the Old Harbour of Alexandria.[24]

In the meantime Coote's force for the west was preparing to embark. The comfortable boredom of the Roman Camp now looked more enticing: 'This service will indeed be wretched. No market . . .'. In the August heat Captain Dalrymple of the Guards would be carrying a greatcoat, a large haversack of ration biscuit, two bottles of wine, and a bottle of water. The force was due to embark on the evening of the 15th, and Hutchinson at last came ashore and joined the army though still sickly and frail. But there was a blunder. The boats arrived from Aboukir bay with no provisions on board. There was not enough stock in the forward depot to provide the necessary three days' field rations, and the boats had to return to the fleet and pick up supplies. This muddle delayed the offensive for twenty-four hours; but on the 16th three of Coote's brigades were relieved in the line by the force from the Nile,

Table 9 New brigading of 9 August (effective rank and file)

Warned for duty under Coote, 11 August				
Brigade of Guards (Cavan)	Coldstream	552		
	Third Guards	590	1,142	
1st Brigade (Ludlow)	25th[1]	526		
	1/27th	538		
	2/27th	465		
	44th	334	1,863	
2nd Brigade (Finch)	2/1st	352		
	26th[1]	438		
	1/54th	381		
	2/54th	384	1,555	4,560 infantry
With Hutchinson east of Alexandria				
3rd (Foreign) Brigade (Stuart)	Stuart's (Minorca)	690		
	De Roll's	383		
	Dillon's	393		
	Watteville's[1]	572	2,038	
4th Brigade (Hope)	8th	285		
	18th	293		
	79th	434		
	90th	437	1,449	
5th Brigade (Doyle)	30th	269		
	50th	337		
	89th	311		
	92nd	414	1,331	
6th Brigade (Blake)	1/20th[1]	604		
	2/20th[1]	484		
	24th[1]	438		
	Ancient Irish[1]	420	1,946	
Reserve (Moore, Oakes)	2nd	327		
	28th	338		
	42nd	490		
	58th	238		
	40th Flank Coys	146		
	23rd	343		
	Rifle Corps[2]	397		
	Chasseurs britanniques[1]	595		
	Corsican Rangers	60	2,934	9,698 infantry
Cavalry	26th Light Dragoons[3]			
At Rosetta				
Cavalry	11th Light Dragoons			
	12th Light Dragoons			
	22nd Light Dragoons			
Infantry	13th			

[1] Reinforcements not previously brigaded.

[2] This unit appears to be Hompesch's (titled in the Army List 'A Regiment of Mounted Riflemen'), presumably augmented by the reinforcements from Britain.

[3] Apparently not sent back to Rosetta: 103 rank and file were later transferred to the western force.

and embarked in the evening under cover of darkness. About 9.30 p.m. the armada of nearly 300 boats and djerms carrying 4,000 troops rowed off and vanished into the west.[25]

Behind them in the eastern sector other forces were moving into action. To deter Menou from moving forces westwards to oppose Coote's landing, pressure in the east was to begin at once with a dawn attack on the outlying French positions. The five eastern brigades had been grouped in two divisions commanded by Cradock and Moore, whose own brigades were taken over by Hope and Oakes. On the left Cradock's division was to seize and hold the Green Hill, the scene five months earlier of the 44th's fight and the death of Lieutenant Brown. In the coastal sector Moore was to drive in the enemy's outposts and dislodge them temporarily from a small sandhill identified as the Sugarloaf Hill 900 yards in front of the French entrenchments. For the Sugarloaf attack he used two battalions of Stuart's Foreign Brigade, the Minorca Regiment and the recently arrived Löwenstein's (Chasseurs britanniques). The troops assembled during darkness in front of their entrenchments, and half an hour before daylight began their advance. Driving in the French outposts, they pushed forward and put a force onto the Sugarloaf. From the crest at daylight Moore had a perfect view overlooking the enemy's main defences, from which a heavy crossfire of artillery came down on his position. The hillock was too small to provide much shelter, and too far forward to be supported if it were counter-attacked; and when the French infantry came out in force an hour after daylight Moore withdrew his troops as had been planned.[26]

Cradock's attack on the left was to be made by Doyle's 5th Brigade. Doyle had hurried forward from convalescence at Rosetta to command the attack, and organised his advance with two battalions forward, the 30th and 50th led by Colonel Spencer. Two small redoubts were cleared and the Green Hill was occupied. But the French, observing that Moore had evacuated the Sugarloaf when a counter-attack was threatened, pushed forward an attack 500 strong against the Green Hill. With colours flying and drums beating, the column breasted the slope, little suspecting that the crest concealed British infantry who were sheltering from cannon fire. The 30th were not more than 250 strong; but Colonel Lockhart hastily formed his men, fired several volleys, and charged with the bayonet. The enemy broke and ran, losing a number of men including eight prisoners who were literally dragged out of the ranks by their pursuers. 'They behaved very ill', judged Moore.[27]

Thus the British remained in possession of the dominating Green Hill, not green in the summer heat but clouded in 'more noxious dust than in any other of the dusty places in this dusty country'.[28] From here siege works could begin, and during the night a battery was dug overlooking the enemy batteries on the heights of Nicopolis. In the meantime Moore's force on the right, retiring from the Sugarloaf, had halted on an intermediate position which they found 400 men already entrenching. Having thus broken ground, regular siege works were pushed forward to a first parallel resting on the sea and defended on both flanks with redoubts. During the night a working party 250 strong was sent forward to construct a two-gun battery and a communication trench.

In spite of this beginning Moore was far from happy about a siege of the heights of Nicopolis whose defences he had now been able to view. The enemy's position was 'very formidable. Nature had made it strong, and they have added to it much by art'.[29] He doubted whether the British engineers were up to attacking the belt of fortifications on the heights: his new battery and trench were faulty to the point of uselessness. On the following night he sent forward 300 men to reconstruct the battery and widen and deepen the trenches; yet when he inspected them by daylight they were 'still extremely defective'. He was also critical of the outpost work along the front. On two successive nights the pickets ran in when they were harassed by the enemy; not from lack of courage, he reflected, 'but our officers and men are extremely ignorant of war, and never have their duties explained to them'. He hoped that the main push would be made against the weaker western face of the city, where Coote was now in action.[30]

20

THE FALL OF
ALEXANDRIA

Dawn broke on 17 August to reveal Coote's armada of boats and little ships widely scattered on the waters of lake Mareotis some three miles west of Alexandria. A change of wind during the night had driven more than half his vessels to leeward, and by the time they were collected again at 10 a.m. the enemy had brought several hundred men and a pair of horse artillery guns to the intended landing point. Coote's last landing had been made on a constricted front in Aboukir bay, but this time he had scope to manoeuvre. Pushing the boats of Finch's brigade towards the shore to pin down the waiting enemy, he moved the rest of his force two miles further west and landed unopposed.[1]

The terrain in which his troops now found themselves was utterly unlike the sandy plains and palm groves to the east of Alexandria. The western isthmus was a jagged ridge of limestone thrusting along the coast from the western desert: treeless, barren, and split by ravines and deep quarries; no sand underfoot, but a fine white dust. At the landing point the breadth of the isthmus from the lake to the Marabout island on the coast was about two miles, with a sandy plain on the seaward side of the ridge; but as one moved eastwards towards the forts of Alexandria the land narrowed to a mere thousand yards of limestone rock, with a narrow coastal strip on each side along which ran a good road. An opposed advance along this narrow, broken isthmus would need the support of gunboats on both flanks; and on the seaward side that would require the capture of the Marabout fort whose guns commanded the entrance to the long lagoon called the Old Harbour.

As the troops came ashore from the lake one battalion remained on the beach to handle the stores, while the remainder took up a right-angled position facing east and north to cover the landing of the stores and guns. During the next twenty-four hours five battalions at a time were detailed for fatigue duties in the heat of the August day and through the night, humping stores and dragging cannon across the ravines and quarries of the ridge. Fortunately the boats were not required to supply water, which was found in plenty in the plain beyond the ridge.

At 5 p.m. on the day after the landing Coote was ready to attack the Marabout, and moved his force a mile and a half to the east to cover the siege, leaving the 1/54th to conduct it. Two 12-pounders and a pair of 8-inch howitzers had been manoeuvred with immense toil over the quarried ridge; and through the night of 18 August artillerymen helped by fatigue parties of infantry laboured to build a sandbag battery. At daybreak on the 19th the guns were in position and the bombardment began. By 7 a.m. they had sunk two French gunboats lying under the fort, and sent the third limping off to Alexandria. But on the solid masonry of the fort the 12-pounders were making little impression, and it was seen that to open a breach heavier battering pieces would be needed.

The guns fell silent to await the arrival of 24-pounders, and infantry took over the siege. The Marabout fort was sited on a rocky peninsula separated from the mainland by a fordable submerged reef. On the landward side was a high rock commanding the island; and on its crest the commanding officer of the 1/54th placed his light company as sharpshooters. The French cannon were on open platforms firing over parapets without embrasures; and the light bobs of the 54th picked off the gunners and drove them from the guns. Soon not a man could show his head above the parapet.

In the meantime no fewer than four British battalions had been recalled from the front to provide a labour force and were hauling a pair of 24-pounders across the precipices from the lake, toiling like the slaves of the Pharaohs. This work took up the whole of 20 August, and the heavy cannon reached the Marabout during the night. By daybreak on the 21st they were in battery positions near the 12-pounders, and the bombardment was resumed. The accuracy of the shooting impressed onlookers, showing 'to what a pitch of perfection the British artillery had arrived'.[2] The first shot from Captain Curry's guns struck the tower of the fort four feet above the ground, and each succeeding shot struck the same spot smashing a hole in the masonry which was gradually enlarged, till at midday the whole tower collapsed with a tremendous crash, filling the ditch and burying stores, provisions, and a 24-pounder. By the evening the garrison had abandoned all its fire-positions and was sheltering under the rocks on the far side of the island. A summons was sent in while four companies of the 54th prepared to storm the fort, and the commandant surrendered with 168 men. The ten cannon taken in the fort had all been scarred by the musketry of the British sharpshooters.[3]

With the silencing of the Marabout fort the entrance to the Old Harbour was open, and during the evening British and Turkish sloops sounded their way through the unbuoyed channel and anchored on the left of the army, ready to support Coote's advance at daybreak. The first French covering line was about two miles east of the British position. Here the isthmus narrowed to slightly less than a mile, and was broken by a ravine formed by the cutting of the canal which had once joined lake Mareotis to the sea. This position was held by 1,200 men commanded by General Eppler, whom we last encountered leading a column of Rampon's division in the battle of Alexandria. His flanks were strengthened with heavy batteries, and field artillery was spaced along his front.

As the sun appeared above the eastern horizon on the morning of 22 August the advance began, with the regularity and magnificence of a military exercise. Two columns of Cavan's Guards formed the right and centre of the advance, with Ludlow's brigade forming the left on the level ground by the Old Harbour, and Finch's brigade in reserve. A strong screen of skirmishers led the advance, supplied on the right by 200 guardsmen, and on the left by the 1/27th from Ludlow's brigade and a detachment of Löwenstein's Jäger which had arrived from the eastern front during the night. Close behind the skirmishing line followed Major Cookson's six field-guns, unlimbering frequently to cannonade the enemy; and on both flanks the navy's flotillas, now expert in co-operating with the army, moved abreast of the troops. On the lake Captain Stevenson, back from the Nile campaign, commanded the gunboats; and Captain Cochrane the sloops in the harbour. On the glittering water sloops and gunboats, with sails set and pennants flying, covered the lake and harbour in drifting smoke as they thundered at the enemy batteries. On the isthmus skirmishing lines and supporting columns advanced confidently into the morning sun, driving back the enemy's pickets with an incessant fire of small arms and cannon. At last the British Army was savouring the exhilaration of certain victory; for once the big battalions were theirs.[4]

The French did not wait to receive the assault. As soon as Eppler knew that a serious attack was coming he withdrew, abandoning his heavy guns in their batteries, and formed again on a rearward ridge from which his troops maintained a galling fire of grape and musketry. Coote was determined to maintain the momentum of his thrust which had begun so well. Joining the skirmishers to reconnoitre the unknown terrain ahead, he commanded the advance with a coolness and judgement which astonished the officers around him.[5] The skirmishing line rushed on at a charging pace, overrunning French tents and baggage. Down on the level by the harbour the squadron of the 26th Light Dragoons charged a body of French cavalry, and pursuing hard found themselves suddenly within thirty yards of a French battalion of infantry. But there was no repetition of Colonel Archdall's disaster five months earlier. The enemy fired a volley, but even at this short range their aim was so unsteady that not a man nor a horse was hit. Evidently the spirit and cohesion of the Army of the Orient was breaking down, as was also suggested by the day's casualties. The French lost about 200 killed, wounded, and prisoners, and seven guns; the British only three killed and forty wounded. The enemy were on the run; and though the British columns were often under heavy fire, they made skilful use of the irregular ground to avoid needless losses.[6]

Coote's headlong rush had carried his force across four miles of broken country and had overrun the French forward positions covering the Alexandria defences. He was now within 1,400 yards of the first defensive work, the Fort des Bains. The time was still only 10 a.m. and most of the long day was in hand. But no heavy cannon were available to batter the fort, and it would take days to bring them up. Coote organised a position within cannon shot of the fort, on a commanding height with a clear view of the crumbling city walls, the shipping in the harbour, and the bustle of the quays. No water was found on the new position, and it had to be manhandled forward from the previous night's camp four miles in the rear.[7] In the desiccating dust and heat Captain Dalrymple was suffering from dysentery: 'I shall never forget the luxury of my tea this evening, for famished with thirst'.[8]

During the afternoon an officer arrived at Hutchinson's headquarters to inform him of Coote's morning advance and the exposed forward position which he now held. Hutchinson had seen signs in the past two days that the enemy was thinning out the force in his eastern defences, suggesting that he was shifting his strength for a counterstroke against Coote. The western force must be reinforced, and pressure increased on the eastern sector. Hutchinson ordered the 6th brigade, now commanded by Colonel Spencer, to embark and join Coote. But boats could not be ready before nightfall; and a diversion had to be mounted quickly to hold the enemy till Coote's reinforcements joined him. Before daybreak on the morning of the 23rd Moore and Cradock drove in the French pickets in front of the heights of Nicopolis, and pushed parties of infantry forward to crawl up close to the French position in the darkness and open fire. One party of Turks crawled right up on to the crest. The enemy beat to arms, and opened a furious fire with all their weapons till daylight revealed that they had been shooting in the air. During the morning Spencer's brigade joined Coote, and the crisis was past.[9]

Coote's dramatic progress presented Hutchinson with a choice between east and west. Should his effort be concentrated on besieging the lines of Nicopolis, or could new siege works be opened on Coote's front? He decided to see for himself, and embarked with Cradock and the Chief Engineer to visit Coote, whom he joined that afternoon. They made a careful reconnaissance of the enemy's fortifications; concluded that they were much weaker than those on the heights of Nicopolis; and took the decision to assault from the west.

The following day, 24 August, was spent in bringing cannon forward, and after stupendous efforts the morning of the 25th saw four 24-pounders and four mortars in bombarding positions. Fire was opened against the Fort des Bains. The beleaguered French, whom Dalrymple considered 'very civil' – 'They never fire except when we begin' – felt obliged to reply, and lobbed shells into the British camp. But their fuses were old, and many failed to explode. One shell dropped through the centre of a bell tent in which eight men of the 3rd Guards were sleeping, took off a guardsman's foot as it fell, and buried itself ten inches in the ground without bursting.[10]

The British bombardment was a failure. The newly constructed gun-platforms soon began to collapse, and firing had to cease. In any case the range of 1,400 yards was too long for a breaching battery, and Coote decided to seize a ridge in front where he could place his batteries 600 yards from the fort. It was held by a strong enemy outpost, much too far forward, which Colonel George Smyth of the 1/20th was ordered to dislodge. The 20th, newly arrived as volunteers from Minorca, was a fine regiment 'that never would be beaten'.[11] At 9 p.m. Smyth formed his battalion in column, supported by a subaltern and thirty men of the 26th Light Dragoons with a second battalion of infantry in reserve. The 20th advanced in the dark along the base of the ridge by the lake with unloaded muskets; and after bypassing the French position they wheeled left into the high ground behind the 100-strong outpost. Surprised and surrounded, the French fired a few shots and tried to retreat, but their escape was barred and all were bayoneted or captured.[12]

With their task completed the 20th were withdrawn, leaving pickets to guard the captured position. Before long the enemy appeared through the darkness with a 1,000-strong counter-attack; and a night action began amid the flash of cannon and the blaze of musketry. The pickets held on stoutly till their supports came up, and after an hour's fighting the French gave up and withdrew behind the Fort des Bains. 'A very beautiful sight', Wilson enthused; and Dalrymple, who had probably never seen a battle by night, had 'never witnessed anything so beautiful as the firing. The shells from our gunboats and the battery had the grandest effect possible'. Beautiful for the spectators; but the darkness hid some brutal fighting with the bayonet. 'One poor old grey-headed Frenchman', a sergeant was told, 'not being able to keep up with the rest, fell on his knees and begged for mercy, but an English soldier, more like a savage than a man, ran him through with the bayonet. Our soldiers all cried "shame" at him.'[13]

The game was nearly over. The prisoners taken by the 20th were all saying that Menou's troops were worn out with incessant duties and would no longer fight, and that he would be forced to surrender. When morning dawned on 26 August Coote pushed his approach trenches forward, and two more strong batteries were erected during the day. That night the first parallel was due to be completed, and thirty cannon, howitzers, and mortars would be ready to open the bombardment in the morning. Coote's plan was to make a lodgement on the hill above Pompey's Pillar, where he would dominate the enemy's defences.

On the eastern face of the city pressure continued. From the Green Hill the British heavy batteries opened against the right of the Nicopolis position, concentrating their fire on a redoubt covering the canal bridge and on the right-hand battery of the French line. Spectators were again impressed by the accuracy of the British 24-pounders. Soon the seven embrasures of the enemy battery were all silenced and the guns withdrawn. This bombardment was the last action of the campaign, and one of the final British casualties was an old soldier whose legs were taken off by a cannon ball as he worked on the parapet of a redoubt. He fell dying into the arms of his son, a corporal in the same regiment. 'An interesting accident', observed Wilson.[14]

About four-thirty that afternoon a French aide de camp came out to Coote's advanced posts under flag of truce to propose an armistice. 'I was never more surprised', Dalrymple wrote; but there had already been a hint that Menou was softening. He had always refused to allow a parley on land; but two days earlier a flag of truce had arrived with a letter of thanks to Hutchinson for saving his wife from the Turkish executioners at Cairo. When the French officer appeared on the 26th Coote sent out his aide de camp, Captain Walsh, to blindfold the Frenchman and bring him in to the lines; and he delivered a proposal for a three days' armistice to draw up terms of capitulation. Firing was at once suspended, while the letter was referred to the Commander-in-Chief; and at 1 a.m. on 27 August Coote learned that the same proposal had been received by Hutchinson and accepted. White flags were hoisted, and hostilities ceased.

Menou's previous behaviour did not promise a speedy agreement, and, predictably, no more was heard from him. In the meantime the British superiority of numbers grew ever stronger, for during the 27th Colonel Montresor arrived from General Baird with the news that his force was due at Rosetta within a couple of days. Hutchinson was as conscious as Menou that time was vital for the peace negotiators in London. On receiving Menou's overture he had rushed off a letter to Lord Elgin in Constantinople, so that the British government could learn with the utmost speed by overland courier that the final surrender of Egypt was imminent.

The armistice was due to expire on 29 August at 11 p.m.; and it had only seven hours to run when a French aide de camp arrived at Hutchinson's headquarters at 4 p.m. But instead of terms of surrender he brought a demand for a thirty-six hours' extension to the armistice, at the end of which Menou would be ready to receive commissioners to treat for a convention. In a fury Hutchinson replied that he required terms for a capitulation, not negotiations for a convention: he would appoint no commissioners, and at midnight would resume hostilities. In the French officer's hearing orders were given for the batteries to be ready to open that night; and he departed with Hutchinson's answer. Time crawled on; and at nine o'clock he returned with a promise that proposals would be sent by 2 p.m. on the following day. Having thus gained an extra day, Menou sent out two officers punctually the next afternoon with articles of capitulation.[15]

Yet even now Menou was wriggling in the net, buying every hour he could for Bonaparte's negotiators. When Hutchinson studied the terms, he found that Menou proposed not only the repatriation of his troops but the return of all warships and other shipping to France, and most of the artillery; the retention of all Egyptian public property in French hands; and, most outrageously, that the armistice should be extended for nineteen days till 17 September, when Menou would be free to resume hostilities if reinforcements reached him.

The suggestion would have been laughable but for the urgent political need for Menou's surrender; and 'in a great rage which frightened not a little the chef de brigade who came with the terms', Hutchinson dictated his own alterations and declared that if they were not immediately conceded he would resume hostilities and storm the town. An aide de camp galloped back to Menou with this ultimatum.[16]

Why was Menou contemplating a capitulation at all? Only extreme necessity could justify surrender, and that necessity was not obvious. On the eastern face of Alexandria Moore believed that Menou could have resisted for two more weeks. When Moore inspected the formidable network of defences, which he was probably shown by their creator Bertrand, he was astonished by their skilful design and construction. 'In every part the superiority of their engineers is apparent', he noted: the sheer labour of the digging was 'prodigious; it is what no other troops would have done'. Admittedly there were weaknesses in the field-works and forts. Constructed of the local dust and rubble, they were under constant repair as they crumbled into the ditches under the weight of the cannon. Heavy British guns would soon have opened a way for storming parties. But Moore believed that bringing siege artillery forward by methodical approaches would have lost a fortnight. Without this preparation no one believed that the heights of Nicopolis could have been stormed. Whether this was true of the entire front remains an open question. The French centre in front of the Rosetta gate, and the coastal sector which Moore faced, had indeed been heavily fortified in depth, with batteries on projecting points to sweep the steep escarpment with flanking fire; and the besiegers' approach trenches from the first parallel would be long and exposed. But Wilson makes a persuasive argument that the French flank on the canal was vulnerable. Here their batteries were dominated at close range from the Green Hill, and the low ground by the canal was easier to bombard and penetrate than the escarpment to the north. Wilson suggested that, had the state of the French defences been known, an attack on the French right flank on the canal, supported at the proper moment by a landing from the lake behind the French front, would have been a surer way to take the town than the double approach from east and west which Hutchinson adopted. But it would certainly have been a more costly operation.[17]

The same question hangs over the western sector. Moore judged that although the approach was easier than in the east, the French might still have kept Coote's force out for a couple of weeks. This does not seem to have been the opinion of those who served in that sector; but there were further fortifications behind those which he was about to assault, and perhaps some regard should be paid to the French engineer who had actually created the defences. General Bertrand admittedly wrote with the hindsight of a Bonapartist groupie on St Helena; but between March and August 1801 he had been the director of the Alexandria fortifications. He asserted that Menou had no right to surrender, and that the favourable terms were offered as an inducement to march out prematurely. He should have fought, wrote Bertrand, till his forward field-works and forts had been overrun, and should then still have fought on till his interior defences were taken or breached: till the Arab walls had been forced, Forts Cretin and Caffarelli taken, and a practicable breach made in the strong inner defence line which barred the way to the New Town on its isthmus.[18]

If the state of the defences dictated no absolute necessity to surrender, neither did the stock of supplies in the city. Though Menou's garrison were hungry and ill dressed – most of them, according to one British officer, clad in cotton 'dressing gowns', presumably the comfortable native djellabah – they were not starving. True, there was much infectious sickness, scurvy was rampant, and the water was bad. But there was enough rice for thirty days, and with horses being butchered at the rate of seventeen a day Menou still had 800 horses and 300 camels to provide meat for seventy days if the beasts could be foddered. Nevertheless on 28 August, having arranged the armistice, Menou had summoned a Council of War and laid before it a list of twenty-one reasons why he should capitulate, blaming Belliard's premature surrender of Cairo for denying him the time to stockpile Alexandria's provisions and complete its defences. Yet in reality his case did not rest on the state of his supplies or ramparts.

What broke Menou's will to fight was the mood of his soldiers. They were exhausted and demoralised. His 9,000 troops of all kinds were too few to man the extensive fortifications, and the whole force had been under arms every night, while each dawn brought incessant labour on the crumbling defences, and this on short rations of poor quality. Well might the British marvel at the French exertions; they were the more astonishing because the soldiers' fighting spirit had sunk so low. The prospect of resisting till they were taken by storm and slaughtered by the Turks appalled them as much as it had appalled the Cairo garrison. A minority of the generals took Bertrand's view that the battle should continue till the inner defences were breached; and no doubt a great fighting leader like Masséna, the defender of Genoa, could have sustained morale and kept the battle going to a bitter conclusion. But the majority opted for the terms which Belliard had accepted at Cairo; terms which a month earlier Menou had rejected. By now his troops had had enough.

When Menou's aide de camp rejoined him on the afternoon of 30 August with the British ultimatum there was no scope left for what Moore called his 'shuffling'.[19] Delaying even now till literally the eleventh hour, he sent his messenger back to arrive at Hutchinson's headquarters at 11 p.m. Menou accepted the British terms: repatriation to France with personal arms, private property, and ten pieces of artillery; but the surrender of the shipping and public property.

On the following day General Hope went into Alexandria to sign the capitulation and dine on horseflesh with Menou; and on 2 September the British entered the city. At 11 a.m. the grenadiers of the army and detachments of Guards and dragoons marched forward to take possession of the enemy's defences, with drums beating and colours flying in the sunshine. At the base of the Nicopolis escarpment which had so long defied the British troops their bands struck up the Grenadiers' March; a moment when the feelings of the army repaid all the hardships of the past six months.[20]

Table 10 Garrison of Alexandria at time of capitulation

Cavalry and infantry	5,965		
Artillery	759		
		6,724	
Corps of dromedaries, Syrians, horse and foot guides		274	
Marine artillery		290	
Sappers and miners		139	
Artificers		122	
Seamen (doing duty in garrison)		1,230	
Greeks		118	
Invalids		240	
Sick		1,387	
Total military			10,524
General hospital		238	
Army commissariat		95	
Marine commissariat		196	
Geographical engineers		9	
Commission of arts and sciences		47	
Clerks of national treasury		17	
Civilians and merchants		83	
Total civil personnel			685
Grand total			11,209

Source: Wilson, 216–17, totals adjusted

21

THE ACHIEVEMENT

'Thus', wrote Colonel Graham, 'terminated a six months campaign of immense importance, in which the character of the British infantry has risen. ... The French cannot deny that ours astonished them by their steadiness and discipline.' Graham himself was to command that infantry with brilliance in the Peninsula. While he wrote, it was marching to occupy the fortifications of Alexandria to the sound of martial music. The drums and fifes played the grenadiers forward with the tune *The Downfall of Paris*; and round Pompey's Pillar the band of the 54th formed a circle and struck up *God save the King*.[1]

They were a lean and hardy race of soldiers who had lived in their clothes by day and night for six months, never undressing except to wash or put on a clean shirt, and sleeping in their equipment. Baird's force from India, coming down the Nile to Rosetta, found Hutchinson's troops 'very dirty, starved and shabby'; without wine, comforts, and even clothing. In contrast the 'Indian' force had brought cooks for the sepoys, while their officers lived in tents like miniature palaces and had brought port and madeira across the desert. British soldiers in the hospital at Rosetta were astonished to see the sepoys removing their uniforms when off duty and walking about in very short white 'drawers'. The King's army jeered at the Company's troops and called them the Army of Darius; 'and not without reason', confessed Surgeon McGrigor, whose own establishment included a dozen Indian servants and their wives, two horses, three camels, and flocks of sheep, goats, and poultry. Hutchinson kept the two forces apart, to avoid exciting jealousy among his unpaid British at the high pay and allowances which the Europeans from India were receiving regularly every month.[2]

Shabby and unpaid the British troops might be, but they were in fair health, thanks to Hutchinson's care and the absence of grog shops in a Muslim country. The French were in much worse case, with many of their sick in the last stages of scurvy. Menou had run out of cash, and asked for a loan to buy provisions; but Hutchinson declined to be fleeced. 'Had they the smallest vestige of truth, moral or military honour remaining', he wrote, 'I certainly should have furnished them with some, but they would have taken the money, laughed at my credulity, and never repaid it. . . . Where they could have collected so many unprincipled vagabonds to make officers of, I cannot imagine. You scarcely ever meet one who has the appearance, trace or vestige of a gentleman.'[3]

The end of the fighting brought modest luxuries to the British which were gratefully welcomed: fresh hot bread for breakfast instead of the biscuit on which Coote's force had been subsisting; for the soldiers, sleeping at night without their accoutrements; and, for all, the morning parade at seven instead of the cold, damp hour of four o'clock. Officers seized their last chance for sightseeing. Moore, who had found no beauty in the Pyramids, was enchanted by Pompey's Pillar, a monument of the classical world which he had discovered in his youth in Rome: 'It is difficult to conceive how a single pillar can convey so much majesty and beauty'. Coote and Ludlow, who had not been up the Nile, contrived a trip to Cairo, where they explored the Pyramids and were entertained by the grateful Grand Vizir to a dinner of eighty dishes washed down with coffee and sherbet. To honour the visitors the one-eyed Vizir sat down for the first time in his life to dine *à l'angloise* at a table specially made for the occasion; and afterwards the party adjourned to a summerhouse on the banks of the Nile for a grand display of fireworks.[4]

For most of the army, however, there was no lingering in the God-forsaken land of the Pharaohs. The Cabinet had long since anticipated the reconquest of Egypt and had planned the redeployment of the force. Hutchinson was to be deprived of his local command when the army dispersed, and General Henry Fox, commanding at Minorca, succeeded Abercromby as Commander-in-Chief in the Mediterranean. Fox was ordered to send 7,000 men to England, which was still plagued with bread-riots and threatened with invasion. Four thousand were destined for the West Indies, to attack Spain's American colonies; and 7,000 for Malta, to secure Sicily and maintain a strong Mediterranean base. The Secretary of State, Lord Hobart, seized the opportunity to favour his old school-friend Cradock with the command of the force for Sicily, to the chagrin of Moore who was to remain at Alexandria with a static garrison of 6,000. 'It has never been my object to remain in garrison anywhere', he complained in his diary.[5]

The dispersal began immediately. Lord Keith departed on 9 September with most of the fleet; and Cradock's force, which had been under notice to embark from the moment of Alexandria's surrender, sailed on 12 September for Malta. Moore, disappointed that he had been denied an active command, avoided being stuck in Alexandria by obtaining leave to go home, and dumped his garrison on Lord Cavan. All ranks embarked in good spirits, thankful as one cavalry officer wrote 'to leave a climate where plague, blindness and disease rage uncontrolled'. The men in the ranks had again to endure the miseries of the troopships, still sleeping in their clothes; for as one of their officers remarked, 'on shipboard private soldiers suffer ten times as much almost, as before an enemy'. But there were consolations. At Malta the soldiers picked up their 'pretty wives' who had been left behind for the duration of the campaign, and after the long deprivation of sex and alcohol became 'scandalously drunk' with them on the cheap wine at Minorca.[6]

They left behind in Egypt 633 officers and men killed or missing in action, and probably another thousand who had died of wounds or disease.[7] Of those who came home some were crippled for life, including 160 blinded by ophthalmia and 200 more who had lost one of their eyes. Of the 3,058 wounded many of the survivors must have been permanently injured, among them the memoir-writing private of the 92nd. We left him six months earlier on the evening of 21 March, wounded that morning in the battle of Alexandria and now being put on board a hospital ship in Aboukir bay. His infected wound soon placed him on the danger list, and with other serious cases he was transferred to the hospital ashore. A couple of the patients, too weak to sit up, were laid on the grating in the bottom of the boat, one dying in the boat and the other on the beach. The survivors were carried to the Aboukir General Hospital, in huts built by the French from split date-palms placed upright in the ground and packed with lime-plaster. Here the highlander suffered a fresh misery for twenty-four hours when he was stung by a small scorpion which had crept into his haversack. But after sixteen days of good nursing the putrid flesh of his leg-wound was cleaned away, leaving a large hole in his heel.

Before long his regiment, the 92nd, was sent down from the line, a skeleton of a battalion after its losses in two battles. Arriving at Aboukir it offered to accommodate its own wounded, as the overcrowded General Hospital was infected with plague which killed 173 patients. In the regimental hospital there was fever, and to keep clear of it the wounded soldier was placed in the convalescent tents some distance away. As his leg healed he began to move about on a crutch, only to fall and reopen the wound which became infected again. He was returned to the hospital tents; and when the regimental hospital was moved to Rosetta he was too ill to travel and was left behind in the General Hospital.

The patients here were tormented by fleas, while swarms of flies hatched their maggots in the wounds. In June conditions improved when the highlander was moved to a new General Hospital in a permanent building in Rosetta. Here the patients lay on blankets folded four-ply to cushion their mattresses of rough-hewn date branches, using their knapsacks as pillows. Sheets were issued, which gave some protection against the clouds of mosquitoes brought out by the warm weather, whose bites blotched the patients' faces like measles. Arab watermen brought fresh water from the Nile in goatskin bags.

By September the Gordon Highlander was well enough to embark with the regiment, repassing the turbulent bar of the Nile in a djerm which sailed along the coast to join the fleet at Aboukir. In spite of the tribulations of his six months in hospital he praised the treatment of the wounded, and felt that no efforts or medicines had been spared to help them. But he never recovered entirely. His wound was still opening when he landed in England; and refusing to stay in the York Hospital in London till it was healed, he made his way home to Glasgow with a permanently shortened leg. He was enrolled as an out-pensioner of Chelsea Hospital, and ended his days in Glasgow as a Tabernacle Christian.[8]

The French Army of the Orient, unlike their British adversaries, landed in a cloud of recrimination. Reynier had made use of his early return to France under arrest to publish his own version of the campaign; self-justifying, libellous about the British Army, and blaming Menou for the French defeat. But the Reynier gang did not have it entirely their own way. Menou, Rampon, and Lagrange all wrote reports blaming Reynier and his supporters Damas and Lanusse for the repulse on 21 March. Bonaparte adopted as the official version Menou's claim that his disaffected subordinates had deliberately lost the battle, and published it in the *Moniteur*. Menou, who had kept faith with Bonaparte's dream of an oriental empire, was rewarded with a succession of interior commands and administrative posts, but was never employed again in the field; a farcical figure who died in 1810 as Governor of Venice.

With Belliard it was otherwise. Bonaparte's first thought had been to disgrace him for the surrender of Cairo; but on reflection he realised that he had been out of his depth in the Cairo command, and that Menou had destroyed the force's morale. Belliard soldiered on under the Empire, serving as chief of staff to Marshal Murat in Spain and Russia; fought in many a great battle; and was wounded at Leipzig in 1813. Created a Count of the Empire in 1810, he played Vicar of Bray to the two succeeding régimes, rising to *Pair de France* under the Bourbon Restoration, while the July Revolution of 1830 made him the Orleanists' ambassador in Brussels, where he died in 1832.

Not all of Menou's lieutenants fared so well. Silly, whose thigh had been shot away in front of the Roman Ruins, retired on a pension; and Destaing was to pay the price for arresting Reynier. Finding in Reynier's book a malicious statement that he had retired from the battle of Alexandria with a light wound, he demanded satisfaction; and in the following May Reynier killed him in a duel.

But most of the generals went on to glory and distinction. Bertrand, Reynier, Friant, Rampon, and Lagrange all became Counts of the Empire; and of these Rampon, like Belliard, made the leap to *Pair de France* under the Bourbon Restoration, as did Lagrange under the Orleanist Monarchy. Donzelot, Valentin, and the cavalry commanders Bron de Bailly, Latour-Maubourg, and Boussart were made Barons of the Empire; but Boussart, *général de division* in 1812, was always unlucky on the battlefield. Wounded in the battle of Alexandria, and again at Pultusk, Lerida, and Torrente, he finally died of wounds in 1813. Rampon held only interior commands; but Bertrand, Reynier, Lagrange, Latour-Maubourg, Bron de Bailly, Valentin, Damas, and Friant all fought with distinction as divisional or corps commanders. Reynier suffered further defeats at the hands of British infantry at Maida and Busaco; Friant was wounded in the last holocaust of the Guard at Waterloo; and Donzelot's division retreated in good order from the stricken field. Bertrand accompanied Napoleon to St Helena, presided at the installation of the Emperor's ashes in the Invalides in 1840, and was buried near him seven years later. The British Army's opponents in Egypt had not been men of straw.

Except, and critically, their Commander-in-Chief. The campaign, young Captain Colborne remarked, had been one 'in which neither the French nor English generals have displayed great military talents'. Of Menou this was unquestionably true. His defects were among the chances of blind fortune in which Abercromby alone had seen hope of success: elements, as Moore phrased it, 'which were not in his power to command'. His hope was realised in Menou's strategic misjudgements and tactical blundering; and in retrospect it became clear that the decisive point of the campaign had been the battle of Alexandria. Up to that moment, it was said, Abercromby had 'never looked forward to final success': after it the French 'lost all hope of keeping their ground'.[9] 'It is perfectly evident', wrote Colonel Graham, 'that they never afterwards chose to fight us.' They showed no desire to protract the campaign and win time, but 'rather a previous determination to *allow* us to come near them and to *surrender* whenever they had a pretence to do so'. For the French the final capitulation at Alexandria was not a mortification but a relief. Their officers sat sociably in the British camp, drinking the health of the King and success to the capitulation; and the diplomatist Mr Hamilton found all but the few immediate friends of Menou 'perfectly contented with this reverse of their affairs which will enable them to return home'. And return they did, 11,000 from Alexandria and 27,000 all told, leaving behind some 4,000 who had been killed or had died of wounds or disease since the British landing.[10]

Wellington was later to perceive a pattern in the French behaviour. He guessed that if he had been allowed to advance after his victory at Vimiero in 1808, the French 'would have acted . . . in Portugal as they did in Egypt; they tried their strength once in the field, and having failed, they would in Portugal have continued to retreat till they could have got into safety'.[11] In Egypt indeed the French had been game for only one full trial by battle. Nevertheless their strength after the battle of Alexandria remained overwhelming until Turkish pressure began to be applied many weeks later; and even then a resolute concentration of force might have torn the allied web asunder.

As Reynier argued, rightly but with his usual ungenerous phrasing, the outcome of the campaign might have been different if the Army of the Orient had been worthily led. The possibility remained, and the careful manner in which Hutchinson played his hand was surely justified. He would not expose his own force to a reverse, which might have cost him casualties he could not afford and would have made a disastrous impression on the Turks and Mamelukes. By methodically separating the enemy forces and removing their advantage of the interior position, he brought superior allied force to bear in succession at Cairo and Alexandria. Cairo fell before he received any reinforcements; and on Belliard's surrender he confidently told the Cabinet that the French could no longer claim Egypt as a negotiating card.

Hutchinson's army gave him little credit. 'Fortune has decidedly been Hutchinson's greatest friend in every instance', seems to have been the general feeling echoed by Captain Colborne. Archibald Campbell agreed that he had received more credit than he deserved, for it was Menou's errors which had lost Egypt; perfectly true, but it was Hutchinson who ensured that the initial errors were not retrieved. The navy's contempt for the general persisted. 'I feel what misery it must be for you', Captain Troubridge wrote to the departing Keith, 'to serve with such a *poor thing, no dash, no exertion*.'[12]

Keith himself had complained, on the eve of Menou's surrender, of Hutchinson's 'unconquerable indolence'; and ill-health certainly had much to do with the general's air of languour: he was still ailing at the time of the final capitulation, and visibly worse at the end of October. His brother, Christopher, though critical of John's personality and manner, vehemently defended his conduct of operations. He told Lord Elgin that he was proud of his brother, and that many people had a vested interest in discrediting him by exaggerating the strength of his force and under-estimating the enemy's. His generals decried him from a guilty wish to justify their disloyalty; and government circles to conceal their own fault in underrating the enemy and assuming that the campaign would be short and easy. Discussing the operations with Elgin and Colonel Graham, Christopher conceded that with better health his brother 'might have used more dispatch, but that I did not even allow that time was lost . . . rash men might have fought battles and lost the country'.[13]

The blame for the risks and difficulties which Abercromby and Hutchinson had faced was laid squarely on the ministers at home by their ablest lieutenant. Goaded by Reynier's strictures on Abercromby, John Moore wrote into his diary a defence of his old chief against the charge of delaying the launch of the invasion. The government, he said, had given Abercromby 'the soldier and his sword', and that was all: not a horse, nor a waggon. 'Thus provided he was ordered to take the field and undertake sieges.' These shortages were the sole cause of the delay at Marmaris, and Sir Ralph's perseverance in overcoming them was 'truly admirable'. Moore bitterly contrasted the British machinery for mounting maritime expeditions with that of the enemy. French expeditions had been planned by soldiers, often the commanders themselves, who took care to provide themselves with what was necessary. 'The military operations of Great Britain have been directed by Ministers ignorant of military affairs, and too arrogant and self-sufficient to consult military men.'[14]

How true this could be. In planning the unfortunate Dutch expedition in the summer of 1799 Pitt had given vent to the memorable boast that 'all military difficulties are completely overruled'.[15] Yet the launching of the Egyptian expedition was different. While the Dutch adventure had been designed by Pitt and his Foreign Secretary, with Dundas at the War Department deferring doubtfully to the Foreign Office and its optimistic sources of intelligence, the Egyptian expedition was Dundas's alone. The Dutch expeditionary force had been a contribution to coalition warfare in Europe, its purpose more political than strategic. But when Dundas demanded the invasion of Egypt, the coalition in Europe had been swept away on a tide of military disasters; Austria crushed, Prussia neutralised, and Russia moving into alliance with Bonaparte. Britain stood isolated in the face of a continent dominated by France, and Pitt declared that the country's bankrupt exchequer called for peace.

To this great crisis Dundas responded boldly; and in the teeth of Cabinet opposition he launched Britain's only striking force into the final offensive of the war to wrest Egypt from French control. It was a choice of doing nothing, or of using the army which chance had collected in the Straits of Gibraltar. The force had been assembled to raid Spanish harbours, not to wage a long campaign in the field; and there was no time to re-equip it. Dundas recognised its limitations when he instructed Abercromby to obtain a foothold and clear the coast, but not to advance into the interior. If he wildly underrated the enemy's numbers, he was not far wrong about their morale. He expected too much of the Turks, but carefully handled they did not prove negligible. After the capitulation of Alexandria Dundas's friends acknowledged his courage and wisdom. But to him the recognition that mattered most was a generous retraction by the King. One hot summer day George III rode out to visit the ageing statesman at Wimbledon, and raised a glass of madeira to the man who had proposed and executed the expedition to Egypt; 'for', said the King, 'when a person has been perfectly in the wrong, the most just and honourable thing for him to do is to acknowlege it publicly'.[16]

It has often been said that Pitt's successor Addington threw away the fruits of the Egyptian victory; and it is true that Bonaparte, with prior knowledge of the fall of Alexandria, jostled the British negotiators into signing the Preliminary Articles on the day before they received the news. But the news was no surprise, for the ministry already knew that Menou's surrender was inevitable. Nor does Bonaparte's haste seem to have been prompted by the news from Alexandria: he was desperate to open the sea to his blockaded fleets, in order to catch the winter campaigning season in the Caribbean and recover San Domingo from its black liberator Toussaint.[17]

The British army in Egypt had not fought in vain, and Egypt was not to be French. The purpose had been accomplished, and British India no longer lay in continual peril of French invasion. When war broke out again in 1803 Bonaparte had a naval squadron and an Anglophobe general ready at Mauritius; but, although a few thousand French soldiers acting with the French-trained Mahrattas could have turned the military balance in India, he had no troops or transports waiting at Suez. In the coming years British ministers were determined to prevent Napoleon from regaining his foothold in Egypt. They showed their concern in 1803 when they retained Malta in defiance of the peace treaty and at the cost of renewing the war; in 1805, the year of Trafalgar, by fixing Nelson's attention on the Levant though Napoleon's true objective was England; and in 1807 by occupying Alexandria in response to Turkey's alignment with France. Dundas had demonstrated the strategic nexus between Europe, Egypt, and India when he launched the convergent assaults of Baird and Abercromby: 'your plan', as a sycophantic naval officer put it, 'of making a Bengal sepoy shake hands with a Coldstream Guardsman on the bank of the Nile'.[18]

And what of the Egyptians themselves, now liberated from the French occupation? A British garrison remained in Alexandria till the peace; but for the population the outlook was a bleak alternative between Turkish misrule and Mameluke oppression. Hutchinson, despairing of Turkey's chaotic armies and lethargic administration, advised his government that the Porte was incapable of retaining Egypt with its Arabs, Greeks, and Mamelukes. To secure Mameluke aid during the Nile campaign he had given their leader Osman Bey Bardussi a guarantee of protection and reinstatement.

This alarmed the British government, which had an obligation to restore the Turkish power in Egypt; and the Turks were outraged when they discovered the extent of Hutchinson's promises to the Mamelukes. Determined to prevent the Beys, who were already masters of all Egypt south of the Pyramids, from regaining control of Cairo and the delta, they planned to arrest them. At Aboukir the Capitan Pacha lured them to a banquet on board his flagship, and in the course of a struggle most of them were massacred. Hutchinson promptly marched a British brigade to Aboukir and forced the Turks to hand over the two Beys who had survived the slaughter; and in Cairo the Grand Vizir was obliged to release the Beys whom he had simultaneously arrested there.[19]

But though some of the Mameluke Beys had been saved, their power had gone for ever. Not that this benefited the Porte for long, for Hutchinson's advice was right and the Ottomans were no longer capable of controlling their outlying provinces. 'The Grand Vizir's army', Captain Colborne reported with the fresh eye of a new arrival, 'is composed of the most despicable rabble ever collected together. The annihilation of Turkey is at no great distance; not even a Belisarius would save this sinking state.'[20] He was not the first, nor by a long way the last, to toll a premature bell for the dying Ottoman Empire. But in Egypt his prediction was rapidly confirmed. The Albanian contingent commanded by Mahomet Ali was not paid, and it mutinied; and being the only disciplined element in the Grand Vizir's army it was victorious. In 1805 Mahomet Ali became Pacha of Egypt and the first founder of its independence.

22

'ABERCROMBY'S SOLDIERS'

In Egypt, wrote General Bunbury, 'our service regained its ancient standing in the estimation of the British people'. For the British Army the Egyptian campaign was a climacteric, when it regained its confidence and was ready to build on the foundations of General Dundas's battle-drill. Seven years later, on the morrow of his first great Peninsular victory at Vimiero, Sir Arthur Wellesley was to praise his troops in glowing terms to the Duke of York: 'Their gallantry and their discipline were equally conspicuous . . . this was the only action I have ever been in, in which everything passed as it was directed, and no mistake was made by any of the officers charged with its conduct'.[1]

It is inconceivable that a British commander could have written thus about his troops before the Egyptian campaign. In those days the army had been dismissed as the laughing-stock of Europe; and in the eyes of Admiral Lord St Vincent the whole infantry of the country was 'totally unfit for a service of hardy enterprise'. After Egypt the soldiers could look the navy in the face again, and had shown the French, Moore told his father, 'that we in red are as stout fellows as our brothers in blue'. And their victory had dispersed the French aura of invincibility, proving that when deprived of superior numbers and unlimited replacements they were not invulnerable; and that 'a Frenchman *beat*, knows as little, perhaps less how to bear and direct his conduct in adversity as his neighbour'. 'It has been the first fair trial between Englishmen and Frenchmen during the whole of this war', wrote Colonel Paget, 'and you may rely upon it, that at no former period in our history did John Bull ever hold his enemy cheaper.' A few years earlier in Flanders the steady gaze of Colonel Arthur Wellesley had perceived the flaws in the French tactical system against steady troops who were not afraid of them, and in Egypt Abercromby tested the French with steady troops and taught his soldiers that discipline would prevail. 'The French', ran Paget's assessment, 'certainly possess the most enthusiastic bravery, and are capable of the most extraordinary exertions, and to these great qualities are they indebted for their unexampled success, but to no other. Of science, system or discipline I am satisfied that they are destitute.'[2]

It may be objected that what really forged Wellington's instrument of victory was not so much the Egyptian campaign as the five years of training after the resumption of the war in 1803, a period uninterrupted by serious European campaigns or by a drain of reinforcements into the noxious West Indian climate.[3] These years were indeed important; for if the Caribbean wastage which had ruined the army in the 1790s had been repeated, it would have undermined the edifice being built on Sir David Dundas's drill and the Egyptian experience.

Nevertheless later drill and training were not the whole story: Egypt had proved the soundness of Dundas's system. Yet perhaps the greatest legacies of the campaign to the British Army were moral: experience, confidence, and above all example. The great Napoleonic military thinker Baron Jomini was to call the Egyptian campaign *'l'époque de sa regénération'*; and British eyewitnesses who rushed into print had no doubt that they had seen a turning point and 'the groundwork of future glory'.[4] All ranks came home with the glow of self-confidence and restored esteem. Lieutenant Caton of the 12th Light Dragoons, though glad to be leaving Egypt and its diseases, yet felt that to serve again in such a campaign and 'to re-establish the glory of the British Army, are such incitements . . . that every soldier feels with me, that he would meet with pleasure double its hardships'. 'Never was there in an army so little plunder', wrote Moore; and Paget of the 28th predicted that 'the example of this army will produce the happiest effects'. They had measured their courage and discipline, and put their tactics to the trial of battle. What was needed now was to spread the word to the rest of the British Army; and to find the right commander. One of Paget's officers in the 28th, Captain Jennings, wrote after the battle of Alexandria that the army had 'manifested to the world what it is capable of performing, at any time, *when properly commanded and united*.[5]

Sir David Dundas must have felt deep satisfaction when he read Abercromby's posthumous letter confirming the success of his tactical system and crediting him with the army's uniformity of practice.[6] The thought of Dundas's pleasure gladdened Colonel Paget, for 'the British troops only wanted what D.D. has given them, to make them in every respect the best troops in the world'. No tactical system will work for unsteady troops; and one of the qualities which the British infantry had demonstrated was their immunity to panic even when a flank was turned: 'A British soldier seems either not to know the fatal consequences to which he is exposed by having his flank turned, or knowing it, is perfectly indifferent to it'. Outflanked in the dawn on 21 March, partly broken, and short of ammunition, Moore's men had fought on to hold their ground and win the battle.[7]

One defect had still to be redressed: the neglect of light infantry training in Dundas's manual. On 21 March the British line on the ridge, particularly the Guards, had suffered needless casualties from French skirmishers because they stood their ground instead of driving off the sharpshooters. At home the Duke of York was aware of the gap in the manual, and looked to Moore to correct it. Moore had learned the importance of light infantry in the West Indian forests and the dunes of Holland. In his brigade in Egypt were the Corsican Rangers whom he described as natural light troops, and he was greatly impressed by their skill when they protected his column from enemy skirmishers in the battle of Mandara.[8]

Moore was also struck by Mackenzie's versatile training of the 90th, a legacy of the American experience of Sir Charles Stuart. When the light brigade was formed at Shorncliffe under Moore's command in 1803, and the 52nd Regiment of which he was Colonel was chosen to be the prototype for new light infantry regiments, it was Mackenzie whom he summoned to command and re-train it. Moore had been convinced for some years past that a light infantry unit should be 'a mixture of the Yager and the Grenadier';[9] in other words, that it should be trained both to skirmish and to act as an élite battalion of the line. When specialist light infantry battalions were belatedly formed in the British Army he recommended that they should be trained 'both in the light infantry manoeuvres and also to act when required as a firm battalion'.[10] Thus were the principles established which were to infuse Wellington's crack Light Division.

The returning army was greeted with acclamation and rewards. Coote received his coveted K.B., as did Cradock. The first peerage earned by the army in the long war went to Abercromby's widow, with the title Baroness Abercromby of Aboukir and a pension of £2,000 for three generations to support the status which Sir Ralph had once refused because he could not afford it. The officers of the Egyptian army received the thanks of the House of Commons; and a separate resolution, thanking the non-commissioned officers and privates for their 'Regularity, Discipline, Coolness and Valour', recognised the qualities which had won the campaign. The regiments in the expedition were awarded the emblem of the Sphinx superscribed *Egypt* to be borne on their colours, the first general battle honour to be awarded in the British Army. The 28th were granted the right to wear their regimental badge on the front and back of their headdress to commemorate the rear rank's repulse of the French cavalry; and the influential Highland Society of London distributed silver and bronze medals to the 42nd Highlanders, including the relations of the many killed in the battle of Alexandria.

The one man from whom the country withheld its gratitude was General Hutchinson. He had already received his K.B. for his service as second-in-command to Abercromby in the opening weeks of the campaign; but for his own victorious operations his immediate reward was to be kicked rudely out of his command, and curtly informed that General Fox was appointed Commander-in-Chief in the Mediterranean while Cradock was to command the expedition to Sicily. Hutchinson was disappointed and hurt by this treatment,[11] which was triggered perhaps by the government's embarrassment over his guarantee to the Mamelukes; though he could fairly reply that their aid had been a military necessity and that at the time the Turks themselves were promising the Mamelukes amnesty and protection.[12] The ministers may have come to see this, and to recognise the merits of Hutchinson's operations, for before long he received a British peerage with the title Lord Hutchinson. He never served in the field again; but after holding a command on the invasion coast of Kent and Sussex in 1803–4, he was sent on a mission during the Third Coalition in 1806–7 to the Prussian and Russian courts, accompanied as usual by his brother Kit. He was with the Russian army at the end of the Friedland campaign.

Unlike the French generals in Egypt, few of the British generals rose much further in their careers. Most of them were older than the French, born in the 1750s and with service going back to the American War; and they were disadvantaged for service in the Peninsula by being senior to Wellington, born in 1769. Moore, born in 1761, went on to high commands but was mortally wounded at Corunna in 1809 at the outset of the Peninsular War, aged only 48. In the same battle Sir David Baird lost an arm and ended his adventurous service in the field. William Beresford, who had commanded one of Baird's brigades from India, rose to distinction in the Peninsula and became a peer and Master-General of the Ordnance;[13] and John Stuart, whose Foreign Brigade had delivered a crucial attack in the valley fighting on 21 March, later commanded in Sicily and defeated Reynier again in 1806 at Maida, where five of his nine regiments had served in Egypt.[14] At Maida Reynier, like Lanusse before him at Mandara and Menou at Alexandria, left a strong defensive position to launch an attack which was shattered in open ground by the fire-discipline of the British line. It was a lesson the French never absorbed.

Abercromby's other brigade commanders gradually faded from sight. Coote commanded a division at Copenhagen in 1807 and was second-in-command of the Walcheren expedition of 1809, but sadly lapsed into scandal and disgrace. Cradock held a command in Portugal in the opening months of the Peninsular War but by then had been 'soured by misfortune' in Wellington's phrase, from being unfairly blamed for the sepoy mutiny at Vellore in 1806. He retired into colonial governorships.[15] Doyle (born in 1750) spent the last eleven years of the Napoleonic Wars as military commander in Guernsey; and Sir Hildebrand Oakes, not in the best of health, held the important civil and military commissionership at Britain's Mediterranean base in Malta. Finch, a Coldstreamer, commanded the Guards brigade at Copenhagen: the same two battalions of the Coldstream and 3rd Guards which had served in Egypt and were to stay together throughout the Peninsular War, proudly calling themselves 'the Egyptian brigade of Foot Guards'.[16] Finch, however, born in 1756, was precluded from serving in the Peninsula by his seniority to Wellington, and remained a courtier and Member of Parliament. Ludlow commanded a division in the Copenhagen expedition but did not serve after that in the field; and Cavan's last appointment was the command of a district at home during the invasion scare of 1803–4.[17]

The heads of the artillery and engineers were relatively older men promoted according to the strict seniority observed in the Ordnance department. Both had done well in Egypt and were commended by Hutchinson for their skill and perseverance in conquering 'difficulties which at first appeared almost insurmountable'.[18] Brigadier Lawson, who had shifted the heavy cannon from Aboukir bay to Alexandria, to Fort Julian, to Cairo and back again, was now aged about 61 and had reached the end of his active career in the field; but George Cookson, whose guns had led Coote's final advance on Alexandria, served at Copenhagen and Corunna and became a general. Colonel Holloway of the Royal Engineers (born in 1749), who, it was said, had practically commanded the Grand Vizir's army in the El Khanka campaign, had also reached the end of his career in the field, and went on to command the Royal Engineers at Gibraltar. But a younger sapper, Richard Fletcher, sorely missed by Abercromby after he was captured on the eve of the Aboukir landing, went on to become Chief Engineer of the Peninsular army.[19] Distinguished in the bloody battles of Talavera and Busaco, he directed the sieges of Cuidad Rodrigo and Badajoz; but his greatest achievement was to design and build the lines of Torres Vedras, which stopped Marshal Masséna on the approaches to Lisbon much as the lines of Nicopolis had baffled Abercromby. Fletcher was wounded in the third and final siege of Badajoz, for which he was awarded a baronetcy and pension; but after surviving the battle of Vittoria he was killed at the capture of San Sebastian in 1813.

It was mainly with field officers of Fletcher's age that the future lay: men who were in their thirties during the Egyptian campaign, born around the year of Wellington's birth and Bonaparte's in 1769. Among Abercromby's staff officers, Anstruther distinguished himself as a brigade commander at Vimiero and in the retreat to Corunna when his career was cut short. Catching an inflammation of the lungs during the terrible march from Lugo, he refused to take to a carriage and remained on horseback, as he had done on the march to Cairo, and died two days before the battle of Corunna.[20] When Moore was killed at Corunna and Baird was wounded, the command of the army fell to John Hope who embarked it successfully. He commanded a division at Walcheren, and again in the Peninsular campaigns of 1813–14, earning Wellington's description 'the ablest man in the Peninsular army'. George Murray, Assistant Quartermaster-General to Abercromby, became Wellington's Quartermaster-General in the Peninsula, where John Macdonald served as Assistant Adjutant-General. The head of Baird's medical staff, James McGrigor, became the head of Wellington's medical department and a pioneer of military medicine. During ten months in the years 1812–13, 95,000 sick and wounded passed through his hospitals, and produced a flow of convalescents to keep up the numbers at the front in the Vittoria campaign.[21]

Three regimental officers of the 90th achieved high distinction. Thomas Graham, who had raised the regiment, and Rowland Hill who commanded it at the battle of Mandara, emerged as brilliant divisional and corps commanders in the Peninsula; and Kenneth Mackenzie, old for his rank when he reconstructed the 52nd as light infantry at Shorncliffe, succeeded Moore as director of the army's light infantry training.[22] One of Mackenzie's successors in command of the 52nd was John Colborne who has been quoted above. He was to break the last charge of the Imperial Guard at Waterloo by wheeling the regiment in line on to the flank of the attacking column.[23]

Edward Paget of the 28th also served in the Peninsula, leading the advance to Oporto in 1809 where he lost an arm. Two years later he was appointed second-in-command to Wellington, but was almost immediately taken prisoner while reconnoitring alone. He later commanded the Burma campaign of 1825. Wellington's divisional commanders included Brent Spencer of the 40th, Hutchinson's Military Secretary Lowry Cole of the Coldstream, Edward Houston of the 58th who had held the Roman Ruins, Charles Colville of the 13th, and Lord Dalhousie of the Queen's.[24] Colonel Alan Cameron, founder and commanding officer of the 79th Highlanders, and the vandaliser of a sarcophagus, commanded a brigade at Talavera and Busaco; but, older than most of his rank, he was invalided home at the end of 1810. His son had followed him in the command of the regiment, and was killed in the following year at Fuentes d'Onoro.

Other Peninsular brigade commanders with Egyptian experience included Sir William Lumley and one of Abercromby's aides de camp, James Kempt, who succeeded to the command of a division at Waterloo on the death of General Picton.[25] Two eclectic officers who served with foreign troops deserve mention. Hudson Lowe remained with the Corsican Rangers in the Mediterranean till 1813, when he was dispatched on missions to the Russian and Prussian armies in the campaigns of 1813–14, and to the Austrians in Italy in 1815; but he is remembered as Napoleon's gaoler at St Helena. Robert Wilson of Hompesch's Hussars, author of the best history of the Egyptian campaign, raised and commanded the Portuguese Lusitanian Legion in 1808–9, but was regarded by Wellington as a *frondeur*, disobedient and unreliable. Like Lowe he served in the last campaigns of the war with the Russians and Austrians. During the allied occupation of Paris after Waterloo, he became involved with a nephew of John and Kit Hutchinson in assisting the escape of the Bonapartist General Lavalette, and was sentenced to three months' imprisonment by a French court. Reinstated in his rank, he ended his career as a General and Governor of Gibraltar.[26]

Of those who did not come home from Egypt, most lay in unmarked graves, or their stripped bones rested on the sea-bed in Aboukir bay. Abercromby's body, however, had been brought to Malta in April in the frigate *Flora*, and there his son asked that he should be buried. In solid rock in the Castle of St Elmo a sepulchre was excavated on a bastion between two cannon; and on 29 April a military procession with muffled drums bore Sir Ralph to his tomb through streets lined by the garrison, while minute guns thundered from the fortress and the warships in the harbour.

Where is he now remembered? There is the inscription on Cleopatra's Needle; and in the south transept of St Paul's Cathedral a monument by Flaxman, on which at one time rested the standard taken by the 42nd on 21 March. The Highland Society of London, formed twenty years earlier to lobby for the repeal of the Disarming Act and the restoration of the highland dress, linked his name with the three highland regiments which had fought under him in Egypt. To this day, at their main annual meeting which is held as near as possible to the anniversary of the battle of Alexandria on 21 March, the Society drink to 'the Immortal Memory of Sir Ralph Abercromby and all Scotsmen who have fallen in defence of their country'.[27]

He was commemorated for a generation by the officers he had trained. A bundle of his letters among the papers of Colonel Alexander Hope is labelled 'from my old commander and first master',[28] and officers like Sir Frederick Maitland and Sir John Macdonald recalled his character with praise and affection in their old age. Yet his memory faded; and though his victory is commemorated on the colours and badges of his regiments, the hero himself who fell in his hour of triumph, the peer of Wolfe, Moore, and Nelson, is almost forgotten even in Scotland, a nation which honours its heroes. Dying quietly in the cabin of the *Foudroyant* a week after he was wounded, his end lacked the drama of Wolfe's death on the field of victory or the poetry of Moore's midnight burial. Yet his victory secured the future of British India, and marked the turning point in the British Army's regeneration.

He may not have been one of the great masters of the battlefield. 'I believe', wrote the Duke of Northumberland on learning of his death, 'we had better talk of the integrity of Sir R. Abercromby's heart, and of his personal bravery, than of his military talents.' Integrity and bravery were not slight virtues in an army and an age when the term 'gentleman' with which General Bunbury described Abercromby denoted principles of honour. To those qualities Bunbury added that 'his justice, his intrepidity, and experience assured him, as a commander, the attachment and confidence of his troops'. As for his professional talents, if he was not a great battlefield commander he was a quiet and courageous leader and a transcendent trainer of troops for war. Of a later British commander in Egypt, Bernard Montgomery, a soldier-historian has written that he was 'the man who gave the British Eighth Army – and through it the whole British Army – restored confidence in itself and its leaders'. The same could have been said of Abercromby and his Egyptian expedition.[29]

When the news of his death reached London the Duke of York drafted, and Pitt amended, a General Order calling on the British Army to admire the conduct of the force in Egypt, and its fusion of discipline and training with activity and courage; and by emulating it, to uphold the glory and honour of the British arms. The Order extolled Abercromby's attention to discipline, and his care for the health and needs of his troops. These qualities, with 'the splendor of his actions in the field, and the heroism of his death, are worthy the imitation of all, who desire like him, a life of honour and a death of glory'.[30]

An authority on the Peninsular War has learned in the papers of Abercromby's disciples, Moore, Hope, and Murray, 'how much they all looked back to Egypt and Abercromby as having set the standard'. But perhaps the last brief, telling phrase should be left to a junior officer who had served with the Coldstream Guards in Egypt. In 1810 Thomas Brotherton was a bold captain of light dragoons with many successful reconnaissance missions to his credit. On one occasion he was nettled by an undeserved reproach from his general that he was fussed by the approach of French cavalry. 'I must say, I was rather annoyed at the remark', he wrote; 'for I was one of Sir Ralph Abercromby's soldiers, and had seen some service before the Peninsula.'[31]

LATER TITLES OF THE BRITISH REGIMENTS

Title 1801	1939	Later amalgamations
Cavalry		
8th or King's Royal Irish Light Dragoons	8th King's Royal Irish Hussars	Queen's Royal Irish Hussars (1958) Queen's Royal Hussars (Queen's Own and Royal Irish) (1993)
11th (Prince of Wales's) Light Dragoons	11th Hussars (Prince Albert's Own)	The Royal Hussars (Prince of Wales's Own) (1969) King's Royal Hussars (1992)
12th Light Dragoons 22nd Light Dragoons disbanded 1802 26th Light Dragoons renumbered 23rd (1803), disbanded 1819	12th (Prince of Wales's Royal) Lancers	9th/12th Royal Lancers (Prince of Wales's) (1960)
Foot Guards		
Coldstream Regiment of Foot Guards	Coldstream Guards	Coldstream Guards
3rd Foot Guards	Scots Guards	Scots Guards
Regiments of Foot		
1st or Royal Regiment of Foot (Royal Scots, 1812)	Royal Scots (The Royal Regt)	Royal Scots (The Royal Regt)
2nd or Queen's Royal Regiment of Foot	The Queen's Royal Regt (West Surrey)	The Queen's Regt (1969) The Princess of Wales's Royal Regt (1992)
8th or King's	The King's Regt (Liverpool)	The King's Regt (1969)
10th Foot	Lincolnshire Regt	Royal Anglian Regt (1968)
13th Foot	Somerset Light Infantry (Prince Albert's)	The Light Infantry (1968)
18th (Royal Irish)	The Royal Irish Regt (disbanded 1922)	
20th Foot	Lancashire Fusiliers	Royal Regt of Fusiliers (1968)
23rd Foot or Royal Welch Fusiliers	Royal Welch Fusiliers	Royal Welch Fusiliers
24th Foot	South Wales Borderers	Royal Regt of Wales (1960)
25th Foot	King's Own Scottish Borderers	King's Own Scottish Borderers
26th Foot	Cameronians (Scottish Rifles) (1st battn)	Disbanded 1968
27th (Inniskilling) Regt of Fusiliers	Royal Inniskilling Fusiliers	Royal Irish Rangers (1968)

LATER TITLES OF THE BRITISH REGIMENTS continued

28th Foot	Gloucestershire Regt (1st battn)	Royal Gloucestershire, Berkshire and Wiltshire Regt (1994)

28th Foot	Gloucestershire Regt (1st battn)	Royal Gloucestershire, Berkshire and Wiltshire Regt (1994)
30th Foot	East Lancashire Regt (1st battn)	Queen's Lancashire Regt (1970)
40th Foot	Prince of Wales's Volunteers (South Lancashire Regt) (1st battn)	Queen's Lancashire Regt (1970)
42nd (Royal Highland) Regt of Foot	Black Watch (Royal Highland Regt) (1st battn)	Black Watch (Royal Highland Regt)
44th Foot	Essex Regt	Royal Anglian Regt (1968)
50th Foot	Queen's Own (Royal West Kent) Regt (1st battn)	The Queen's Regt (1969); The Princess of Wales Royal Regt (1994)
54th Foot	Dorset Regt (2nd battn)	Devonshire and Dorset Regt (1958)
58th Foot	Northamptonshire Regt (2nd battn)	Royal Anglian Regt (1968)
61st Foot	Gloucestershire Regt (2nd battn)	Royal Gloucestershire, Berkshire and Wiltshire Regt (1994)
79th Foot or Cameronian Volunteers: Cameronian Highlanders 1804, Cameron Highlanders 1806	Queen's Own Cameron Highlanders	Queen's Own Highlanders (1961); The Highlanders (Seaforth, Gordons and Camerons) (1994)
80th Foot	South Staffordshire Regt	Staffordshire Regt (Prince of Wales's) (1959)
86th Foot	Royal Ulster Rifles (2nd battn)	Royal Irish Rangers (1968)
88th or Connaught Rangers	Connaught Rangers (1st battn) disbanded 1922	
89th Foot	Royal Irish Fusiliers (Princess Victoria's) (2nd battn)	Royal Irish Rangers (1986)
90th Foot or Perthshire Volunteers	Cameronians (Scottish Rifles) (2nd battn)	Disbanded 1968
92nd (Highland) Regt of Foot (1794–8, 100th (Gordon Highlanders) Regt of Foot)	Gordon Highlanders (2nd battn)	The Highlanders (Seaforth, Gordons and Camerons) (1994)

NOTES

ABBREVIATIONS

BL	British Library, London
NAM	National Army Museum, London
NLS	National Library of Scotland, Edinburgh
NMM	National Maritime Museum, Greenwich
NRA	National Register of Archives, London
NRAS	National Register of Archives (Scotland), Edinburgh
PRO	Public Record Office, Kew
RO	(County) Record Office
SRO	Scottish Record Office, Edinburgh

1 'SIR RALPH IS NOT A COURTIER'

1 Holland, II.62; Cornwallis, III.300.
2 *Parliamentary History*, XXXV.1065; Donoughmore MSS, 1 Dec. 1800, diary of Christopher Hely-Hutchinson; James, 118.
3 The savagery of the storm is recorded in *Moore*, I.380–1; Anderson, 87–90; Wilson, 1n.; Wyvill, *Sketch*, 390; Melville MSS (SRO), GD51/1/774, 23 Oct., John Hope to Dundas.
4 *Narrative*, 59; Church, 3; Campbell MS (NAM).
5 Hoskins, 33–4, 52–3.
6 Dunfermline, 251. The political decision to send an expedition to Egypt is described in Mackesy 1984a.
7 Melville MSS (SRO), GD51/1/703, 10 Jan. 1800, Abercromby to Dundas; Dunfermline, 217–18.
8 George III, *Later Corr.*, no. 1709.
9 Cornwallis, III.127.
10 Hope of Luffness, MSS, 1 Dec. 1799, Abercromby to Col. Alexander Hope; Melville MSS (SRO), GD51/1/774, 4 and 30 Aug., 15 Sept. 1800, Abercromby to Huskisson.
11 Dunfermline, 201.
12 Castlereagh, II.488; WO 1/179, ff.41–2. For the planning of the Dutch expedition in 1799 see Mackesy 1974, chs 9–11.
13 Dunfermline, 148–9; Dropmore V.217, 224.
14 Dropmore, V.386–8.
15 For Abercromby's refusal of a peerage see Dunfermline, 212–16; Melville MSS (SRO), GD51/1/703, 11 Sept., Alexander Hope to Dundas, 10 Oct., Dundas

NOTES

to Duke of York, and 30 Nov., Dundas to Abercromby; George III, *Later Corr.*,
no. 2054; Hope of Luffness MSS, 26 Sept., Abercromby to Dundas, and 1 Dec.,
same to Alexander Hope.
16 Dropmore, V.221, 237.
17 George III, *Later Corr.*, no. 1161.
18 For an admirable account of Abercromby's West Indian command, see Duffy,
Soldiers, Sugar and Seapower.

2 A LOOK AT JOHN TURK

1 Melville MSS (SRO), GD51/1/774, 23 Oct., John Hope to Dundas.
2 *Moore*, I.381–2; Campbell MS (NAM), 20 Dec., Archibald Campbell to Lord
Breadalbane.
3 Elphinstone MSS, KEI/1/13, 12 Oct., Abercromby to Keith; Mackesy 1984a,
157–9. Had it not been for Abercromby's understanding of Dundas's mind,
there might have been no army available for the Egyptian expedition. In July and
August, after the Austrian defeat at Marengo, he had been put under heavy pressure by the Austrians, the Queen of Naples, Lord Keith, and British diploma-
tists to commit the force in the Mediterranean to Italy. Although the first priority
in his instructions was to aid the Austrians, he realised that the collapse of the
war on the continent prefigured a change in British strategy: 'I am no longer at
liberty to commit the small corps under my command to any uncertain undertaking on the continent' (Minto MSS, 11252, f.213, 21 July to Lord William
Bentinck). See also Minto MSS, 11254, 16 July, Minto to Abercromby; Spencer,
IV.125–6; Dunfermline, 222–4; Melville MSS (SRO), GD51/1/774, 24 July,
Abercromby to Dundas; Hopetoun MSS, 170, 3 Aug., Abercromby to John
Hope; Arthur Paget, I.262; *Moore*, I.366 (that Abercromby was being urged 'to
sacrifice a corps which ought to be reserved for better purposes').
4 Melville MSS (SRO), GD1/1/174, 27 Oct., Abercromby to Huskisson; Mackesy
1984a, 157 and n.34.
5 Melville MSS (SRO), GD1/1/174, 27 Oct., Abercromy to Huskisson;
Dunfermline, 241–2; WO 6/21, 104 et seq.; Dunfermline, 245 et seq.; Lowe
MSS, Add. MSS 20107, W. Gifford to Hudson Lowe.
6 FO 78/30, f.274, 25 Oct., Abercromby to Anstruther; FO 78/31, passim; Keith
II.281–2.
7 Hopetoun MSS, 170, 1 Nov., minute of Hope's conversation with Keith; Wyvill,
Sketch, 403; Dunfermline, 254; Melville MSS (SRO), GD51/1/774, 27 Oct.
and 5 Nov., Abercromby to Huskisson. The Duke of York and Anderson do not
show the 54th as a regiment enlisted for service only in Europe, but Atkinson
(II.74) confirms Fortescue's statement that it was mainly composed of volunteers
from the militia, with service restricted to Europe, who volunteered for Egypt.
8 Dalhousie journal, f.125.
9 Parsons, 78–81; Smyth, 142; Inglis, 339; Harley, 121. Anderson states (187) that
the best entrance, the eastern one, was about a mile wide at the narrowest;
Hudson Lowe (Lowe MSS, Add. MSS 20107, f.19) that the entrance chosen was
not half a mile wide. Beaver states that Keith learned of the Marmaris anchorage
by a note from Sir Sidney Smith; but Captain Hallowell had mentioned it to the
Admiral on 31 Oct. (WO 1/344).
10 Dalhousie journal, 133; Brodie journal, 31 Dec.; Walsh 45–6.
11 Wyvill, *Sketch*, 404–6; Anderson, 188–90; Wilson, 3–5; Dalhousie journal,
133–4; Walsh, 46; Brown MSS; Rooke MSS, 11 Jan., Capt. J.C. Rooke to Capt.
Willoughby Rooke.

12 FO 78/31, 2 Jan., Anstruther to Elgin; WO 1/345, 11 Jan., Abercromby to Dundas; Wilson, 4–5; Walsh, 48–9.
13 Mackesy 1979, 234–42.
14 FO 78/30, 21 Nov., Elgin to Grenville.
15 For Smith's later gasconades in the Mediterranean see Mackesy 1957; and for Elgin's views on him, Shankland, 131.
16 Information from the present Earl of Elgin and Kincardine. For Sir Sidney Smith's military evaluation of the Turks, Sidmouth MSS, 27 June 1800, Smith to Lord Wellesley.
17 Information from Lord Elgin.
18 FO 78/30, 4 and 5 Dec., Elgin to Abercromby; FO 78/31, 21 Dec., 2 Jan., Anstruther to Elgin, and 6 Feb., Elgin to Abercromby; Elgin MSS, 13 Jan., Elgin to Abercromby.
19 FO 78/31, 21 Jan., Abercromby to Elgin, and 6 Feb., Elgin to Abercromby; Smyth, 141; Anderson, 193; Walsh, 50.
20 Lawson, 209.
21 Anderson, 194; Brodie journal, 12 Jan.; Wilson, 21; Walsh, 53.
22 FO 78/30, 22 Dec., Elgin to Grenville; Campbell MSS (SRO), 11 Jan., Archibald Campbell to Major Campbell; Wyvill, *Sketch*, 409; Lowe MSS, Add. MSS 20107, f.20; Maule, 194–7; Brown MSS.
23 Elgin MSS, 13 Jan., Elgin to Abercromby, and 6 Jan., Abercromby to Elgin.
24 Wittman, II.62; WO 1/345, 11 Jan., Abercromby to Dundas; Keith, II.258–9; Dundas of Beechwood MSS, 16 Feb., Abercromby to General Dundas.
25 Elgin MSS, 6 Jan., Abercromby to Elgin. For the growing Russian threat, Mackesy 1984a.
26 Wittman, II.1–2; Leake MSS, 85483, 17 Feb., letter of William Leake (copy).
27 Dropmore, VI.91.
28 Leake MSS, 85483, 17 Feb., letter of William Leake.
29 Ibid.
30 Walsh, 148–9.
31 Maule, 194–7; Lowe MSS, Add. MSS 20107, f.20.
32 Wittman, II.186; Walsh, App. 3–7.
33 WO 6/21, ff.104 et seq. See also Mackesy 1984a, 159.
34 *Moore*, II.55.
35 FO 78/31, 2 Jan., Abercromby to Elgin; WO 1/345, 11 Jan., Abercromby to Dundas.
36 Wilson, xvii, 7; Baldwin, 74; WO 1/345, 15 Jan., Abercromby to Dundas.
37 Wilson, xvii, 7.
38 Adm. 1/404, 21 Jan., Keith to Admiralty; WO 1/345, 21 Jan., Abercromby to Dundas.
39 FO 78/30, 21 Nov., Elgin to Grenville; FO 78/31, 2 Jan., Anstruther to Elgin; Elgin MSS, 2 Jan., Abercromby to Elgin.
40 WO 1/345, 11 Jan., Abercromby to Dundas; Hopetoun MSS, 170, 3 Jan., Moore's instructions; *Moore*, I.390–3. Lawson (216) alludes to the Turks' reluctance to operate during Ramadan.
41 FO 78/34, 4 Feb., Holloway to Grenville; *Moore*, I.393–4; Walsh, 54–5, and App. 3–7.
42 Oman, 247–8.
43 *Moore*, I.395–7; Brodie journal, I.99, 101. Sir Sidney Smith, who knew the Turks well, had described their army as 'a multitude of barbarians within an inch of famine or insurrection'.
44 *Moore*, I.398; WO 1/345, 21 Jan., Abercromby to Dundas.

3 THE FORGING OF THE BLADE

1 Lawson, 208–9, 211; Wyvill, *Sketch*, 408; Brodie journal, I.104; Walsh, 66.

2 Anderson, 197; Brodie journal, I.104.

3 Rooke MSS, 11 Jan., Capt. J.C. Rooke to Capt. Willoughby Rooke.

4 Quot. Clode, II.355; Mackesy 1984b, 204; Glover, passim.

5 Spencer, III.346; Wortley, 318.

6 Dundas, i–iv, 5–6, 11–13, 16.

7 Gurwood, 650; Mackesy 1974, 57; Dropmore, V.386.

8 Dropmore, VI.237; Keith, II.110–11.

9 Donoughmore MSS, Christopher Hutchinson's journal, 1 Sept. 1800 and 29 March 1801; Harley, I.136; Dalhousie journal, 110; Macdonald, 837–40. Abercromby's easy social manner was contrasted with that of the commander at Minorca, General Henry Fox (brother of that charmer Charles James Fox): 'I rather think he means civility', wrote Christopher Hutchinson, 'but he appears naturally so very unsociable and awkward that it is really very ennuyant to be of his parties'.

10 Bunbury, 29, 76; Simcoe MSS, 24 June 1799, Moira to Simcoe.

11 Melville MSS (NLS), 3835, f.119; Hope of Luffness MSS, 20 Nov. 1799, Abercromby to Alexander Hope.

12 Dalhousie journal, 4 Aug. 1799.

13 Duke of Northumberland in Simcoe MSS.

14 Melville MSS (SRO), GD51/1/703/11, 26 Oct. 1799 (misquoted in Dunfermline, 202); George III, *Later Corr.*, no. 2113. For the army's condition in the spring of 1800, Mackesy 1984a, 78–9.

15 Wyvill 212; *Moore*, I.370. For the order of battle and provenance of Abercromby's regiments, see p. 70. The 79th Highlanders were confusingly designated Cameronian Volunteers until 1807 when they first appeared in the Army List as Cameron Highlanders. The 92nd did not become Gordon Highlanders in the Army List until after the Crimean War, but none the less appeared in unofficial lists in 1800 (e.g. in Anderson) as 92nd or Gordon Highlanders. The names Cameron and Gordon Highlanders will be used in the text below.

16 See also Mackesy 1984a, 165; George III, *Later Corr.*, No. 2113 (Duke of York's lists, in which the strength of the 2/Royals is wrongly printed as 124 instead of 624).

17 Anderson, 40 et seq.; Dalhousie journal, 3 Aug.; Brodie journal, I.35.

18 E. Paget, 54; Huskisson MSS, Add. MSS 38736, f.239, 24 Oct., Doyle to Brownrigg; Dalhousie journal, 117.

19 Brown MSS.

20 Dunfermline, 241–2, 280n.; Dalhousie journal, 3 Dec.; Macdonald, 838–41; Wortley, 337; *Moore*, II.56; Rose, 241. Carola Oman, who lost no opportunity to slight Abercromby for the advantage of her hero Moore, suggested in defiance of all the evidence that his poor eyesight made him incapable of inspecting troops (p. 242).

21 *Moore*, I.208; Duffy, 286.

22 Dunfermline, 138; Dundas of Beechwood MSS, bundle on tactics.

23 Gardyne, I.67. For Sir David Dundas, the Duke of York, and light infantry, see Mackesy 1984b, 204–13; Gates, passim.

24 Fuller 1925a, 43; *Gentleman's Magazine*, April 1834, 441–3; Teffeteller 26. Light infantry regiments were not officially listed as such until 1813, and the 90th not until 1 May 1815; but their historian regards the change as formal recognition of the regiment's own training policy (Johnston, 178, 181, 225). See also Gates, 93–4, 112, 127.

25 Bunbury, 30.
26 *Moore*, II.56; Dalhousie journal, 135. I have been unable to find evidence whether Dundas's three-deep line was used in battle in Egypt. Though Parsons (p. 99) claims to have seen from the deck of his ship the 42nd forming in three ranks on the Aboukir beach to repel cavalry, the two-rank line is likely to have been the norm. It had been used increasingly in India for the past forty years, and in the West Indies (Duffy, 65) in the 1790s. It had received official sanction at home for most purposes (though not to resist cavalry) despite Dundas's manual (Evelyn, 19). From Sept. 1801 reviewing generals were authorised to allow an under-strength regiment to be drawn up in two ranks: an instruction which, Gates has pointed out, was misrepresented by Fortescue (IV.921).
27 *Moore*, II.55; Melville MSS (SRO), GD51/1/774, 13 Dec., Abercromby to Huskisson. Abercromby's historical imagination had already been fired by Bonaparte. 'If I had accepted the command in India', he had written two years earlier on news of the French invasion of Egypt, 'I might have had the glory of being opposed to Bonaparte, who they say is to tread in the footsteps of Alexander, Gengis Khan, Tamerlaine and Koobli Khan' (Melville MSS (NLS), 3835, f.167).

4 REHEARSING INVASION

1 This account of the Cadiz operation is based on Mackesy 1991. Keith's orders for the boats are in Elphinstone MSS, KEI/19/13.
2 Nepean MSS, NEP/5, 22 Sept. 1800, St Vincent to Nepean.
3 Donoughmore MSS, Christopher Hutchinson's journal, 7 Nov. 1800.
4 Ibid, 25 Nov.; Keith, II.235, 311–12.
5 Huskisson MSS, Add. MSS 38736, f.252, 17 Nov., T. Maitland to Huskisson.
6 Ibid.
7 Hope of Luffness MSS, 31 Dec. 1796 and 21 March 1797, Abercromby to Alexander Hope.
8 Melville MSS (SRO), GD51/1/774, 27 Dec., Dundas to Abercromby; Dropmore, IV.401; George III, *Later Corr.*, No. 2291; Spencer, IV.136–43, 291; Keith, II.149, 265.
9 Sidmouth MSS, 29 Jan. 1799, Simcoe to Addington.
10 Moore, I.377–8; Dalhousie journal, 120.
11 Elphinstone MSS, KEI/1/15; Keith, II.252; Young MSS, Add. MSS 46714, 18 Feb.; Wortley, 337. 'Captain Beaver is a most indefatigable officer but his inferior rank exposes him to envy and creates jealousy' (Althorp MSS, G216, 1 Nov. 1800, Keith to Spencer). Beaver's new appointment gave him post rank, and at Marmaris Keith reported that he was working harmoniously with Young. The term *beach-master* was used by Seaman Nicol (192) to describe Cochrane's appointment.
12 A plan of shipping dispositions for the landing, with written explanation, is in Dalhousie MSS, GD45/4/17/25.
13 Brodie journal, I.102; Dalhousie journal, 137; Walsh, 52–3.
14 Wyvill, *Sketch*, 408; Dalhousie journal, 137, 139. There are accounts of the rehearsals in Wilson, Walsh, and Anderson; and the instructions to the boats are printed in Bunbury, 103–6. Each company of infantry had a camp colour (still used today by the Foot Guards as markers and called company colours). They were used by the quartermasters to mark the battalion positions when camp sites were chosen.
15 The boat tables are printed in Anderson, 218–20.

16 Lawson, 209–10.

17 Adm. 1/404, 21 Jan., Keith to Admiralty; FO 78/31, 5 Feb., Elgin to Grenville.

18 WO 6/21, 6 Oct., Dundas to Abercromby; WO 1/345, 21 and 31 Jan., Abercromby to Dundas; Hopetoun MSS, 170, 3 Dec., examination of Greek sailors and memo. of Capt. Boyle's information; FO 78/31, f.195; FO 78/34, f.27.

19 Hope of Luffness MSS, 17 March, John Hope to Alexander Hope; Hope of Luffness MSS, 8 Sept., Graham to Alexander Hope; Mackesy 1984a, 160–1.

20 Elgin MSS, 26 Jan., Abercromby to Elgin; WO 1/345, Abercromby to Dundas. Abercromby considered (at any rate by the time of the landing) that only one attempt to land on the Alexandria sector would be feasible: if that failed he would have to try the Damietta option (Hopetoun MSS, 170, 7 March, Abercromby to Hutchinson).

21 Melville MSS (SRO), GD51/1/774, 20 Dec., Abercromby to Dundas or Huskisson; Adm 1/404, 20 Jan., Keith to Admiralty (encl. notes of proceedings of conference); *Moore*, I.397–8.

22 Keith, II.258–9, 262–4.

23 WO 1/345, 21 Jan., Abercromby to Dundas; FO 78/31, 21 Jan., Abercromby to Elgin; Elgin MSS, 26 Jan., Abercromby to Elgin.

24 Napoleon, 17.

25 *Moore*, I.398.

26 Donoughmore MSS, C. Hutchinson's journal, 9 Feb.

27 Melville MSS (SRO), GD51/1/774, 16 Feb., Abercromby to Huskisson; Dundas of Beechwood MSS, 16 Feb., Abercromby to Sir David Dundas.

28 Coote Transcripts, 10 Feb., Coote to Prince William.

29 Moore, II.55. Lord Cornwallis's phrase 'laughing-stock' had been echoed by Colonel Paget of the 28th: 'A British army, if we do not speedily change our passive system, will become the laughing-stock of Europe' (E. Paget, 56).

30 *Moore*, I.398.

31 Walsh, 67; Melville MSS (SRO), GD51/1/774, 16 Feb., Abercromby to Huskisson; Dalhousie journal, 16 Feb.; WO 1/345, 16 Feb., Abercromby to Dundas, and memo. of 10 Feb. on water; Hopetoun MSS, 170, 14 or 15 Feb., instructions for Major McKerras.

32 Dalhousie journal, 141.

33 Keith, II.267; Walsh, App. 10; Hopetoun MSS, 170, f.154 (list of small vessels with place of origin); Dunfermline, 273–4.

34 Dunfermline, 273–4; Walsh, 68–9.

5 THE EVE OF BATTLE

1 Dalhousie journal, 28 Feb.; Walsh, 69.

2 *Moore*, I.401; Dalhousie journal, 1 March.

3 Wilson, 10–11; Wyvill, *Sketch*, 411–12; Anderson, 214; Inglis, 341–2; Landmann, II.335. Fletcher, whose distinguished later career is recorded below (p. 238), was a serious loss. Abercromby had retained him at Marmaris when he arrived from the mission at Jaffa 'as we are short in the Engineer department': he was 'an officer . . . of whose experience we stand in need' (FO 78/34, 9 Feb., Abercromby to Holloway).

4 Dalhousie journal, 2 March; *A Faithful Journal*, 29; Dropmore, VI.469; *Moore*, II.1.

5 Anderson, 214; Inglis, 343; Walsh, 73; *Moore*, II.2.

6 Inglis, 343; Elphinstone MSS, KEI/L/147D, journal of *Foudroyant*; Wilson, 11–12; *Moore*, I.402.

7 Anderson, 215–16; Dunfermline, 275; E. Paget, 59; Walsh, 73–4; Sibthorpe MSS, '28 Feb' (*sic*), Henry Sibthorpe to his sister.

8 Anderson, 216; Oakes MS, Add. MSS 36747, f.44 (17 March, Oakes to Gen. (?)); Brodie journal, 7 March.

9 For Menou's character and relations with his officers, see Herold, Derrécagaix, Rigault, Dumas (IV.150–2), Marmont (I.409–11).

10 The first author in modern times to mention the Valley of the Kings was Richard Pococke, who visited the valley in 1757; James Bruce discovered the tomb of Ramesses II in 1769, and several more tombs were discovered by Bonaparte's *savants*. The *Description de l'Égypte* was published between 1809 and 1820.

11 *Moore*, II.50.

12 Account of Menou's decisions based on Reynier, François, and documents printed in Rigault and Derrécagaix.

13 For Friant's numbers, see p. 62.

14 Anderson, 201.

6 ASSAULT LANDING

1 Anderson, 70 et seq., 201; Walsh, 75; Brodie journal, I.51–64.

2 Elphinstone MSS, KEI/L/147D (journal of *Foudroyant*).

3 Baldwin, 102; Dropmore, VI.469.

4 Elgin MSS, 12 March, Abercromby to Elgin; Baynham, 29; Wilson, 30; Moore MSS, Add. MSS 57329, notes by (?) Capt. Anderson attached to Moore's diary.

5 Wilson, 13.

6 *Narrative*, 72; Brodie journal, I.122.

7 Dunfermline, 280; Macdonald, 842–3; Brownrigg, 114; David Stewart, I.444n.

8 Anderson, 222; Dropmore, VI.470; Wilson, 14; Thornton, 34; *Narrative*, 72; Baldwin, 106; Walsh, 76–8; Moore MSS, loc. cit.

9 Brodie journal, I.129–30; Lowe MSS, Add. MSS 36297, 29 March, Hudson Lowe to father; Wyvill, *Sketch*, 414; Wilson, 15; Walsh, 78; Inglis, 344; Brodie journal, I.124–6; Dropmore, VI.470; Vincent diary, 8 March.

10 Brodie journal, I.127.

11 Harley, 125–6; Dunfermline, 280n.; Macdonald, 842–3. Harley says that the delinquent officer resigned his commission rather than face a court martial. The anecdote of Colonel Hall of the 23rd is related by Macdonald, 13. By 'abuse you' Abercromby must have meant 'abuse your regiment'.

12 Inglis, 344; Young MSS, Add. MSS 46714, Capt. Young's orders of 18 Feb.; Thornton, 36; Anderson, 201.

13 Orders for boats in Bunbury, 103–4; additional instructions in Wilson, 275–80.

14 Gardyne, I.84; Church, 4; Robertson, 7.

15 Walsh, App. 12–13; NAM, Acc. 6807–74 (naval casualties). Meade matriculated at Wadham College in 1797, aged 16. At the time of his death he had been promoted to lieutenant in the 23rd, but was probably not aware of this. I owe the information that he was said to be the only Oxbridge death to Dr A.D. Harvey.

16 Dropmore, VI.470.

17 Allardyce, 261 (quoting Bertrand).

18 Coote Transcripts, 15 March, Coote to Prince William.

19 Oakes MS, Add. MSS 36747, f.44 (17 March, Oakes to Gen. (?)).

20 A. Paget, I.325; Sidmouth MSS, OM5; Dundas of Beechwood MSS, 18 March, Abercromby to Sir David Dundas; Anderson, 388–90. 'There is no event in *our* military history to compare with it', John Hope wrote to his brother, particularly

stressing the very limited naval fire support that was possible in the shallow bay (Hope of Luffness MSS, 17 March).
21 Donoughmore MSS, C. Hutchinson diary, 99; Wilson, 16.
22 Wilson, 17.

7 'WE SHALL ALL FARE ALIKE'

1 *Moore*, II.4–5.
2 Dunfermline, 199; Bunbury, 180, 210. Bunbury served under Moore in Sicily as Quartermaster-General in 1807.
3 *Moore*, II.4–5; Wilson, 18.
4 Baldwin, 115; Walsh, 81–2.
5 Anderson, 238–9; Robertson, 9.
6 Inglis, 345; Wilson, 275–80.
7 Spencer, IV.148–9.
8 Adm. 1/404, 2, 10, 12, and 14 March, Keith to Admiralty.
9 Dundas of Beechwood MSS, 17 March, Anstruther to Sir David Dundas; Keith, II.272.
10 Wilson, 275–80.
11 Wilson, 18; Keith, II.273.
12 Walsh, 82; Inglis, 245; Williams, 98–9.
13 *Moore*, II.6.
14 Wilson, 19; Wyvill, 416; P.F. Stewart, 47; Lawson, 216. I am grateful to Brigadier K.A. Timbers of the Royal Artillery Historical Trust for information about the British howitzers.
15 Wilson, 290; Anderson, 232–4. For the unsuitability of the sand for training in 1915, see *Staff Officer: The Diaries of Lord Moyne, 1914- 1918*, ed. Brian Bond (1987), pp. 74, 86.
16 *Narrative*, 79; Walsh, 84–6; *Moore*, II.6.
17 Dropmore, VII.1; *Moore*, II.6–7; Lowe MSS, Add. MSS 20107, 23 March, Lowe to (?).
18 Maule, 83, 85; Davis, IV.21–2; The Queen's are not shown on plans of the battle of 13 March, though Maule, who was one of them, records the regiment leading their brigade in the advance to the Green Hill. Nor indeed are the 2/27th shown, though Walsh states that they had joined Cavan's brigade on 10 March.
19 Walsh, 86; *Moore*, II.7; Macdonald, 843–4.

8 'A COOL INTREPIDITY': THE MANDARA BATTLE

1 Robertson, 12. Walsh (86) refers to 'untoward circumstances' delaying the planned 5 a.m. advance: the troubles of the 90th coming off picket duty, mentioned below, suggest lapses in staff work.
2 Hope of Luffness, 17 March, John Hope to Alexander Hope; Dropmore, VI.471; Wilson, 19; Walsh, App. 16. The Alexandria canal, seven feet wide and lined with brick, had been created in order to bring the annual overflow of the Nile to fill the city's cisterns; it was now silted up and no longer navigable.
3 Lowe MSS, Add. MSS 36297, f.13; Walsh, 87; Anderson, 227–8. The terms 'first line' and 'second line' to denote the right and left columns produced some writing which is confusing to the modern reader. One reads that when the columns deployed, 'the first line formed two lines to the front of march' (*A Faithful Journal*, 29).
4 Anderson, 227–8; Johnston, 185; Wilson, 19, 290.

5 Thornton, Ch. iii; *Moore*, II.9; Dropmore, VI.471; Walsh, 89, 92; Maule, 85; Reynier, 202, shows twenty-two guns and howitzers.

6 *Moore*, II.8; Dropmore, VI.471; E. Paget, 60–1. Phoenix Park in Dublin was one of the few permitted areas in the British Isles where there was space to hold a brigade exercise.

7 Bertrand, 442–3.

8 Bertrand, 432–3; Reynier, 201–5.

9 Hope of Luffness MSS, 8 Sept., Graham to Alexander Hope.

10 Graham MSS, NLS 3604, f.18, 4 Apr., Hill to Graham; Delavoye, 39; Johnston, 186; *Narrative*, 80; *Moore*, II.7. According to his obituary in the *Gentleman's Magazine* (Apr. 1834, p. 442) Mackenzie was commanding the advance guard of the 90th with the two flank companies, two battalion companies, and a troop of cavalry, while Hill commanded six companies in support.

11 North MSS, c.18, f.3, part of an account of the battle by (?) Doyle; Delavoye, 39. Reynier (205) provoked British indignation with a claim that the 22nd Chasseurs had caused two British battalions to lay down their arms before the chasseurs were forced to retire and abandon their prisoners by the accurate fire of the British second line. This story illustrates Reynier's untruthfulness.

12 *Narrative*, 81–2; Walsh, 88; Brodie journal, II.4–9. The Marines lost fifty-nine of all ranks killed and wounded (Adm. 1/404, no. 77).

13 The 90th lost ninety-one killed or invalided in the battle (Hope of Luffness MSS, 8 Sept., Graham to Alexander Hope).

14 Ibid.; Gardyne, I.86; Graham MSS, NLS 3604, f.18, 4 Apr.; Wilson, 20. The 92nd had been weakened in numbers by sickness during the voyage from England, exacerbated (it was alleged) by exchanging the kilt for thick trousers. On the kilt in the three highland regiments, see David Stewart, II.265–6.

15 North MSS, c.18, f.3; Walsh, 15; Thornton, Ch. iii; Oakes MS, Add. MSS 36747, 17 March, Oakes to Gen (?). Lawson, 216, lamented that if only a part of the artillery had been well horsed Alexandria might have fallen.

16 Dunfermline, 286: the story was evidently current in the force, and Dalrymple and Graham both heard it on their later arrival from England (Dalrymple journal, 24 July; Hope of Luffness MSS, 8 Sept., Graham to Alexander Hope).

17 *Moore*, II.8.

18 Ibid.; Wilson, App. 17.

19 D. Stewart, I.471; Wyville, *Sketch*, 418; Walsh, 81; Brown MSS, encl. in Isaac Worthington to Mr Harrap, 20 May.

20 Walsh, 81; *Moore* II.8–9; Wilson, 21–2; Donoughmore MSS, Christopher Hutchinson's journal, 13 March; J.C. Moore, I.288. Thornton states that Abercromby's horse was killed at this stage; but Johnston indicates that it happened earlier during the advance to the Roman Camp ridge. According to Walsh Abercromby received a contusion of the thigh from a musket ball during the battle.

21 *Moore*, II.10.

22 Wilson, 22; Wyvill, *Sketch*, 416; *Moore*, II.10.

9 'WE MUST MAKE THE ATTEMPT'

1 *Narrative*, 87; Robertson, 14; Harley, 129; Wyvill, *Sketch*, 419.

2 Wilson, 26; *Moore*, II.11; Walsh, 93; Daniel, 79; *A Faithful Journal*, 35; Robertson, 15.

3 *Narrative*, 90; Wilson, 25–6; Anderson, 243–4.

4 Anderson, 240–3; Brodie journal, II.11–12; Gardyne, I.91.

5 Thornton, 59; Wyvill, *Sketch*, 419; Walsh, 94.
6 E. Paget, 60; Lowe MSS, Add. MSS 20107, f.50; Dropmore, VI.471–2; Maule, 90; Wyvill, *Sketch*, 418; Dundas of Beechwood MSS, 17 March, Anstruther to Sir David Dundas; Hope of Luffness MSS, 17 March, J. Hope to Alexander Hope.
7 Lowe MSS, Add. MSS 20107, f.50, and Add. MSS 36297, f.13; Oakes MS, Add. MSS 36747, f.44.
8 E. Paget, 60. John Hope wrote in the same vein, conveying the regularity of a field day: the infantry's 'order and regularity' had astonished everyone, 'advancing rapidly in two lines and at the same time almost as regularly as they could have done in the neighbourhood of Windsor' (Hope of Luffness MSS, 17 March, to Alexander Hope).
9 Abercromby MS (NAM), 16 March, Abercromby to Brownrigg; Dundas of Beechwood MSS, 17 March, Anstruther to Sir David Dundas, and 18 March, Abercromby to Sir David Dundas.
10 Walsh, 91, App. 18–19; Oakes MS, 36747, f.44.
11 According to Reynier (207–8) Lanusse did not hold the edge of the escarpment in strength, but with a strong advance guard, making his main defensive position the line of the Arab walls which he repaired.
12 Dundas of Beechwood MSS, 17 March, Anstruther to Sir David Dundas; *Moore*, II.11. Though Moore reported that the lake-bed could be crossed, the French 18th Dragoons, which Lanusse had sent away to Damanhur to conserve forage in Alexandria, had to go as far west as the Marabout to find a route across the lake; and a few days later Rampon's reconnaissance led to a similar route being adopted (Reynier, 208–9).
13 Dundas of Beechwood MSS, 17 March, Anstruther to Sir David Dundas; Hope of Luffness MSS, 17 March, John Hope to Alexander Hope.
14 Hope of Luffness MSS, 17 March, John Hope to Alexander Hope; Dundas of Beechwood MSS, 17 March, Anstruther to Sir David Dundas; *Moore*, II.11; Coote Transcripts, 15 March; Oakes MS, Add. MSS 36747, f.44.
15 Dundas of Beechwood MSS, 18 March, Abercromby to Sir David Dundas.
16 Ibid.; Elphinstone MSS, KEI/18/7, 14 March, Abercromby to Keith; Brownrigg, 123; Dropmore, VI.472.
17 Hope of Luffness MSS, 17 March, John Hope to Alexander Hope; Macdonald, 846.
18 General O'Hara's nickname for Cradock (Teffeteller, 22).
19 Abercromby MS (NAM), 16 March, Abercromby to Brownrigg; Donoughmore MSS, C. Hutchinson's journal, 8 March.
20 Wilson, 26–7, 292; Reynier, 210; *Moore*, II.11–12; Walsh, 95–6.
21 Smith MSS, f.11, 20 March, Sir Sidney Smith to Bickerton (referring to the French cutting the British land communication with the Arabs, which was in reality a consequence of Menou's approach); *Moore*, II.10.
22 Keith, II.275.
23 Baldwin, 124; *Moore*, II.12; Dropmore, VI.476.
24 Wilson, 371; Walsh, 96; Gardyne, I.92 n.1.
25 *Parliamentary History*, XXXV.1172.

10 SURPRISED IN DARKNESS

1 The terrain and entrenchments are described in Wilson, 23–4, and Walsh, 97. Wilson states the width of the front from sea to canal to be about a mile, but all maps including his own show it to be about 3,000 yards, or a mile and three-

quarters. Christopher Hutchinson (Donoughmore MSS, C. Hutchinson journal, 94) criticised the slightness of the new fieldworks, forgetting that the army's first priority in the use of labour was to bring up material for the planned offensive. Jennings describes the redoubt: it is usually stated that two 24-pounders were mounted in it; but David Stewart (I.251), who was present with the 42nd, wrote that one of the pair had not been mounted.

2 *Moore*, II.13; Williams, 99.

3 *Moore*, II.16; WO 1/345, pp. 111–13 (returns of 18 March). The dismounted men of the 26th Light Dragoons were still at Aboukir.

4 François, I.462.

5 Rigault, 296; Rousseau, 399.

6 François, I.460; Reynier, 200–1.

7 Reynier, 201. Herold suggests that the Mameluke chief Murad Bey (of whom more later) would have held Cairo for the French if Menou had concentrated his whole force against Abercromby. He also points out that the French had lost Cairo before and had regained it; but since that time extensive base-establishments had been created whose destruction would have been serious for the isolated Army of the Orient.

8 Walsh, App. 41–2.

9 It is impossible to establish the exact numbers in the line on both sides on the morning of 21 March. The numbers detached from each unit, and the sick on the actual day, are figures lost in the turmoil of battle. My computation of the French relies on Reynier's figures of 1 March, and may be too high in spite of allowance for casualties. Prisoners stated the French strength as 12,000–14,000, Bertrand as 10,800; while on the British side Walsh called it 12,000–13,000 excluding artillery, Wilson 9,700 (like Moore he puts the British at under 10,000), Anstruther 9,000 at most.

10 Hope of Luffness MSS, 8 Sept., Graham to Alexander Hope.

11 François (I.462) says that Menou was pressed by Lanusse and Reynier to attack, in order to forestall the advance of the Grand Vizir and the Red Sea expedition.

12 Reynier, 210–11; François, I.462.

13 Menou's orders (printed in Walsh, Wilson, and Anderson) should be read in conjunction with Reynier's description (211–14) of Menou's intention, though his account is not disinterested. Menou blamed Reynier's passivity for the defeat, and Reynier's description of the plan and the course of the battle is designed to exonerate himself. There is a contentious critique of the plan in Bertrand, 443.

14 Reynier, 213. Reynier indicates that Rampon was not in overall command of the centre, and the written orders do not mention his holding that command; neither, however, do they accord Reynier the command of both divisions of the right wing, though he certainly held and exercised it, as Rampon appears to have done in the centre.

15 *Moore*, II.12–13; Wyvill, *Sketch*, 421.

16 Walsh, 97–8.

17 Walsh, 98; Thornton, 62; *Narrative*, 93.

18 Wyvill MS, 263; Baldwin, 124 et seq.; Gardyne, I.92; *Narrative*, 93; Walsh, 100n.

19 *Moore*, II.13; Wyvill MS, 263.

11 THE BATTLE IN THE DAWN

1 Wilson, 31; *Moore*, II.13–14; David Stewart, I.453.

2 *Moore*, II.13; Campbell journal, 31.

3 *Moore*, II.13–14. The printed text of Moore's diary misleadingly reads that

Anderson was sent *to* the right wing, instead of *for* the right wing (i.e. of the 42nd) as in the original (Moore MSS, Add. MSS 57329).

4 Wilson, 31; Walsh, 99–100; Reynier, 214.

5 Rigault, 303.

6 Reynier, 214; Wilson, 372 (narrative of 42nd).

7 Wilson, 372–3. According to David Stewart (I.453) the companies of the 28th which had been stationed outside the redoubt were ordered into it when the 42nd came up. *Moore* however (II.14) describes part of the 28th charging with the 42nd a little later.

8 *Sic* in Melville MSS (SRO), GD51/1/786 (narrative of 42nd): Wilson transcribed it as *loaded.*

9 Wilson, 372–4. David Stewart (I.453) states that only the rear rank of the 42nd turned about and charged; but the narrative of the 42nd implies that the whole wing charged.

10 *Moore*, II.14; Inglis, 347. David Stewart's account of the 42nd's movements (I.453) differs from Moore's. According to Stewart the right wing was echelonned 200 yards in rear of the left wing and parallel with it; and the enemy column penetrated between the two wings.

11 Wilson, 31; Hill MSS, Col. Hill's statement of services; Wyvill, *Sketch*, 422; Smyth, 148.

12 Wilson, 373; *Moore*, II.14; Hill MSS, Col. Hill's statement.

13 Wilson, 373; *Moore*, II.14, 18; David Stewart, I.455.

14 Wilson, 373; *Moore*, II.14; Walsh, 102n. According to David Stewart the order for the 42nd to rally on the redoubt was given by Moore and repeated by the commanding officer. The accounts of this confused fighting in Wilson, Walsh, and Oman contain errors or contradictions; and the official narrative produced by the 42nd strangely refers to only one cavalry charge though the regiment was charged twice.

15 Gardyne, I.92; *Narrative*, 94.

16 Reynier, 214–19.

17 Wilson, 34; Walsh, 100. Walsh wrote with the first-hand authority of an aide de camp to Coote.

18 *Moore*, II.15.

19 Ibid.

20 Reynier, 217–18.

21 Reynier, 218–19.

22 Dundas of Beechwood MSS, Col. Paget to Lord Paget.

23 Campbell journal, 31; David Stewart, I.457; Wilson, 33; *Moore*, II.15, 18.

24 Daniel, 81–2; Jennings microfilm.

25 Reynier, 220–1.

26 Wilson, 33n.

27 Walsh, 104; David Stewart, I.458, 460–1.

28 *Moore*, II.15–16; Dropmore, VI.476; Walsh, 104–5; David Stewart, I.459.

12 THE PRICE OF VICTORY

1 *Moore*, II.16–17.

2 The casualty figures and distribution are based on MS Casualty Returns in NAM.

3 Wilson, 38n., 39; Bunbury, 180.

4 *Moore*, II.17; Wyvill, *Sketch*, 422; Duncan, II.128.

5 Wilson MSS, Add. MSS 30095, diary for 21 March; Dalhousie journal, 167;

Moore, II.16; Smyth, 147–8; Inglis, 347; Dropmore, VI.477 (my italics).

6 Wilson, 38, 372–8; Dawson and Conway, 124–6. The captured standard was claimed in 1947 from the Royal Hospital, Chelsea, by the Manchester Regiment, whose 2nd battalion, the 96th, were successors to the Queen's German Regiment, which had been numbered 96th for two years before its disbandment in 1818. General David Stewart of the 42nd (I.454n., 479–81) dismissed the quarrel about the standard, which for some years caused a breach between the regiment and the Highland Society of London, as a fuss about nothing fomented by young officers of the 42nd and the journalist William Cobbett. The outstanding performance of the 42nd seems to have aroused some jealousy: Captain Jennings of the 28th recorded that 'an entire column of chosen men who endeavoured to turn our rear were cut to pieces, chiefly by the 58th Regiment, tho' the 42nd Regt. attributed this action to themselves' (Jennings microfilm).

7 *Moore*, II.16–17; Dropmore, VI.476; Walsh, 65.

8 *Moore*, II.17; Oman, 277–80.

9 Haddington MSS, 29 March, Hope to Dundas; Huskisson MSS, Add. MSS 38739, Col. Robert Abercromby's journal.

10 Huskisson MSS, ibid.; Macdonald, 845. Macdonald later became General Sir John Macdonald, Adjutant-General.

11 Baldwin, 133; Huskisson MSS, Add. MSS 38739, Col. Robert Abercromby's journal; Gardyne, I.94; Robertson, 18–19. Dr Green was named, and described as a surgeon in the Guards and 'a very experienced professional man', by Colonel Robert Abercromby; and it was probably from him that his brother Lord Dunfermline derived the description 'a skilful surgeon of the Guards'. But there is no Green listed as a surgeon in either the Coldstream or the Third Guards, and I have not identified him with certainty in the Army Lists or in Drew. The only Green whose dates could fit was Ralph Green, Inspector of Field Hospitals in 1801 and therefore not attached to a regiment: he never served in the Guards.

12 Wilson MSS, Add. MSS 30095, f.112; Wilson, 36–7.

13 Dalhousie journal, f.166.

14 Harley, 140.

15 Wilson, 36; Thornton, 72.

16 Thornton, 66.

17 Gardyne, I.95–6.

18 *Narrative*, 96–8.

19 Young MSS, Add. MSS 46714, March 11, 20, 21, 23, 24; Althorp MSS, G222, 29 Apr., Nepean to Spencer.

20 Parsons, 112.

21 Melville MSS (SRO), GD51/1/787, 23 March, Keith to Dundas.

22 Huskisson MSS, Add. 38739, Col. Robert Abercromby's journal, ff.85–8; Dalhousie journal, f.168.

23 Huskisson MSS, Add. 38739, Col. Robert Abercromby's journal.

24 Maitland MSS, note on character of Abercromby.

25 Brodie journal, II.44–5; Dalhousie journal, 29 March; Thornton, 74; Inglis, 347.

26 Simcoe MSS, 1038M/F7A, 24 June 1799 and 24 June 1801, Moira to Simcoe.

27 Bute MSS, 3 Apr., Doyle to Moira; Wilson MSS, Add. MSS 30095, f.118.

28 *Moore*, II.18; Haddington MSS, 29 March, Hope to Dundas.

29 Brownrigg, 122.

13 'UNGRACIOUS MANNERS AND A VIOLENT TEMPER'

1 Bunbury, 76, 85; Donoughmore MSS, C. Hutchinson diary, 10 Feb., and citations below, note 2. Christopher (Kit) became much liked by General Cradock and Sir Robert Wilson, both of them slightly odd characters (Wilson MSS, Add. MSS 30111, f.247, Aug. 1826, Cradock (Caradoc), by then Lord Howden, to Wilson). Although referred to as Colonel, his name does not appear in the Army List.

2 Donoughmore MSS, C. Hutchinson diary, 26 Nov. and 8 Dec. 1800, and 22 Feb. 1801; Brodie journal, II.45–6; Elgin MSS, 28 July 1801, Hamilton to Elgin; *Moore*, II.32.

3 Bunbury, 76; above, p. 104; Cornwallis, III.360; Brownrigg, 122. The rebarbative Lord Buckingham, head of the Grenvilles, who will have known the Hutchinsons during his Lord-Lieutenancy in Dublin, commented: 'I dread Hutchinson; for he is a Gascon, and has as much of the family madness as may play the divil with his army' (Grenville MSS, AR30/63, 17 May 1801, to Thomas Grenville).

4 Hope of Luffness MSS, 8 Sept., Graham to Alexander Hope; Donoughmore MSS, E 10c, f.256.

5 Dalhousie journal, 29 March.

6 Anderson (250) prints the General Order in full, and attributes it to Abercromby; but internal evidence confirms the attribution to Hutchinson and the date 21 March given in Wilson (App. 295), Brodie journal (II.31), and Donoughmore MSS, C. Hutchinson diary, 95–6.

7 Wilson, 44–5; Walsh, 109; Fraser MSS, General Order of 8 Apr.

8 Wilson MSS, Add. MSS 30095, ff.116, 118; Wyvill, *Sketch*, 425; Fraser MSS, General Orders of 30 March and 8 Apr.; Miller, 27; WO 1/345, 3 Apr., Hutchinson to Dundas.

9 Walsh, 115; Wilson MSS, Add. MSS 30095, f.122.

10 Above, p. 23.

11 Elgin MSS, 2 Apr., Hutchinson to Elgin; Coote Transcripts, 30 March, to Prince William; Brownrigg, 122; Dropmore, VI.476; above, pp. 25–6.

12 Wilson MSS, Add. MSS 30095, 21 March; Wyvill, *Sketch*, 425; Rooke MSS, 1 Apr., Capt. J.C. Rooke to Capt. W. Rooke; Donoughmore MSS, C. Hutchinson diary, 93.

13 Wilson, 45–6; Elgin MSS, 2 Apr.,Hutchinson to Elgin.

14 Wilson MSS, Add. MSS 30095, ff.119–20; Dalhousie journal, 29 March; Wyvill MS, 267.

15 Reynier, 243–4.

14 'MUCH MORE AT EASE IN HIS COMMAND'

1 Donoughmore MSS, C. Hutchinson diary, 96, 101; Elgin MSS, 2 Apr., Hutchinson to Elgin; WO 1/292, 21 March, Hutchinson to Pigot. The 1/27th, which had been left at Malta to recover from sickness, were forwarded in response to Hutchinson's appeal, and arrived on 20 May.

2 Keith, II.270.

3 Melville MSS (SRO), GD51/1/788, 30 March, Cochrane to Dundas; Smyth, 151; A. Paget, I.340–1; Donoughmore MSS, C. Hutchinson diary, 97.

4 Bertrand, 428, 445; Reynier, 222–3.

5 Reynier, 222; Charles-Roux, II.188–9.

6 Melville MSS (SRO), GD51/1/789, 5 Apr., Anstruther to Brownrigg. Anstruther believed that the remaining enemy forces in Egypt were only 8,000

French and 3,000 natives: in reality after losing further men through wounds and disease the French eventually embarked some 23,500 military personnel for France.

7 Brownrigg, 123; Hopetoun MSS, 170, c.24–7 March; Keith, II.279; Walsh, App. 42.

8 Wilson, 55–6; WO 1/345, 2 June, Hutchinson to Hobart; Loveday, 40.

9 Anderson, 252; Walsh, 96; WO 1/345, 3 Apr., Hutchinson to Dundas; Donoughmore MSS, C. Hutchinson diary, 98.

10 Donoughmore MSS, C. Hutchinson diary, 98 and 100.

11 WO 1/345, 3 Apr., Hutchinson to Dundas; Melville MSS (SRO), GD51/1/755, Graham's annotated sketch map.

12 Maule, 96–7; Wilson, 51; Donoughmore MSS, C. Hutchinson diary, 103–5.

13 Lawson, 219; Duncan, II.116. Lawson's paper implies that his artillerymen organised the overland movement of the gunboats.

14 Walsh, 117–18; Wilson, 58–9; Duncan, II.128.

15 *Moore*, II.22; Donoughmore MSS, C. Hutchinson diary, 113; Dropmore, VII.9; Melville MSS (SRO), GD51/1/791, 21 Apr., Hutchinson to Dundas; WO 1/345, 20 Apr., Hutchinson to Dundas, and 2 June, to Hobart; Melville MSS (SRO), GD51/1/789, 5 Apr., Anstruther to Brownrigg; Keith, II.284; Wilson, 55–6.

16 Walsh, 118–19; Wyvill MS, 270; Wilson, 62; Melville MSS (SRO), GD51/1/789, 5 Apr., Anstruther to Brownrigg; Anderson, 287–8. Of Hutchinson's health his brother wrote, 'I do not think he looks bilious, but he does not appear strong' (Donoughmore MSS, C. Hutchinson diary, 122). Coote's brigade was taken over by Finch, whose cavalry brigade was broken up on the departure of part of it to the Nile. While the new lake was filling, the level of lake Aboukir did indeed fall for a time, and the supply boats repeatedly grounded.

17 Donoughmore MSS, C. Hutchinson diary, 102; Wilson, 183; Coote Transcripts, 4 and 13 June; Walsh, 173.

18 Coote Transcripts, 17 May, 4 July; Dyott, 156–60.

19 Keith, II.321–3; Hope of Luffness MSS, 8 Sept., Graham to Alexander Hope.

20 Walsh, 186–8; Coote Transcripts, 1 July.

21 Walsh, 173–4.

22 Rooke MSS, 9 May, 13 June, Capt. J.C. Rooke to Capt. W. Rooke; Dalrymple journal, 86–9; Dyott, 156–60; Smith, 26; Walsh, 185; David Stewart, I.474n.

23 Coote Transcripts, 1 July; Young MSS, Add. MSS 46714, 8 Apr., 14 June; Keith, II.234–6; Dalrymple journal, 97–8.

24 Randolph, I.164–5; Keith, II.236–8, 283–5; Wilson, 65; Walsh, 121; Donoughmore MSS, C. Hutchinson diary, 95; Elgin MSS, 60/6/7, Hamilton to Elgin. At the end of the campaign Sir Sidney Smith went home, at his own request, as the bearer of Keith's despatches. He arrived at the Admiralty still wearing his huge mustachios, and in Turkish dress with turban, robe, and shawl; with a girdle round his middle holding a brace of pistols.

15 THE THRUST ON THE NILE

1 Rousseau, 404–5.

2 Reynier, 243–4; François, 473.

3 Reynier, 237.

4 Jollois, 136–61; Keith, II.334–5.

5 *Moore*, II.22; Melville MSS (SRO), GD51/1/791, 21 Apr., Hutchinson to Dundas; WO 1/345, same; Keith, II.284; Dropmore, VII.8–10.

6 *Moore*, II.22; WO 1/345, 3 Apr., Hutchinson to Dundas; Melville MSS (SRO), GD51/1/791, 21 Apr., Hutchinson to Dundas; WO 1/345, same; Dropmore, VII.10.

7 Walsh, 247; Dalrymple journal, 94.

8 Wilson, 328–9; Donoughmore MSS E 10c, f.123; Randolph, I.168; Keith, II.287–91.

9 Lawson, 212–13, 218.

10 Wyvill, *Sketch*, 432–4; Wilson, 70–1; Walsh, 122–3 and App. 55. William Stewart, senior lieutenant-colonel of the 89th, is to be distinguished from Lt Col. the Hon. William Stewart who had raised the Rifle Corps (later the 95th). The returns of 30 March (Wilson, 275) show 4,894 rank and file of infantry fit for duty in the regiments which were to be sent to the Nile, and 510 cavalry. Hutchinson and Wilson (who was with the Nile force) both give the British strength on the Nile in May as 4,500.

11 Campbell journal, 36.

12 Donoughmore MSS, E 10c, ff.127, 246, 250 (Christopher Hutchinson's sketch of the campaign). *Moore* (II.34) later suggested that General Hutchinson ought to have closed up to the enemy on the previous day, the 8th, and attacked on the 9th. This opinion, however, is based on after-knowledge of Lagrange's position and of his withdrawal in an unexpected direction during the night of the 9th. Moore also mistakenly assumed that Hutchinson had intended on the 9th to approach, reconnoitre and attack in a single day – a degree of haste unnecessary on Hutchinson's reading of the situation.

13 *Moore*, II.34. Reynier (240–2), prejudiced against Lagrange who was a supporter of Menou, assumes that he intended to fight for Rahmanieh but bungled his choice of ground.

14 I have no evidence on who ordered Lagrange's retreat to Cairo. The decision must have been taken before the allies approached the Rahmanieh position; otherwise Lagrange would have taken up different ground and made his escape to Alexandria sooner. As chief of staff Lagrange is likely to have known Menou's mind, and it is possible (though unlikely since Menou does not mention it) that the retreat to Cairo and concentration against the Turks was Menou's own design. Colonel Hill heard noise while on duty during the night which suggested that the French were moving off, and reported it to Cradock; and according to his diary Wilson had observed the French retreat before dark from a minaret on the far bank of the Nile, and returned to inform Hutchinson (Sidney, 42; Randolph, I.172–3). There is much that remains obscure about the Rahmanieh action, for the outline of which I have used Wilson supplemented by Walsh, Wyvill, and Maule.

16 THE VERGE OF MUTINY

1 E. Paget, 62; Dalhousie journal, 10 June; Dalhousie MSS, GD45/4/48, n.d., Dalhousie to (?); Wilson, 93–7 (who indicates that the view was widely held, though he does not support it).

2 *Moore*, II.34.

3 Donoughmore MSS, E 10c, f.250.

4 *Moore*, II.34; Donoughmore MSS, E 10c, f.246 (Christopher Hutchinson: 'It was said in the heat of the moment, but since apologised for, that an opportunity was lost at Rahmanieh, when the enemy ought to have been immediately attacked. No one ever suggested this upon that day . . .'); Maule, 40; Randolph, I.172–3.

5 David Stewart, II.249n.; Liverpool MSS, Add. MSS 38357, 24 May, unidentified correspondent from Algam.

6 Dalhousie journal, 10 June.

7 Elgin MSS, 25 Apr., Hutchinson to Elgin. Belliard's true strength was not revealed till his force was counted after the surrender of Cairo (below, p. 203).

8 All British sources describe the French detachment as part of the 22nd Dragoons, a regiment which was not in Egypt: presumably they were the 22nd Chasseurs à cheval. Though all authorities agree (including the commanding officer of the 12th) that the British watering party belonged to the 12th Light Dragoons, the historian of the regiment names their officer as Lieut. Drake (P.F. Stewart, 50). The only likely officer of that name is Lieut. William Drake of the 26th Light Dragoons, which indeed had a detachment of eighty with the Nile force.

9 Wilson, 328–9, 29 May, Hutchinson to Hobart.

10 Dalhousie journal, 11 May.

11 Donoughmore MSS, E 10c, f.229 (C. Hutchinson's conversation with Elgin, Oct. 1801); Huskisson MSS, Add. MSS 38736, f.330 (7 Aug., Brownrigg to Huskisson, enclosing an earlier letter from Anstruther expressing a want of confidence in Hutchinson, and asking for a discretionary authority to come home: Brownrigg feared that without Anstruther 'Hutchinson would be dreadfully at a loss, and . . . unequal to the arduous task he has to perform').

12 Dalhousie journal, 11 May; Donoughmore MSS, E 10c, f.229, 249; Hope of Luffness MSS, 1 Aug., Graham to Alexander Hope.

13 Randolph, I.177, Wilson's journal for 12 May.

14 Bunbury, 85n.

15 Donoughmore MSS, E 10c, f.249 ('in their zeal for self preservation they were ready and anxious generously to sacrifice the Vizier's army who was advancing upon our solicitation and our friends from India too . . .').

16 Lowe MSS, Add. MSS 20107, f.60; Keith, II.310; Donoughmore MSS, E 10c, ff.229, 243, 259–60; Melville MSS (SRO), GD51/1/795, 22 May, Anstruther to Brownrigg.

17 For Hutchinson's changes of plan see *Moore*, II, 23–4; Keith, II.300; Hook, 294–5.

18 FO 78/34, 4 Feb., Colonel Holloway to Lord Grenville.

19 There is no means of establishing the exact strength of the Grand Vizir's force. Walsh (139, 155n.) suggests that an original force of 15,000 rose to 30,000 during its advance. Wittman, who was present with the Turkish army, puts it at only 10,000 at Jaffa, rising by reinforcement to 12,000 at Gaza and 16,000 at El Arish. Hutchinson, after visiting the Turkish camp and consulting the British Mission, concluded that there were not more than 15,000 of which 8,000–9,000 were mounted (below, p. 186).

20 Browning MSS, Add. MSS 35894, ff.166–7.

21 Holloway's entry in *Dict. of National Biog.* is to be found in Suppl. Vol. II. He was a captain with the local rank of colonel (Porter, I.229, 231).

22 Accounts of the Turkish advance are in Wilson, Walsh, and Wittman (the only eyewitness of the three); and in Leake's journal and reports to Holloway (Leake MSS, 85487 and 85489).

23 Derrécagaix, 207.

24 Derrécagaix, 234; Walsh, App. 77–84 (Belliard's despatch).

25 François, 472.

26 Melville MSS (SRO), GD51/1/795, 22 May, Anstruther to Brownrigg.

27 Brownrigg, 126.

28 There are accounts of the battle of El Khanka in Wilson, Derrécagaix, and Bertrand. Belliard's despatch is in Walsh (App. 79–80), and further material in Anderson, 418 (21 June, Elgin to Hawkesbury) and François, 478–9. Bertrand (434) subsequently challenged Belliard's apologia, and interprets the battle as a further instance of the French higher command's strategic mismanagement which exercised a decisive influence on the Egyptian campaign. He argues that if Belliard had not been obsessed by the vulnerability of Cairo he could have collected 10,000 troops to fight the Turks instead of 5,500, and could still have left 3,000 veterans, armed civilians, convalescents and depot men to garrison Cairo with a mobile reserve of 1,000 infantry and cavalry. In any case, wrote Bertrand, Belliard had enough men at El Khanka to rout the Grand Vizir if he had resolutely sounded the charge; and after driving the Turks back to Salahieh he could have returned to Cairo, and attacked Hutchinson at the end of May. Instead, Belliard '*se laissa imposer*' by the Turkish *canaille*, and allowed himself to be distracted by Hutchinson's threat to his rear though the British were still six marches from Cairo. In short, argued Bertrand, Belliard's irresolution had lost the opportunity to crush the Turks and turn on Hutchinson. Bertrand's calculations, however, are questionable in the light of the numbers who eventually surrendered.

17 ONWARD TO CAIRO

1 Hope of Luffness MSS, 22 May, Anstruther to Alexander Hope.
2 Wilson, 127.
3 WO 1/345, 2 June, Hutchinson to Hobart; *Moore*, II.25; Randolph, I.176; Wilson, 321. Bertrand criticises Lagrange for losing a three weeks' opportunity to bring in the Damietta garrisons; but perhaps Menou should be blamed for not delegating authority to do so.
4 Wyvill, *Sketch*, 442.
5 Accounts of the capture of Cavalier's convoy are in Walsh, App. 63–4 (Doyle's report); Wilson, 104–9; Randolph, I.183–4; P.F. Stewart, 52–3; Lowe MSS, Add. MSS 20107, f.60 (Hudson Lowe to Giffard); Reynier, 242–3, 249–50 (characteristically cooking the figures). Bertrand (433–4) condemns Cavalier for receiving a parley in view of the known feelings of his men. I have not identified the incident involving Sir William Erskine to which Wilson refers.
6 P.F. Stewart, 51.
7 Brownrigg, 126–7; *Moore*, II.24. As late as 22 May Anstruther still believed that Hutchinson intended to wait at Algam for Baird's arrival (Melville MSS (SRO), GD51/1/795, to Brownrigg).
8 *Moore*, II.26.
9 WO 1/345, 2 June, Hutchinson to Hobart; Walsh, 178.
10 WO 1/345, 2 June, Hutchinson to Hobart.
11 Only Dalhousie makes this point, but it seems to be valid.
12 WO 1/345, 2 June, Hutchinson to Hobart; Hook, 297–8. Wilson's discussion of the alternatives which Hutchinson faced telescopes arguments which developed over a period of weeks.
13 *Moore*, II.25–6. The summons for the siege train had reached Rosetta by 1 June.
14 Walsh, 145–6.
15 Wilson, 123–4; Randolph, I.189–91; Walsh, 157. The British were fascinated by the Mamelukes – their skill, bearing, and way of life: see for example Dalhousie's journal for 2 June; P.F. Stewart, 54; Walsh, 156–72.
16 *Moore*, II.25–6; Wyvill, *Sketch*, 445; Anderson, 310–11; Wilson, 137; Teffeteller, 23.

17 Hope of Luffness MSS, 29 June, Hutchinson to Alexander Hope; Teffeteller, 23;
   P.F. Stewart, 51; Melville MSS (SRO), GD51/1/795, 22 May, Anstruther to
   Brownrigg; Maule, 108, 110, 134–5; Wyvill, *Sketch*, 448. Cantlie (I.269) states
   that 1,000 were sent down the Nile to Rosetta besides 800 in the new hospital.
18 Wyvill, *Sketch*, 447.
19 Keith, II.310–11; Dalhousie journal, 11 June. Wilson dates Lloyd's junction
   with Stewart 16 June, but Dalhousie seems conclusive.
20 Dalhousie journal, 10, 11, and 20 June; Lawson, 219; Teffeteller, 23.
21 For Hutchinson's intentions see WO 1/345, 21 June, Hutchinson to Hobart;
   Wittman, II.313.

18 FORTY CENTURIES LOOK DOWN

1 Rousseau, 406–8, 410–11.
2 Derrécagaix, 252.
3 For the decision see Walsh, App. 81–4 (Belliard's despatch); François, 480 et seq.;
   Derrécagaix, 257; Bertrand, 434–41. The Bonapartist Bertrand is very critical of
   Belliard; but the soldierly appraisal of Dumas (*Précis* IV.165) endorses his decision.
4 The documents on Hope's negotiations are in Hopetoun MSS, 171. See also
   WO 1/345, 21 June, Hutchinson to Hobart; Wilson, 131–4; Walsh, 182–4;
   Wyvill, *Sketch*, 456–7, 465; *Moore*, II.31.
5 Wilson, 145; Dalhousie journal, 5 July.
6 By Giovanni Belzoni about 1818.
7 Stair MSS, Dalrymple journal, 109; Robertson, 18–19. Robertson says that the
   whole party from the 92nd were equipped with hammers, and all, including
   himself, acquired souvenirs.
8 Robertson, 28; Jennings microfilm; Dalhousie journal, 5 July; Maule, 118–19.
   Wilson judged the base of the Great Pyramid to be 'prodigiously vast, but the
   altitude is by no means imposing' (Randolph, I.196).
9 Harness, 158; *Moore*, II.30; Johnson, *Rasselas*, 105.
10 Wyvill, *Sketch*, 456–7, 461; *Moore*, II.31.
11 *Moore*, II.30–1.
12 Dalhousie MSS, GD43/4/41, 5 Aug, (?) Dalhousie to LFM.
13 WO 1/345, 29 June, Hutchinson to Elgin; Elgin MSS, 29 June, Hutchinson
   to Elgin; Wilson, 157–9; Hope of Luffness MSS, 29 June, Hutchinson to Elgin;
   Donoughmore MSS E 10c, f.245 (undated note by C. Hutchinson).
14 Wilson, 166.
15 Hook, 355–8; Keith, II.229, 286, 290–1; Mackesy 1984a, 159.
16 Fortescue, IV.719; Stowe MSS, Box 156, 7 March, Wellesley to Elgin; Walsh,
   195–200 and App. 104–5.

Table 11 Baird's force, effective rank and file, Rosetta, 24 August

British infantry	2,609
Native infantry	1,994
Total infantry	4,603
Artillery	1,014
British cavalry	80
Royal Engineers, Pioneers	125
Total	5,822

17 Marlowe, 29.
18 Hook, 355–8; WO 6/21, 19 May, 10 and 16 July, Hobart to Hutchinson; Sidmouth MSS, 16 July, Hobart to Addington; WO 6/55, 22 July, Hobart to General Fox. For Baird's march: Hook, 299–332; Walsh, 196–207; Wilson, 169–70; Phipps, 31–2. At this stage the intended future destinations of Hutchinson's forces were: Corfu; a garrison for Sicily; attacks on Spanish American colonies; and reinforcement of the British Isles against a threatened invasion.
19 Elgin MSS, 4 Sept, Hamilton to Elgin.
20 *Moore*, II.32. Bunbury (94) says that the British and French troops intermingled and laughed together; but he was not present, and this probably occurred only at the final French camp near Rosetta.
21 Melville MSS (SRO), GD51/1/781, Graham to ? (extract); Bertrand, 340–1.
22 The sailors' syndicate made a considerable impression on army officers: Thornton, 78; Wilson, 61n.; Burgoyne, 135. For the conduct of the march from Cairo: *Moore*, II.32–9; Wilson, 172–8; Walsh, 191–4; Anderson, 347–9, 355–6; Wyvill, *Sketch*, 465–71; Miller, 32.

19 THE FINAL MANOEUVRE

1 Dropmore, VII.11–12, 18; Grenville MSS, AR41/63, 7 May, Lord Grenville to Thomas Grenville.
2 Brown Transcripts.
3 Sidmouth MSS, 10 May, Dundas to Addington; Pellew, I.392; Matheson, 307.
4 *Parliamentary History*, XXXV.1427–9; Pellew, I.394–5; George III, *Later Corr.* no. 2415; George III MS (NAM), 15 May, George III to Duke of York.
5 George III, *Later Corr.* nos 2415, 2420, 2423; WO 6/55, 19 May, Hobart to Gen. Fox. For composition of the reinforcements, see note 8 below.
6 Walsh, App. 84–5.
7 Derrécagaix, 259–68; Rousseau, 412–13.
8 From the British Isles came the 22nd Light Dragoons (dismounted), and the 24th, 25th and 26th Foot; from Minorca, the 20th (two battalions, which volunteered though enlisted for Europe only), Ancient Irish Fencibles, Watteville's (an ex-Imperial regiment of Swiss); from Trieste, Löwenstein Jäger or Chasseurs britanniques (men re-enlisted from Condé's French émigré force which had been disbanded when Austria made peace with France in Feb. 1801).
9 Elgin MSS, 16 Aug., Hutchinson to Hobart; Smith, 26; Wilson, 174–5; Dalhousie MSS GD45/4/41, (?) Dalhousie to LFM (extract). Bertrand (428ff.) acknowledged the risks of Hutchinson's advance to Cairo, and even argued that he should have withdrawn Coote's force from the Roman Camp to Aboukir during his absence.
10 Rooke MSS, D1833, f.14, 1 June, Capt. J.C. Rooke to Capt. W. Rooke; Brodie journal, II.62–3; *Moore*, II.31–2; Coote Transcripts, 7 and 9 July; Dalhousie journal, 5 July.
11 Dalrymple journal, 90, 105.
12 Ibid., 98; Loveday, 40; Dyott, 155.
13 Keith, II.300, 306–7.
14 Keith, II.315–16; Elgin MSS, 22 May, Keith to Elgin.
15 Sidmouth MSS, 12 June, Keith to Addington; Keith, II.327–31.
16 Keith, II.336–7.
17 Coote Transcripts, 7 July; Walsh, 189–90; Wilson, 200–1; Dumas, IV.162.
18 *Moore*, II.39; Coote Transcripts, 9 Aug.

19 Dalrymple journal, 104; Dyott, 161.
20 Wilson, 214.
21 Hope of Luffness MSS, 8 Sept., Graham to Alexander Hope; Anderson, 361; Randolph, I.201; WO 1/345, 19 Aug., Hutchinson to Hobart; Keith, II.347.
22 Wilson, 187, 192.
23 Wilson, 186; Melville MSS (SRO), GD51/1/781/1, Graham's narrative.
24 Wilson, 187; Walsh, 209–10.
25 Dalrymple journal, 108, 112; Wilson, 187; Coote Transcripts, 30 Aug.; Melville MSS (SRO), GD1/1/781/1, Graham's narrative.
26 Ibid.; *Moore*, II.40–1, 214–15.
27 Walsh, 215–17; Wilson, 188–90; Melville MSS (SRO), Graham's narrative (Graham had a good view of the attack); *Moore*, II.41.
28 Hope of Luffness MSS, 8 Sept., Graham to Alexander Hope. David Stewart (I.471) suggests that 'Green Hill' was a 'jocular' description, and that the hill was covered with white sparkling sand.
29 Elgin MSS, 21 Aug., Moore to Elgin.
30 *Moore*, II.41–2; Wilson, 191–2; Elgin MSS, 21 Aug., Moore to Elgin.

20 THE FALL OF ALEXANDRIA

1 Walsh, 212–13; Dyott, 163.
2 David Stewart, I.472–3.
3 Walsh, 217–21; Wilson, 192–4; Miller, 33. Wilson states that the submerged reef which separated the fort from the shore was 150 yards wide; while Walsh, who was present at the siege as aide de camp to Coote and was involved in negotiating the capitulation, says that the sharpshooters of the 54th were firing at pistol range.
4 Dyott, 166–7; Wilson, 195; Elgin MSS, 23 Aug., Coote to Hutchinson (copy).
5 Randolph, I.203.
6 Wilson, 197–8.
7 Wilson, 199.
8 Dalrymple journal, 22 Aug.
9 *Moore*, II.42–3; Wilson, 199.
10 Walsh, 225–7; Wilson, 203.
11 Bunbury, 6.
12 Rolle MSS, 3 Sept., I.M. Cutcliffe to Lord Rolle; Wilson, 203–4. *Moore* (II.45) visited Coote's front on the 25th and judged the French pickets to be 'infinitely too much advanced'.
13 Dalrymple journal, 25 Aug.; Wilson, 204; Rolle MSS, 3 Sept., I.M. Cutcliffe to Lord Rolle; Miller, 34. The supports were either the 1/20th (Wilson) or a battalion of the 54th (Rolle MSS, 3 Sept, I.M. Cutcliffe to Lord Rolle).
14 David Stewart, I.472; Walsh, 230–1; Wilson, 205. *Moore* (II.45) writes that the firing from the Green Hill was unauthorised and foolish. Colonel Graham and David Stewart judged otherwise; but Moore was General of the Day.
15 Wilson, 205; Walsh, 230; Elgin MSS, 27 Aug., Hutchinson to Elgin; Rolle MSS, 3 Sept., I.M. Cutcliffe to Lord Rolle; *Moore*, II.46; Dalrymple journal, 29 Aug.
16 Walsh, 232–3; Rolle MSS, 3 Sept., I.M. Cutcliffe to Lord Rolle.
17 Walsh, 239; *Moore*, II.47, 50–1; Wilson, 209–14; Wyvill, 323.
18 Bertrand, 447. A note on a map, probably by John Hope, states with reference to the works in front of the Arab walls, 'an attack in front would have been madness' (RHP 43890, in West Register House, Edinburgh). Graham also regarded the French fortifications as very formidable (8 Sept., to Alexander Hope).

19 *Moore*, II.46.
20 Wilson, 206–9, 213; Dyott, 173; Wyvill, *Sketch*, 476; Rolle MSS, 3 Sept., I.M. Cutcliffe to Lord Rolle.

21 THE ACHIEVEMENT

1 Melville MSS (SRO), GD51/1/780, Graham's narrative; Wyvill, *Sketch*, 476; Coote Transcripts, 30 Aug. (postscript of 3 Sept.).
2 Hill MSS, Col. Hill's of 25 Dec. 1801; *Narrative*, 114; Harness, 158; Phipps, 61; McGrigor, 114.
3 Elgin MSS, 6 Sept., Hutchinson to Elgin; Huskisson MSS, Add. MSS 38736, f.337.
4 Dalhousie journal, 30 Aug. and 3 Sept.; *Moore*, II.50; Coote Transcripts, 9 Oct.
5 Dropmore, VII.28; WO 6/21, 22 July, Hobart to Hutchinson and WO 6/55, to Fox; *Moore*, II.48.
6 P.F. Stewart, 55–6; *Moore*, II.48–9; Hill MSS, Col. Hill's of 25 Dec. 1801; Wyvill MS, 338.
7 The deaths from wounds and disease are difficult to establish precisely: the figure given here relies on a summary of losses in Dundas of Beechwood MSS.
8 *Narrative*, 98–119, 129–30.
9 Smith, 28; Elgin MSS, 13 Sept., Hamilton to Elgin.
10 Melville MSS (SRO), Graham's narrative; Elgin MSS, 13 Sept., Hamilton to Elgin. Wilson's figures for the disposal of the French forces are in Table 12.

Table 12 Disposal of French forces in Egypt by end of campaign

Cairo garrison	13,600	
Alexandria garrison	10,500	(including seamen)
Prisoners of war	3,500	
Total returned to France	27,600	
Killed or died of wounds	3,000	
Died of disease	1,500	
Total force in March 1801	32,100	

11 I owe this quotation to Mr S.G.P. Ward. Both Wellesley and General Dalrymple cited the Alexandria convention as a model in their defence at the enquiry into the Convention of Cintra.
12 Reynier, 282–3; Smith, 28; Campbell MSS (SRO), GD13/358, 22 Feb. 1802, Archibald Campbell to Lt Col. Campbell; Keith, II.354.
13 Minto MSS, 11195, f.33, 27 Aug., Keith to Minto; Donoughmore MSS, E 10c, ff.229–30, 240.
14 *Moore*, II.53–8.
15 Above, p. 10.
16 Mackesy 1984a, 207.
17 The point is discussed in ibid., 214–15.
18 Melville MSS (SRO), GD51/1/805, 19 March 1802, Capt. Home Popham to Dundas.

19 Marlowe, 81–92. For contemporary British accounts and views of the massacre, Walsh, 167n., 169n.; Wyvill, *Sketch*, 485–9; Donoughmore MSS, E 10c, ff.262 et seq.
20 Smith, 29.

22 'ABERCROMBY'S SOLDIERS'

1 Bunbury, 102; Gurwood, 213.
2 Brownrigg, 123; Dundas of Beechwood MSS, Aug. 1801, Col. Paget to Lord Paget; E. Paget, 65.
3 I am grateful to Dr Michael Duffy for putting this point to me.
4 Glover, 3; Wilson, 39; Walsh, 235.
5 P.F. Stewart, 56; *Moore*, II.51; Dundas of Beechwood MSS, Aug. 1801, Col. Paget to Lord Paget; Jennings microfilm, 21 March (my italics).
6 See above, p. 101.
7 Dundas of Beechwood MSS, Aug. 1801, Col. Paget to Lord Paget.
8 *Moore*, II.62; above, p. 88. The twelve battalions of *voltigeurs* in the French army before the Revolution had included two of Corsicans. The Corsican Rangers were disbanded at the peace, but raised again at Malta and commanded by Hudson Lowe, of whom Moore had written: 'when Lowe's at the outposts I'm sure of a good night'.
9 Quot. Gates, 110.
10 Ibid., 90. For Mackenzie at Shorncliffe, 116–23, 128–9.
11 Elgin MSS, 16 Sept., Hamilton to Elgin.
12 Christopher Hutchinson made the point to the Porte (Donoughmore MSS, E 10c, 208–10).
13 General William Carr Beresford, Viscount Beresford (1768–1854).
14 Lt Gen. Sir John Stuart (1759–1815), Commander-in-Chief in the Mediterranean, 1808–10; Lt Governor of Grenada, 1811.
15 Sir John Francis Cradock (1762–1839) changed his name to Caradoc 1820; created Baron Howden (Irish peerage 1819, British peerage 1831): Governor of Gibraltar 1809, and of the Cape 1811–14. For his treatment in the Vellore case see E. Talbot-Rice, *Army Museum '85*, 19–30.
16 Maurice, I.267. Ludlow addressed the brigade in Egypt as the Second Brigade of Guards.
17 Gen. Sir John Doyle (1750?-1834). Lt Gen. Sir Hildebrand Oakes (1752–1822). Gen. Edward Finch (1756–1843). Gen. George Ludlow (1758–1842), who succeeded his brother as Earl Ludlow in 1811. Gen. Richard Lambart, seventh Earl of Cavan (1763–1836).
18 Duncan, II.128.
19 Lt Gen. Robert Lawson (c.1740–1816) had accumulated fifty-six years' service when he died. Lt Gen. George Cookson (1760–1835). Maj. Gen. Sir Charles Holloway (1749–1827). Lt Col. Sir Richard Fletcher, Bt (1768–1813).
20 Information from Mr S.P.G. Ward.
21 Gen. Sir George Murray (1772–1846), Governor of Canada 1814; Colonial Secretary 1828–30; Master-General of the Ordnance; edited Marlborough's despatches. Sir James McGrigor, Bt (1771–1858), director-general of army medical department 1815–51.
22 Gen. Sir Thomas Graham, Baron Lynedoch (1748–1843). Gen. Sir Rowland Hill, Viscount Hill (1772–1842). Lt Gen. Sir Kenneth Mackenzie (1754–1833), who took the surname Douglas on being made a baronet, 1831: though he had a short spell in command of a brigade in the Peninsula, his health had been

damaged by an earlier fall from a horse.

23 Field Marshal Sir John Colborne, First Baron Seaton (1778–1863).

24 Gen. Sir Edward Paget (1775–1849). Gen. Sir Brent Spencer (1760-1828). Gen. Sir Galbraith Lowry Cole (1772–1842), Governor of Mauritius and of the Cape. Gen. Sir William Houston, Bt (1766–1842), Governor of Gibraltar. Gen. Sir Charles Colville (1770–1843), Commander-in-Chief Bombay, Governor of Mauritius. Gen. Francis George Ramsay, ninth Earl of Dalhousie (1770–1838), Governor of Canada, Commander-in-Chief in East Indies.

25 Lt Gen. Sir Alan Cameron of Erracht (1753–1828). Gen. Sir William Lumley (1769–1850), Governor and Commander-in-Chief of Bermuda. Gen. Sir James Kempt (1764–1834), Governor of Nova Scotia, Governor-General of Canada, Master-General of the Ordnance.

26 Lt Gen. Sir Hudson Lowe (1769–1844), Governor of St Helena and of Antigua. Gen. Sir Robert Wilson (1777–1849).

27 Campbell of Airds, 16, 62. On the first anniversary of 21 March the 79th Highlanders 'drank to the immortal memory of General Sir Ralph Abercromby with all our medals on' (Wyvill MS, 343).

28 Hope of Luffness MSS, Section A, Bundle 1 (letters of Nov.-Dec. 1799).

29 Simcoe MSS, 1 June 1801, Duke of Northumberland to Simcoe; Bunbury, 76, and above, p. 31. Northumberland and Simcoe had served in the American War and identified themselves with the 'American' school of soldiers. The parallel drawn with Montgomery quotes General Sir David Fraser.

30 Wilson, 319. A draft with Pitt's amendments is in Hope of Luffness MSS, GD363/1122.

31 Personal letter from Mr S.G.P. Ward; Combermere, I.166–7 (a reference for which I am also indebted to Mr Ward). Captain Brotherton (later Gen. Sir Thomas Brotherton, 1785–1868) had exchanged into the 14th Light Dragoons.

GUIDE TO CITATIONS

For abbreviations see p. 244

MANUSCRIPT MATERIALS LISTED AS CITED

Abercromby: letter to Col. Brownrigg, NAM, Acc. 7301–94.

Adm.: Admiralty records in PRO, Adm. 1/404.

Althorp: papers of Earl Spencer from Althorp, now in BL.

Brodie journal: Journal of Egyptian Expedition by Col. George Brodie, Brodie Castle, Moray (via NRAS).

Brown: letters from Lieut. James Brown, 44th Regiment, and concerning his death, NAM, Acc. 8011–40.

Brownrigg: see Hardwicke.

Bute: summary of papers of the Marquis of Bute at Mount Stuart, NRA.

Campbell (SRO): papers of Archibald Campbell, SRO, GD13/306, 358.

Campbell (NAM): letter of Archibald Campbell, NAM, Acc. 6807–456.

Casualty Returns: casualty returns for Abercromby's actions, NAM, Acc. 6807–74.

Coote: transcripts of letters from General Sir Eyre Coote to Prince William of Gloucester, NAM, Acc. 8806–28 (another set in Middle East Centre, St Antony's College, Oxford).

Dalhousie: papers of the Earl of Dalhousie, SRO, GD45/4/22 (journal), GD45/4/23, –25, –30, –31, –41.

Dalrymple: diary of Capt. Robert Dalrymple, Third Guards, SRO, Stair MSS, GD135, vol. 152, part 3.

Donoughmore: diary and notes of the Hon. Christopher Hely-Hutchinson 1800–1, in papers of the Earl of Donoughmore, Trinity College Library, Dublin.

Dundas of Beechwood: papers of Gen. Sir David Dundas, Beechwood, Comrie, Perthshire (via NRAS).

Elgin: papers of the Earl of Elgin and Kincardine, Broomhall, Fife.

Elphinstone: papers of Visct Keith, Elphinstone MSS, NMM.

FO: Foreign Office records in PRO, FO 78/30–34 (Turkey).

Fraser: papers of General Mackenzie Fraser, Castle Fraser, Aberdeenshire.

George III (NAM); unpublished holograph letter to Duke of York, NAM, Acc. 6208–21.

Graham: papers of Gen. Sir Thomas Graham, Lord Lynedoch, NLS, 3590, 3603–4.

Grenville: papers of Thomas Grenville, Buckinghamshire RO, Aylesbury.

Haddington: papers of the Earl of Haddington, Mellerstain, Berwickshire (via NRA).

Hardwicke: MSS of the Earl of Hardwicke, BL, Add. MSS 35894.

Hill: papers of Col. J.C.E. Hill, in the possession of Mrs Enid Case, Brampford Speke, Devon.

Hobart: papers of Lord Hobart in Buckinghamshire RO, Aylesbury.

Hope of Luffness: papers of Col. Sir Alexander Hope, NRAS, GD364/1122.

Hopetoun: papers of General Sir John Hope, Earl of Hopetoun, Hopetoun House, West Lothian (via NRAS).

Huskisson: papers of William Huskisson, BL, Add. MSS 38736 and 38759.

Hylton: papers of Lord Hylton, Somerset RO, Taunton.

Jennings: memoir of Capt. Peter Jennings, 28th Regiment, NAM, Acc. 8301–102 (microfilm).

Leake: papers of William Martin Leake, Hertfordshire RO, Hertford, 85483–9.

Liverpool: papers of first Earl of Liverpool, BL, Add. MSS 38357.

Lowe: papers of Col. Sir Hudson Lowe, BL, Add. MSS 20107, 36297c.

Maitland: notebook of Gen. Sir Frederick Maitland (note on character of Abercromby, 1844), NAM, Acc. 7902–13, No. 46.

Melville (SRO): Melville Castle muniments, papers of Henry Dundas, first Visct Melville, SRO, GD51/1/768, 774, 780–1, 784–91, 794–5, 798–9, 804.

Melville (NLS): papers of above, NLS, 2956, 3835, 5319.

Minto: papers of first Earl of Minto, NLS, 11195, 11252, 11254, 11256, 11259.

Moore: papers of Sir John Moore, BL, Add. MSS 57329–30 (original diaries with variants on printed edition), Add. MSS 57321.

Nepean: papers of Evan Nepean, NMM.

North: papers of Lord North, Bodleian Library, c.18, f.3.

Oakes: letter of Sir Hildebrand Oakes, BL, Add. MSS 36747c.

Peacocke: diary of Capt. and Lt Col. William Peacocke, Coldstream Guards, NAM, Acc. 8209–28 (microfilm).

Rolle: Rolle Papers, letters from Cornet I.M. Cutcliffe, 26th Light Dragoons, Devon RO, Exeter.

Rooke: Rooke Papers, letters of Col. J.C. Rooke, Gloucestershire RO, Gloucester.

Sibthorpe: Sibthorpe Papers, letters of Midshipman Henry Sibthorp (*sic*), Lincolnshire RO, Lincoln.

Sidmouth: papers of Visct Sidmouth, Devon RO, Exeter.

Simcoe: papers of Gen. John Graves Simcoe, Devon RO, Exeter.

Smith: letters from Adm. Sir William Sidney Smith, BL, Add. MSS 37778.

Stowe: Stowe Papers, Huntington Library, San Marino, California.

Vincent: journal of Capt. Exham Vincent, 54th Regiment, NAM, Acc. 7611–24 (typescript copy).

Wilson: papers of Gen. Sir Robert Wilson, BL, Add. MSS 30095 (diary), 30111.

WO: War Office records in PRO, WO 1/292, WO 1/344–5, WO 6/21, WO 6/55.

Wyvill: 'The Memoirs of an Old Army Officer', by R.A. Wyvill, Library of Congress, Peter Force Collection, series 8D, No. 191 (in a few instances varies from the text of the printed version).

Young: papers relating to Vice-Adm. William Young, BL, Add. MSS 46714.

PRINTED MATERIALS

* denotes original source

A Faithful Journal of the Late Expedition to Egypt by a Private on Board the Dictator (1802), London.

Allardyce, Alexander (1882): *Memoirs of the Hon. George Elphinstone, KB, Viscount Keith*, Edinburgh.

*Anderson, Lieut. Aeneas (40th Regiment) (1802): *A Journal of the Forces which sailed from the Downs, in April 1800 . . .* , London.

*Annual Register, 1801, London.

Atkinson, C.T. (1947): *The Dorsetshire Regiment*, Oxford.

*Baldwin, George (1802): *Political Recollections Relative to Egypt*, London.

*Baynham, Henry (1969): *From the Lower Deck: The Old Navy, 1780–1840*, London.

*Bertrand, Gen. Henri Gratien (1847): *Campagnes d'Égypte et de Syrie*, Paris.

Brownrigg, Beatrice (1923): *Life and Letters of Sir John Moore*, Oxford.

*Bunbury, Sir Henry (1927 edn): *Narratives of some Passages in the Great War with France (1799–1810)*, London.

Burgoyne, J.M. (1885): *Short History of Naval and Military Operations in Egypt, 1798–1802*, London.

*Campbell, Lieut. A.: 'Journal of Lieut. A. Campbell, 42nd R.H. Regt.', *The Red Hackle*, nos 162, 167–8, 170, Perth.

Campbell of Airds, Yr, Alastair (1983): *Two Hundred Years: The Highland Society of London, 1778–1978*, Inverness.

Cantlie, Sir Neil (1974): *A History of the Army Medical Department*, Edinburgh.

*Castlereagh (1849): *Memoirs and Correspondence of Viscount Castlereagh, Second Marquess of Londonderry*, ed. Charles Vane, Marquess of Londonderry, London.

Charles-Roux, F. (1925): *L'Angleterre et l'expédition française en Égypte*, Cairo.

Church, E.M. (1895): *Chapters in an Adventurous Life*, Edinburgh.

Clode, C.M. (1869): *The Military Forces of the Crown*, London.

*Collingwood, Lord (1957): *The Private Correspondence of Admiral Lord Collingwood*, ed. E. Hughes, (Navy Records Society), London.

*Combermere (1866): *Memoirs and Correspondence of Field Marshal Viscount Combermere*, ed. Mary, Viscountess Combermere, London.

*Cornwallis (1859): *Correspondence of Charles, First Marquis Cornwallis*, ed. Charles Ross, London.

Daniell, D. Scott (1951): *Cap of Honour: the Gloucestershire Regiment, 1694–1950*, London.

Davis, John (1887–1904): *Historical Records of the 2nd, Queen's Royal, now the Queen's (Royal West Surrey) Regiment*, London.

Dawson, W.P., with Conway, O.P.M., collaborating (1970): 'The capture of "The Invincibles" standard, Alexandria, 1801', *Journal of the Orders and Medals Research Society*, no. 3, vol. 9, 1970, London.

Delavoye, Alexander M. (1880): *Records of the 90th Regiment – Perthshire Light Infantry, 1795–1880*, London.

Derrécagaix, V.B. (1908): *Les états-major de Napoléon: le lieut. gen. comte Belliard*, Paris.

*Doguereau, Gen. J.-P. (1904): *Journal de l'expédition d'Égypte*, Paris.

Doyle, Col. Arthur (1911): *A Hundred Years of Conflict*, London.

Drew, Lt Gen. Sir William R.M. (1968): *Commissioned Officers in the Medical Services of the British Army, 1660–1960*, London.

Dropmore: see Fortescue, J.B. (1905–8).

Duffy, Michael (1987): *Soldiers, Sugar and Seapower: the British Expeditions to the West Indies and the War against Revolutionary France*, Oxford.

Dumas, le comte Mathieu (1816–28): *Précis des événements militaires de 1799 à 1814*, Paris.

Duncan, Francis (1873): *History of the Royal Regiment of Artillery*, London.

*Dundas, Colonel David (1788): *Principles of Military Movement, chiefly applied to

Infantry, London.

Dunfermline, J.A. Abercromby, Lord (1861): *Lieutenant General Sir Ralph Abercromby, KB, 1793–1801: A Memoir by his Son*, Edinburgh.

*Dyott, Gen. William (1907): *Dyott's Diary, 1781–1845*, ed. R.W. Jeffrey, London.

Evelyn, G.J. (1990): ' "I learned what one ought not to do": the British Army in Flanders and Holland 1793–95', *The Road to Waterloo: The British Army and the Struggle against Revolutionary and Napoleonic France, 1793–1815*, ed. Alan J. Guy (NAM, London).

Forbes, Archibald (1896): *The 'Black Watch'*, London.

*Fortescue, J.B. (1905–8): *Report on the Manuscripts of J.B. Fortescue, Esq., Preserved at Dropmore*, Hist. MSS Comm., vols V–VII, London.

Fortescue, J.W. (1915): *History of the British Army*, vol. IV, London.

*François, C.F. (1903): *Journal du capitaine François, dit le Dromedaire d'Égypte, 1792–1830*, Paris.

Fuller, J.F.C. (1925a): *Sir John Moore's System of Training*, London.

Fuller, J.F.C. (1925b): *British Light Infantry in the Eighteenth Century*, London.

Gardyne, C.G. (1901): *The Life of a Regiment: The History of the Gordon Highlanders from its Formation in 1794 to 1816*, Edinburgh.

Gates, David (1987): *The British Light Infantry Arm, c. 1790–1815: Its Creation, Training and Operational Role*, London.

Gentleman's Magazine (1834): obituaries of Lt Gen. Sir Kenneth Douglas and Gen. Sir John Doyle, London.

*George III (1962–70): *The Later Correspondence of George III*, ed. A. Aspinall, Cambridge.

Glover, Richard (1963): *Peninsular Preparation: The Reform of the British Army, 1795–1809*, Cambridge.

Gordon, Thomas C. (1960): *Four Notable Scots*, Stirling.

*Graham of Fintry (1901–9): *Manuscripts of Graham of Fintry*, Hist. MSS Comm, London.

Griffith, Paddy (1981): *Forward into Battle: Fighting Tactics from Waterloo to Vietnam*, Chichester.

Gurwood: see Wellington.

*Harley, John (1838): *The Veteran, or Forty Years in the British Service*, London.

*Harness, William (1957): *Trusty and Well Beloved*, ed. C.M. Duncan-Jones, London.

Herold, J.C. (1962): *Bonaparte in Egypt*, London.

*Hill, Col. J.H.E. (1988): *Letters to a Vicarage, 1796–1815*, selected by Enid Case, ed. Jenny Currie, Exeter.

*Holland, Elizabeth Lady (1908): *Journal of Elizabeth, Lady Holland (1791–1811)*, ed. Earl of Ilchester, London.

Hook, T.E. (1912): *Life of Sir David Baird*, London.

Hoskins, H.L. (1928): *British Routes to India*, New York.

Howard, Hon. E.G.G. (1839): *Memoirs of Admiral Sir Sidney Smith, KCB*, vol. I, London.

*Inglis, Cmdr (1912): 'Operations on the Egyptian Coast, 1801', *The Naval Miscellany* II (Naval Records Society XL), London.

James, Adm. Sir William (1950): *Old Oak: The Life of John Jervis, Earl of St Vincent*, London.

Johnson, Samuel (1923 edn): *Rasselas, Prince of Abyssinia* (Carlton Classics edn, intro. by Hannaford Bennett), London.

Johnston, S.H.F. (1957): *The History of the Cameronians (Scottish Rifles)*, Aldershot.

*Jollois, J.B.P. (1904): *Journal 1798–1801*, ed. P. Lefèbre-Pontalis (in vol. VI of Bibliothèque Égyptologique, ed. G. Maspero), Paris.

*Keith, Admiral Visc. (1950): *The Keith Papers*, ed. Christopher Lloyd (Navy Records Society), London.

*Landmann, Col. George T. (1852): *Adventures and Recollections of Landmann*, London.

*Landmann, Col. George T. (1854): *Recollections of my Military Life*, London.

Laws, Lt Col. M.E.S. (1952): *Battery Records of the Royal Artillery, 1716–1859*, Woolwich.

*Lawson, Lt Gen. Robert (1884): 'Memorandum by Brig. Gen. Lawson on artillery arrangements in Egypt', *Proceedings of Royal Artillery Institution* XII, Woolwich.

Loveday, Arthur F. (1964): *Sir Hilgrove Turner*, Alkham.

*Macdonald, Sir John (1915): 'Sir Ralph Abercromby by a contemporary', *Blackwood's Magazine*, Dec. 1915, pp. 836–46, London.

*McGrigor, Sir James (1861): *The Autobiography and Services of Sir James McGrigor, Bart*, London.

Mackesy, Piers (1957): *The War in the Mediterranean, 1803–10*, London.

Mackesy, Piers (1974): *Statesmen at War: The Strategy of Overthrow, 1798–99*.

Mackesy, Piers (1979): *The Coward of Minden: the Affair of Lord George Sackville*, London.

Mackesy, Piers (1984a): *War without Victory: the Downfall of Pitt*, London.

Mackesy, Piers (1984b): 'What the British Army learned', *Arms and Independence: the Military Character of the American Revolution*, ed. Ronald Hoffman and Peter J. Albert, Charlottesville, Va.

Mackesy, Piers (1991): ' "Most sadly bitched": the British Cadiz expedition of 1800', *Les Empires en Guerre et Paix, 1793–1860*, ed. Edward Freeman, Vincennes.

Marlowe, John (1971): *Perfidious Albion: The Origins of Anglo-French Rivalry in the Levant*, London.

*Marmont, Marshal (1857): *Mémoires du Maréchal Duc de Raguse*, Paris.

Matheson, C. (1933): *Life of Henry Dundas, first Visct Melville, 1742–1811*, London.

*Maule, Capt. Francis (Queen's Regiment) (1806): *Memorials of the Campaigns of North Holland and Egypt*, London.

Maurice, Frederick (1934): *History of the Scots Guards*, London.

*Miller, Benjamin (1928): 'The adventures of Serjeant Benjamin Miller during his service with the 4th Battalion, Royal Artillery, from 1796 to 1815', intro. M.R. Dacombe and B.J.H. Rowe, *Journal of Society for Army Historical Research*, VII, London.

*Miot, J.F. (1814): *Mémoires pour servir à l'histoire des expéditions en Égypte et en Syrie*, Paris.

*Moore, Sir John (1904): *The Diary of Sir John Moore*, ed. J.F. Maurice (cited as *Moore*), London.

Moore, J.C. (1834): *Life of Sir John Moore*, London.

*Napoleon I (1897): *Lettres inédites de Napoléon I (an VIII-1815)*, ed. Leon Lecestre, Paris.

Narrative (1820): *Narrative of a Private Soldier in HM's 92nd Regiment . . . 1798–1815*, Glasgow.

*Nicol, John (1822): *Life and Adventures of John Nicol, Mariner*, Edinburgh.

Oman, Carola (1953): *Sir John Moore*, London.

*Paget, A. (1896): *The Paget Papers*, ed. A.B. Paget, London.

*Paget, E. (1898): *Letters and Memorials of Gen. the Hon. Sir Edward Paget*, coll. and annot. Harriet M. Paget, ed. Eden Paget (for private circulation).

Parliamentary History (1806): *The Parliamentary History of England*, ed. William Cobbett, London.

*Parsons, G.E. (1843): *Nelsonian Reminiscences*, London.

Pellew, George (1847): *Life and Correspondence of Henry Addington, first Visct Sidmouth*, London.

Phipps, Pownoll W. (1894): *The Life of Col. Pownoll Phipps*, London.

Porter, W. (1889): *History of the Corps of Royal Engineers*, London.

*Randolph, Herbert (1862): *The Life of Sir Robert Wilson*, London.

*Reynier, Count J.L.E. (1802): *De l'Égypte après la bataille d'Héliopolis, et considerations générales . . .* , Paris

Rigault, G. (1911): *Le général Abdallah Menou et la dernière phase de l'expédition d'Égypte (1799–1801)*, Paris.

*Robertson, Sgt J. (1842): *Journal of Sgt. D. Robertson, late 92nd Foot: Comprising the Different Campaigns between the Years 1797 and 1818*, Perth.

Rose, J. Holland (1911): *William Pitt and the Great War*, London.

*Rousseau, F.R. (1900): *Kléber et Menou en Égypte* (Société d'Histoire contemporaine, 24), Paris.

Shankland, Peter (1975): *Beware of Heroes: Admiral Sir Sidney Smith's War against Napoleon*, London.

Sherrard, O.A. (1933): *Life of Lord St Vincent*, London.

Sidney, Edwin (1845): *Life of Lord Hill*, London.

Smith, G.C. Moore (1903): *Life of J. Colborne, Field Marshal Lord Seaton*, London.

Smyth, W.H. (1829): *Life and Services of Capt. Philip Beaver*, London.

Smythies, R.H.R. (1894): *Historical Records of the 40th (2nd Somersetshire) Regiment . . . 1717–1893*, Devonport.

*Spencer (1913–24): *The Private Papers of George, second Earl Spencer, 1794–1801*, ed. J.S. Corbett and H.W. Richmond (Navy Records Society), London.

*Stewart, Gen. David (1822): *Sketches of the Character, Manners, and Present State of the Highlanders of Scotland with Details of the Military Service of the Highland Regiments*, Edinburgh.

Stewart, P.F. (1950): *History of the XII Royal Lancers (Prince of Wales's)*, London.

*Teffeteller, G.L. (1983): *The Surpriser: the Life of Rowland, Lord Hill*, Newark, NJ.

*Thornton, William (1933): *The British Campaign in Egypt in 1801, as Recorded in the Diary of Surgeon William Thornton*, ed. Lt Col. W.H. Thornton, MC (printed for private circulation: copy in Middle East Centre, St Antony's College, Oxford), Alexandria.

*Walsh, Capt. Thomas, 93rd Highlanders (1803): *Journal of the Late Campaign in Egypt: Including a Description of the Country*, London.

*Wellington, Duke of (1851): *Selections from the Dispatches and General Orders of Field Marshal the Duke of Wellington*, ed. Lt Col. Gurwood, London.

Williams, G.T. (1908): *Historical Records of the XI Hussars (P.A.O.)*, London.

*Wilson, R.T. (1803): *Narrative of the Expedition to Egypt* (2nd edn), London.

*Wittman, William (1803): *Travels in Turkey, Asia-Minor, Syria and Across the Desert into Egypt, during the Years 1799–1801*, London.

Wortley, E. Stuart (1925): *A Prime Minister and his Son*, London.

*Wyvill, R.A. (1820): *Sketch of the Military Life of R.A. Wyvill*, London.

INDEX

Note: Sub-entries are arranged chronologically within most entries, but where this is inappropriate alphabetical order is used.